High on the Hogs

High on the Hogs

A Biker Filmography

by DAVID STIDWORTHY

McFarland & Company, Inc., Publishers
Jefferson, North Carolina, and London

Library of Congress Cataloguing-in-Publication Data

Stidworthy, David, 1947–
High on the hogs : a biker filmography / by David Stidworthy.
p.   cm.
Includes index.

ISBN 0-7864-1418-9 (softcover : 50# alkaline paper) ∞

1. Motorcycle films—Catalogs. I. Title.
PN1995.9.M66 S75   2003   791.43'655—dc21   2002152179

British Library cataloguing data are available

©2003 David Stidworthy. All rights reserved

No part of this book may be reproduced or transmitted in any form or by any means, electronic or mechanical, including photocopying or recording, or by any information storage and retrieval system, without permission in writing from the publisher.

On the cover: poster art from *The Wild Angels* (1966)

Manufactured in the United States of America

*McFarland & Company, Inc., Publishers
Box 611, Jefferson, North Carolina 28640
www.mcfarlandpub.com*

Dedicated to the following screen artists whose work enriched the biker film genre: Al Adamson, Bambi Allen, Tom Baker, William Bonner, Marlon Brando, Regina Carroll, John Cassavetes, Richard Compton, Roger Corman, Bruce Dern, Robert Dix, Peter Fonda, John Garwood, Claire Hagen, Ross Hagen, Dennis Hopper, Steve Ihnat, O. Dale Ireland, Laszlo Kovacs, Gary Kent, Stanley Kramer, Gary Littlejohn, Lee Marvin, Arlene Martel, Jack Nicholson, Stephen Oliver, Michael Pataki, Stu Phillips, Adam Roarke, Des Roberts, Alex Rocco, Richard Rush, Sabrina Scharf, Jeremy Slate, William Smith, Joe Solomon, Jack Starrett, Valerie Starrett, John Stephens, Tom Stern, Russ Tamblyn, Robert Tessier and James Gordon White.

Acknowledgments

Academy of Motion Picture Arts and Sciences, Mike Accomando, the late Samuel Z. Arkoff, Cape Copy Center, Richard Compton, Roger Corman, Eddie Brandt's Saturday Matinee, Gene Freese, John Garwood, Jerry Ohlinger's Movie Material Store, David Konow, the late John Lawrence, Johnny Legend, Ron Main, Movie Poster Palace, Fred Olen Ray, Samuel M. Sherman, Joe Solomon, the late Jack Starrett, Tom Stern, Burt Topper and James Gordon White.

Contents

Acknowledgments
vii

Introduction
1

The Filmography
3

Chronology of Films
209

Index
211

Introduction

Often cavalierly critiqued in other books linking them to various types of wild youth drama, the history of motorcycle films—Bikers—covers the heyday of a group of people who were made out to be more than they actually were, thanks to a spontaneous early postwar event. That event inspired a short story retold with considerable modification as *The Wild One* (see the entry beginning on page 191 for details of the incident). The real outlaws took that film's concepts of them and evolved into the Hell's Angels. While impressions of the old Brando image lingered, outlaws appeared in movies that were rarely full-fledged cycle dramas as the filmmakers often depended on other interests to sell their pictures—be it sports cars (*Dragstrip Riot*), airplanes (*The Hot Angel*), caper crimes (*Ivy League Killers*) or even sci-fi (*These Are the Damned*).

Most basic Biker conventions took hold in the early pre–Angels features. With their clannish mindset, regimental structure, fetishistically observed club rituals and willingness to fight at the drop of a pin, outlaws seem like one part urban youth gang, one part Mafia and one part period horde. Treated as both romantics and vermin, film outlaws were a source of crisis, a target of prejudice or the answer to someone's problem. In a single story, they could be bullies or victims, rapists or people falsely accused of a sex crime. Mad dogs or underdogs, outlaws never left a town or other gathering places (diners, hippie communes, Indian reservations, movie sets) the way they found it. If they had a fixed base, they were considered a local blight or part of a generally depressing landscape.

An outlaw leader may have been a cool, reflective thinker, a confused hunk with a soft side or a conscienceless sociopsychopath—perhaps a full maniac in the making. What a leader had his people do—or what he didn't want them to do—was often a prime plot mover. A president was someone who rose above his mindless confederates or dragged followers down some calamitous path. Women were usually the "taken for granted old lady," the "naïve small town girl" or the "spunky chick" who could get down and dirty. Police were "wimps," "facist pigs" or detached "Robocops."

American International Pictures (A.I.P.) handled the two earliest exploitation movies with bikers, *Motorcycle Gang* and the borderline *Dragstrip Riot*. When the fifties image of outlaws grew moldy, A.I.P. satirized it in Eric Von Zipper and his club. Essential beach party characters, they were not a strong enough presence to render the beach pix a legitimate hybrid of Bikers.

Motor Psycho contemporized the degrees of Biker sex and violence, opening up what was credited to the next classic Biker, *The Wild Angels*, stylizer and solidifier of the Angels movie phenomenon. With full creative license came designer label Bikers. The category that developed first, girl Bikers, was tuned to the vibrations of feminism. *The Mini-Skirt Mob* and the super-gory *She-Devils on Wheels* indirectly led to the sporadic wave of porno Bikers originated by *Sisters in Leather*.

A movie that shook up the whole Hollywood establishment, *Easy Rider*, wasn't a gang movie, but to much of the public, morality-flouting longhaired potheads on choppers were born to be wild. *Easy Rider* precipitated films with outlaws and hippies that dodged hybrid-theme identification because the exploitation campaigns of *Angel Unchained*, *The Peace Killers* and *Angels—Hard as They Come* acknowledged *only* outlaws.

The *Black Angels* darkened theater screens only months before the song of Sweetback ushered in the start of serious blaxploitation. Black Bikers, mostly, were only support figures. *Werewolves on Wheels* meant that virtually no class of humanity is immune to becoming monsters. Horror Bikers, though, were merely genre jokes of no sociological value.

During the 1966–1972 vogue phase of Bikers, much was written about their box-office clout—none, in the sixties at least, had ever lost money—and their presumed moral negativity. These Bikers were the first wholesale lot of films to show blasé drug use, the cruelty of the Establishment to counterculture societies and the polarization effect of a war that helped destroy the reputations of two presidents. What the grundies really reacted to was the terror that outlaw clubs represented then. Prohibition gangster and juvenile delinquency movies had been similarly attacked during the thirties and fifties. Even fair appraisals of Bikers untainted by bourgeois distaste felt the trend was prone to early burnout while vicious commentaries eagerly anticipated it.

When outlaws lost their shock value, Biker films finally ran out of road. Other protest pictures of the era were doomed by swollen, obsolete moral and social pretensions. It is easy to laugh at some unhip producer's silly notion of a love-in or acid trip, but not a graphic gangbang. Able to touch things both elemental and topical, Bikers were the most durably thrilling action pieces of their time, helping to create or advance the careers of many gifted performers and technicians.

Still among us, real outlaws have outlived other fringe organizations, drawing their generational resiliency from the undying appeal of the motorcycle itself and the retention of a central sense of identity. After all, does anyone fantasize about being a gridlocked commuter?

The Filmography

Angel Unchained

American International 1970. Presenters: H. Nicholson, Samuel Z. Arkoff; Executive Producer: Hal Klein; Producer-Director: Lee Madden; Co-Producer: Norman T. Herman; Screenplay: Jeffrey Alladin a/k/a Allen Fiskin; Story: Lee Madden, Jeffrey Alladin Fiskin; Production Executive: William J. Immerman; Cinematography: Irving Lippman; Film Editor: Fred Feitshans, Jr.; Musical Supervision: Al Simms; Music-Lyrics: Randy Sparks; Arranger-Conductor: Jim Helms; Post Production Supervisor: Salvatore Billitieri; Post-Production Manager: James Honore; Production Manager: Rusty Meek; Camera Operator: High Gaghier; Gaffer: Ralph McCarthy; Property Master: Arthur Frederick; Key Grip: John Hennessy; Costumes: Oscar Rodriguez; Makeup: Fred Blau, Jr.; Sound Mixer: Brad Trask; Script Supervisor: Stu Lippman; Special Effects: Roger George; Transportation Captain: George Baer; Stunt Coordinator: Bud Ekins; Still Man: Jack Albe; First Aid: George Cook; Man in Arizona: Jerry Haml; Title Design-Optical Effects: Cinefx; Sound: Ryder Sound Services; Sound Effects: Edit International, Ltd.; Locations: Cinemobile Systems, Inc.; Songs: "Following a Dream," "In Your New World," sung by Randy Sparks, Karen Rondell; "Bad Fish Blues," Music-Lyrics: T.C. Ryan, Yehudi Kazootie, Performed by T.C. Ryan, J. Cosgrove Butchie; "Blackbird in Despair," Music-Lyrics: Martin Stebler, Gilbert Avila, Performed by The Drivers, Featuring Chuck Freeman. Movielab Color; Running Time: 90 minutes.

Cast: Don Stroud (Angel); Luke Askew (Tremaine); Larry Bishop (Pilot); Tyne Daly (Merrilee); Aldo Ray (Sheriff); Neil Moran (Magician); Jean Marie (Jackie); Bill McKinney (Shotgun); Jordan Rhodes (Tom); Peter Lawrence (Dave); Pedro Regas (Injun); Linda Smith (Wendy); Nita Michaels (Matty); J. Cosgrove Butchie (Ray); T.C. Ryan (Hood); Alan Gibbs, J.N. Roberts (Duners); Bill Burton (Marauder); Bud Ekins (Speed); Jerry Randall (Candy); Dirty Dozen of Arizona (Bikers).

A.I.P.'s *The Wild Angels* was followed by the Fanfare picture *Hell's Angels on Wheels*, and *Hell's Angels '69* was the A.I.P. version of the Fanfare movie. Usually a helmer for hire, *Angels '69* director Lee Madden produced and co-wrote *Angel Unchained*, an A.I.P. counterpart of Fanfare's *Run, Angel, Run*, whose identically named hero was running from violence itself, not a betrayed gang. Real Danger rolled on dune buggy power, the force of good in a lesser Fanfare release, *Wild Wheels*.

At an amusement park, Angel and his gang rumble with their opposition. Angel's leader, Pilot, faces certain death atop a roller coaster until Angel throws his attacker to the ground. While they hide from the police, strung-out Angel decides to ride alone. He will be just another citizen. "Have a good trip," wishes Pilot.

On his aimless, unfulfilling journey, Angel stops for gas at a rural station where commune hippies Merrilee and Hood are refused service. Angel buys them gas, paying scornful proprietor Tom, who drops his money. "Keep the change," sarcastically remarks Angel. Grateful Merrilee rides with Angel to the commune. "Damn hippies!" curses Tom. "We're just gonna have to do somethin' about them!"

Angel meets the commune leader, Jonathan Ravenell Tremaine III. Son of a rich Louisiana family, he owns a dirt bike. Angel decides to stay. The eldest commune inhabitant is an aged Yacqui named Injun.

Angel and Merrilee become more intimate while skinny-dipping. At the commune, the locals attack in dune buggies, tearing up crops. Angel jabs a pitchfork into one man's arm. "Next time, we'll be back for your blood!" Tom threatens. "One week!"

Having until next Saturday to do something, the communers consider resistance. Tremaine wants Angel to summon his gang for help. "You bring a bike club in here and you're gonna have a lot of

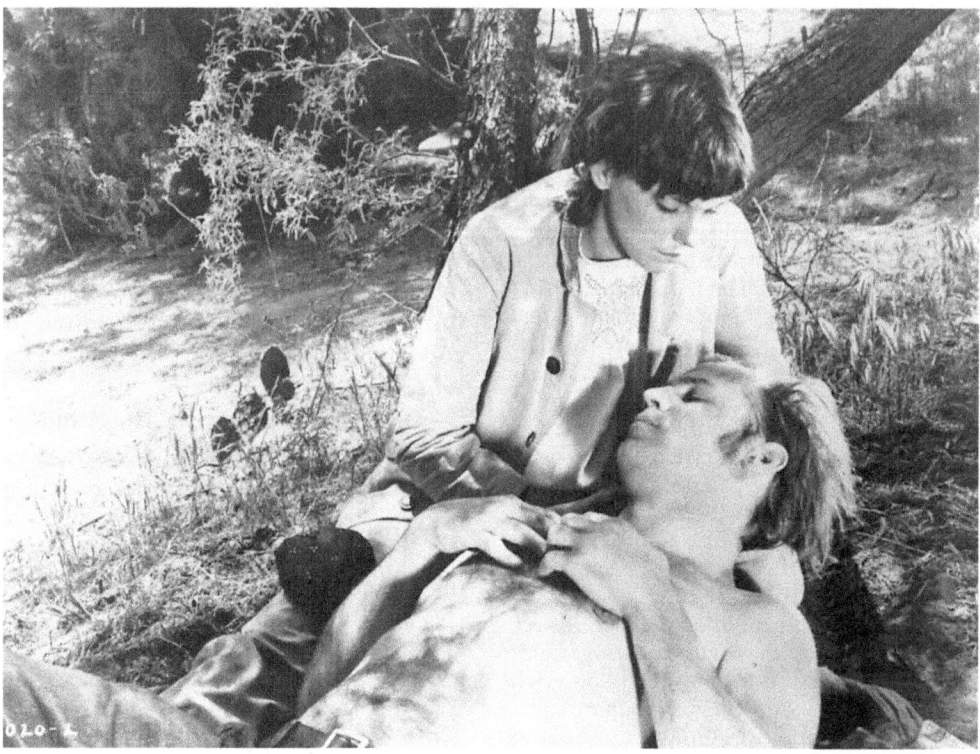

Merrilee (Tyne Daly) and Angel (Don Stroud) in love.

trouble on your hands," warns Angel. Tremaine turns to Merrilee for persuasion. She approaches Angel and, for the first time, they kiss.

Hoping diplomacy will work, Angel apologizes to the duners at a cattle yard—but they don't take kindly to "pigs." Under attack, Angel defends himself with an electric prod, loosing the steers. Tackling Tom, Angel yells, "Eat dirt, pig!"

Pilot still owes Angel for saving his life and the gang follows Angel to the commune. With them is Angel's ex–old lady, Jackie, now the property of Shotgun. She reveals the scars of an old tattoo Shotgun didn't like and removed. Shotgun, sizing up Merrilee, suggests a swap to Angel—warning him to keep away from Jackie.

Peering into his private domain, Pilot, Shotgun and Magician watch chanting Injun bake chocolate chip cookies and eat one. They sample the cookies, which contain a potent hallucinogen, and get high on the stuff named Whammo.

The bikers chaperone the communers when they go into town for supplies. Pilot and the Sheriff have a lazy chat while duner Dave maliciously trips a hippie. Biker Candy shoves a half-eaten peach into his face and a brawl breaks out. "Too much activity isn't good for you," says the Sheriff. Borrowing his gun, Pilot fires three shots into the air to end the fight. "Nice talkin' to you," the Sheriff says. "Toodle-oo," bids Pilot.

The self-defense course laid out by the bikers amounts to basic dirty fighting and traps are set up for the duners' expected return. Pilot regards all this as a "bad joke," asking Angel, "What are you doing here, man? You give up motorcycles for parsley!"

Shotgun still digs Merrilee, approaching her as she tills a vegetable patch. She treats his playfulness in good spirit, offering him canteen water. As she takes a drink, he gets grabby. Just teasing, he walks away. Taking it differently, Angel lunges at Shotgun. Shotgun slugs Angel, raising a club with seeming lethal intent, but laughs and walks off.

Wanting to split, the gang would like to take a "memento"—the Whammo. Angel tells Merrilee that Tremaine is asking for "too much," not sure if the commune will make it.

Coming back early, the duners beat up Hood and chase Wendy in their speeding buggies. One duner lassos her to the ground. Meanwhile, the bikers ransack the commune for Whammo until Angel has Pilot stop them. Battered, dazed Hood and Wendy stagger into view, warning of the duners. Angel wants to give the gang the Whammo, but Tremaine intends to hold it for now.

Merrilee asks Tremaine if he is quitting. "I'd ask you what a good pacifist would do," he says, "but I don't care." As long as he has the Whammo, the gang will have to wait until he gets back from where he plans to hide.

As Tremaine races out into the desert on his dirt bike, Angel chases him on his chopper. They see the duners coming. The bikers and the communers are ready for them. One buggy makes Tremaine fall off his bike and he is killed. Merrilee hands Angel Shotgun's weapon. He shoots Tom, who falls before his buggy crashes into a building, causing an explosion. Angel attends to dead Tremaine. "We're even," Pilot tells him. The gang and the duners leave.

Manson and Altamont brought about the downfall of the Age of Aquarius. Only in the Biker category that *Angel Unchained* started were there still any Flower Friendlies. *Angel Unchained* was moderately aware of things from *Easy Rider* that would work within the formula patterns of a gang movie, like the lake version of the waterhole scene. Water plus carefree young people meant nudity and nudity here promised the beginning of a romance. Intelligent, fully emotional and attractive in other places besides beaver country, Merrilee had more substance in her earwax than all the *Easy Rider* girls had in their collective air-retainer of a head.

Hippies made it challenging for audiences to see them as a genuine oppressed minority. Mostly from the privileged middle class, discontented communers could always drop back into the mainstream if they felt like it. The trick to making bike drama hippies look worthwhile was to cast them as beleaguered homesteaders. Rooting for its communers all the way, *Angel Unchained* wasn't meant to end like *The Savage Seven*, where the villain-duped outlaws and Indians who occasionally got along wiped themselves out. Leary of hallucinogens taken by the wrong people, the story gave up that concern once the bikers fulfilled their obligations.

Angel (Don Stroud) is just another citizen now.

Much of it the usual A.I.P. stuff, *Angel Unchained* featured two surprise participants *Easy Rider* might have found room for in its looser narrative. *Angel Unchained* was made near Apache Junction, Arizona. Going there to scout locations, Lee Madden met Max and Maria West. En route to Florida, the couple was traveling by prairie schooner. With their mules, Dawn and Bruce, the couple established camp on the mockup commune set and charged visitors a fee for their photos and a tour of the place. In the film, the Wests appeared as travelers just arriving at the commune.

The biker extras belonged to the Dirty Dozen Motorcycle Club, guarding their privacy by first-name-only identification, signed on their federal income tax withholding forms such unusual aliases as "Caveman," "Cheetah," "Pappy," "Bombo," "Burr," "Rush," "Al" and "LBJ."

Don Stroud was an ex–Universal contract actor who played a hippie in *What's So Bad About Feeling Good?* (1968) and the biker thug, Ringerman, in *Coogan's Bluff* (1968). For Roger Corman, Stroud portrayed Herman Barker in *Bloody Mama* (1970). He became Capt. Pat Chambers on *The New Mike Hammer*. When star Stacy Keach's London coke bust disrupted production, Stroud was offered the Hammer role. Daughter of the late *Medical Center* star James, former New York stage actress Tyne Daly won two Emmys for the role of Mary Beth Lacey on *Cagney and Lacey*, later taking the part of Maxine Gray on *Judging Amy*.

Bill McKinney became one of the mountain men in *Deliverance* (1972). Robert's son, T.C. Ryan, belonged to an Oregon commune and composed a song for *Angel Unchained*, singing it with player J. Cosgrove Butchie.

Downplaying its resemblance to *Run, Angel, Run* once it got its own story going, *Angel Unchained* made its communers the smartest ones in a bike drama because they knew from the outset that aggression was their only hope. Setting aside their belief in peace, they opted for the ploy of praising the Lord while passing the ammunition.

Angels Die Hard

New World 1970. Presenter: James Tannenbaum; Executive Producers: James Tannenbaum, Jane Schaeffer; Producer: Charles Beach a/k/a Beach Dickerson; Director-Screenplay: Richard Compton; Cinematography: Arch Archembault; Film Editor: Tony DeZarrago; Music Director: Richard Hieronymous; Unit Production Manager: Michael Stringer; Key Grip: David Atkins; Script Supervisor: Barbara Peeters; Production Stills: Joel Sussman; Sound Mixer: James Evergreen; Sound Boom: James Heinlen; Assistant Editor: Bill Tremberth; Assistant Director: John Rico; Titles-Opticals: Modern Film Effects; Songs: "Kern County Line," "Questions," "Someday Soon" composed by Marcia Waldorf; "Changes," "Something's Wrong" composed by Bill Cone; "The Man Who Kills Ants" by Tom Hill; sung by Dewey Martin; "Death Is a Dancer" by R. Landes, S. Holtzman, W. Holtzman and sung by Fever Tree; "Night of the Lions" by S. Holtzman and sung by Marc Eric; "I Want to Take You Higher" by M. Malmberg and sung by Sylvanus; "Tendency to Be Free" composed and sung by Rabbit McKay; Instrumental Music composed by Richard Hieronymous; Soundtrack Coordination: Marcia Waldorf—Pettipoint Prods. Movielab Color; Angels Productions; Running Time: 86 minutes.

Cast: Tom Baker (Blair); William Smith (Gentleman Tim); R.G. Armstrong (Mel Potter); Alan DeWitt (Sparagut); Connie Nelson (Nancy); Carl Steppling (Sheriff Dan Davis); Frank Leo (Deputy Johnny Martin); Beach Dickerson (Shank); Gary Littlejohn (Piston); William Bonner (Houston); Rita Murray

Monk (Michael Donovan O'Donnell) watches Deputy Johnny Martin (Frank Leo) and Gentleman Tim (William Smith) converse at the roadblock. In the background is Sparagut (Alan DeWitt).

(Naomi); Mikel Angel (Dirty Davie); Les Otis (Tommy); Dianne Turley (Patsy); Michael Donovan O'Donnell (Monk); Dan Haggerty, Michael Stringer (Seed); Bambi Allen (Wife); and David Schaeffer.

Richard Compton and Roger Corman regular Beach Dickerson came together on the set of the *The Savage Seven* when Dickerson was doing a supporting role and Compton was working as the assistant property master. Most of Compton's early credits, other than the story of *Run, Angel, Run*, were in the adult market. Roger Corman wanted the first New World movie to be a Biker, as there was still money in that field. Since *Easy Rider* was fated to be imitated, Compton wrote *Violent Angels*, which began with an *Easy Rider*-type highway murder. Renamed *Angels Die Hard*, it was budgeted at sixty-five thousand dollars. For the distribution rights, Corman raised an additional ten grand.

Angel chieftans Blair and Gentleman Tim lead the Angels into the lakeside mountain town of Kernville. Answering a riot call, Sheriff Dan Davis and Deputy Johnny Martin break up a street fight between the Angels and the friends of Mel Potter and Shank. Davis takes an Angel, Seed, hostage and makes the gang leave, promising to free him in two days.

Davis' teenaged daughter, Nancy, and her boyfriend, Tommy, attend the annual Whiskey Flats Parade. Davis releases Seed, whose idle chopper stalls. Borrowing a phone to call the Angels, he meets Nancy. Davis sternly orders Nancy to go home, wanting Seed out now. Seed gets the bike started. At the county line, he gives the finger to someone before there is a crash.

Tim brings Seed's body back to the Angels' junkyard headquarters. He was deliberately run off the road. "We've got to get somebody's ass for this," Blair intently tells Tim. "You know that, don't ya? I don't care whose. Anybody's!"

Funeral arrangements are handled by undertaker Sparagut, who joins the Angels' procession. Piston and Dirty Davie square off over who inherits Seed's old lady Naomi. Swarming into a closed restaurant, the Angels subdue the owner and gangbang his wife in a spaghetti orgy. Forced to let the Angels pass, Davis gives them a stay deadline of noon tomorrow. In his fiery graveside eulogy, Tim warns, "Every outlaw rider in the State of California is fair game!" To give his send-off "class," the Angels pee on Seed's coffin.

The Angels hold a wake involving some local kids, including Nancy. Monk gets Sparagut zonked on pills. Stumbling into town, he runs after Johnny's squad car, yelling, "Taxi!" Davis has Sparagut put on a late bus for home.

Potter fans the flames of community hostility. Johnny asks the Angels, "What do you want?" "A piece for a piece," answers Blair. When a small boy is trapped in an abandoned mine shaft, the Angels help in the child's rescue. This doesn't sit well with Davis. Blair meets Nancy.

Tommy takes Nancy to lovers' lane, sensing why she shrinks from his clumsy, over-aggressive affection. "You saving it for that bike guy?" Nancy understands the Angels' need for revenge: "Maybe they have that right!" She leaves Tommy, joining Blair at the Angels' camp. Intruding Tommy refuses to go without Nancy until Tim beats him up. Leaving camp, Nancy runs into insanely jealous Tommy, who asks, "You've been with him, haven't you?" He slaps Nancy, who bumps her head. She appears dead.

Tommy claims that the Angels kidnapped Nancy. Outraged Davis authorizes a vigilante posse and Johnny ineffectually protests. Tommy tells Johnny he lies and they follow Davis in Johnny's car. Lying in wait, the Angels ambush the vigilantes, shouting, "Kill the pigs!" Potter guns down Tim before he is slain by another Angel. Blair is one of the few who manage to escape.

Near the massacre scene, Davis spots Nancy collapsing by the road. "Don't go out there!" she pleads. When Blair passes on his bike, inflamed Davis takes pursuit. Instead of Blair, flash-back-tortured Davis sees finger-waving Seed from the killer's perspective—his own. Before Davis can kill Blair, Johnny shoots him. Davis' car rolls down an embankment and explodes.

The sentiment of hate kept the plot of *Angels Die Hard* going more than motive. Immediately antagonistic, the rednecks established where trouble would go, making the assassination of a lone outlaw not a revelation like the finale of *Easy Rider*, but the premise for a long-anticipated showdown. The Angels were upset by Seed's death, but not overly surprised because self-preservation, according to the script, was what drew outlaws into clubs in the first place.

This was Dick Compton's first major directorial job and in his ambition he felt he had to ratchet up every point of sensationalism. Comic relief Sparagut was a crude spoof of George Hanson. The restaurant rape was tastelessly jokey. Seed's funeral was ritualistically vulgar, not a sudden reaction to hypocrisy like the one in *The Wild Angels*. The mine rescue was a heavy-handed acknowledgement that even Angels can be angels. Meant to expose who snuffed Seed, Davis' hallucination was startling because it made Seed appear as an actual ghost.

The funniest sight gag was that of a helmeted Angel who was a "blockhead" for walking around with a piece of broken board (inflicted during the first fight) stuck to the helmet's spike. On the back of a rotund booger-eater's trike, the Ichabod Crane–like Sparagut resembled a stiff swaybacked dummy.

Once a frontier gold mining town

Vigilante leader Mel Potter (R.G. Armstrong) is killed by an angry Angel (Dan Haggerty).

where silent westerns were made, Kernville donated the best production value in its Whiskey Flat celebration, *Angels Die Hard*'s version of the *Easy Rider* Mardi Gras. The junkyard belonged to extravagant bric-a-brac collector Al Coe. Built by Gary Littlejohn, the masterpiece bike was the Cinderella cart, an orange trike with a pumpkin-shaped cowl. Behind it was towed Seed's pine box casket, bedecked with a bouquet of purple flowers.

Some Angels were the Bakersfield Knight Riders. During the filming of the scene where Davis ordered the Angels out of town, they got high on pills, demanding pay-off money from the producers until the real Kernville cops threw *them* out. Scenes at the Angels' camp were done in the backyard of Compton's Laurel Canyon home. For pick-up shots that couldn't be done in Kernville, Compton photographed scenes against the L.A. sky. One Knight Rider was killed in a way similar to Seed's homicide and network TV covered his funeral. Al Coe lost all but three acres of his pack rat's paradise to the Bureau of Land Management.

Gentleman Tim was apparently written with William Smith in mind for his bombasity, reflectiveness, brutality and kindness. Laidback prez Blair was breezily played by former Jim Morrison drinking buddy Tom Baker, star of Andy Warhol's *I, a Man* (1967). Baker's aboveground film career, unfortunately, didn't prosper at a lead level. Baker produced *Bongo Wolf's Revenge* (1971), a documentary on William Donald Grollman, a Hollywood freak who thought he was a werewolf. A drug overdose killed Baker in 1982.

Outgrossing *Woodstock* in Texas, *Angels Die Hard* made two million. Not only the movie that began New World, it formed the cornerstone of Dick Compton's obsession with freaked-out fuzz in such films as the true-life *Macon County Line* (1974), his biggest hit, the exciting, Compton-scripted TV movie *The California Kid* (1974) and *Macon's* 1975 sequel *Return to Macon County*.

Angels from Hell

American International 1968. Executive Producer: Joe Solomon; Producer: Kurt Neumann; Director: Bruce Kessler; Screenplay: Jerome Wish; Cinematography: Herman Lee Knox; Film Editor: William Martin; Music: Stu Phillips; Cycle Art: Von Dutch; Technical Consultant: Sonny Barger; Assistant Director: Ray Gosnell; Assistant Cameraman: Ross Kelsey; Art Director: Wally Moon; Script Clerk: Bri Murphy; Makeup: Richard Scarso; Sound Mixer: Keith Wester; Recording: Producers Sound Service; Post-Production: Synchro-Film Inc.; Sound Effects: Edit-Rite Inc.; Hair-Pieces: American Fashion Products; Songs: "No Communication" by Jerry Styner, Stu Phillips; "Angels from Hell" by Stu Phillips, Guy Hemric, Byron Cole; "Crystal Tear" by Stu Phillips, Guy Hemric and sung by the Peanut Butter Conspiracy; "Who's It Gonna Be," "Mr. Madison Avenue" written and sung by the Lollipop Shoppe Courtesy Lord Tim Prods.; Perfect Color; A Fanfare Production; Running Time: 86 minutes.

Cast: Tom Stern (Mike); Arlene Martel (Ginger); Ted Markland (Smiley); Stephen Oliver (Speed); Paul Bertoya (Nutty Norman); Jimmy Murphy (Tiny Tim); Jack Starrett (Bingham); Jay York (George); Pepper Martin (Dennis); Bob Harris (Baney); Saundra Gayle (Clair); Suzy Walters (Millie); Luana Talltree (Angry Annie); Rod Wilmoth (Cop); Ginger Snapp a/k/a Suzzanne Sidney (Buff); Lori Hay (Go-go Dancer); Lee Stanley (Reynolds); Doug Hume (Crowley); Jim Reynolds (Durkens); Steve Rogers (Dud); Susan Holloway (Jennifer); Judith Garwood (Louise); Tony Rush (Hippie Child); Maureen Heard (Hippie Girl); Barry Feinstein (Prophet); Dodie Warren, Wally Berns (Hippie Girl's Parents); Cynthia McAdams (Pearl); Bud Ekins (Scrambler); the Madcaps of Bakersfield.

U.S. Films handled the earliest Joe Solomon movies. About to make Fanfare a self-distributing entity, Solomon released his second Biker, *Angels from Hell*, through A.I.P. Richard Rush was off making *The Savage Seven* and on *Angels from Hell*, direction went to Bruce Kessler, a successful racecar driver of the fifties who had been Dan Gurney's partner for some events. Kessler had done second-unit work for Howard Hawks and helped on the car chase scenes from *Bonnie and Clyde*.

In *Angels from Hell*, Jack Starrett reprised the character of Bingham from *Hell's Angels on Wheels*. Now a captain, Bingham worked in Bakersfield, whose local bikers, the Madcaps, played a gang kicked out of Riverside who moved to that city in the absence of their fictitious first leader, Mike Connery. Bingham was more patient with Mike than he had been with Angel Buddy, but this president was an out-and-out megalomaniac.

Home from Vietnam, Mike enters a bar, where two rednecks beat up a black biker in the restroom. Mike karate chops the duo, carrying the injured biker to his concerned friends.

Mike meets up with his old sidekick, Smiley, who will tell the club he is back. Mike arouses the wariness of a police sergeant, staring at him tauntingly as he lewdly strokes his bike. As Mike roars off, the sergeant reports in to Bingham.

At the go-go joint where the Madcaps hang out, Mike is welcomed by his followers, who heard that Mike won a medal. "They give you a medal if you don't catch the clap," Mike cracks. Current prez Big George wants to maintain the good relationship the Madcaps have with the Bakersfield cops. Eager to reclaim his throne, Mike pushes George into a fight and applies a leg-break move. Mike takes George's prez colors before Bingham arrives.

A sexy farm owner who lets the Madcaps stay at her place, Ginger is "a woman of independent means." Bingham shows up to lay down certain ground rules.

On a road trip, the Madcaps tease a scrambler who leads them on a good chase. The wily scrambler escapes but things look up for Mike romantically when Ginger invites him into her bedroom.

In Beverly Hills, the Madcaps pay a surprise visit to an ex-member, movie star Dude Marshall. Dude's producer, Sol Joseph, is inspired to make a film about the club. For research, Joseph's buxom secretary, Louise, ushers Speed into a private room to tape his words. "You smell beautiful," she tells Speed, making herself comfortable. Overwhelmed, Speed mumbles, "I love my chopper," as Louise goes down on him. The Madcaps have a movie deal.

Back in Bakersfield, Mike goes out with a go-go girl while rookie cop Reynolds hassles the gang over a parking violation. He attacks playful Speed and pulls his gun, calling in for backup. Mike's lovemaking with the dancer is interrupted when her butch "mother" arrives and presses a knife to his throat, dragging the dancer away. Mike is amused—until he hears the cutting laughter of Ginger, standing in a corner. Arrested, Speed was beaten by two cops who were supposed to take him in but didn't. Mike complains to Bingham.

Smiley's girl, Claire, comes on to Reynolds at a refreshment stand. Out of the back of a panel truck, some hippie-disguised Madcaps suddenly fake Clair's abduction. Responding, Reynolds starts his bike, moving only a few feet before he is thrown off by an attached chain moored to a pipe.

Trouble erupts amongst the Madcaps when Dennis is caught fitting his bike with a part stolen from Smiley's. Investigating the commotion, Mike tells George to fade and "leave your colors." As Mike turns his back, Dennis throws his knife, but Smiley warns Mike. Mike grabs the knife, taunting Dennis, who attacks with a bigger blade before Mike kung fus him senseless.

Speed is approached in town by two cops who set him up on a pot charge. An urgent phone call sends Mike racing to where Speed was fatally shot for supposedly resisting "routine questioning." "When it becomes a crime to ride a motorcycle," declares appalled Bingham, "by God, that's a sad day for us all."

The Madcaps visit some city hippies enjoying the pastoral pleasures of a country retreat. "It's the same sick bag no matter where you go in this country," gripes Prophet. "Hey, everybody's uptight about property rights. What about civil rights?" "The squares run the scene," says Mike. "The trick is you gotta show 'em you got the same rights they do. We don't want 'em to love us—just leave us alone." Nutty Norman digs a hippie girl who gives him her peace necklace and he exchanges his Iron Cross pendant.

Alarmed, Smiley summons Mike and Ginger, taking them to Nutty and the girl, whom he has murdered. "Oh my God!" cries Ginger. "Yeah, God," laughs insane Nutty. "She kept yelling about God over and over. That's all she talked about—God and love. Well, I showed her about love … and she kept screamin' for God. So I told her if she wants God to love her, she's gotta get in the right position and see God." The Madcaps make a discreet exit. "They're good people," the hippie leader says.

Five hundred outlaws are expected to attend Speed's funeral. Sol Joseph will film the procession for his movie. Smiley and Ginger fear a possible riot. "You know how many slobs are out there that have no place to go to?" raves Mike. "Wow! Dig! Television! Radio! Newspapers! Why, when they see that in the headlines, man, they'll be knockin' down our doors to get in! I'll take this chapter and make fifteen, twenty clubs! I won't have five hundred bikes! I'll have a thousand! A whole mother-lovin' army!" "You're insane!" cries Ginger. "I'm brilliant!" grins Mike.

Suddenly, the police raid the farm and line all the men up against a wall.

Mike (Tom Stern) clobbers the menacing Dennis (Pepper Martin).

Bingham makes them peel their colors. Methodically, he walks by each man and glances at their chests ... looking for something. He finds it on Nutty—the dead girl's necklace. As Nutty is led away, Bingham tells the gang he wants them out tomorrow. "There's no place for you! Nowhere! I don't event think the zoos would want you!"

Mike pulls Bingham's gun on him, vowing to bring in all the funeral bikers and wreck the town. Bingham tells his men to let Mike go, but as Mike rides off, the Sergeant shotguns him. "Come Now, And Let Us Reason Together. Isaiah I, 18," reads a Biblical caption.

Sonny Barger was the technical consultant of *Angels from Hell*, which in production scope and degree of on-screen violence was a lesser film than *Hell's Angels on Wheels*. First, to show black bikers, it made Ginger an outlaw feminist men had to take on her own terms, though Mike was able to press the right compromise buttons.

Another wild man of the military-industrial complex like Brahmin of *Motor Psycho*, Mike operated on purpose, not animal impulse. Expected to come home docile and drained of hostility supposedly well spent, Mike self-servingly revived the old club spirit to feed a battle-acquired sense of invincibility, incurring extralegal action from Bingham's men. The Madcaps would have been harmless without their favorite leader, and if not for behaviors Mike encouraged or excused, Bingham wouldn't have been the only reasonable cop in an out-of-control department.

Angels from Hell was the first piece of bike fiction via the spoofing of Joe

Solomon to indicate the fascination Hollywood had with outlaws. Solomon hired actors who became known for bike roles while Joseph contractee Dude Marshall *had been* an outlaw in his "flaming youth." Secretary Louise may have been conceived as a swinging version of Solomon's valued assistant Pearl Kempton.

More and more, the police of North America were confronting a population that no longer adhered to an old sense of place. Mike expressed that feeling in legal babble. It was when the Madcaps took physical license that the Bingham cops would take no more. Mike's death prevented an all-out town invasion, but all the cops had to do was radio ahead to the Highway Patrol for his apprehension. The disobedient Sergeant hid his vigilante urge in plain sight. A savior, maybe ... Hero?

No Richard Rush imitator, Bruce Kessler kept his direction clean and simple. Overscored by the tune "No Communication," the first encounter between Mike and the sergeant was intercut with pop paintings of a demon Mike humping a half-beast, half-bike thing ... like a cycle centaur. The sarge was a fascist ogre. Nude paintings compensated for the lack of full-frontal skin. On his office desk, Bingham kept a framed picture of Alfred E. Neumann.

Wardrobe touches were sometimes pointed. The confiscation of George's colors denoted Mike's official return to power. An old man wore a tiny Iron Cross around his neck, showing his youthfulness of heart. Under her prim dress jacket, braless Louise wore a semitransparent white blouse. The hippies favored period pageant costumes. And the respective

Mike (Tom Stern) takes Bingham (Jack Starrett) hostage.

necklaces of Nutty and the hippie girl were relevant murder clues like the hunting medal in *The Savage Seven*.

Tom Stern was a former agent for New England Mutual Insurance who got his nose smashed during a Dodgers tryout in Vero Beach, Florida. Drafted, Stern went to Germany and joined the Army's Special Forces. He acted in the plays *Twelfth Night, The Moon Is Blue* and *Detective Story*. Upon return to civilian life, Stern sold more Mutual insurance, then studied at the Stella Adler School and the Actor's Studio. Stern was TV's Chesterfield Man, an understudy to Alan Arkin and Gabriel Dell in the off-Broadway bomb *Man Out Loud: Girl Quiet,* and he appeared in the London stage presentation of *Never Too Late*. After doing the TV series *Espionage*, Stern was in *The Spy Who Came In from the Cold* and *The Hallelujah Trail* (both 1965). This led to the lead in *You've Got to Be Smart* (1967). Stern was then married to Samantha Eggar and fathered their two children.

Since Mike was so much the center of things, nobody less than Stern could have brought the role its essential grandstand level of acting. Arlene Martel, the French resistance fighter Tiger on *Hogan's Heroes* and Mr. Spock's wife, T'Pring, on *Star Trek*, was just as heady, Ginger being steel panties to Mike's iron drawers. With more room to enact Bingham, Jack Starrett gave him an element of pathos missing from his first appearance.

Mr. Motor Psycho, Steve Oliver, was the more mellow and lovable Speed. Richard Rush's son, Tony, played a child hippie. Bud Ekins, the harassed scrambler, was a motorcycle dealer and repairman in San Fernando who coached many bike rider celebrities, designing bikes and coordinating stunts for films.

Sol Joseph was Joe Solomon being himself. He accompanied Tom Stern, Jack Starrett, Ted Markland, Jimmy Murphy and Luana Talltree to the premiere of *Angels from Hell* at the Meadowlark Twin Drive-Ins in Wichita.

Before 1968 was out, Fanfare would be ready to stand on its own two feet. On his next film, *The Devil's Brigade* (1968), Tom Stern met Jeremy Slate and they would make the next Biker Sonny Barger appeared in, *Hell's Angels '69*.

Angels—Hard as They Come

New World 1971. Producer: Jonathan Demme; Director: Joe Viola; Screenplay: Jonathan Demme, Joe Viola; Cinematograthy: Steve Katz; Supervising Film Editor: Joe Ravitz; Music: Richard Hieronymous, Performed by Carp Titles; Designer-Photographer: Don Record; Art Director: Jack Fisk; Production Manager: Donald Heitzler; Assistant Director: Lorenzo Barzaghi; Stunt-Motorcycle Coordinator: Gary Littlejohn; Stuntman: Bobby Clark; Sound Man: Peter Pilifian; Camera Assistants: John Swain, Lynn Ellsworth; Set Design: John Lynch; Wardrobe-Makeup: Jodi Tillen, Claudia Ellsworth; Key Grip: Jim Morris; Gaffer: Don Clark; Script Girl: Connie Graver; Sound Mixer: Richard Brummer; Editorial Assistant: Anthony J. Ciccolini III; Music performed by Caleb Deschenal; Special Effects: Immagic Inc.; Music Producer: T.C. Corbett; Metrocolor; Running Time: 90 minutes.

Cast (in order of appearance): Dennis Art (Rings); Larry Tucker (Lucifer); Cheri Latimer (Lucifer's Girl); Scott Glenn (Long John); Bill Carter (Charlie); Charles Dierkop (General); Gary Littlejohn (Axe); Brendan Kelly (Brain); Steve Slauson (Magic); John Taylor (Crab); Marc Seaton (Louie); Niva Davis (Clean Sheila); Ronn Starr (Ron); Frank Charolla (Frank); Evelyn Littlejohn (Evi); William Gray (Gas Station Attendant); Gilda Texter (Astrid); Gary Busey (Henry); Janet Wood (Vicki); Brendan Burns (Tim); Sharon Peckinpah (Sharon); Lynn Ellsworth (Lynn); Pete Loman (Pete); James Iglehart (Monk); Don Carrera (Juicer); Mike Shack (Gordon); Becki Borland (Carol); Hal Marshall (Jagger); Jim Morris (Bike Rider); Frank Kimberly (Angel); Lance Springer (Cloud); John Spence (Angel).

Before getting into the "Lights! Camera! Action!" end of film, Jonathan Demme had been a critic and publicity man at United Artists. Producer and co-writer of his first film, *Angels—Hard as They Come*, Demme left the direction to his fellow author, TV commercials veteran Joe Viola. It had been called *The Savage Angels* until New World substituted *Angels—Hard as They Come* ("hard" and "come" obvious innuendoes). Dramatically and pictorially reminiscent of Italian westerns, *Hard as They Come* was *Rashomon* (1954) in the modern American West, *The Outrage* (1964) a nineteenth century remake.

In their adaptation, Demme and Viola rained on the pretensions of two bike clubs, the Angels and the Dragons, and some hippies trying to start a commune in the ghost town of Lost Cause. The

Angels were "honorable" outlaws pushing drugs; the Dragons were everybody's enemy. Compulsory truces between the sympathetic opposites to stop a mutual foe were the common theme of most of Demme's exploitation movies.

Pusher Lucifer and his lady drive to a hillside where Long John, accompanied by Charlie, arranges a coke deal. Their lookout, Rings, spots two unmarked police units parked on either side of the highway below. Long John instructs Lucifer to bring the money to Cloud's in three days. To throw the cops off-balance, Long John and Charlie take off in separate directions. Rings cripples the car chasing Long John by tossing a riot control gas bomb through an open back window.

Fifty miles away, the Dragons stop at a gas station, noticing a van owned by the Lost Cause hippies, en route to their new home.

The next day, Long John, Monk and Juicer meet Dragons Brain and Magic at the station and are invited to joint them at Lost Cause. On its main street, General beats his lieutenant Axe in a race. General challenges Long John to a race. Long John wins. Petulant General demands a rematch.

Long John sees Astrid up in a loft sketching the bikers. "Which one is me?" he asks. "I don't know," she answers. "I can make you anyone I want." "I'm me!" Long John testily insists. After introductions, he questions life in a ghost town while Astrid asks, "Why do you do the things you do?"

"You mean cop-stompin' baby rapin' town burning shit?" Long John retorts. "You tell me why you hippies are chuckin' acid in the reservoirs and ballin' in the park." What Astrid means is all the violence. "What about Altamont? You know a guy was killed there," she says.

"I was never at Altamont," Long John states. "Are you with them hippies' chicks who chopped up those Hollywood types?" He asserts under his breath, "What works is what's right."

Long John spots a towering sluice and in the town church meets Vicki and the hippie leader Henry. "Where's his head at?" wonders Henry. "I don't think he knows," replies Vicki.

In the evening, the bikers and the communers party. Axe wants to race Long John. "Why Long John?" Monk asks. "Let's say I want to bring home the trophy," infers Axe. Long John accepts Axe's

Long John (Scott Glenn) races General (Charles Dierkop).

offer. They will go up to the end of the road and back twice.

During the race, General, Brain and Crabs drag Astrid into the candlelit church to gangbang her. Axe finishes the race first. Sensing Astrid's peril, Long John dashes into the church with Monk and Juicer. As they interrupt the rape, the lights go out. Someone flashes a knife. The melee ends with sore tempers on the part of the Dragons. Henry steps out of the darkness carrying the stabbed body of Astrid. Brain thinks Long John accidentally knifed her trying to murder General. General vehemently concurs and the Angels are carted off to the jail.

General presides over the Dragons' kangaroo court. Axe is sergeant at arms, Brain the "persecutor" and Magic the token defense. "We treated you like brother outlaws should!" General rails. "You hassled us! You busted up our party! You spoiled our train! *You tried to kill me!* And you snuffed out my new mama!" Brain reinforces the assassination theory. Henry tries to instill reason, but General cuts him off. Long John thinks either Brain or Axe used the knife, feeling neither wants to kowtow to General. Before sentence is passed, the Angels are returned to jail, where Long John maps out an escape plan.

The Angels are condemned to chopper polo. "You guys are the balls," General explains. During the game, Long John cues Juicer to grab a bike, but he falls and a hog wheel crushes his hand. Monk flees on a bike with a half full tank. Long John and Juicer are returned to jail. Henry wants the confiscated van rotor, but won't get it back until tomorrow. General wants a rope put around the sluice to make it "a roller coaster—a going away present for our guests."

On the dunes, Monk bogs down. He meets Gordon and Carol, a sadistic dune buggy couple who taunt him racially. Gun-toting Gordon will offer gas for Monk's colors. Carol goes topless to tease him. As Monk walks away, Gordon runs him down a dune bank.

At the jail window, Henry tells Long John, "There's been too much damn blood. Because of that, we're gonna help you. If we can." Back on his feet, Monk joins a doctor who gives him water and commandeers his camper. Vicki drops acid into the coffee she gives jail guards Crabs and Louie. As they trip out, Louie imagines himself a school classroom monitor and Long John tricks him into unlocking the cell door. Monk joins the other Angels at Cloud's.

While Vicki takes on Clean Sheila in a lively strip battle, Henry goes to Long John and Juicer. They hide in the church belfry, where Long John tells Henry to get a lantern and some items to fix Juicer's hand.

Morning sees most of the Dragons still hung over. Going to the jail, General explodes when he discovers Long John and Juicer have escaped. In the belfry, Long John uses the lantern, a Coke bottle and a rag to make a Molotov cocktail. Vicki is dragged to General to make her tell where Long John and Juicer are. Her hands are bound to a raised rope running to a bike Crabs starts. General threatens to burn her bare breasts with a torch until Long John calls down from the belfry. From his colors, he produces the bomb—threatening to burn the Dragons' bikes if they come any closer.

While Juicer gets the van rotor, Axe subdues Long John with his hand axe. General orders that the Angels be taken to the sluice. Axe announces he is taking over. Henry brandishes a knife to defend Long John and Juicer until Brain overpowers him. Magic recognizes it as Axe's knife. Henry confirms this to General. Axe killed Astrid. Removing his Kaiser helmet, infuriated General drives the spike into Axe's heart.

The cavalry in the presence of Monk and the other Angels arrives. Demented General tries to kill unconscious Long John by dragging him to the sluice. Juicer brains Brain in the face with a Coke bottle. Long John pushes General into the path of blinded Brain's veering bike. Brain flies over the handlebars and General is hurled against the sluice, which collapses, burying him under falling debris.

Soon after the massacre is over, the Angels and the hippies prepare to leave Lost Cause. Henry and Long John turn to each other for a moment. On highway, the groups go their separate ways.

Angels—Hard as They Come took to heart the lesson of Altamont that even rebels feel they are not all created equal. Even in underbelly realms, segregation may be best for those whose forms of anarchy mix like gasoline and fire. Since the Angels and the Dragons were both bikers, trouble at Lost Cause might have been avoided if it was just their party or if fraternizing had only been between the hippies and the Angels.

If most of the Dragons were foolish in letting themselves be wrapped around the finger of little Hitler General, the hippies were naïve in thinking everyone would come around to peace if exposed to their brand of hospitality. Not all hippies lost faith at the same time, so those in *Hard as They Come* were the last bastions of Pure Dreamers—not pragmatists like the Tremaine colony in *Angel Unchained* who lived with danger knowingly. In the skeleton of a town created by industry and killed by the cave-in of its mine, Henry's group hoped to pursue their rose-colored, unworkable belief they were the hope of mankind.

Monk (James Iglehart) is about to "tour" the town.

The debate between Long John and Astrid over Altamont was checkmated by the guilt both divisions of longhairs had to own up to concerning how each overbearingly practiced expressions of freedom. The Altamont statement would have been wiser if the *Hard Angels* had a different name, as any movie bike gang called Angels is usually perceived as being a counterpart of *the* Hell's Angels. The Dragons were the outlaws who behaved like Meredith Hunter's killers.

Astrid was the sacrificial lamb for a Hunter-like death that was obscured so confusion would lend righteous anger to the Dragons. As paranoid about personal safety as most dictators are, General was too rabidly biased to consider what Long John suggested—a power play within his ranks. In their resistance against the Dragons, the hippies fared best at sneak strategy. Once Axe was exposed, the Dragons were in group disarray and defeat was inevitable. The Angels could return to their life, but the hippies felt they had betrayed theirs. The shame was lessened by knowing they had in them the guts the Angels helped bring out.

As with the best westerns, *Angels—Hard as They Come* swelled with effects pop psychology could glom on to. The stink bomb Rings threw turned a police weapon on the cops. The hippies adopted a painted sunburst as their cheery commune logo. A reminder of Lost Cause's former business, the sluice appealed to the artistic sensitivity of Astrid and the fiendishness of General. The American flag was an altar cloth for Astrid's "train" and decorated the Dragons' court. Behind it was a wall cross the General posed in front of in Messianic contortions. When the Angels couldn't hide underground, they found heavenward sanctuary in the church belfry. The collapse of the sluice upon General saw him done in by his own guillotine.

Art Director Jack Fisk met future wife Sissy Spacek on the set of *Badlands* (1973), art directed her breakout film *Carrie* (1976) and directed Spacek in his own film, *Raggedy Man* (1981).

Credited with music work, Caleb Deschenal attended U.C.L.A. with George Lucas and was second-unit cameraman on *Apocalypse Now* (1979). As D.P., he won an Oscar nomination for *The Right Stuff* (1983), with Scott Glenn as Alan Sheppard and Deschenal's wife, Mary Jo, as Annie Glenn. Deschenal turned director with *The Escape Artist* (1982) and helmed a few episodes of *Twin Peaks*.

Scott Glenn made Long John a different sort of inner-centered leader. Long John had the individuality to survive without a club, but belonged to one to protect his right to do what he wanted. Gary Busey drummed for Carp, the band that performed for *Hard as They Come*. Only adequate as Henry, Busey looked more like a commune follower, as hippie leaders in Bikers usually affected a Christ aura.

Charles Dierkop had played Mr. Clean in *The Sweet Ride* (1968). Dierkop bounced all over the screen as General, doing everything but standing on his head (easy, when there's a spike on top of it) to exploit General's nuances. Retaining the twisted merriment of hairless Clean, Dierkop, with General's helmet, once again made a condition of his head his prime visual feature.

Gilda Texter, the film's violently terminated notion of a heroine, had shown all of herself throughout the role of the nude hippie bike girl in *Vanishing Point* (1971).

Guest star Larry Tucker, playing Lucifer, was Paul Mazursky's writing partner on *I Love You, Alice B. Toklas* (1968), *Bob & Carol & Ted & Alice* (1969) and *Alex in Wonderland* (1970). Lucifer's girl was Cheri Latimer, whose role in *Alex* was cut, but acknowledged in Mazursky's words in a *Playboy* spread. Dennis "Dirty Denny" Art was Rings and Gary Littlejohn had his most important role as Axe. Littlejohn's wife, Evelyn, was a Dragon mama.

Jonathan Demme and Joe Viola paired on *The Hot Box* (1973), bringing back Charlie Dierkop, and wrote the story of *Black Mama, White Mama* (1973). *Caged Heat* (1974), the New World women's prison classic shot in the U.S. instead of the Philippines, was the first picture Demme directed. Scott Glenn appeared in Demme's Peter Fonda vehicle *Fighting Mad* (1976). Demme's upward screen credits *Citizen's Band* (1976), a/k/a *Handle with Care*, *Melvin and Howard* (1980) and *Swing Shift* (1984) were low frequency at the box-office. After the luckier *Something Wild* (1987), Demme put Scott Glenn in the much wilder movie about a charismatic cannibal name Hannibal.

Angels' Wild Women

Independent-International 1972. Executive Producers: Samuel M. Sherman, Dan Q. Kennis; Producer-Director: Al Adamson; Screenplay: D. Dixon, Jr.; Cinematography: Louis Horvath; Production Manager: Erik Lidberg; Sound: Bob Dietz; Script Girl: Sandy Portelli; Stills: Hedy Dietz; Stunt Coordinator: Erik Cord; Key Grip: F.A. Miller; Makeup: Lee James; Titles-Opticals: Modern Film Effects; Music: Quasar Prods.; DeLuxe Color; An Al Adamson Production; Running Time: 86 minutes.

Cast: Ross Hagen (Speed); Kent Taylor (Parker); Preston Pierce (Turk); Regina Carroll (Margo); Maggie Bembry (Cool Chick); William Bonner (King); Arne Warda (Slim); Jill Woelfel (Donna); Vicki Volante (Terry); Albert Cole (Weasel); Claire Polan (Love Child); John Bloom (Big Foot); Gus Peters (Preacher); Linda Gordon (Sue); Erik Lidberg (Freak); Margo Hope (Orphan Girl); Ervin Saunders, Tony Lorea (Sheriffs).

For Al Adamson, the Spahn Ranch had almost become a shrine. In 1970, he went back there one more time to make *Screaming Angels*. Convinced that Bikers were dead, Sam Sherman pulled it out of play schedules. Meeting Larry Woolner of New World, he heard about its upcoming *The Big Doll House* (1971). As far back as the fifties when he directed his own girl action movies, Roger Corman—who was able to secure better distribution deals than I.I.—knew that sex could always tweak tired male macho formulas. Sherman felt he could turn Corman's World upside down by copying its Lib-ertenarianism more cheaply.

Sherman had the women of *Screaming Angels* form an independent sisterhood. Only thirty pages long, the new script, *Angels' Wild Women* was a mostly improvised bridge between feminist and hippie bikers, siding with the outlaws and making the hippies Manson people. In this inversion of Adamson's *The Female Bunch* (1971), the babes were the good guys.

Across an open field, black Cool Chick runs from two horny farmhands who rape her. Elsewhere, biker boss Speed and his old lady, Donna, visit a film set where extra Turk moves in on Donna until Speed punches him. Cool Chick's attackers are dealt with by whip-cracking Margo, Terry, Sue and Joy. Cool Chick gets some kicks in too.

Turk springs a rope ambush on cycling Speed and Donna. Speed fights Turk, who dramatically kisses Donna and escapes by jumping his bike across a wide crevasse. Salute gestures indicate that Speed and Turk know and respect each other.

Peace also eludes Speed and Donna on a beach where Speed battles the men of rival Weasel. Girls cause fights, so Weasel proposes a stag run.

While Donna fixes their bikes, Margo, Terry and Sue aggressively seduce a dumb, virginal farm boy. Obviously stoned, cycle straggler Terry is busted by two cops for drug possession. Cries of rape distract the cops, who cuff Terry to their car steering wheel. Both disappear.

The girl's visit crippled old Parker's ranch. Margo knows Love Child, a member of the King cult. Heavy into dope since the violent death of her sister, Terry craves serenity and King gives her an injection. A King pusher, Turk notices Donna, who stays aloof. Aware of King's vice operation, Parker attempts blackmail.

Terry becomes gravely ill and King locks the girls up. Turk objects. King and henchman Slim kill Parker. Donna squeezes through a wall hole and sees Parker's burial. Love Child surprises her, holding a gun.

Bike trouble hampers Cool Chick. A bad Samaritan who happens by expects a favor for a favor. Stringing him along, Cool Chick partially disrobes, slugs him and takes his pickup.

Top: Cool Chick (Maggie Bembry), Margo (Regina Carroll) and Terry (Vicki Volante) avenge Cool Chick's honor.
Bottom: Drugs are a "friend" to Terry (Vicki Volante), the first victim of King (William Bonner).

In love with Margo, Turk is knocked out by King and Slim, who tie him up. Margo escapes, hailing Cool Chick on the road and they summon their men. King knifes drugged Donna in a fake human sacrifice. The arriving male bikers fight King's followers. Speed and Margo free Turk and view dead Donna. Turk tries to stop King and Slim as they flee in a station wagon. Speed chases them while Turk tells Margo he and Speed are brothers.

On straight, open highway, Speed roars ahead of King and Slim up a mountainside road and crashes his bike down on their car. They roll to their fiery doom down a canyon. Speed leaves with the gang while Turk and Margo go off together.

Sam Sherman's ideas vastly improved the female characterizations, helping to make *Angels' Wild Women* the only I.I. film about sympathetic bikers. Lovers Speed and Donna were an item fated for tragedy like Rommel and Rita of

Five the Hard Way—Donna being Speed's Rita. King was not the only Manson type. Slim and Love Child were his Tex Watson and Susan Atkins. Parker, also a surrogate for Monty, the stable groom who got dragged behind a horse for trying to shake down *The Female Bunch*, was a George Spahn stand-in (the sign of the ranch was plainly visible).

Al Adamson met Ross Hagen while Hagen was making *Brad Charleston Charlie* (1973). Taking a shine to Adamson's dog Stupie, he agreed to play Speed and rounded up some Sunset Boulevard Hell's Angels to play gang members. The Angels were a no-show. The next night, Hagen confronted them, reminding them of their agreement. The Angels were afraid to comply because they thought Hagen was an undercover cop. Hagen so impressed the Angels with his toughness they made him and wife Claire honorary members.

Regina Carroll brought some of her real self into Margo when Margo spoke of how her mother died young—as did Carroll's mom when Carroll was fifteen. Adamson was patriotically upset by a scene where Gus Peters, playing Preacher, described some pills as "reds, whites and blues." Adamson changed the line to "upways, downways and sideways." He also couldn't abide the open hanky-panky that occurred during breaks and made the hankers pank in private. For the big brawl, a rooftop jumper was supposed to land on a mattress and a pile of cardboard boxes, but he missed his mark and fell on the shoulders of Gus Peters.

Carroll was the best actress, but the wildest woman anatomically was Meggie Bembry as Cool Chick. Sold on a face compared to Diana Ross', she was more akin to the thin Oprah Winfrey except for a forty-eight inch bust.

Fire destroyed the Spahn Ranch in September 1970. Manson's evil karma survived the blaze and his conviction, seeming to hurt others besides principal players in his story. Bill Bonner was permanently paralyzed from the waist down in a car wreck. Divorcee Gus Peters was going through child-custody grief. Chain-smoker Regina Carroll, inheriting her mother's fatal habit, suffered her first brush with cancer.

Al Adamson associate produced the Leonard Freeman TV-movie *Cry Rape!* (1973), but further jobs for Freeman were flatlined by Freeman's death during open-heart surgery. Vilmos Zsigmond, the cinematographer of *The Sugarland Express* (1974), gave Gus Peters a copy of the script. At the Universal commissary, Peters approached Steven Spielberg and several executives about getting a part, but two tourists openly recognized Peters from his role in an Adamson horror movie. Peters missed the *Express*—indirectly because of Al Adamson.

Adamson stopped directing to pursue real estate. A recurrence of her cancer claimed Regina Carroll in 1992. Adamson ended his long self-imposed exile to direct and love again. Love with a "new Regina," opportunistic Stevie Ashlock, broke Adamson's heart—and nearly his wallet in a palimony suit.

Owner of various properties, including a house in Indio he wanted to sell, Adamson threatened to charge Fred Fulford, the contractor renovating it, unless he paid back the money Fulford stole by using Adamson's credit card. When Fulford intercepted a script Gary Kent sent Adamson, one scene gave him the idea to kill Adamson that June of 1995. Sixty-six year old Adamson, who sustained blunt force head trauma—but not enough to cause immediate death—was found buried beneath the circular foundation of his home's Jacuzzi on August 2. Fulford incriminated himself by forging Adamson's signature on checks, running up bills on his credit cards and selling four of Adamson's cars in Florida. When he was arrested in St. Petersburg, Fulford was wearing one of Adamson's suits.

Gary Kent was subpoenaed to testify in the Adamson murder trial in 1999. Fulford, who maintained his innocence, was convicted of first-degree homicide.

The Angry Breed

Commonwealth United Entertainment 1968. Executive Producers: Frank Brandt, Fred Maisel; Producer-Director-Screenplay: David Commons; Story: Rex Carlton; Associate Producer: Sally Goldwater; Cinematography: Gregory Sandor; Film Editor: David Saxon; Musical Score: Lawrence Brown for Mike Curb Prods.; Music Coordinator: Morris Diamond; Art Director–Production Design: Leon Erickson; Camera Operator: Frank Ruttencutter; Assistant Cameraman: Marcel Shain; Co-Producer–Unit Manager: Jack Bohrer; First Assistant Director: Elliott Schick; Second Assistant Director: William Lasky; Casting: Marvin Paige; Assistant Editor: Marvin Goldberg; Music Editor: Edward Norton; Dialogue Director: Thomas Markus; Script Supervisor: Joyce King; Sound: Frank Murphy; Gaffer: Aggie Aguilar; Key Grip: Jack Oliver; Makeup: Louis Laine; Hairdresser: Gretchen Moon; Wardrobe: Dodie Warren; Props: Robert O'Neill; Electrician: Foster Denker; Grip: Tom Coleman; Transportation: Tony Vorno; Special Effects: Gary Kent; Accessories: Jaceranda Nephew, Peter McCloskey; Vocalist: Joniman Bahlo Musical Group, Jamie and the Jury, The Orphan Egg; Color: David Commons and Associates Inc. in association with Commonwealth United Productions; Running Time: 90 minutes.

Cast: Jan Sterling (Gloria Patton); James MacArthur (Deek Stacey); William Windom (Vance Patton); Jan Murray (Mori Thompson); Murray MacLeod (Johnny Taylor); Lori Martin (Diane Patton); Melody Patterson (April Banner); Karen Malouf (Jade); Suzie Kaye (Ginny Morris); Russ McCubbin, Hagen Smith, Arthur Wong, Burt Taylor, Morris Diamond, Thomas Markus, Kent Kim, Hal Marshall, Frank Ruttencutter, Natasha Kelly, Jenny Sullivan, Meryle Dee, Kip Lewis, Roland Burnett, Laura Hilliard.

Outlaws were used for low comedy and to solve a mysterious attack on call girl–starlet Vicki Cartwright in *The Sweet Ride*, a 1968 adaptation of William Murray's novel. Dumped from a Rolls in the middle of a Malibu highway, assault victim Vicki had earlier attracted surfer Denny McGuire and bald-pated biker Mr. Clean. Already abused by Denny, Vicki let Clean rape her near the beach house of the man who had beaten Vicki, blackmailing TV exec Brady Caswell. Denny clobbered Caswell, but lost Vicki and went to work in a hardware store.

Show biz chicanery was also part of *The Angry Breed*, David Commons' celluloid Rolodex of every bad youth film cliché. Commons felt that bikers wearing SS paraphernalia on denim were old "German helmet." His gang wore full Gestapo gear. Their leader was a dilettante outlaw, actor Deek Stacey, not readily discernable because of his leisure look.

Deek, Go-Go and a third guy molest teenage Diane Patton on a private beach until Johnny Taylor fends them off. "I know you, war hero," says Deek, "and I know where to find you. It's been kicks. I'll be seeing you—Johnny Wild." After the gang leaves, Diane tends to Johnny's cut arm and picks up the script he was carrying. Called "Johnny Wild," it is his biography. Struggling actor Johnny became a Marine and in Vietnam saved the life of the script's late author.

In Diane's house, Johnny meets her sad alcoholic mother, Gloria, and Jade, a sexy Asian maid who gives first aid. Diane's father, studio head Vance Patton, shows interest in the script Johnny wants to star in.

Johnny's agent, Mori Thompson, also

handles Deek and starlet April Banner. Vance feels that Johnny is no good for Diane. Gloria warns Johnny, "The jungle can be anywhere." Vance tries unsuccessfully to bribe him away from Diane. Mori can produce the film if he helps Vance get rid of Johnny. Deek will replace him. The plan will commence during a Halloween party at Mori's castle. Diane misconstrues the platonic affection between Johnny and Jade.

Cat-costumed Jade attends the party. Deek's men grab Diane, taking her to an altar, and slug Johnny. Nazi-uniformed April, who likes Diane, tells Deek to let her go. In the dungeon, Deek prepares to give Johnny a heavy dose of LSD. "You're going on a publicity trip," taunts Go-Go. Jade creates a blackout, knocking Deek unconscious. Diane's friends help her escape while Johnny and Jade elude Deek and his goons.

Johnny reports to the studio for his insurance physical. Mori tells Vance "some cat" spoiled their plan. Vance gets the meaning. Johnny meets Deek without disguise for the first time. Deek starts an antagonistic fencing match that becomes a brawl. Johnny wants him off the picture.

Diane wants to wed marriage-shy Johnny. Vance has found Jade's cat suit—allegedly under Johnny's bed—and tells him to leave. Distraught Jade runs down to the beach. Johnny comforts Jade, creating more jealousy in Diane to Vance's delight. Vance has gone too far with Gloria.

Over the phone, Vance tells Mori the film is canceled. Present in Mori's office, Deek is plotting "Doomsville."

When Vance decides to take his usual dip, drunken Gloria oils the defective beach cable car so it will crash. Shocked by her own action, quickly sobered Gloria

Diane (Lori Martin) is attacked by Deek Stacey (James MacArthur).

stops departing Johnny from using it. Deek and his gang break in. Gloria seduces Deek to protect Johnny and Diane. When Vance is grabbed, Deek plans to send him away on the cable car. Seeing the oil, Vance realizes what Gloria tried to do, telling Deek he will expose Johnny in return for Diane. Vance lures Deek to the cable car, but Deek touches the oil—knowing Vance was going to kill them both.

Johnny is caught. "It's you and me," says chain-swinging Deek. "The best man gets the girl. You're cattle and I'll put you in the cattle car." "You need killing," grins uncowed Johnny. Vance helps Johnny fight the whole gang before throwing Deek and himself into the plummeting cable car, which kills Deek. "The Fuehrer is dead!" announces Go-Go. "Long live the Fuehrer! That little old cycle pusher … me!" The gang splits while Johnny revives injured Vance, who will let Diane marry

Deek (James MacArthur) holds a knife to Johnny (Murray MacLeod).

the rightful star of the on-again "Johnny Wild."

Most of the "angry" characters were just a bunch of costume freaks from the formative phase of Mod. In love with the *idea* of rebellion, theirs was nothing but nitwit conformity. If Deek and his storm troopers had considered Hassidic clothes provocative, they would have probably worn those instead. The person most entitled to anger was Gloria—ignored by a business barracuda husband, the Brady Caswell of this drama.

A St. George up against dragons overt and covert, Johnny Taylor was a surfnick Billy Jack depicted as a kind of Nam-age Audie Murphy aspirant to acting ... valued for his written exploits, not for who could play Johnny Wild best. If *The Angry Breed* had been pitched a little later, no one would have bought it. Duke Wayne had gotten away with his Green Berets valentine because he was long established box-office and a hawk icon. *Angry Breed* expected kids to idolize a young star who willingly participated in a war most producers avoided until it became history.

Even though it was spam camp rather than steak, *Angry Breed* had enough laughs to fill half a barrel. The Mike Curb sound in Biker rock was quickly becoming stale and its use in the first scenes made the early action seem lampoonish. And almost buffoonish was Johnny's sudden bolt-from-the-blue entrance. Deek was a semi-travesty of Marlon Brando the public oddball in such stunts as ordering mashed potatoes and strawberry Jell-O mixed with gravy (wavy gravy?). For the Halloween party, Johnny wore a clown suit, Deek presided as a de Sade ringmaster, April had her Nazi outfit, Jade's costume you already know, Mori dressed in drag and Deek's co-dirty workers were Tweedledee and Tweedledum. Somebody's dog wore a mask.

Two stars, Jan Sterling and Jan Murray, shared the same first name while Murray MacLeod, the second Murray, was surnamed Mac like James MacArthur. MacLeod, who was well showcased on a *Run For Your Life* episode, should have become the success that his well-played character Johnny was going to be. Would a convenient marriage have helped—say, to a studio president's daughter? Before Deek went to the Casting Audition in Hell, James MacArthur found ways of getting into the swing of an atypically unsavory role for him.

Working on *The Angry Breed* enabled MacArthur to meet his future ex-wife, Melody Patterson, Wrangler Jane of *F Troop*. She later graced *The Cycle Savages* while he was booking felons on *Hawaii 5-0*.

Black Angels

Merrick-International 1970. Executive Producer-Director-Screenplay-Cinematography: Laurence Merrick; Associate Producer: Leo Rivers; Film Editor: Clancy Syrko; Musical Director: Lou Peralta; Cameraman: Paul Hipp; Assistant Cameraman: Henning Schellerup; Sound Mixer: Ted Botkin; Costumes: Blue Bell (Wrangler); Makeup: Gerald Sutcliffe; Continuity: Jill Murphy; Effects Editor: Dan Finnerty; Titles: Photo Effex; Bikes: D & M Enterprises; Stunts: George Baudin; Re-recording: T.V. Recorders; Songs: "What's Going On," Bobby Steven, Checkmates Ltd., sung by Tom Markham; "What You Don't See Won't Hurt You Is a Lie" composed and performed by Bobby Steven, Checkmates Ltd.; "Cigarettes" composed and performed by Smokey Roberds, Pequod Music Inc.; "Black Angel," "Confrontation" written and performed by Morgan Cavett, Golden Age Prods.; "Beautiful" written and performed by Jack Bendient, Diogenes Music; "Lord Give Us Peace" written and performed by Alan Brackett, Four Star Music; "Multileveller Conversational Tightrope Walking Shoes" composed and performed by Judy Fine, Golden Age Prods.; "Military Disgust," "Everything Is Alright" performed by Mad Dog, Golden Age Prods.; Movielab Color; Running Time: 92 minutes.

Cast: Des Roberts (Chainer); John King III (Johnny Reb); Linda Jackson (Jackie); James Young-El (Jimmy); Clancy Syrko (Lt. Harper); Beverly Gardner (Wallflower); James Whitworth (Big Jim); John Donovan (Frenchy); Gene Stowell (Fixer); Miller Pettit (One-Eye); Channon Scott (Jawbone); Robert Johnson (Knifer); Frank Donato (Clyde); Sumner Spector (Daddy); Choppers Gang (Themselves); Harry Hampton (Drunk); Irma Smith (Waitress); Charlie James, Nate White (Black Panthers); Fabian Cantivella (Machetti); Joanne Strum, Margaret Kingman (Club Girls); Bill Hooks (Knifer's Right Hand); Mark Ross (Singer); Sandy Friedberg (Nun); Kent Wyatt (Chauffer); Adam Lahav (Boy on Bike); Dee Blauser, Marni Pepper, John Wheeler, and John Landon.

Laurence Merrick was an honored

Hollywood drama coach and theater director who made movies with some of his students. A Bikerese omen of the forthcoming Blaxploitation trend, Merrick's *Black Angels* was a primitively baroque, crazily fanciful tale of rivalry between the white Satan's Serpents and the real-life black Choppers. Out to destroy both was a cop named Lt. Harper ("black angel" was this film's euphemism for police). *Black Angels*' message was that in the seventies it was almost impossible for the races to differ on anything without color staining the issue.

Serpents leader Chainer makes love to his kinky socialite girl Jackie in her cozy pad. Militant Jimmy of the Choppers breaks a window to lure Chainer outside. "Somebody wants to play games," says Chainer, telling Jackie to meet him at a park where the other Serpents are. Chainer pursues Jimmy while Harper and a sergeant watch.

Flashback to a beach, where excited, newly initiated Jimmy joins his girlfriend, sunbathing nude. They romp by the water and have sex. Flaunting his colors afterward, Jimmy feels that Knifer, head of the Choppers, is getting soft and plans to kill Chainer. "Why, Jimmy?" the disturbed girl asks. "Because Chainer is *all*-white!" he acidly replies. "His white is pale! And pale is sick! And I hate all sickness!" "You hate too much!" the girl feels. "Not enough, baby!" retorts Jimmy. "You've changed," regrets the girl. "I'm a new shade of black!" Jimmy rails. "An all-new breed!"

Jimmy leads Chainer on a long, wild chase until his bike gives out. Jimmy fixes it as incensed Chainer catches up. Chainer will settle for an apology, but the word "boy" provokes Jimmy into attacking him and Chainer chains Jimmy unconscious.

Quickly rebounding, Jimmy picks up on Chainer, who leaps across a deep ravine. Regarding this as a challenge, Jimmy races toward the abyss over Chainer's unheard plea, "Don't try it!" Jimmy falls to an explosive death. Chainer goes down to the body ... brains spilled all over.

Harper decides to check out the park, where the rest of the Serpents eye his passing car with loathing. Risking death, Chainer reports Jimmy's death to Knifer and hands over his colors. Admiring his guts, Knifer barks, "Split, Chainer!" Harper tails Chainer as the Choppers leave to claim Jimmy's body.

In the park, Serpents vice-president Big Jim is hit in the face by a stream of yellow liquid spraying down from a treetop. It isn't beer. Perched on a high branch, Frenchy says it is "champagne." Big Jim shakes Frenchy down and they fight until Chainer breaks it up. Down the road, Harper blocks the Serpents for a mild roust.

The Serpents return to their ghost town commune, greeted by hanger-on Wallflower. Running from Harper on a limey bike is wild Johnny Reb, whom the Serpents hide in a barn. Harper warns that Knifer may be planning payback for Jimmy. Chainer, Big Jim and Frenchy interrogate Johnny, wanted in Dallas for assaulting an ex-girlfriend. Suspicious Frenchy thinks he may be a Harper plant. "Any cat that would work over his old lady with a baseball bat can't be all bad," muses Chainer.

Harper tells Knife that Chainer is planning war. The Serpents ride to a bar where Knifer has a waitress spy.

Johnny's strident racism offends Chainer—who argues that trouble with the Choppers is merely territorial. Going to an alley restroom, Chainer is jumped by some Chopper while the other Serpents are busy fighting redneck customers. Johnny saves Chainer.

When Jackie appears, Chainer berates her for standing him up at the park. Their violent spat leads to Chainer balling Jackie atop a table as everyone leaves, except a

Chainer (Des Roberts) examines dead Jimmy (James Young-El).

still-dancing go-go girl. Jackie's father and Harper arrive as Chainer and Jackie ride off. Jackie's father asks Harper to stop them, but he refuses.

Johnny attends a Serpents commune barn party with a bag of uppers, meeting Wallflower—herself a bigot. As the drugs are passed around, they groove. Chainer wants to make peace with Knifer. Frenchy wonders how Johnny could have scored the pills since he was broke during the interrogation. Chainer concedes this is odd, telling Frenchy to watch Johnny. As the uppers make everyone else drowsy, Frenchy follows Johnny outside. Frenchy sees him signal the waiting Choppers with his bike's blinking headlight and don their colors. The Choppers roll down in slow procession as Frenchy confronts Johnny, shouting "Why?" "Black, baby, black!" proclaims Johnny, who stabs Frenchy.

The pills were really downers. Roused by Chainer, the Serpents take on the Choppers. "I've been fooling Mister Charlie for years," Johnny brags to Knifer in earshot of Big Jim, whom Johnny knifes before Wallflower drives a pitchfork into his back. Chainer battles Knifer, who flashes his blade, crying, "Burn, baby, burn!" Even the Serpents' pet cougar, breaking loose, joins the fray. Chainer and Knifer play lethal tug of war with Chainer's chain until they roll into a ditch. Knifer stabs Chainer before a rattler bites him. Jackie is taken away by her father while Harper contentedly surveys the gruesome spectacle of war and leaves. His rear bumper sticker reads "Support Your Local Police."

Touted as the *Gone with the Wind* of Bikers, *Black Angels* was an almost unfathomable tangle of coincidences, con-

The Serpents and the Choppers at war.

spiracies and ironies—powered by more exploitation moxie than a single Biker had a right to have. Punctuated by memory shots, the drawn out vehicular fencing between Chainer and Jimmy began it with a burst of energy meant to parrot of the *Bullitt* car chase. The funniest chase bit was a muddled nun swearing a blue streak—conveyed by purely visual suggestion—while another sister registered shock in a close-up of beautifully spontaneous dismay.

Merrick made the Serpents more sympathetic while one-sidedly picturing the Choppers as rabid honky-haters. Jimmy's girl was a weak voice for black moderation and Knifer stood above his fellow Choppers as a diplomat with limited patience. Harper seemed to spend his every duty hour monitoring the gangs. Perhaps telepathic, he was almost everyplace where something was going on.

Frenchy, who pegged Johnny as an undercover man, was half right in sus-pecting Johnny of ulterior motives. Being a Choppers spy was the big surprise. While many blacks who pass *do* look white, Johnny was hard to accept as a secret Chopper. The Serpents and the Chopper had brushed with each other for years. Wouldn't the only light-skinned member of a black gang been noticeable long before the current trouble? If the makeup budget had been higher (most effectively spent on Jimmy's facial mutilations), Johnny could have been a dark black wearing a whiteface mask. The removal of such a disguise might have been more startling.

The most convincing of Merrick's spirited troupers was raw-boned, crackly Des Roberts as the volatile yet at times thoughtful Chainer. He had played a flamboyantly mod vampire in Merrick's *Guess What Happened to Count Dracula?* (1970) and composed the music. Roberts was hardly one of the better Draculas, but he possessed a definite something and should have gone further, like tall, hirsute, gravel-voiced James Whitworth, who became Jupiter in *The Hills Have Eyes* (1977).

Merrick didn't win any awards for *Black Angels* or *Guess What Happened to Count Dracula?*, but his 1973 documentary *Manson* won him an Oscar nomination and praise at the 1974 Venice Film Festival. Few people in California saw *Manson* because it was banned there. Merrick's actress wife, Joan Huntington, who helped research *Manson*, became his widow one evening in January 1977 soon after midnight when Merrick was shot in the back in the parking lot of his North Vine acting academy (en route to a bathroom just like would-be murder victim Chainer). Merrick died at Hollywood Presbyterian Hospital. Some blamed *Manson* for Merrick's homicide.

Nearly five years later, unemployed cannery worker Dennis M. Mignano confessed to the crime. A long-term head case who auditioned for him, Mignano claimed that Merrick cast magic spells that ruined his voice and made his body shrink. Not guilty by reason of insanity, Mignano was remanded to a state psychiatric facility.

Still remembered, Laurence Merrick received a memoriam tribute from his associates in a page of *Variety*.

The Born Losers

American International 1967; Re-released in 1974. Presenters: James H. Nicholson, Samuel Z. Arkoff; Executive Producer: Delores Taylor; Producer: Don Henderson a/k/a Tom Laughlin; Director: T.C. Frank a/k/a Tom Laughlin; Screenplay: James Lloyd a/k/a Elizabeth James; Associate Producer: Jay Loughrin; Cinematography: Gregory Sandor; Film Editor: John Winfield; Music Supervision: Al Simms; Music Composer-Conductor: Mike Curb; Production Coordinator: Alan Chase; Production Manager: Paul Lewis; Assistant Director: Jonathan Hayes a/k/a Haze; Production Designer: Richard Beck-Meyer; Script Supervisor: Joyce King; Casting: Armie Associates; Sound: Leroy Robbins; Makeup Supervision: Louis Lane; Wardrobe: Katherine Free; Property Master: Mike Ezzes; Special Costuming: Switched-On Ltd.; Optical Effects: Westheimer Corp.; Sound Effects: Edit-Rite Inc.; Production Assistant: Barbara Bouyet; Pathecolor; An Otis Pictures Production; Running Time: 112 minutes.

Cast: Tom Laughlin (Billy Jack); Elizabeth James (Vicky Barrington); Jane Russell (Mrs. Shorn); Jeremy Slate (Danny Carmody); William Wellman, Jr. (Child); Jack Starrett (Deputy Fred); Paul Bruce (District Attorney Davis); Robert Cleaves (Mr. Crawford); Paul Prokop (Speechless); Robert W. Tessier (Cueball); Jeff Cooper (Gangrene); Stuart Lancaster (Sheriff); Anne Bellamy (Mrs. Prang); Susan Foster (Linda Prang); Janice Miller (Jodell Shorn); Julie Cohn (LuAnn Crawford); Ruth Warshawsky, Bill Carey, Paul Naplier, Art Eisner, Michael Ivey, Edwin Cook, Timothy a/k/a Tex Hall, Robert Coutu, Susan Baumann, Susan Winfield, Robin Corum, Tom Middleton, Wayne Capasso, and James Smith.

Minneapolis native Tom Laughlin played college football and wanted to become a priest before he discovered acting. A James Dean fanatic, Laughlin married actress-painter Delores Taylor. While she was pregnant with their first child, the couple moved to Hollywood in 1955. That year, Robert Altman starred Laughlin in their mutual first feature, *The Delinquents*. It was unreleased until 1957, by which time Laughlin had done *Tea and Sympathy* (1956). His other bit movie credits were *Lafayette Escadrille*, *South Pacific* (both 1958), *Gidget* (1959) and *Tall Story* (1960).

Laughlin wrote, produced, directed and starred in two obscure independents, *The Proper Time* (1960) and *The Young Sinner* (1965). Neither film went anywhere. In their Santa Monica home, the Laughlins ran a Montessori school until Laughlin became disenchanted with the movement.

Introducing the character that made Laughlin a Somebody, *The Born Losers* was an anti-crime Biker that painted Good and Evil in basic black and white. Laughlin claimed it was inspired by the case of a Pittsburgh ex-marine who saw a trio of punks menacing three teenage girls. When the police he called were late in coming, the man injured two of the assailants in self-defense. Charged with aggravated assault, the man was fined fourteen hundred dollars and spent one hundred eighty days in jail. Also an inspiration was the 1964 Kitty Genovese homicide, passively abetted by thirty-eight witnesses. Another story is that during a 1966 plane trip, Laughlin met stewardess Elizabeth James. Accepting Laughlin's offer that she write a short story for him, the budding authoress penned *The Contrary*, the purported literary basis of *Born Losers*.

When Laughlin agreed to cast James as heroine Vicky Barrington, her moneyed Colorado family raised financing. Delores Taylor was executive producer of Laughlin's first feature for Otis Productions. Starring under his own name, Laughlin produced *Born Losers* as Don Henderson and directed as T.C. Frank. Elizabeth James' screenplay credit was James Lloyd. Once the James money was spent, Laughlin sneaked a print of the half-finished film out of the lab and showed it to Jim Nicholson and Sam Arkoff, who put up another three hundred thousand.

In the Big Sur mountains, a man at peace with nature is described by narrator Vicky. "He had just returned from the war—one of those Green Beret rangers ... a trained killer people would say later. Before the war, he had hunted down and broken wild horses in these mountains. Some said the reason he was so good at these things and the reason why he lived alone was that he had some Indian blood in him. Others said that he simply didn't like people. All I knew was his name ... Billy Jack."

Billy drives his Jeep into busy downtown Big Rock, a nearby recreational community. At an intersection, a young Volkswagen driver distracted by Child's old lady rear-ends Danny Carmody's hog. Seeing no damage, affable Danny says, "You were lucky." "You're the one who's lucky, man," sneers the boy. Insults intensify and the boy spits at Danny's feet. Exploding, Danny roughly extricates the boy from his car. In a feint of returned good humor, Danny sucker-punches the boy, throwing him to the rest of the gang.

The bloodied boy staggers into an eatery where Billy is and tries to call the police, but the gang drags him outside for a stomping. At rifle point, Billy tells them to disperse and wings a Loser swinging a broken bottle. The Sheriff and Deputy Fred arrive—busting also chagrined Billy.

Tom Laughlin's franchise justice fighter Billy Jack.

Billy has five days to pay a one thousand dollar assault fine. The Losers got a mild fine and suspended sentence. "Go help someone else again sometime," sarcastically remarks Billy's lawyer.

Rich coed Vicky plans to holiday at Big Rock with her father, but at the airline terminal where he fails to show she learns of his extended Asian business trip.

The Losers flaunt their bikes on the Big Rock strip, eliciting mixed responses from Jodell Shorn, LuAnn Crawford and Linda Prang. Danny's brutal dad is beating up his kid brother Jerry, who accepts Danny's offer to go with him. Vicky rides to Big Rock on her bike.

In the parking lot of their bar, the Losers racially taunt Billy, slashing one of his Jeep tires. Danny remembers Billy from back "when I had to settle for second best." Fred investigates the theft of a hot tape recorder. Clearly, he despises the gang. Finishing a swim on a quiet beach, Vicky chases her windblown shift, which alights on a rotting seal carcass.

On the main strip, the Losers start a race. Some riders stacked-up by traffic ahead cause mute Speechless to swerve into a pond. The Losers spot Vicky passing on her bike and chase "first prize." Vicky hides in a gas station restroom until the gang leaves. She calls the cops, but they are busy.

Vicky is tricked into taking a dead-end route. Menacingly, the Losers loom over the crest of the road. Confident Speechless struts forward to molest Vicky, who attempts to ride around him and tumbles down an embankment. A tenuous ally, Danny's wife Hazel says, "I think she'd like to become legal." Vicky must "turn out a little," hints Cueball.

The Losers escort Vicky to their beachside "Pleasure Palace" where Jodell, LuAnn and Linda are part of a violent orgy in progress. Sized up for initiation, Vicky dares the gang to try LSD with amphetamines supposedly stashed in her bike. Accompanied by Hazel and Crabs, Vicky conks Crabs with a wrench. Hazel gives her time to escape.

Speechless and Jerry chase Vicky. Out of gas, she sprints to the door of a lady who locks her out. Vicky runs into the hands of laughing, wild-eyed Speechless—who rapes her as revolted Jerry looks away.

Six Losers are arrested for rape. Positively identified Speechless and Jerry are held without bail. Trauma is worst for LuAnn. To protect Jerry, Danny wants the girls silenced before Monday's court hearing.

Jodell's mother, Mrs. Shorn, is, by turns, harsh and loving. After she goes to work, Jodell erotically entertains a stuffed toy dog. Someone tampers with a fuse. Jodell goes out to fix it. She strips down for the toy dog before two Losers creep up from hiding and scare her.

Though untouched, Jodell regresses to a semi-infantile state. Despite promised protection from District Attorney Davis and the Sheriff, Mrs. Shorn refuses to let Jodell testify. "And you swear to God right now that if she helps you, you'll protect her completely? *Look at her!*" Screaming, "Get out!" Mrs. Shorn shoves Davis and the Sheriff through the nearest door. "Excuse me," apologizes Davis sheepishly. "This is the bedroom." Mrs. Shorn doubles up in an emotional fit of loud laughter.

Haunted by her rape, Vicky won't testify, telling Davis and the Sheriff, "I'm not much of a person for social causes." Billy sells his Jeep to LuAnn's father to pay his fine. "If only one of us had the guts to just cut 'em down," wishes Crawford. "Yeah—I tried that once," recalls Billy.

Crawford drops Billy off at a café opposite a motel where Vicky is staying under customer Deputy Fred's guard. Gangrene hotwires his car so Danny can lure Fred away while Child, Cueball and

Tex grab Vicky. Breaking free, she collides with Billy, who punches Cueball and breaks Tax's arm. On her bike, Billy takes numb Vicky to his cliff top trailer home.

Bringing Billy his money, Crawford recognizes Vicky, whose refusal to testify angers him. "Don't you have some sense of responsibility?" To myself—yes!" retorts Vicky. Nonjudgmental Billy wraps the money in a folded newspaper and tucks it under a trailer cushion. He puts on a magic show for Vicky, who collapses.

Danny visits the jail to see Jerry. Raising a Billy club to his cheek, Fred warns, "All I need is one person who saw you steal that car—just one—and I'd even settle for a liar." In a restaurant, Billy and Vicky meet an astrologer who sees their signs as incompatible for now. As Danny leaves Jerry's cell, Fred viciously clubs him in the abdomen. "Nobody steals my car, punk, and gets the last laugh!" The astrologer likes Billy and Vicky—but feels the stars are against them.

The Losers beat the bushes for signs of Billy and Vicky until Gangrene finds the money. Returning with Vicky, Billy discovers the theft. Billy wants Danny to return the money by tomorrow. Subtly, Danny initiates a pain contest by placing his lit cigar between their arms on the bar counter. Billy stuffs the cigar in Danny's drink. "Be interesting to see what it's like to be hunted for awhile," he says.

At a remote gas station, the Losers surround Billy and Vicky, who slip Billy a hammer. Crabs grabs Billy's hat so Cueball can fill it with gasoline Billy pours on the ground. Gangrene sneaks up on Billy, who hammers and karate-chops him. Threatening to burn Gangrene unless he is compensated, Billy takes a three thousand-dollar trike.

In the woods that night, Vicky tells Billy, "You know, I feel like stars are up there inside of me ... just glowing softly. I've always felt that I had a light bulb–like thing inside me and all of my seeds were in it. If I ever let the wrong person in, the little light bulb would be jabbed ... and broken! Oh, Billy, Billy, Billy, Billy ... what am I going to do?" "You do what you have to," answers Billy.

Fred and Deputy Bill are guarding the Crawford place. Child fires diversionary rifle shots while Danny and Gangrene snatch LuAnn. Vicky still won't testify, but Danny wants to see her and Billy. Danny threatens to kill LuAnn unless Crawford goes to the Pleasure Palace alone.

Billy and Vicky are already there. Arriving, Crawford is overpowered by Gangrene, who takes his concealed gun, pointing it at him. LuAnn is close to getting raped again. To save her and Vicky, Billy challenges Danny. He gets slugged as Vicky sneaks away to the front gate, where Gangrene catches her. Crawford agrees to drop the charges. For Billy's freedom as well, Vicky stays. Danny comes on to Vicky, who tells him, "Go to hell!"

Billy and LuAnn are taken to the hospital. Sole remaining witness Linda schizophrenically hates the Losers for what they did to Jodell and LuAnn—and her mother. "That's not true, I guess," Linda says, relieving Mrs. Prang—then admits that since the rapes she has been with the Losers twice. "I like it! I really do!" "Why? Why?" shouts Mrs. Prang. "Because," softly vents Linda, "They're everything you hate!" Davis' case is shot. "Suddenly the whole system is upside-down!" He cries, " I have to open the gate and let the animals out! Where did the Goddamn system go wrong?"

Gangrene attempts to force himself on Vicky, who declares, "I don't choose scum!" Spitting in Gangrene's face, she knees him, getting her jaw punched. "Get up!" Gangrene roars.

Billy learns that Vicky is still at the Pleasure Palace. The police can't move until the Highway Patrol arrives. Appalled by their slowness and cowardice, Billy determines to rescue Vicky over the Sheriff's protest. "Whatever they've done to your women," he hisses, "you deserve!"

Outside the Pleasure Palace, Billy starts a gasoline fire around Danny's bike. While he sneaks inside, the alarmed Losers put it out. "Who would burn your bike?" Child asks comprehending Danny, who orders a search for Billy. Inside the Palace living room, Billy crouches over nude, unconscious Vicky and covers her with a jacket. The Losers enter, noticing the jacket before Billy lines them up against a wall at rifle point. Two girls will take Vicky to the hospital and call from there. After fifteen minutes, one Loser a minute will die until the phone rings. "That would be murder," Danny tells Billy, who would be acting in self-defense since his life was threatened. Pulling a knife, advancing Danny swears, "I'll carve your bowels out!" before Billy shoots him between the eyes.

Put in charge, Child oversees Vicky's immediate removal. Billy herds the other Losers toward the door, keeping Child in front of him. Cueball slams the door on Billy and the Losers make a break, but the police have them surrounded. Billy takes off on the trike to see Vicky, but Fred mistakes him for a fleeing Loser. Before Crawford can stop him, Fred shoots Billy in the back.

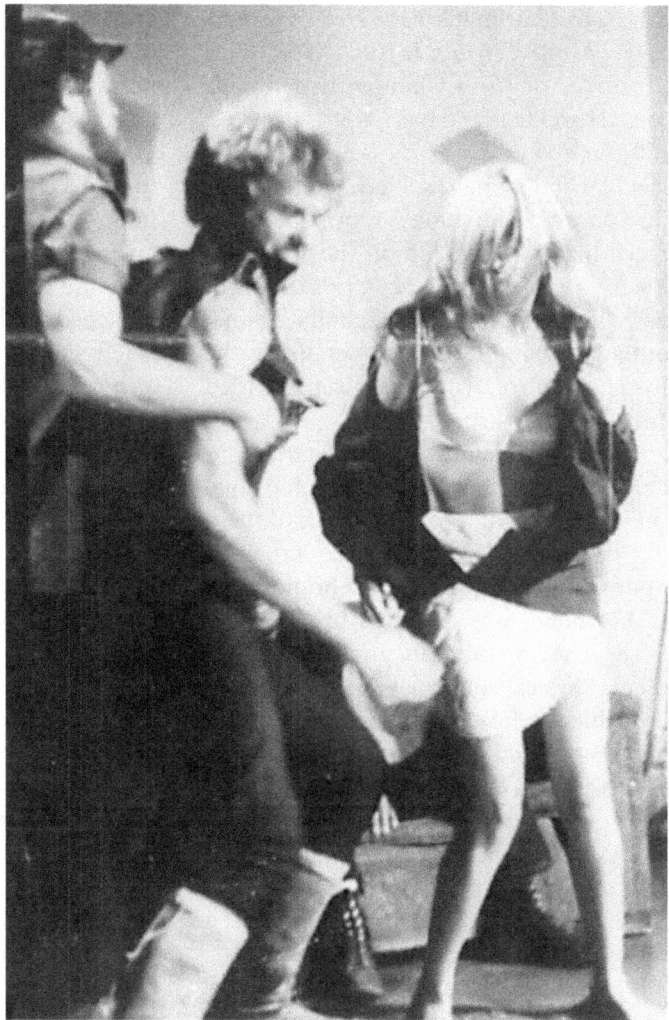

Danny (Jeremy Slate) stops Gangrene (Jeff Cooper) from attacking LuAnn (Julie Cohn).

In dismal rain, Vicky joins a rescue party who find wounded Billy lying in the woods. "I love you," Vicky tells him. "This is the closest I've ever been to a real home," says Billy. "You crazy Indian!" says smiling Vicky, "You and I—we are the sunset—and the stars—and... Oh, Billy, Billy, Billy!" A helicopter airlifts him away as the sun begins to set.

Whatever version of the genesis of *The Born Losers* is true, public apathy gave rise to a new strain of ferocious, dedicatedly antisocial misfits Hunter Thompson grimly foresaw in his tome *Hells Angels: A Strange and Terrible Saga*. A New West precursor of Kwai Chang Caine for his mixed parentage and martial-arts prowess, Billy Jack could hold his own in both outlaw turf and straight society when his Indian ancestry didn't make him an object of racial bigotry. As down on the establishment as either *The Wild Angels* or *Devils Angels*, *Born Losers* was equally against outlaws, basing its exposé details on the Lynch report (mamas were called "mamas," but also "sheep").

Collecting enough negative traits for a dozen gangs, the Losers were terminal sinners with moral rot flaking off of them like dead skin. Their emblem, a crucified nude woman with a swastika brand stuck to her body, was crowned by "Born to Lose"—not a real club title but a statement. Physical abnormalities were part of Speechless, whose stepfather had cut out his tongue, and Crabs, a blithe carrier of venereal disease who *liked* showers ... as long as they were communal. While generally hetero, the Losers also flirted with homosexuality for its kink kick. Rather than police, these guys should have been busted by the Board of Health.

In its cross-section dramaturgy, *Born Losers* bubbled over with family dirt soapsuds. Poor little rich girl Vicky was the daughter of a loved but lacking father who was off somewhere in the Far East. Danny and Jerry were the sons of an abusive father. Jodell was the daughter of an antsy, aging whore and Linda's mom ... it's a wonder that Linda didn't actually join the Losers to get away from *her*.

Born Losers reserved political contempt for a clumsy, skewed, impotent legal system, which was more about statutory bullshit than sane safety. Deputy Fred would have gladly blitzed Loser ass any time, but only in jail did he have full autonomy. D.A. Davis was handcuffed by protocol and nobody respected the Sheriff. Efforts to stop the Losers were so frustrating that after his arrest, Billy gave up until he had to reclaim the money stolen by the guys who got him in trouble.

Vicky was not only someone for Billy to protect with a personal stake in her welfare, but a human incentive for Billy to emerge from his tranquil wilderness womb for reasons other than consumer or financial needs. Billy couldn't return the vanished wild horses or undo the tourist atmosphere that changed Big Rock's character, but he managed to make the Losers wish they had never been born ... causing some civilized citizens to look at themselves differently in the mirror. The Carmodys, the Shorns and the Prangs were three families who would never find the closure that the Barringtons and the Crawfords would.

Producer Tom Laughlin made a quantum leap from uncommercial, obscure cheapies to a Big-B movie. At one hundred twelve minutes, *Born Losers* was the longest Biker with more varied characters and backdrops than any Biker set mainly in one locality. The picturesque tour of Billy's world, evidence of his self-sufficiency, and brief narration placing the story as a past event remembered by another key character, were to establish the feeling of an epic morality play, bringing the camera to awesome nature vistas, the nerve center of a large little town and homes with Good Housekeeping seals or proof of how their occupants let themselves go.

Director Laughlin wouldn't deplore the detestable unless he could objectify obscenities for all their titillating worth. The beating of the intersection youth testified to the insane savagery of the Losers, the complacency of people like the Prangs, the courage of Billy and the stupidity of the System all within one scene. Starting with a white-booted and bikinied Vicky, every young girl was an embodiment of sex crisis. Little more than child molesters with bravado, the Losers were the only people other than Billy who could be efficiently aggressive. Only as a whole gang or when they could get the drop on him were they able to beat Billy, a non-cyclist Biker movie hero who could even handle bikes when it was required by the script.

The most stressful tensions were enacted within the Pleasure Palace's walls. What a place for Danny and Hazel to raise their toddler: snake dancers, protest scrawlings, gangbangs. Laughlin's favorite person killed in a Porsche, James Dean, was a poster neighbor of Joan Baez. "Down With Fuzz" were words made to come out of her mouth via one scrawl. When Billy shot Danny, the blood-stained bullet also smacked into Dean's two-dimensional face—as if Laughlin had decided that his former hero was now an unacceptable role model, meant to be symbolically assassinated.

Several seconds of Billy showering under a waterfall and unclad, knocked-out Vicky offered a Biker first: nudity. Vicky's prominently angled rump was sodomy sirloin.

Laughlin didn't pay much attention to cycle spectacle except when he brought some Hell's Angels to the main street of Seal Beach. The town authorities were upset because Laughlin didn't tell them in advance that the Angels were coming. Someone who saw the police carjack as it was being filmed called the cops, who reacted as an army, believing the Angels had stolen one of their own cars. Seal Beach finally forced the filmmakers to leave town.

If Laughlin overstated behind the camera, he underplayed Billy to the effect that he was a gene-carrier for all laidback do-gooders who can turn both cheeks until repeated slapping rubs the skin too raw. Elizabeth James, injecting post-adolescent feminism without raising the issue politically, misplaced some of her spunk in leadenly poetic declarations ("When I come back as a horse, *then* I'll let you inspect me ... maybe") and the impossible star light bulb soliloquy.

Danny was played by nordically handsome Jeremy Slate, a World War II veteran who spent three years aboard one of the four destroyers that survived the Normandy D-Day landing. He majored in English at St. Lawrence University, was listed in the 1952 *Who's Who in American Colleges*, worked as a radio announcer and sportscaster at Watertown, New York, and Stamford, Connecticut, and became an employee of the Grace Line. Doing publicity for the line and Panagara Airlines in Lima, Peru, Slate joined the caudrilla of a local matador. Part of an amateur theatrical group, Slate stayed with the Grace Line while studying at the New York Actor's Studio. The supporting role of Luke Grant in the Broadway play *Look Homeward Angel* was Slate's pass to Hollywood, where he played Larry Lahr on the TV series *Malibu Run*. Slate's second wife was Tammy Grimes, whom he divorced in 1968.

Child was William Wellman Jr., who acted in dad William Sr.'s final film, *Lafayette Escadrille* with Laughlin. He costarred in *The Young Sinner* with James Stacey, his fellow lead in both *A Swingin' Summer* and *Winter A-Go-Go* (both 1965). Wellman was also in most of the forthcoming Billy Jack films.

Robert Tessier was similar to Billy Jack in his own Native-American heritage and conspicuous military service. The Algonquin Tessier was an Army paratrooper in Korea, winning two Bronze Stars, one Silver Star and four Purple Hearts, as well as sustaining a leg injury. He was a carpenter, a furniture maker and a gym owner who befriended Dan Haggerty when Haggerty was a Venice leather smith. Tessier did circus stunt cycling, which led to Tom Laughlin hiring him as both an actor and a technical advisor for *Born Losers*.

As Fred, Jack Starrett was allowed to be more emotional than his Bingham character. Jeff Cooper was a screaming phallic torpedo as Gangrene and Paul Prokop's pixie face made Speechless initially ingratiating. Susan Foster and the late Paul Bruce joined Bill Wellman Jr. in the next Billy Jack picture.

Doing her two scenes in only one day, Jane Russell took special guest billing in the small but scorching role of Mrs. Shorn, deliberately putting on twenty-five pounds.

Laughlin and Delores Taylor planned five more Otis opuses and, after his assassination, a screen Martin Luther King Jr. tribute that was to feature Elizabeth James. In his first namesake movie, Billy Jack was reintroduced as an Arizona desert loner much closer to his Indian ties who traded in his *Born Losers* white Stetson for a black Indian hat. Delores Taylor originated her role of the embattled Freedom School teacher, Jean Roberts, Billy's lasting love interest.

American International was the first sponsor of *Billy Jack*, but when it disregarded contractual agreements and tampered with the product, Laughlin took it to Avco Embassy, Twentieth Century–Fox and, finally, Warner Bros., which released *Billy Jack* in 1971 and again in 1974. A.I.P. took ownership advantage of *Born Losers* to re-issue it in '74 with a new ad campaign emphasizing Billy. Laughlin resented A.I.P.'s plug that *Born Losers* was the first Billy Jack picture—alleging it was just a motorcycle film that just happened to include someone named Billy Jack. Despite Laughlin's transparent denials, most facets of Billy were there. Unsuccessfully, he sued for five million in damages.

Identifying with his alter ego *too* much, Laughlin played him in *The Trial of Billy Jack* (1974), stepping out of the role long enough to portray *The Master Gunfighter* (1975). There was *Billy Jack Goes to Washington* (1977). All of these films were critical and commercial flops, the Washington fiasco not even getting a commercial release. A fifth Billy Jack vehicle was to pit him either against child pornographers or pedophiles in a McMartin school–type case. Entering the 1992 Democratic convention, Tom Laughlin found in politics some measure of renewed prestige—even though his movie creation is better left as a memory of the Sixties and Seventies.

Bury Me an Angel

New World 1971. Executive Producers: Rita Murray, John Meier; Producer: Paul Nobert; Director-Screenplay: Barbara Peeters; Associate Producer: Charles Beach Dickerson; Cinematography: Sven Walnum; Film Editor: Tony DeZarrago; Musical Director–Theme Composer: Richard Hieronymous; Art Director: Laurence Paul; Sound Mixer–Assistant Special Effects: James Tannenbaum; Effects Editor: Jay May; Music Editor: Jack Cheap; Special Effects: Harry Woolman; Opticals: Cinefx; Sound: Ryder Sound Assoc.; Assistant Director: Donjean Gardner; Assistant Editor: William Tremberth; Assistant Cameraman: Michael Stringer; Second Assistant Cameraman: Leslie Otis; Boom Operator: Jim Heinlein; Script Girl: Connie Graver; Gaffer: Mike James; Grip: Les Irving; Best Boy: Al York; Production Coordinator; Nicole Scott; Production Assistant: David Atkins; Still Photographer: Elizabeth Plumb; Publicist: Rachel Silverman; Songs: "So Here We Are," "Let It Be," "Flaming Groovie," "Free as a Child," "Daughter of Loneliness" composed and performed by East-West Pipeline, Producer: T.C. Corbett; Eastman Color; A Meier and Murray Production; Running Time: 86 minutes.

Cast: Dixie Peabody (Dag); Terry Mace (Jonesy); Clyde Ventura (Bernie); Stephen Whittaker (Killer); Joanne Moore Jordan

(Annie); Marie Denn (Bernice); Dennis Peabody (Dennis); Gary Littlejohn (Bike Shop Proprietor); David Atkins (Preacher); Janelle Pransky (Young Dag); Wayne Everett Chesnut (Young Dennis); Corky Williams (Sheriff); Beach Dickerson (Hary); Dan Haggerty (Ken); Maureen Math (School Girl); Dianne Turley (Secretary); Alan DeWitt (Principal); Richard Compton, Dan Knapp (Pool Players); Joan Gerber (Op's Voice); Angel Colbert (Op).

Barbara Peeters was an actress in one of Dick Compton's skin flicks and the production secretary of *Angels Die Hard*. Many on that film—including Compton—were part of Peeters' *Bury Me an Angel*. The first woman to direct a Biker, Peeters devised a vigilante drama, but one that considered how eye-for-an-eye can permanently blind the avenger—often leaving him or her a ruined mess.

Dag Bandy and her brother Dennis celebrate her birthday with a biker party in their home garage; Dag's present is a chopper Dennis stole. The rightful owner, carrying a shotgun, breaks down the front door of the house. During a struggle, the weapon explodes in Dennis' face.

For months, the case goes down as unsolved. Getting a sawed-off shotgun, Dag learns that the killer is a drug dealer headed for Canada. On her revenge ride are Bernie, who loves Dag, and footloose Jonesy.

Camped at a park, Dag, Bernie and Jonesy encounter a hostile, diminutive Sheriff and towering, sharp-tongued Dag puts him down. In a bar, she becomes the center of a brawl. In a river, Dag takes a tension-relieving skinny dip, but Bernie and Jonesy tease her too violently. The unpleasant memory of a childhood bath causes Dag to run away.

Losing their bearings in a fierce sandstorm, Dag, Bernie and Jonesy find refuge

Jonesy (Terry Mace), Dag (Dixie Peabody) and Bernie (Clyde Ventura) pursue the killer of Dag's brother.

in the care of Op, a too-wise Indian witch. Her insight into their motives prompts them to accuse the witch of having harbored the killer. Upset Dag thrusts Op's hand into a flaming fireplace ... nearly burning it. Before Dag, Bernie and Jonesy leave the next day, Op gives Dag a cryptic note.

In a mountain town café, Dag asks the proprietor if he has seen a stranger on a chopper. Ken, an artist and art teacher, says a guy fitting this description is the high school handyman. Going to the school, Dag leans on the principal and his secretary to learn where the killer is. He is not expected back until Monday. Ken joins Dag, Bernie and Jonesy at dinner and invites Dag on a tour of the town. She beds Ken—whose gentle lovemaking stirs traumatic thoughts about Dennis.

Ever more impatient, Dag takes Bernie and Jonesy to the killer's home, a deserted turkey ranch. In a cabin, Dag confronts the frightened killer, who only meant to scare Dennis. As Dag presses the trigger of the sawed-off, the killer, surmising her passion for Dennis, cries "Incest!" Now totally insane, Dag scrapes the ground with the butt of the shotgun so she can "bury me an angel!" Stressed to complete exhaustion, she collapses.

As much inside the head of Dag as an external account of her vendetta, *Bury Me an Angel* kept the true relationship between Dag and Dennis under carefully-tied wraps. A psychic virus ate Dag's spirit while rage-pumped adrenalin kept her Amazon body going. Companion crutches Bernie and Jonesy couldn't shield Dag from inner and outer forces eroding her soul. She had known the social meaning of the abnormal brand of attraction she and Dennis felt, but it took the killer to make Dag *hear* why no other man could make her love as well again.

The incest was veiled for surprise first. A second reason was that Dag and Dennis were played by real-life sister and brother Dixie and Dennis Peabody—who couldn't have been expected to actually bounce the bedsprings on-camera. A longing gaze by Dennis in the last flashback was the nearest thing to open lust.

Dixie Peabody, a mama in *Angels Die Hard*, was a six-foot Sagittarius who owned a 1948 Indian with a suicide clutch. She juggled tough girl Camp with touching sadness in an unrefined but honest performance. Ken was the only Biker character of any substance Dan Haggerty ever got to play.

New World built its image on subversiveness, championing female causes while exploiting women, often-violent women who got away with killing. With *Bury Me an Angel*, Barbara Peeters created her own subversion—glorifying a powerful woman ultimately destroyed by her own act of deadly closure. The advertising—perhaps more of Jack Hill's provocative prose—built up healthy anticipations of excitement in the alliterative, posterity-worthy blurb: "She took on the whole gang! A howling hellcat humping a steel hog on a roaring rampage of revenge!"

C.C. and Company

Avco Embassy 1970. Presenter–Executive Producer: Joseph E. Levine; Producers: Allan Carr, Roger Smith; Director: Seymour Robbie; Story-Screenplay: Roger Smith; Cinematography: Charles Wheeler; Film Editor: Fred Chulak; Music Composer–Conductor: Lenny Stack; Musical Sequence Choreographer: Walter Painer; Production Supervisor: Frank Baur; Assistant to the Producers: Walter Rachmil; Sound Mixer: Robert Martin; Continuity: Meta Wilde; Camera Operator: Roger Sherman, Jr.; Construction Supervisor: Bob Krume; Property Master: Allan Gordon; Set Decorator: Ted Mossman; Chief Set Electrician: Harry Sundby; Assistant Editors: Howard Deane, John Hanley; Assistant Directors: Dennis Donnelly, Joe Nayfack; Makeup: Joe DiBella; Key Grip: Art Brobker; Special Effects: Harry Millar, Jr.; Transportation: Ray Tostado; Location Manager: Bob Shelton; Unit Publicist: Bob Yaeger; Casting: Phil Benjamin; Location Casting: Frank Kennedy; Location Auditor: Elton McPherson; Wardrobe Supervisor: Ron Ross; Stunt Coordinator: Paul Nuckles; Location Secretary: Jo Worner; Production Secretary: Vera Armen; Ann-Margret's ensembles created and designed by Jon Shannon; Sound Effects Editing: Edit-Rite Inc.; Producers Sound Service; Songs "Today" by Lenny Stack, Janelle Cohen and sung by Ann-Margret; "Jenny Take a Ride" by Jonson/Tennian/Crew and sung by Mitch Ryder; "I Can't Turn You Loose" by Otis Redding and sung by Wayne Cochran and the C.C. Ryders; filmed on location in Tucson, Arizona, and the Flamingo Hotel in Las Vegas; Movielab Color; A Roger Smith–Allan Carr Production; Produced by Rogallan Productions in association with Namalco Productions Inc.; Running Time: 90 minutes.

Cast: Joe Namath (C.C. Ryder); Ann-Margret (Anne); William Smith (Moon); Jennifer Billingsley (Pom Pom); Mike Battle (Rabbit); Greg Mullavey (Lizard); Teda Bracci (Pig); Don Chastain (Eddie Ellis); Sid Haig (Crow); Bruce Glover (Capt. Midnight); Kiva Kelly (Tandalaya); Jackie Rohr (Zit Zit); Bob Keyworth (Charlie Hopkins); Alan Pappe (Photographer); Ned Wertimer (Motorcycle Dealer); William Baldwin (Night Watchman); Shirley Eder (Lady Ticket Seller); John Wasserman (Store Manager); Bonnie Emerson, Paula Warner (Models); Wayne Cochran and the C.C. Ryders (Themselves).

Ann-Margret's husband, Roger Smith, is remembered by fans of *77 Sunset Strip* for the role of private eye Jeff Spencer. When his acting orbit waned, he became Ann–Margret's manager. Going into partnership with Allan Carr, who also managed his wife, Smith co-wrote and co-produced the sexual coming of age story *The First Time* (1969)—a better name than its risible working title *You Don't Need Pajamas at Rosie's*.

Locking himself away in a hotel room, Smith knocked out in three days the first draft of *C.C. Ryder and Company*. Retitled *C.C. and Company*, this was a serio-comic tale combining the outlaw-straight girl romance of *The Wild One* with the revenge-for–club betrayal slant of *Run, Angel, Run*.

Although the script had been prepared before he signed on, Joe Namath's relaxed, friendly demeanor seemed to influence the personality of lovable hero C.C. Broadway Joe's first coming out as an actor had been in the comedy *Norwood* (1970), where he was basically himself. Namath's rousing football victory for the Jets was a major point of exploitability. Keen on bikes, to Smith's later dread, Ann–Margret was cast as C.C. Ryder's love interest, Eastern fashion coordinator Anne McCalley.

Entering a supermarket, C.C. shoplifts a sandwich, washes it down with a stolen carton of milk and tops it off with a filched cupcake, fastidiously wiping his mouth with a paper napkin. At the checkout stand, C.C. hides a pack of gum under stamps. Slipping on the colors of the Heads, C.C. joins his roving gang.

On a lonely highway, C.C., Lizard and Crow spot a stalled limousine whose chauffer left to get a mechanic. Anne pokes her head out of the back seat and asks, "Are you just gonna sit there like the wild ones or are you gonna give a girl a hand?" While C.C. fixes the engine, Lizard and Crow gorge themselves on the luxuries of the limo. They also want Anne. "I think you guys have seen too many motorcycle movies!" she protests as Lizard and Crow try to rape her. C.C. keeps his cool until Anne bites Crow's hand and Crow slaps Anne. Chivalrous C.C. beats up Lizard and Crow. After the sore Heads leave, C.C. gets cozy with Anne, asking, "How do you know I wasn't saving you for myself?" The chauffer returns in a tow truck. "Win a few, lose a few," C.C. tells Anne nonchalantly—but the essence of chemistry is there.

At the campground home of the Heads, leader Moon asks for C.C.'s version of the limo incident, which doesn't sit well with Moon. "I mean, like we got the club over here, see," he complains, gesturing, "and here you are way over there. It just don't seem to blend!" Moon's old lady, Pom Pom, is caught taking a bath in a pond ... her first this month. The club kitty is tap city. On Moon's order, the girls go a-hustling.

While most of the other Heads are asleep, restless, horny Pom Pom tries to seduce disinterested C.C. Pom Pom accuses him of avoiding her because every guy is afraid of messing with Moon's property. C.C. shows Pom Pom how unafraid he is by screwing her on the spot.

The Heads attend a motocross race where Anne is with male model Eddie Ellis readying preliminaries for a modeling session. A race begins as the Heads watch from a hilltop. C.C. and Anne see each other again at a distance. "Those guys over there," judges disdainful Eddie, "that's what gives motorcycling a bad name." Moon wants to "show these mini-motors what a *real* bike can do." Riding toward the "minis," the Heads make the obstacle course a disaster area. C.C. is embarrassed because Anne is watching.

C.C. shops for a racing bike. The dealer lets him take his choice for a test spin around the building. Gone a long time, C.C. reappears with the bike tied to the rear of his hog. Waving goodbye, he leaves an envelope with five dollars' down payment and an I.O.U. on the rest.

Truly a May-December match: fashion coordinator Anne McCalley (Ann-Margret) and C.C. Ryder (Joe Namath).

While Anne is arranging some photo setups, C.C. shows his track stuff. "Isn't it strange how our paths keep crossing," she tells C.C. "I have a strange feeling you're following me," he says. "I was here first," states Anne. Eddie tells her, "Did anybody tell you you're known by the company you keep?" Impressed by C.C.'s skill, bike distributor Charlie Hopkins advises C.C. to enter next Sunday's race.

All the Heads enthusiastically back C.C. except jealous Moon. C.C. makes a track jump shot that includes the models. In the last lap he makes a flying leap, breaking off the front wheel of his bike. By dragging it across the finish line, he wins.

Moon spoils the campsite victory celebration by demanding the prize money. C.C. submits a portion, keeping one hundred. Moon tries to encourage "share and share alike." When C.C. turns his back on him, Moon slugs C.C. and gives the withheld money to Pom Pom. C.C. retaliates, but Moon knocks him out.

That night, Pom Pom looks in on recovered C.C. who knows, "You came here to get laid." C.C. obliges so he can lift the money from Pom Pom's purse.

C.C. wants to see Charlie about a career racing job. Anne needs his signature to release a story on him. Also needing a pad, C.C. thinks, "We can work something out." Moving into Anne's rented house, C.C. becomes Anne's lover.

Anne will be returning to the Madison Avenue rat race soon. She is curious about why C.C. became a Head. "You like just drifting around?" "I think looking is a better word," explains C.C. "For what?" Anne asks. "If I knew that," replies C.C. "I wouldn't be looking now, would I?" Not giving up on Anne romantically, Eddie feels she can't have a permanent relationship with a guy like C.C. "I'm not looking for anything permanent," says Anne, "because nothing is."

C.C. leaves the house to buy food, watched by the Heads. Anne hears someone enter. Thinking it is C.C., she asks, "What did you forget?" Moon, the foremost intruder, remarks menacingly, "Well, little lady, I'll tell ya what he forgot."

Coming back, C.C. finds no Anne, but the Heads. Hostage Anne is at camp. Moon discovers the money theft and demands one thousand. "This chick is C.O.D. You get her back when we get the bread." C.C. proposes that he and Moon settle this in a flat track grudge race on choppers. The danger visibly unnerves Moon, who tries to evade the challenge by threatening Anne. C.C. ups the stakes to two grand—double or nothing. He phones Charlie so the money will come out of a pay advance.

The race will commence midnight at the stadium of the University of Arizona.

C.C. (Joe Namath) and Anne (Ann-Margret) share poolside talk.

First rider who passes Lizard on the tenth lap wins. Anything goes. Under the switched-on field lights, the race begins. Moon attempts to kick C.C. off balance, causing both to crack up on a turn. Quickly, they remount. The lights bring a campus security guard whom Pig and Zit Zit immediately distract. They say they are student filmmakers shooting a motorcycle movie documentary. "A cross between Antonioni and A.I.P," pretends Zit Zit.

Moon is slowed down by fuel line trouble and grabs another bike as C.C. moves ahead. Struggling to catch up, Moon loses control on the next lap turn and slams broadside into a parked convertible. Catapulted over the exploding vehicle, he hits the ground, breaking his neck. Pom Pom cries for dead Moon while most of the enraged male Heads take after escaping C.C. and Anne.

The Heads chase C.C. and Anne out into the desert, where they reach a dead end. C.C. uses their slight gain to fake a canyon accident. While he and Anne hide in the brush, the Heads investigate. C.C. moves one bike away from the others, detaches the fuel lines of the rest and with a flare blows them up. The startled Heads are left in the lurch while C.C. and Anne exit on the remaining chopper.

C.C. pauses at a stoplight. He wants to return the money to Charlie. "And then what?" asks Anne. "Then I gotta split for awhile," plans C.C. "Where?" Anne inquires. C.C. shrugs. "Remember we talked about looking for something?" reminds Anne. "Well, I'd—I'd like to look with you … for awhile anyway." The light changes to "go" and the couple go on their uncertain quest.

C.C. and Company was designed as comedy-drama because Smith and Carr wanted it a few notches above quickie Bikers and this one would gain by sending them up. Knowing too openly what it was, *C.C.* was corny and condescending, and treated its outlaws (described in publicity as "a hippie motorcycle gang") as clownish sociopaths only one step removed from the Ratz. Starting with the deftly droll way C.C. prepared himself a five-finger discount lunch, materialism permeated the film—mostly product tie-ins presented with obnoxious flattery.

All we knew about C.C.'s past was that he joined the Heads after getting into a fight with them and they appreciated how well he handled himself. Oh yes— C.C. used to work at a bike shop, but he and the owner were not compatible. His idyll with Anne meant returning to the Establishment, but unlike Bill Smith's poignant Angel, C.C. was not a character in torturous transition, being pretty much the same happy-go-lucky guy as before.

Neither C.C. nor Anne planned their romance to be much more than a vacation from their normal routines. C.C., to Anne, was the Complete Biker stud—not a sleaze like his fellow Heads or a plastic quiche eater like Eddie Ellis. The only thing that made C.C. more than a kept man was that he was now motorcycling professionally. The only thing that an audience could connect with was C.C. and Anne's strong sexual attraction, spiced up by their oppositeness and how non–class conscious they were. C.C. was only a casual outlaw, so the Heads should have been glad to have been rid of him, but the Moon-perceived misappropriation of money was an issue set aside like a little bomb waiting to go off. C.C. showed more by being Moon's only independent satellite … who could get to Anne and everything in her sumptuous world by ingratiation … not intimidation.

A graduate of its University, producer Roger Smith picked Tucson as the primary location, with an additional scene at Las Vegas' Flamingo Hotel. Near Tucson, the production company built a half-mile motocross track where twenty-five pro bike riders raced, one of them champion John DeSoto.

Bruce Glover, who played Capt. Midnight, was the first pick for the role of Moon until he met Joe Namath, who felt Glover wasn't big enough to convincingly beat up C.C. The part went to William Smith. During production, a cow obstructed Glover's path and he ran his bike into the ground, turning off the motor before it could catch fire. Nobody saw the accident and Glover went back to shooting. Not until eight o'clock that evening did Glover feel any real pain. Going to the hospital, he discovered he had broken his arm.

Since Bill Smith was now Moon, Glover had to totally improvise Capt. Midnight. He and Sid Haig (Crow) made up as they went along the scene where mama Tandalaya was supposed to have "Property of the Heads" tattooed on her belly. Crow suggested, "This Property Condemned."

C.C. and Company made the living room rug sex scene between C.C. and Anne a good inducement to see it, whereas all the ground rutting by the Heads was a turn-off, especially when it involved frequent dirt-crawler Pom Pom. Ann-Margret had done some nude scenes as the slovenly, repellent grad student Rhoda in R.P.M. (1970). However, she developed stage fright the day before the shooting of the rug scene and Roger Smith had to plead with her for five hours until she relented. Even Joe Namath—whose favorite indoor sport uncovered him to a lot of sated dates—was hesitant, although there was much more of Ann-Margret to view. For personal modesty, she wore a crotch shield—yet even with tastefully subdued lighting, the film was hit with an "X" until the groping was trimmed.

Namath had a tall order to fill: learning to ride a chopper, fighting William Smith and dry-humping the wife of one of the producers. He was up to most of what was expected of him and was most comfortable at being funny. Ann-Margret's own performance was unexceptional but for her show of skin.

While Bill Smith copped the drama award, hilarity hosannas went to Ted Bracci, who had played one of the radicals in R.P.M. Decked out in Dogpatch chic from her toes to her Bull Shirt, she was a comic nightmare with an abrasive, husky voice that rubbed like burlap on a baby's behind. Bruce Glover did one of his best roles right after C.C. in Diamonds Are Forever (1971) as the comic gay assassin Mr. Wint. Deputy Coker in the first two Walking Tall movies, Glover is the father of Crispin Glover.

Greg Mullavey, who was married to Meredith MacRae, became Tom Hartman on Mary Hartman, Mary Hartman. Sid Haig, who was also in Diamonds Are Forever, was a regular on the last season of the show. Another football star, Mike Battle, was acrobatic but little else as frisky Rabbit.

Even though he tried, Joe Namath must have felt like Ann-Margret did after all the bad press she received in her early career. She managed to quiet her detractors when she brought profound sex appeal to the character of Bobbie in Carnal Knowledge (1971). Namath took another leading role in The Last Rebel (1971)—once again hearing boos from the critics' corner. Television was a mixed adventure. Namath's show The Waverly Wonders wasn't wonderful, but he touched down in those popular male panty hose ads.

Roger Smith left films altogether to manage Ann-Margret's career full time while rancid celluloid pastry became glitter nerd Allan Carr's stock commodity, from the extremely successful Grease (1978) to the disco dud Can't Stop the Music (1980)—the career-killer for the Village People that tried to convince us the execrable Eighties would be a great decade—to the sterile, stupid *Where the Boys Are '84* (1984). Producing the Broadway smash *La Cage aux Folles* made up for much of the trash. Carr died of cancer in 1999 while Roger Smith has long battled the debilitating disease Myasthemia Gravis.

Chrome and Hot Leather

American International 1971. Presenter: Wes Bishop, Lee Frost; Producer: Wes Bishop; Director-Cinematography: Lee Frost; Screenplay: Michael Alan Haynes, David Niebel, Don Tait; Story: Michael Alan Haynes, David Niebel; Film Editors: Alphonso P. LaMastra, Edward Schryver; Music Composer–Conductor: Porter Jordan; Music Arrangers–Composers: Billy Sprague, David Angel; Production Manager: Donald Baker; Assistant Director: William E. Martin III; Second Assistant Director: David Carey; Costumes: Chris Morris; Second Unit Cinematography: Jack Steely; Assistant Cameramen: Chuck Minsky, Edward Schryver, Henry Fusco; Still Photography: Elliott Marks; Wardrobe-Makeup: Judy Redlin, Katie Coyle; Grips: Brad Bunch, Wayne Deats; Special Effects: Modern Film Effects; Production Sound: Mike Fenton, John Toll; Stunt Coordinator: Bud Ekins; Electricians: Jim Stemme, Herman J. Solomon; Special Effects: Unlimited Sound; Ryder Sound Services; Movielab Color; A Wes Bishop–Lee Frost Production; Running Time: 91 minutes.

Cast: William Smith (T.J.); Tony Young (Mitch); Michael Haynes (Casey); Peter Brown (Al); Marvin Gaye (Jim); Michael Stearns (Hank); Kathy a/k/a Kathrine Baumann (Susan); Wes Bishop (Sheriff Lewis); Herb Jeffries (Ned); Bob Pickett (Sweet Willy); George Carey (Lt. Reardon); Marland Proctor (Capt. Barnes); Cherie Moor a/k/a Cheryl Ladd (Kathy); Ann Marie (Helen); Robert Ridgeley (Sgt. Mack); Lee Parrish (NCO Club Bartender); Larry Bishop (Gabe).

Experts in softcore S & M, Robert Cresse and Lee Frost turned out various types of skinflicks from their company Olympic-International, starting with innocuous nudie cuties. Frost was also associated with Wes Bishop and the pair moved out on their own. Most of the Frost oeuvre, both in and out of porn, showed a certain fascination with Army or paramilitary activity.

Billy Jack, Johnny Taylor, Johnny Martin (the *Satan's Sadists*, Johnny), Phil Duncan and—until he went bad—Joe Grady were nice Nam vets. In their first GP venture, *Chrome and Hot Leather*, producer Bishop and director-cinematographer Frost presented four macho but likeable Green Berets. *The Losers* had gotten away with its Army orientation by making outlaws themselves the heroes. *Chrome* dispensed with depressing Vietnam politics for basic justice, playing as a detective-cum-vigilante-cum–war epic.

A G.I. squad approaches some Vietnamese peasant farmers who open fire with hidden guns. The G.I.s shoot back, decimating the enemy. One soldier stands over the body of a Vietnamese, pointing his gun at it before he is ambushed by another. "Get up!" orders towering taskmaster Sgt. Mitchell. So does the man who was playing dead in what was a California Army base training exercise. Mitch reprimands the incompetent private for his failure to shoot. He and co-instructor Jim join fellow Sergeants Al and Hank, who report how their pupils fared. The outfits return to Fort Hanson.

T.J., leader of the Wizards, and his gang roar down a mountain highway ahead of Helen and Kathy, who try to pass in their car. Brash Casey, packing Susan, yells, "Pull over! I'll give you a ride!" Politely refused, he gets nasty. "I said pull over!" Waiting for Casey to drop back, Helen and Kathy tear down a side road, knocking Casey and Susan to the pavement. Maddened Casey chases the girls. *"Pull over now!"* he demands. Casey chains the car's windshield—blinding driver Helen. She and Kathy bounce helplessly in their seats as the car runs down a steep canyon, overturns and stops upright.

Casey joins the other Wizards as they view the wreckage. "If those people are alive, we're gonna help 'em," put-out T.J. tells Casey. "And if they're not?" Casey asks. "Then you've got yourself a problem, boy," warns T.J., who sends Casey to check the girls before he spots a distant car coming and shouts an alarm. With no time to retrieve his chain, Casey follows the rest of the fleeing Wizards. The motorist watches their escape before the car wreck catches his eye and he goes down to investigate. Helen is dead. Kathy is alive ... just barely.

At an NCO club, Mitch shows the bartender two snapshots of his fiancée ... Kathy. Mitch is ushered to a booth by Capt. Barnes, who gives him the grim news from Lt. Reardon of the Leedsville Sheriff's department that Kathy is dead.

After the service for Helen and Kathy, Mitch talks to Lt. Reardon. All the police have to go on are the word of the witness and Casey's chain. Its fingerprints are untraceable. Reardon is short on men. Reservedly, he sanctions Mitch's idea of him, Al, Jim and Hank conducting their own private investigation.

The Wizards rowdily return to their pool hall hangout in Piru. The rest of the hated gang is camped somewhere in the Superstition Mountains. Tension is thick between Casey and T.J., who says, "Now you wanna be the big man. You just take your best shot!" Casey pummels T.J. before the Sheriff complains of the gang's hellraising.

Kathy died repeatedly uttering "devils" ... thought to be the Wizards' name. Mitch sees a Kawasaki dealership, getting an idea. He talks to the dealer about a cheap multi-bike purchase deal. "What do you plan to use it for?" asks the dealer, "Street or dirt?" "Hunting," answers Mitch.

Mitch puts Al, Jim and Hank through an intense instructional course so they can pass as outlaws. Wearing sergeant's stripes on the backs of their jackets, they split up, planning to meet at the gas station in Rainbow in three days.

The Wizards stop at the Rainbow station, where Mitch reacts to their red devil insignia—what Kathy really meant. He tries to call Lt. Reardon, who is unavailable, leaving a message with the station attendant. Susan moseys over to Mitch, mentioning where the Wizards are from. Jealous Casey calls her back. "You like that?" he asks and then slaps Susan.

Mitch follows the Wizards to the pool hall, where T.J. hassles him. Distracted by pinball fanatic Gabe's game, T.J. yells, "Can't you see we're menacing someone?" Mitch seems okay. "You've been accepted," Susan tells Mitch, inviting him to the Wizards' house. "I wonder where Casey is," smirks T.J. In a bedroom, Susan strips for mildly shocked Mitch, finding him "square but nice."

Casey comes back to the pool hall, looking for Susan. "You mean that chick who used to be your old lady?" teases T.J. Al, Jim and Hank pick up Mitch's message. In the house, Casey overhears Susan discussing the car accident with Mitch. Breaking into the bedroom, he kicks and beats Mitch unconscious.

T.J. takes over and Mitch's army ID is found. T.J. will question him further at the camp in the Superstitions. From there, the gang will head for Mexico. Taking bound Mitch outside, Gabe and Willy are subdued by Al, Jim and Hank.

Mitch, Al, Jim and Hank lead the

T.J. (William Smith) grimly ponders the future with Susan (Kathy Baumann).

pursuing Wizards to the flats and split up. Soft, muddy ground bogs down the Wizards' big choppers. Overheard by Mitch, T.J. mentions the mountains.

At a field bivouac, Mitch launches offensive measures by requisitioning search and destroy equipment for purported maneuvers. Brooding T.J. and Casey glare at each other across the camp during a party. The Berets establish a command post. T.J. tells Casey he is leaving. "It's for your own good, kid." "You've decided, huh?" objects Casey, who summons Susan. "She ain't your old lady anymore," declares T.J. Casey rips into him.

Explosion simulators force the startled Wizards to move up the canyon. T.J. knows a back way out. Some Wizards are knocked off their bikes by a trip wire. Willy escapes, telling the others he recognized one of the Berets. "Mitch," pertinently mutters T.J.

As the Wizards break camp the next morning, the Berets attack with mortar rounds and tear gas. Gas-masked, they flex karate to neutralize the confused, vulnerable Wizards. Casey chokes Mitch with a chain, but Mitch breaks free and beats up defeated T.J. Casey flees as T.J. tells Mitch, "He's the one you want!" Casey has a head start on Mitch as they rush into a cave. Casey braces for a knife ambush at the end of the tunnel, but Mitch's reflexes are too fast. "I take it," laughs Casey, "that you found my chain." Arms tied, the Wizards are herded away.

Bishop and Frost showed high initiative attempting a Biker for the A.I.P. label rather than a gore and tits New World–type item. Unless a spinning roulette wheel signifying Mitch's grief counts, this was not a "sensitive" Biker but a restrained action piece. None of the Wizards—even unpleasant Casey—were the usual Bishop-Frost degenerates and the Berets didn't embark on a blood for blood manhunt. The real tension existed in the Wizards between T.J. and Casey, exacerbated by the outlaw code of protecting a wanted member.

Unused to bikes, Mitch's comrades got entangled in slapsticky mistakes during the elementary phase of their bike-riding education. A one-word clue put them onto the general identity of the Wizards, its misconstruement a detection obstacle. The collapse of Mitch's cover put him at temporary risk but made the Wizards retreat into an area where the Berets launched a cartoon war almost as perkily light as the cycle school sequences. Mitch got his man and didn't have to kill anybody to do it.

Chrome and Hot Leather acknowledged Bill Smith's impact on Bikers by introducing T.J. in a stark, protracted freeze-frame closeup. As the camera zoomed back for a high group shot, the Wizards were put into motion. A like shot began *The Jesus Trip*, but Lee Frost's copy image

No magic can save the Wizards.

was more forceful. Such a zestful lenser, Frost shot *three* consecutive bikes popping wheelies in rapid succession and photographed the long dialogue scene with Lt. Reardon in one unbroken follow focus set-up. Unable to film real sex between Mitch and Susan, Frost substituted innuendoish close-ups of the flashing pinball machine.

Reunited with his *Laredo* pal Peter Brown, who played Chad Cooper on the show, William Smith had only minimal screen time with Tony Young. The son of film and radio actor Carlton Young, Tony was a very stoic actor whose composure played well against the occasional overacting of Smith. Michael Haynes was a stuntman who helped write the script, playing Casey. His male model looks made him a Marlboro man. Kathy Baumann had been an Ohio representative in the Miss America contest.

Motown star Marvin Gaye, who had done a role in the Nam vet Biker drama for TV, *The Ballad of Andy Crocker* (1969), was *Chrome and Hot Leather*'s hoped-for casting sensation as Jim. The agreeable Gaye here was not the coked-up madman who died at the hand of his father in 1984. Two other music names were Bobby "Boris" Pickett of "The Monster Mash" and dialogue-deprived jazz great Herb Jeffries.

Cherie Moor was Cheryl Ladd, who in between Moor (a name forced on her by her agent) and Ladd had acted under her real name of Cheryl Jean Stopplemoor. Dan Haggerty was a Wizard and Erik Estrada a G.I.

William Smith cameoed in two other Bishop-Frost films, producing and starring in the Jack Starrett–directed *Hollywood Man* (1976), where Smith played an ex-biker turned movie mogul. Wife Michelle was in the cast. With the role of Arthur Falconetti in *Rich Man, Poor Man*

(1977) and as the father of *Conan the Barbarian* (1982), Smith found a measure of fame beyond *Laredo* and his bike pics. On the last season of *Hawaii 5-0*, he was Kimo and starred on *Wildside* as Brodie Hollister.

Wes Bishop and Lee Frost broke up in the late Seventies. After his 1988 motorcycle accident, Gary Busey played a Desert Storm vet seeking to avenge his brother's murder with the aid of three Nam vets in *Chrome Soldiers*. The 1992 cable film was a *Chrome and Hot Leather* for the Nineties —meaning it was typically charmless, synthetic, drabber than worn paint post–Seventies action. Only an all-out nude scene by Kathy Baumann, now a successful accessories designer, could have made this dull *Chrome* sparkle.

When Wes Bishop died in 1993, *The New York Times* reported that he had been nominated for an Oscar for *Chrome and Hot Leather*!

The Cycle Savages

Trans-American 1970. Executive Producers: Mike Curb, Casey Kasem; Producer: Maurice Smith; Director-Screenplay: Bill Brame; Associate Producers: Arthur Gilbert, Frank Ragusa; Cinematography: Frank Ruttencutter; Film Editor–Production Manager: Herman Freedman; Music: Jerry Styner—Sidewalk Prods.; Art Director: Ray Markham; Script Supervisor: Sarah Pierson; Gaffer: John Murray; Key Grip: Ross Nannarella; Assistant Cameraman: Marcel Shain; Sound: Joe Dixon; Wardrobe: Billy Jordan; Makeup: Louis Lane; Visual Effects: Modern Film Effects; Art Work: Roger Robles; Still Photos: Tom Hohl; Special Effects–Stunt Coordinator: Charles Bail; Technical Advisor: Lynn Steed; Filmed at Hollywood Stage; Movielab Color; A Maurice Smith–Ray Dorn Production; Running Time: 82 minutes.

Cast: Bruce Dern (Keeg); Melody Patterson (Lea); Chris Robinson (Romko); Casey Kasem (Keeg's Brother); Maray Ayres (Sandy); Karen Ciral (Janie); Mich Mehas (Bob); Jack Konzal (Bartender); Walter Robles (Tom); Joe McManus, Jerry Taylor (Storekeepers); Tom Daly (Docky); Denise Gilbert (Little Girl); Daniel Gaffouri (Marvin); Anna Sugano (Motorcycle Girl); Gary Littlejohn (Motorcycle Boy); Ron Godwin (Walter); Lee Chandler (Doug); Marjorie Dayne (Motorcycle Girl); Lydia Banks, Randee Lynn (One of the Girls); Peter Fain (Sam—Police Detective).

Rejecting the role of George Hanson in *Easy Rider* kept Bruce Dern away from quality stardom for the next few years. Maurice Smith, the executive of Dennis Hopper's first Biker, *The Glory Stompers*, produced *The Cycle Savages*, whose executives were *Stomper* associates Mike Curb and Casey Kasem. Kasem played the unnamed underworld brother of Keeg, Bruce Dern's version of the Hopper flesh peddler Chino.

Romko Pietrandre, a young escapee from East Berlin, has been sketching Keeg's gang. In a corner bar with his nympho old lady Sandy, Keeg warns him to quit. In Romko's apartment building, Keeg does some "art work" on his belly with a razor, stealing his sketchbook.

Prostitute tenant Lea takes Romko to her room and summons Docky, an unlicensed physician. Lea does Kaag's bidding because Sandy is her sister. The white slavers he supplies want a new girl for this weekend.

Lea urges Romko not to call the police. Keeg considers breaking Romko's hands in a vice. Lea diverts Romko with a nude posing session while the bikers trash his studio and take more drawings and a war sword awarded to his father. Discovering the thefts, Romko forcefully reclaims his possessions.

Keeg (Bruce Dern) and his old lady Sandy (Maray Ayres).

Keeg learns about Romko's visit. On other business, he wastes a park employee who stole a bike. Teenage Janie is initiated into the gang and given LSD. Two vice cops hear from arrested Docky about Romko's assault and catch him in bed with Lea. They are arrested, she for prostitution.

Acid-ill Janie looks for Docky and collapses in the park. Tired of insatiable Sandy, Keeg abuses her. Romko posts Lea's bail. Out of guilt for her actions, she shuns him.

Back in his studio, Romko is kidnapped for the big "squeeze play." Packing a gun in her purse, Lea pretends she wants to see meddlesome Romko suffer. Allowed to work the vice, Lea fakes hurting his hands. Keeg catches the ruse. Cornered, Lea pulls the gun, but Keeg manipulates Sandy into taking it from her. Janie has been taken to the hospital and the cops are coming. Keeg tells everyone to stay put so he can sneak away. Abandoned Sandy shoots Keeg in the back as a speeding sports car cuts him off. Keeg crashes into a trash heap. Sandy mourns Keeg as their image becomes a drawing.

Showing an ugly part of America through the eyes of a sensitive foreigner was not enough of a vivid novelty, nor was the previously tried white slavery theme exploited provocatively enough in something like a descriptive title. If *The Glory Stompers* was too outdoorsy, *The Cycle Savages* showed how urban settings tend to dilute the visual flexibility of an action form that creates greater tension when the innocents are far from home or home is some isolated spot with minimal or nonexistent police protection. Scratch bikes and *Cycle Savages* seems like a film about street punks ... lacking even the subculture color of a film dealing with hippie degenerates.

Romko revered the beauty of the female form. To Keeg, it was just a toy and something to sell as merchandise. An unintentional danger to Keeg's girl-pushing, Romko was more a "heroine" than love interest Lea, being the true party at risk for physical violation. With Romko, menace to his creative digits was almost tantamount to a threatened gangbang. Chino-style, Keeg died from the violence of his own woman.

Mostly, what *The Cycle Savages* had going for it were the acceptable performances of Bruce Dern, Chris Robinson and Melody Patterson. From a poolside table, Casey Kasem took that easiest of roles—a phone-in part talking into a real phone. Unbilled Scott Brady was the head vice cop and Steve Brodie was another detective in a cut role.

So grubby was *The Cycle Savages* that A.I.P. wouldn't show it under the company's real name, distributing it through one of the A.I.P. dummy outfits, Trans-American, which usually handled foreign sleaze. Mike Curb, converting to Republican politics, got out of films and became lieutenant governor of California.

Devil Rider

Goldstone 1971. Producers: Brad F. Grinter, Charles G. Ward; Director: B.F. a/k/a Brad Grinter; Screenplay: Carole McGowan, B.F. Grinter, C.G. a/k/a Charles G. Ward; Second Unit Director: Ted Botkin; First Unit Crew: Cinematography: Barry Mahon; Production Manager: Heather Hughes; Assistant Director: Randy Grinter; Script Supervisor: Carole McGowan; Sound: Larry Fisher, Jon Williams; Gaffer: Dan Wright; Set Construction–Fight Choreography: Tim Aycock; Grips: Kenny Dudley, Barnett Millman; Makeup: Julie Ward; Assistant to Producer: Lary Wright; Second Unit Crew: Cinematography-Lighting: Pete Kauppi; Sound: Earl McClintock, Ted Botkin; Assistant Director–Assistant Cameraman: James Scott; Wardrobe-Properties: Julie Ward; Makeup: Sharon Scott; Other Assistants: James Murphy, Bob Lynn, Dan Lynn; Still Photography: Nelson Cooper; Production Manager: Charles G. Ward; Music Recording: Shadow Recording, Fort Lauderdale, Florida; Lab Processing: Capitol Lab Inc.; Soundwork: Criterion Sound Studio, North Miami, Florida; Song: "The Wind" written by Heroes of Cranberry Farm Music, written-directed by Gyl Ward; Music Arranger–Special Guitar Work: Dave Chiodo; Eastmancolor; Running Time: 74 minutes.

Cast (in order of appearance): Sharon Mahon (Kathy Holliday); Ridgeley Abele (Jim Aldredge); Johnny Pachivas (Himself); Larry Parmillo (Karate School); Ross Kananza (Champ); Chris Martell (Sarge); Wayne Hagen, Patty Scanlon (Mama); John Donnell, Wes Dunbar (Biker); Phyllis Purviance (Mama); Ernie Falco (Biker); Michael Martin (Biker); Steve Misen (Biker); Joan DeCamp (Mama); Poppy Little, Frank Hatton (Karate School); Mike Arma, Dee Dee Andrade (Mama); Cherill Honor (Mama); Robert Stark (Biker); Gaye Gipson (Mama); Heather Hughes (Penny Holliday); Brad Grinter (John Holliday); Gyl a/k/a Charles Ward (Roger Kimbrough); Pat McCarron, Janice Kerr, Robert Doran, Sy Prescott, Harry Hall, Nelson Cooper, Warren Ellsworth; Special Guest Stars: Heroes of Cranberry Farm.

New York soft-core veteran Barry Mahon retired to Miami but he and his actress daughter Sharon got involved with Brad F. Grinter's *Devil Rider*. Its draw kung fu against bare knuckles, *Devil Rider* was largely paid for by the expensive tuition fees of Grinter's Viking Cinema Workshop. All the recompense his students received was getting their names on

Champ (Ross Kananza) dukes it out with Duke.

the screen. *Devil Rider* was a bicoastal movie since Grinter directed its Florida parts and second-unit director Ted Botkin shot other scenes in Los Angeles.

Black belt Jim Aldredge dislikes his girl Kathy Holliday mingling with "freaks." She goes off with a bike gang led by ex–Navy boxer Champ. Clobbering the challenger, Champ offers Kathy a "happiness bomb" (pill) that makes her pass out. Kathy's rich father John hires private eye Roger Kimbrough to find Kathy, whose missing big sister Penny, John recently learned, is a hooker.

Posing as a reporter researching prostitution, Roger meets Penny, who tells him she was raped by another bike gang on her eighteenth birthday.

Locating Champ's gang, would-be infiltrator Roger is given away by his fake disguise. Thought to be a cop, he is tied to a tree and riders viciously poke spears at him. Outraged Kathy refuses to be Champ's old lady and is in danger of becoming a mama. Arriving in secret, Jim frees Roger, but two outlaws deflate his bike's tires. The girl culprit clubs Jim unconscious. To save Kathy, Roger threatens Champ by holding a coral snake from the back of its head. Champ casually bites off the head, spitting it out.

Recovered Jim dares obliging Champ to a test of judo and pugilism for Kathy. Jim gets the upper hand, but Champ's main man, Sarge, fatally stabs him in the heart. As Sarge turns to Kathy, who is cradling Jim's body, he asks, "What about her?" "She stays," replied Champ. "He won didn't he."

Devil Rider had a good idea for a sex-oriented Biker: the destiny of one prodigal daughter foreshadowing the possible fate of another by their shared association with a particular type of bad company. The fall of Penny pointed to the fact that so many street women have turned to whoring after early sexual trauma (Penny was a virgin). And what about the gang girls who give themselves freely to outlaws? Do they move on to another life with practical wisdom or end up becoming other "bad Pennys"?

It was California director Ted Botkin who realized much of the film's sex value when he photographed the rape of Penny with the camera taking her point of view. In the meantime, her narration described the crushing suffocation caused by her immediate molester's weight.

Barry Mahon photographed Brad Grinter's scenes. The karate school footage was done in front of a public restroom. A reptilian wrinkle on Man Bites Dog, the snake scene was toothlessly executed and the clumsy battle between Champ and Jim was dulled by the incongruous rhythm of slow, lazy guitar chords.

Champ was played by stuntman and alligator wrestler Ross Kananza, the double in the scene from *Live and Let Die* (1973) where James Bond jumped across the backs of multiple gators. During one gator match, Kananza died of a heart attack.

After playing John Holliday, Grinter hosted his next film, *Blood Freak* (1972). In his campy, weirdo take on grass and Gospel, consumption of pot and additive-tainted poultry made a lapsed lamb-of-God biker a turkey man thirsty for junkie jugulars.

Devil's Angels

American International 1967. Presenters–Executive Producers: James H. Nicholson, Samuel Z. Arkoff; Producer: Burt Topper; Director: Daniel Haller; Cinematography: Richard Moore; Film Editors: Ronald Sinclair, Kenneth Crane; Musical Score: Sidewalk Prods.; Written by: Mike Curb; Production Manager: Jack Bohrer; Assistant Director: Dale Hutchinson; Production Assistant: Jack Cash; Sound Mixer: Phil Mitchell; Properties: Karl Brainard, Richard M. Rubin; Script Supervisor: Bonnie Prendergast; Lighting Gaffer: Lloyd Garnell; Key Grip: Chuck Hanawalt; Design Service: Leon Erickson; Costumes: Richard Bruno; Makeup: Jack Obringer; Hair Stylist: Ray Forman; Construction Coordinator: Ross Hahn; Theme Song: "Devil's Angels" written by Mike Curb, Guy Hemric, Jerry Styner, performed by Jerry and the Portraits; Additional Music by Dave Allen and the Arrows; Panavision and Pathecolor; A Roger Corman Production; Running Time: 83 minutes.

Cast: John Cassavetes (Cody); Beverly Adams (Lynn); Mimsy Farmer (Marianne); Maurice McEndree (Joel the Mole); Leo Gordon (Sheriff Henderson); Russ Bender (Royce); Marc Cavell (Billy the Kid); Buck Taylor (Gage); Marianne Kanter (Rena); Kip Whitman (Roy); Mitzi Hoag (Karen); Nai Bonet (Tanya); Buck Kartalian (Funky); George Sims (Leroy); Salli Sacshe (Louise); Wally Campo (Grog); Dick a/k/a Richard Anders (Bruno); John Craig (Robot).

A.I.P. would dominate Bikers for the next two years following *The Wild Angels*. An in-name-only sequel, *Devil's Angels* was produced by Burt Topper and directed by Roger Corman's former set designer Daniel Haller. Topper, when he had been a full-time director, established himself with several grim, taut combat quickies. A.I.P. promoted Topper to head of its theatrical production. Once an actor, he injected himself into A.I.P. films as the announcer of many of its trailers, including the one for *Devil's Angels*.

Peter Fonda had become involved with *The Wild Angels* while trying to finance a movie. More seasoned in the unstable independent field, John Cassavetes was busy making *Faces* (1968) when he took the role of Cody, president of the Skulls—partly out of the desire to learn how to ride a bike. Cassavetes was allowed to direct a few scenes of *Devil's Angels* without credit.

Since Charles Griffith's script was not a reject like the ones he had done for *The Wild Angels*, it was his only Biker scenario ever filmed. He tried to compare the Skulls to the Okies, who had the misconception that California would afford them a new and better life. The imagined paradise for the Skulls was Hole-in-the-Wall, the fabled sanctuary of the Butch Cassidy gang. Out of his contempt for Bikers, maybe, Griffith gave the plot the pervasive sense of an era coming to an end.

Various Skulls are en route to a club meeting: Cody, Leroy, Joel the Mole and Billy the Kid. Racing down a hilly residential street, Gage and Louise strike a pedestrian standing in front of them. Citizens gather as a cop examines the dead man and fires at the escaping couple. Cody and Leroy look on.

In the Skulls' headquarters, Cody announces the incident. The Man will be coming and he orders the disassembly of the hit-and-run bike. "We are washed up!" feels Joel. Over five years, the Skulls have dwindled from three hundred members to twenty-six. Cody asks Joel to repeat the story of Hole-in-the-Wall. Accessible only by a pass, no posse could ever touch the Cassidy gang. Cody decrees, "We're gonna pick up our old ladies and whatever little else we have and we're gonna roll—and neither man nor beast is gonna stop us until we find a place where we can blow our own peace ... and we're gonna love each other!" With his old lady Lynn, Cody plans to take the Skulls to Hole-in-the-Wall.

The Skulls pause in Lenning City to pick up ex–Skull Funky DiVico, who was busted for painting graffiti on city hall. The Skulls spring overjoyed Funky by yanking out the cell bars with ropes tied to their bikes.

Stopping for gas, the Skulls loot a general store. When the owner complains, Cody bemusedly threatens him, then does an about-face and asks the gas attendant, "How much do I owe you?" A couple exiting in a camper accidentally knock over Gage's new composite hog. Chasing the camper, the Skulls demolish it as the couple watch from safety. "I hope you got this camping business out of your system," the wife tells the husband. "Okay, honey," he says, "Next year we'll get a boat."

In Brookville, the people are holding a local celebration. Up for re-election, Sheriff Charlie Henderson lets bikinied beauty contestants pelt him with tomatoes to show he is a good sport. Cody tries to get lodging at a local campground but is turned down. Emcee Royce introduces the beauty finalists. One is new resident Marianne Fielding. Alarmed by the Skulls, Royce sends for Henderson.

The only girl willing to accommodate the Skulls at the kissing booth, Marianne meets Roy, who offers her a bike ride. Royce harasses Funky over some prizes he won, thinking he stole them. Henderson agrees to let the Skulls spend the night on the beach of the town park if they leave at sunup. He makes Cody promise no trouble. "You've got my word on it," Cody pledges. "They're not going to give you any votes, Charlie!" criticizes Royce. Henderson fears the Skulls' riot potential, hoping isolation will contain them. "I know my job, Royce!"

Marianne joins the Skulls' beach party. Lynn doesn't share Cody's utopian dream: "There's no place that doesn't have good things that doesn't have cops." Joel tells a ghost story. The Skulls discuss "quail-hunting" with Marianne as she tries marijuana. Roy initiates the start of group molestation, kissing her too hard. Gage, the scariest figure in her pot-distorted vision, picks up Marianne to kiss her—triggering a violent panic raction. Wriggling free of restraint, Marianne flees.

Stumbling into a saloon, Marianne looks like she has been raped. "They didn't," Marianne quietly tells Royce and the Mayor. Royce feels the Skulls may have well have. Summoned, Henderson races to the beach as Royce shouts, "You're finished, Charlie!"

Arriving at the park with a posse,

Lynn (Beverly Adams) and Cody (John Cassavetes) in a rare moment of privacy.

Henderson tells Cody, "Your word lasted about two hours, but mine's a little more durable." Despite denials of rape, Cody is arrested. Henderson sends the other Skulls packing. "Another mistake, Charlie!" yells Royce. Joel dispatches Roy to summon the Stompers. Billy has devised a plan.

Henderson hears the truth from Marianne and frees Cody, warning that the Skulls never return. "There was no rape!" he tells Royce. "You knew that!" Royce argues, "Your job—your real job—is not to interpret a set of books nobody bothers to read anyway … to make us feel safe and comfortable in our beds at night!"

Rejoining his group, Cody hears Billy's "righteous" idea: take over Brookville. A vote has already been passed. Joel advises Cody not to call another. Cody insists they aren't strong enough. "Oh, yes we are," chortles Joel, who leads Cody down the road apiece to show him "Two hundred Stompers, baby!" Led by Cain, they are also hot for some "razzle-dazzle." Okay," reluctantly concedes Cody, "razzle-dazzle."

Mechanized thunder awakens early morning Brookville as the Skulls and the Stompers infest its empty streets. Royce, the Mayor and Marianne are snatched from their homes. A rock tossed through a window draws Henderson and his deputies out of his office. "You're under arrest!" declares Henderson. "All two hundred of us?" arrogantly asks Billy, who tells the men to drop their weapons. Henderson is brutally beaten until Cody makes Billy stop the attack. Billy is to keep an eye on the Stompers, who will be needed only if there is trouble.

The Skulls hold court in the saloon, putting Marianne, Royce and the Mayor on trial before prosecutor Joel. The defendants are forced to admit they knew a rape didn't happen. Royce and the Mayor are hustled out. Cody turns to Henderson, who admonishes, "You boys are diggin' a big hole." "You know, we came to this town in a peaceable manner," protests Cody. "All you nice citizens did was insult us and rough us up and throw us out of here like a pack of mad dogs!" "You say we're guilty of rape," excoriates Joel,

"Well, I say we got a rape comin' to us!" "Overruled," objects Cody, "Forget it!" "Let's ask the jury!" suggests Joel. Poor Marianne is ravaged.

Out front, Cain tells Billy, "My boys aren't too crazy about playin' cops," asking, "Is that invite still open?" "Any time," answers Billy, "the town's all yours."

As Brookville is being destroyed, Cody asks Joel, "Where is Hole-in-the-Wall anyway?" "There's no such place," answers Joel. "I made it up. Cody, you're the only one who needs a Hole-in-the-Wall—just like you need Funky and you need Leroy and all the rest of us to pat you on the back!" "*Just like I need you?*" roars Cody. "*Just like you need me!*" retorts Joel. Cody slaps Joel to the ground. Passing on a second swipe, he joins Lynn, who is enjoying herself. "We're goin' to Hole-in-the-Wall, you and me," says Cody. Lynn is not interested and Cody turns his back on her as she joins the fun.

Deposed, ignored Cody rips off his colors and leaves town. On the freeway, he spots Highway Patrol cars heading for Brookville to restore order. Heartsick, stone-faced Cody rides on.

Hole-in-the-Wall is an abstract western landmark, but Charles Griffith managed to sustain the wishfulness of Cody's vision. Even if the Skulls had found it, how would they have supported themselves? What would they have done for kicks in a place without modern conveniences? In Butch Cassidy's day, lawmen had less advanced means of ferreting out and subduing criminals—so there went supposed impregnability. Joel was remiss in telling Cody it was only legend and Cody accepted his tale without even pausing to consider its direction ... let alone credibility. Once the Skulls left home, their travel became as existential as a typical Black Rebels (*The Wild One*) run ... only the Rebels had addresses to return to and, until Wrightsville, they were not major felons.

Beneath their disparate exteriors, Cody and Henderson were alike. Common sense placed them above the rest of their people, but prudent decisions threatened their peer group popularity. Henderson stood to lose re-election. Cody's half-hearted sanction of the Brookville raid failed to restore his command. When the Skulls went Stomper, they forefeited their own club identity so they could regain their previous sense of status. In a turnabout on the fate of Heavenly Blues, Cody escaped "The Man"—but as a captain without a crew.

Devil's Angels and *The Wild Angels* were the only studio Bikers from A.I.P. *Devil's Angels* was supposed to create the protest mood of *The Wild Angels* but leave out the extreme morbidity. For the Black Rebellish attire of some of the Skulls, *The Wild One* seemed to have a marked influence. Inside the Skulls' clubhouse was a Brando poster with a beard drawn on his face. Most welcome was what *The Wild Angels* lacked completely; some funny citizens.

Among the people from *The Wild Angels* who returned was cameraman Richard Moore, who did some Corman-worthy tracking shots, including an extremely intricate moving angle shot of the Highway Patrol cars crossing an overpass. The music twice reprised "Blues' Theme" and "Bongo Party" was heard on a record.

Playing Funky, Buck Kartalian nearly collided with a car while learning to ride his bike when he mistook the gas for the brake. Sliding under the car, Kartalian hung on, tearing a muscle in his right hand. He and John Cassavetes changed a scripted scene to everyone's enthusiastic reaction except Burt Topper, who was only interested in violence. Cassavetes and Kartalian rode to Nogales one day, but border guards who thought they may have been drug smugglers held the pair and searched them. Cassavetes phoned the production company to gain their release.

The Skulls and the Stompers turn Brookville into another Wrightsville.

The young John Cassavetes had made an impact in both the TV and motion picture versions of Reginald Rose's *Crime in the Streets* as the vengeful, reckless gang leader Frankie. Cody was an older, more cautious hoodlum honcho entertaining some notion of comfortable retirement. Maurice McEndree had helped produce Cassavetes' historic art film *Shadows* (1960) and sparked the inception of *Faces* when he unearthed a Cassavetes play script called *The Marriage*. Through Cassavetes, McEndress got to play Joel the Mole.

Lovey Kravzitt in the Matt Helm spy spoofs, Beverly Adams married and later divorced Vidal Sassoon, who gave her a new hair style for *Devil's Angels*. Mimsy Farmer had been the wild Gloria in *Hot Rods to Hell* and the tragic Andi in *Riot on Sunset Strip* (both 1967). Farmer planned to quit acting and train in Canada, Beverly Adams' birthplace, to become an LSD therapist. However, Farmer appeared in another Dan Haller film, *The Wild Racers* (1968), and found stardom in Europe. Nai Bonet was the eminent navel-shaker from Saigon who had been Shirley MacLaine's belly dance trainer for *John Goldfarb, Please Come Home* (1965).

Marc Cavell and Buck Taylor had been Frankenstein and Dear John of *The Wild Angels*, Cavell the more dominant player here. Kip Whitman took the early acting name of big brother Stuart.

From Maine, Richard Anders had been the lead in the off–Broadway play *The Sunset* and did some TV contract work at Columbia before teaming with director Richard Rush. A biker extra was chopper-builder Gary Littlejohn, who appeared with Anders in *Hell's Angels on Wheels* and *The Savage Seven* before doing many others.

John Craig, the moronic Robot, was a Marlboro man who thought he found his own Hole-in-the-Wall—and died for it in 1998—when he joined the Heaven's Gate cult.

The Dirt Gang

American International 1972. Executive Producer: Ron Jacobs; Producers: Joseph F. Bishop, Art Jacobs; Director: Jerry Jameson; Screenplay: William Mercer, Michael C. Healy; Associate Producer: Paul Carr; Cinematography: Howard A. Anderson, Jr.; Film Editor: Byron Brandt; Music: The Harvest; Music Editor: Ken Johnson; Art Director: Thomas Hasson; Special Photographic Consultant: Darrell A. Anderson; Sound Recordist: James G. Stewart; Sound Mixer: Clark D. Will; Sound Editor: John Hall; Unit Manager: Robert O'Neill; Stunts: Stunts Unlimited and Friends; Stunt Coordinator: Ronnie Rondell, Jr.; Assistant Director: Tom Powell; Key Grip: Tom Doherty; Gaffer: Mel Maxwell; Script Supervisor: Richard Chaffee; Makeup: Bob Sidell; Still Photos: Dene B. Hilyard; Casting: Karen Davis; Production Secretary: Carle Smith; Motorcycle Helmets: Champion Helmets; Titles and Effects: Howard A. Anderson Co.; Recorded: Glen Glenn Sound; Transportation Vehicles: Ford Motor Company; CFI Color; A Roger Corman Production; Running Time: 89 minutes.

The Gang: Paul Carr (Monk); Michael Pataki (Snake); Lee DeBroux (Jesse); Jon Shank (Padre); Nancy Harris (Big Beth); T.J. Escott (Biff); Jessica Stuart (Stormy); Tom Anders (Marty); Joe Mosca (Willie); The Movie Company: Michael Forrest (Zeno); Jo Ann Meredith (Dawn Christian); Nanci Beck (Mary); Charles MacCauley (Curt); Hal England (Sidney); Ben Archibek (Jason); William Benedict (Station Attendant).

Jerry Jameson was a director on *The Mod Squad* and Paul Carr a favorite guest heavy. They were the director and star of *Brute Corps* (1972), the chronicle of a platoon of degenerate mercenaries in Southern Mexico who whiled away their free time by tormenting a young American draft dodger and his hippie girlfriend. One of the few times he came close to playing a hero, creep specialist Carr portrayed the major fed up with the corps' wanton cruelty.

Another "Corp-man," Roger, was the sponsor of *The Dirt Gang*. Helmed by Jerry Jameson and associate produced by leading man Carr, *The Dirt Gang* was like a working vacation for some of the *Mod Squad* crew. Visually, the film resembled an episode called "The Thunder Makers" and cast from that some of its performers, ubiquitous Paul Carr included (an earlier bike story on *Mod Squad* guest-starred Tom Stern and *Dirt Gang* actor Lee DeBroux). Present also in *The Dirt Gang* were *Brute Corps* members Mike Pataki and Charles MacCauley.

The persona non grata of the scramble circuit, the Dirt Gang are led by steel eyepatch–wearing Monk, who pulls into a gas station with Snake, Jesse and Willie. They rob and kill the owner. Monk spots a deputy sheriff coming, splitting with Snake and Jesse while Willie is swiping some valuable garage tools. Willie injures the cop, who shoots him dead and radios another deputy.

The second deputy sees Monk, Snake and Jesse, and goes after them. Jesse takes a fall. When the deputy tries to arrest him, Jesse laughs and points to Monk, who blindsides the officer with a deadly wheelie. Snake pins his badge on Jesse. The cop's body is put in the back seat of his car, which is set on fire and pushed down a hill. The vehicle explodes.

Monk, Snake and Jesse join the rest of the gang at camp, hoping Willie will come. Monk's astrologer old lady Stormy shares her bad vibes with hefty Big Beth: "We're doomed." Monk is closer to Biff, who sees Monk staring bitterly at an old racing poster with a picture of Zeno, the racer Monk blames for the loss of his eye. Biff thinks Zeno may be dead. "He ain't dead baby," says certain Monk, "and maybe we're gonna find him sooner than you think." Biff says that accidents are part of the game. Baring his vacant, droop-lidded socket, Monk shows Biff "the prize." It's off to Mexico.

From the top of a mesa, the gang spots some filmmakers shooting in a mockup western town and invade the set. Leading lady Dawn Christian is lashed to a post. "Untie that wench," commands Monk. Zeno, the production stuntman, uneasily watches the proceedings. Monk says all the gang wants is food and director Curt Gilroy sends them to the mess tent, hoping they will be gone soon. "They're looking for action," warns Zeno. "What do you know about it?" asks male star Jason. Zeno feels the sheriff should be called, confiding in script girl Mary that he used to be a biker.

At the mess tent, Big Beth calls Mary over for some "girl talk"—throwing her down on a table to give her a lesbian kiss. Hanging from the balcony of the hotel, Dawn blows her corny line, "Help me White Feather!" and laughs. She argues with Curt, who feels the actress is over-the-hill. "I should've become a nun like mama wanted," gripes Dawn.

"We've got an audience," Monk tells the gang when Zeno intently stares at them, insisting, "I'm a peace-lovin' man." He has heard that Monk has been looking for him. Monk shows Zeno his eye. "There's nothing here for you," says Zeno. "Wrong, baby," Monk retorts. "Everything is here for me," telling Biff "We're home." Stormy tries to seduce Monk, who physically rejects her. To her, this is a "suicide trip."

The gang disrupts the shooting of a street scene so Jesse can "direct" a love scene between Big Beth and reluctant Jason, whom Snake threatens with a knife. Sidney, the assistant director, sends Mary to call the sheriff. Monk wants Zeno's ass "bike style." Snake catches Mary trying to call the sheriff, asking, "Wanna be my mama?" Meeting her violent rejection with a lustful kiss, he gets slugged by Zeno. Zeno and Mary flee in a dune buggy, but Zeno is jumped by one of the pursuit riders.

"Little boys and dirty old men all want the same thing," knows Dawn—believing she can handle the gang. Monk gets his hands on a scattergun, aiming it at unconscious Zeno. The sheriff is coming. Concealing their bikes, their gang hides with all of the company except Curt and Sidney, who tell the sheriff the gang is not around.

After the sheriff leaves, the company is herded into a big tent for a game of numbered partners. "It's the way you wanted it," Monk tells tied Zeno, "you know that." "If we can be alone," Dawn tells Monk, "I think we can arrange a little something that might make everyone happy." "Your place or mine?" cracks Monk.

In her private dressing room, Dawn slips into something more comfortable. "How may I serve you?" she asks. Monk's answer is the beginning of hot sex between them while the others engage in an orgy.

One man tries to escape, but Monk, who boasts, "I just had me a movie star!" expects him back. Gunshots ring. "I told you he'd be back," says Monk, before Marty brings the man's body. Mary frees Zeno, helping him sneak out. Monk notes his absence, brutalizing cowardly Sidney, who says Mary aided Zeno. Monk hits Sidney. "That's for being a fink!" Some riders with flares chase Zeno into the nighttime desert. Grabbing a flare, he torches a rider who plunges off a cliff. Zeno is captured.

Dragged back to the set behind a bike, Zeno is tied to a hitching post. Snake spreadeagles Mary on the ground, eagerly awaiting permission from Monk to rape her at knifepoint. Zeno finally agrees to challenge Monk. Jesse firmly but gently wrestles the knife out of worked-up Snake's hand.

At high sunup on Main Street, Monk and Zeno prepare for battle. Monk removes his eyepatch. "Zeno's no ordinary dude," admits nervous Biff. Monk and Zeno face off on their bikes, swinging chains. The biking turns to brawling. Zeno grabs an Indian spear. Hitting him with a plank, Monk remounts his bike and charges at Zeno—who impales him on the spear. The demoralized gang mourns Monk's death. Biff cries.

The Dirt Gang was almost a vision of the later Road Warrior–type sagas about marauding wasteland nomads. Leather was preferred over denim, Monk was a psuedo–Toecutter/Lord Humungous and the movie set a besieged "settlement" thrown together out of makeshift odds and ends. The set's nineteenth-century architecture created a blurring of time like that seen in futuristic citadels assembled from pieces of twentieth century junk.

Those whom the Dirt Gang preyed on were the weakest collection of terrorized people in a Biker hostage situation. Hippies, rednecks and Indians, all of whom belonged to the land where outlaws met them, had something to defend and they were either accustomed to fighting or could adapt quickly. Except for Zeno, who found himself haunted by his past, the movie crew were not used to real-life mayhem. Isolated from the rest of Hollywood, they couldn't rely on studio security, powerful attornies or generous bribes to make this problem go away. Zeno's was the only spine supported by backbone, but his butt needed some motivation before he would take on Monk. Had he complied sooner, Zeno might have prevented a few tragedies.

Category swansong films from A.I.P. sometimes debunked their form by presenting the final entry as one big charade. *The Dirt Gang* was serious about terror, but denuded cinematic artifice by juxtaposing the gang's harassment with the making of a hack horse opera. Where the MGM ranch of *Angels—Hard as They Come* was an "authentic" ghost town, the

Monk (Paul Carr) wields a big double-barreled stick.

lesser-known Bell Ranch was seen here as the sham structure it was. The gang caught a group of dream merchants and enlivened the drama of their own existences by involving them in the axiom that all the world is a stage.

Now that permissiveness was here to stay and this was their last Biker, A.I.P. didn't care if this one was an R film. Much of *The Dirt Gang* looked like a TV-movie full of network no-nos of the time like nudity, copulation and gore. In balling Dawn Christian, Monk fulfilled the fantasy of screwing a celebrity. One male rider at the tent orgy spoofed Gilda Texter's nude cycling in *Vanishing Point* (1971). Besides Big Beth, two other mamas (played by a pair of familiar soft-core actresses) dug lesbianism.

The tent surroundings gave the orgy surreal furnishings like a brothel and surreal too were the flare illuminations brightening the desert canvas like glows from a horde of malevolent fireflies. The rider who burned was completely garbed in protective gear which obscured all signs of a *man* in flames—as though the operator of the bike was a robotic attachment. When the attrition between Monk and Zeno escalated into a mechanized joust, *Dirt Gang* beat George Romero to his

Back row: Big Beth (Nancy Harris), Jessie (Lee De Broux), Snake (Michael Pataki), Biff (T.J. Escott), Padre (Jon Shank), Marty (Tom Anders). Front row: Stormy (Jessica Stuart), Monk (Paul Carr).

Biker Camelot *Knightriders* (1981). In one of the weirdest fights ever staged, Monk and Zeno punched each other while still wearing their helmets, making them appear as berserk automatons. With the Indian lance, Zeno killed Monk with a symbol of his movie protagonist's racial identity. It was the second time, following *The Savage Seven*, such a weapon killed a biker story villain.

On *The Gallant Men*, Paul Carr played another handicapped man on a dangerous hate trip—a G.I. whose boxing hand was maimed by the Nazis. Like Michael Pataki, Carr became a sleaze casting desirable in the early and mid-seventies.

Dragstrip Riot

American International 1958. Released in England as *The Reckless Years*; Executive Producers: Jonathan Daniels, Victor Purcell; Producer: O. Dale Ireland; Director: David Bradley; Screenplay: George Hodgins; Story: O. Dale Ireland, George Hodgins; Additional Story–Dialogue: V.J. Rhems; Associate Producer: Basil Bradbury; Cinematography: Gil Warrenton; Film Editor: John A. Bushelman; Music Composer–Conductor: Nicholas Carras; Lyrics: Carl Eugster; Production Manager: Mack V. Wright; Story Editor: Robert Kirch; Script Supervisor: Bobbie Sierks; Sound Effects Editor: Allen Antics; Prop Master: Jack Owens; Custom Motorcycles: Tony Sloan; A Trans-World Production; Running Time: 68 minutes.

Cast: Yvonne Lime (Janet Pearson); Gary Clarke (Rick Martin); Fay Wray (Mrs. Martin);

Silva (Gabe DeLutri) gets creamed by "Curly," Rick Martin (Gary Clarke).

Bob Turnbull (Bart Thorson); Connie Stevens (Marge); Gabe DeLutri a/k/a John Garwood (Silva); Marcus Dyrector (Cliff); Ted Witherspoon (Gramps); Barry Truex (Gordie); Marilyn Carroll (Rae); Marla Ryan (Helen); Tony Butula (Joe); Carolyn Mitchell (Betty); Steve Ihnat (Dutch); Marc Thompson (Gary); Allen Carter (Mike); Joan Chandler (Lisa); Aileen Carlyle, Anton Van Stralen.

Tops at creating low-budget action and suspense, savvy sensation-monger O. Dale Ireland let David Bradley direct his first production, *Dragstrip Riot*. No dragstrip and a riot on a beach instead, its semi-misleading title fulfilled expectations of speed and mayhem in the inimitable Dale Ireland style.

New to Los Angeles, Rick Martin is liked by everyone in a Corvette club except Bart Thorson, current beau of Janet Pearson. Rick's widowed mom Norma and grouchy grandpa try to cope with a family scandal in San Francisco for which Gramps blames Rick.

Several times, Bart attempts to rile Rick. Real trouble comes in a bike gang led by Silva. From behind, Bart jostles Silva so Silva will blame Rick. Rick runs away, followed by Janet. When Silva makes a pass at her, Rick demonically clobbers him. "That was only round one, Curly," threatens scowling Silva.

Not wanting Rick to ever fight, Norma takes his car keys. Hotwiring his 'vette, Rick sneaks off to a big road race. Dirty driver Bart makes him lose. Rick demands satisfaction. "Martin, you've just invited yourself to a train drag," dares Bart.

Rick and Bart park on the tracks of a railroad crossing. Cocky Bart panics as the train nears—taking off in a cloud of dust. Winner Rick dates Janet.

Bart tells Silva where "Curly" will be. After taking Janet home, Rick is chased by the gang and Bart. Silva swings a lug wrench—missing Rick, but hitting Gordie, who plunges off a cliff. Gordie dies in Silva's arms. Silva turns to blood on his palm.

"Gordie's blood," he intones, "and I swear … on Gordie's blood … *I'm gonna kill you Curly!*"

Since it will be Silva's word against his, Rick heads for Mexico. Janet's remembered pleas echo. "You can't keep running away! Don't you see that I love you?" Turning back, Rick reports the accident.

Facing new charges, Rick had once done three months in detention for killing a boy in a fight. Out on bond, he calls Janet to arrange a secret meeting. Bart overhears, phoning Silva. Rick bridles at bullying Gramps—walking out on him and Norma.

While Norma and Gramps look for Rick, Bart tries to divert Janet until Rick beats him off. Rick tells Janet that "that innocent boy" was a deadly, knife-armed thief whose dad was a politician. The bikers join Bart. Smooching on the sand, Rick and Janet hear them calling his name. They are caught. Silva levels a speargun at Rick, vowing to inflict "the round I'm never gonna forget."

Thrashing Janet's screams are heard by the other kids. Rick breaks free of Bart just before Silva accidentally spears Bart's shoulder. Norma, Gramps and the cops arrive at the ensuing free-for-all. Snivelling Bart fingers Silva for Gordie's death as they are led away. Gramps hails Rick a "chip off the old block."

Balsa light in its almost satirically puerile hijinks, *Dragstrip Riot* carved its conflict from the dark wood of the woes of causeless rebel Jim Stark. Ireland's favorite theme was the bond between manly malefactors like Silva and wimpy big shot wannabes like Gordie. The term "Curly" suggested that Silva felt more for Rick than just hate. The device of a hurled metal object killing someone in such a way to implicate the hero was a chipping from *The Wild One*.

Dragstrip Riot's greatest claim to originality was how its dramatic framework blueprinted the eternal enmity between the A.I.P surfers and the Eric Von Zipper gang. The clash of classes differed only in that these "surfers" were car cultists and

Silva (Gabe DeLutri), Gordie (Barry Truex), Dutch (Steve Ihnat), Rae (Marilyn Carroll) and two pals eye the passersby.

the bikers were earnestly deadly. Endowing some of the Vetters with professional entertainer's voices, *Dragstrip* itself was a near-musical.

Cameraman Gil Warrenton combined the excitement of both Vettes and bikes in some nail-biter chase setups. Nicholas Carras' kicky "Teenage Rumble" theme should have been a hit record.

Steve Ihnat appeared with *Dragstrip Riot* lead Gary Clarke in Dale Ireland's *Date Bait* (1960), Ted V. Mikels' *Strike Me Deadly* (1963), which he co-wrote, *Passion Street U.S.A.* (1966), co-produced and directed possibly by Ireland as "Oscar Daley," and the TV pilot *The Police Story*. The Czech-Canadian Ihnat saw his talent ripen in the late Sixties and it promised success in direction with *The Honkers* (1972). Promoting it at Cannes, Ihnat died of a heart attack. He was just thirty-seven.

Born in Brooklyn, Baptist preacher's son Gabe DeLutri fought in Korea, earned a bachelor's degree in theater arts at the Pasadena Playhouse and worked as a studio electrician, prop man and carpenter. He was discovered in his evening drama class by Dale Ireland, who found a fabulous Silva. Also outstanding as drug pusher Nico Martinelli in *Date Bait*, DeLutri co-starred with another Ireland actor, Anton Van Stralen, in *The Jailbreakers* (1960). Becoming John Garwood, DeLutri joined the Richard Rush team. Thanks to *Dragstrip Riot*, the underrated Garwood managed to get a long head start on other Biker familiars.

Easy Rider

Columbia 1969. Executive Producer: Bert Schnieder; Producer: Peter Fonda; Director: Dennis Hopper; Screenplay: Peter Fonda, Dennis Hopper, Terry Southern; Associate Producer: William L. Hayward; Cinematography: Laszlo Kovacs; Film Editor: Donn Cambern; Production Manager: Paul Lewis; Assistant Editor: Stanley Siegel; Consultant: Henry Jaglom; Sound Effects: Edit-Rite, Inc.; Music Editing: Synchrofilm, Inc.; Re-recording: Producers Sound Service, Inc.; Sound: Ryder Sound Service; Titles: Cinefx Color Processing, Consolidated Film Industries; Post-Production: Marilyn Schlossberg; Art Director: Jerry Kay; Assistant Cameraman: Peter Heiser, Jr.; Sound Mixer: Leroy Robbins; Gaffer: Richard Aguilar; Key Grip: Thomas Ramsey; Script Supervisor: Joyce King; Location Manager: Tony Vorno; Transportation: Lee Pierpoint; Stunt Gaffer: Tex Hall; Second Assistant Director: Robert O'Neill; Makeup: Virgil Frye; Special Effects: Steve Karkus; Still Man: Peter Sorel; Electrician: Foster Denker; Best Boy: Mel Maxwell; Sound Boom: James Contrares; Generator: Guy Badger; Songs: "The Pusher," "Born to Be Wild," "I Wasn't Born to Follow," "The Weight," "Do You Want to Be a Bird," "Don't Bogart Me," "If Six Was Nine," "Let's Turkey Trot," "Kyrie Eleison," "Flash, Bam, Pow," "It's Alright Ma (I'm Only Bleeding)," "Ballad of Easy Rider," by Gerry Goffin, Carole King, Jaime Robbie Robertson, Antonia Duran, Elliott Ingber, Larry Wagner, Jimi Hendrix, Jack Keller, David Axelrod, Mike Bloomfield, Bob Dylan, Roger McGuinn, Performed by Steppenwolf, the Byrds, the Band, the Holy Model Rounders, Fraternity of Man, the Jimi Hendrix Experience, Little Eva, the Electric Prunes, the Electric Flagg, Roger McGuinn; Technicolor; Presented by Pando Company in association with Raybert Productions; Running Time: 95 minutes.

Cast: Peter Fonda (Wyatt); Dennis Hopper (Billy); Antonio Mendoza (Jesus); Phil Spector (Connection); Mac Mashourian (Bodyguard); Warren Finnerty (Rancher); Tita Colorado (Rancher's Wife); Luke Askew (Stranger on Highway). Commune: Luana Anders (Lisa); Sabrina Scharf (Sarah); Sandy Wyeth (Joanne); Robert Walker (Jack); Robert Ball, Carmen Phillips, Ellie Walker, Michael Pataki (Mimes). Jail: Jack Nicholson (George Hanson); George Fowler, Jr. (Guard); Keith Green (Sheriff). Café: Hayward Robillard (Cat Man); Arnold

Hess, Jr. (Deputy); Buddy Causey, Jr., Duffy LaFont, Blasé M. Dawson, Paul Guedry, Jr. (Customers); Suzie Ramagos, Elida Ann Herbert, Rose LaBlanche, Mary Kay Hebert, Cynthia Grezaffi, Collette Pupera (Girls). House of Blue Lights: Toni Basil (Mary); Karen Black (Karen); Lea Marmer (Madame); Cathe Cozzi (Dancing Girl); Thea Salerno, Ann McClain, Beatriz Moniel, Marcia Bowman (Hookers). Pickup Truck: David C. Billodeau, Johnny David.

The differences between something like *The Hellcats* and *Easy Rider* are like, say, the infinite gap between early stop-motion and computer graphics. Seeing celluloid itself as an external hallucinogen, Dennis Hopper acknowledged its power of enrapturement when he wrote the screenplay of *The Last Movie*. Not filmed until the year after *Easy Rider*, one of its characters was a Peruvian priest who regarded cinema as a tool of Satan. Jack Valenti, president of the Motion Picture Association, wasn't such an absolutist since he felt high-budget family fare was still what real Hollywood was all about. At the Showarama film exhibition in Toronto, Valenti defended his show business Republicanism in a speech trying to assure everyone that only extremist youth got off on sex and psychedelia (Valenti was also an outspoken critic of skinflicks). One who listened but didn't agree was Peter Fonda.

Later that evening in his hotel room, Fonda drank some Heineken beer and took a sleeping pill. Under their combined influences, he looked at a still of him and Bruce Dern from *The Wild Angels* on bikes against an oddly-compelling washed-out background. Inspiring a different Biker—one where the search for freedom created a bondage in its unrealistic attainment—an inner voice shouted "Eureka!" That voice, however, carried inflections of *Free Grass*.

While reveling in his revelation, Fonda envisioned two counterculturites working as circus stunt drivers who decide to plan for the rest of their lives. On coke money, they would go to New Orleans on choppers, expecting to settle in the palmy paradise of Florida rather than some illusory Hole-in-the-Wall. Since the actual journey was its own special "trip," the two would try to groove on the best they could find in reality with an occasional pot picker-upper.

Fonda phoned Dennis Hopper at three a.m. to describe his vision, making it sound feasible commercially by reminding him of how successful their respective Bikers *The Wild Angels* and *The Glory Stompers* had been. Interested in producing *Easy Rider*, Fonda was willing to let Hopper direct after Hopper requested the job, hoping it would lead to *The Last Movie* as his next movie. Brooke Hayward's brother William would be associate producer of *Easy Rider*, Roger Corman the executive and American International the distributor.

Sam Arkoff cared little about the artistic pretensions of *Easy Rider*, but sensed a mega-hit. The New Orleans scenes had to be shot in conjunction with the 1968 Mardi Gras festival since the characters had to interact with the festivities and stock shots or studio mockups were unacceptable. Arkoff did not trust Hopper as a director, wanting a backup replacement if he fell more than one day behind schedule. Fonda and Hopper were not amenable to this condition and the stipulation queered a lost opportunity at greatness for A.I.P. Since *Easy Rider* evolved from the genre advanced by *The Wild Angels*, and A.I.P. had made mass-market Bikers commercial, the company wasn't completely removed from having a hand in the hit that got away.

Jack Nicholson was at Columbia helping Bob Rafelson write their production *Head* (1968) and told Fonda and Hopper to go with that company. Bert Schneider, the son of former Columbia board chairman Abraham Schneider and brother of studio chief Stanley, had grown up with Rafelson and they formed Raybert Productions to create and produce *The Monkees*. Schneider flipped for the idea of *Easy Rider*—initially budgeted at sixty thousand dollars—but felt that six hundred thousand would guarantee Columbia backing. *Easy Rider* would be a joint venture of Peter Fonda's Pando Company and BBS Productions, named after the initials of Bert Schneider, Bob Rafelson and Steve Blauner. A seven-week shooting schedule was desired so no scrutiny from the home office would inhibit creativity.

The script was credited to Fonda, Hopper and Terry Southern, the co-author of the book *Candy* (made into a 1968 film written by Buck Henry) and several previous films, including Jane Fonda's *Barbarella* (1968). His actual contribution mostly negligible, Southern agreed to help so financing would benefit from the stature of the man whose screenplay credits included *Dr. Strangelove: Or How I Learned to Stop Worrying and Love the Bomb* (1964), *The Loved One* and *The Cincinnati Kid* (both 1965). For several weeks, the trio met in New York, thrashing out ideas on tape. Although it carried with it the thrill of Prohibition defiance, dope-dealing was only an act to start the plot—its money the lubricant, choppers the propulsion. The Fonda character, Wyatt, was a self-contained brooder, Hopper's Billy a wacky wild man. Their types were essentially the essences of Heavenly Blues and the Hopper Chino. Fonda was the box-office name.

The one vital and completely defined character was the alcoholic civil liberties lawyer, George Hanson, whom Southern saw as a variation on Gavin Stevens, the attorney created by William Faulkner. What Southern definitely contributed was the term "Easy Rider" ... Dixie slang for guy living with a chick—usually a hooker—who sponges off her money. Rather than peddled flesh, Wyatt, alias Captain America, and Billy sponsored their sojourn on the profits of a different kind of "lady." The female script typist belonged to a U.F.O. cult and she contributed that interest held by George. Not really that enthused, Terry Southern drifted away from the project.

Fonda and Hopper wanted Rip Torn to play George. Torn seemed willing at first, but passed because all salaries were for scale. Rumor claimed he dismissed the film as "shit" while at a party. Bruce Dern was considered, only he wanted more money also. Hopper didn't care for Fonda's recommendation of Jack Nicholson, because Nicholson wasn't a Texan, until Fonda made Hopper change his mind. In crash preparation for his role, Nicholson adopted the traits of Lyndon Johnson.

Tired of Bikers, Laszlo Kovacs demurred on the offer of being cinematographer until he was finally talked into participating. Besides Nicholson and Kovacs, other names associated with Richard Rush who were hired were Sabrina Scharf of *Hell's Angels on Wheels*, Robert Walker of *The Savage Seven* and nine Rush production staffers: Paul Lewis, Robert O'Neill, Peter Sorel, Leroy Robbins, Tex Hall, Foster Denker, Peter Heiser, Richard Aguilar and Joyce King. Henry Jaglom, who played the deranged hippie Warren in *Psych-Out*, had shot some impressive footage of the Six-Day war with a sixteen millimeter camera, getting close with hand-held movement rather than zoom work. He was made an editing consultant. After New Orleans, filming would continue in Los Angeles and Dennis Hopper's home town of Taos, New Mexico.

On stock bikes, Wyatt and Billy go to a desert garage and join their Mexican contact Jesus. Before leaving with their precious coke stash, they have a pause that refreshes. In the noisy parking lot of Los Angeles International Airport, they meet the chauffered connection, who samples the merchandise approvingly in the back seat of his Rolls and pays them. In a pickup, Wyatt and Billy return to the desert, where the cash is wadded up into plastic tubes inserted in the gas tanks of their new choppers. Disassociating himself from temporal time, Wyatt jettisons his wristwatch before he and Billy begin their travel east.

After dark, Wyatt and Billy pull into the parking lot of a motel with the neon Vacancy sign on. Wyatt asks if he has a room, but the owner flashes "No."

The next day, Wyatt gets a flat tire near the home of a hospitable rancher who lets him and Billy fix the bike in his barn. They are invited to lunch with the rancher and his large family. Once, he wanted to see L.A., but didn't: "… you know how it is." "You've got a nice place," compliments Wyatt. "It's not every man who can live off the land. You do your own thing on your own time. You should be proud."

Farther along, Wyatt and Billy pick up a hitchhiking stranger from a distant commune. At a gas station, he repays the courtesy by fueling Wyatt's tank, making Billy uneasy about the money within. They spend the night in an adobe ruin. High on pot, Wyatt sees things, asking the withdrawn stranger, "Where you from?" "Hard to say," answers the stranger. Pressed, he admits, "It's hard to say because it's a very long word." Basically, his origin is "a city," adding, "Doesn't make any difference which one." "You want to be somebody else?" Wyatt asks. "I wanted to be Porky Pig," the stranger confesses. "I never wanted to be anyone else," says Wyatt.

Wyatt, Billy and the stranger arrive at the open, barren commune. Washing his hands, the stranger wipes them on his jacket. A hippie girl, Lisa, shows a quiet interest in Wyatt. The stranger's woman, Sarah, functions in a housemother capacity. Members of a mime troupe arrive to perform. Though dedicated, the inexperienced communers have trouble growing crops. "Nothin' but sand," negatively observes Billy. "They're gonna make it," contradicts hopeful Wyatt. The mime leader presides over a mealtime prayer, telling God, "We ask simple food for simple tastes." Lisa comes on to Wyatt, asking, "Are you an Aquarius?"

Billy wants to leave, but Lisa suggests a trip to a canyon where they, Wyatt and Sarah go skinny-dipping. The stranger gives Wyatt a hit of acid cut for four trips to be used "at the right time with the right people," hinting, "this *could* be the right place." "I'm hip about time," Wyatt tells him, "but I just gotta go."

In a small Texas town, Wyatt and Billy prankishly ride behind a high school band on Main Street and are arrested for parading without a permit. Recovered from a drunk, fellow prisoner George Hanson wakes up Billy by accidentally

Billy (Dennis Hopper) and Wyatt (Peter Fonda) with the stranger (Luke Askew).

slamming a steel door, irritating him. A guard frees George. He couldn't save two other longhairs from the jail's Beautify America campaign—forced haircuts with a rusty razor.

George doesn't want his father to know where he spent the night because Hanson senior is ill. Curious about Wyatt's bike, he pulls out a fifth, offering a toast to D.H. Lawrence. Several times, he started out for Mardi Gras. A cousin had given him a card to Madame Tinkertoy's House of Blue Lights, a popular New Orleans brothel. George would like to accompany Wyatt and Billy. "Got a helmet?" asks Wyatt. "Oh," laughs George, "I've got a helmet."

Wearing an old high school football helmet, George packs with Wyatt and is exhilarated by his first bike ride. At camp, George says he threw the helmet out a week ago but found it on a pillow with a note from his mother saying, "Save It for Your Son." Offered a joint by Wyatt, George declines until assured it is safe and he is taught how to puff. Billy claims he just saw a U.F.O. that flashed three times, then zig-zagged and vanished. George says it was beaming Billy, and notes he saw forty in Mexico. Venusians, asserts George, have been living among earthlings and our leaders have suppressed this because it would stagger our antiquated system. "Grass," Wyatt tells George, "gives you a whole new way of looking at the day."

At a Louisiana café, Billy and George raise eyebrows, attracting a gaggle of teenaged girls seated in a booth. "They look like a bunch of refugees from a gorilla love-in," cracks one redneck. "A gorilla wouldn't love that," sneers another. Refused service, Wyatt, Billy and George leave. The redneck leader infers they won't make it past the parish line.

Wyatt, Billy and George camp in a wooded clearing outside of town. "You know," laments George, "this used to be a helluva good country," telling Wyatt and Billy, "They're not scared of you. They see a free individual, it's gonna scare 'em ... make 'em dangerous. They're scared of what you represent to them and what you represent is freedom. Oh, they say they're free, but talking about it and being it, that's two different things. Being bought and sold in the marketplace, it's real hard to be free. Course don't tell anybody they're not free, cause they're gonna get real busy killin' and maimin' just to prove to you that they are."

While Wyatt, Billy and George are asleep, the café rednecks brutally beat them with axe handles and quickly vanish. George is dead. Wyatt collects his wallet to send it back to his family and notices the card for Madame Tinkertoy's.

In New Orleans, Wyatt and Billy visit the garishly decorated bordello, where they meet two hookers, Karen and Mary. Karen gets cozy with raucous, horny Billy

George (Jack Nicholson) anticipates his own kind of freedom ride, with Wyatt (Peter Fonda).

while Mary tries to warm up detached Wyatt—who bought her company for Billy. On Wyatt's idea, the four go out among the Mardi Gras revelers and visit a cemetery to trip out. Afterwards, elated Billy tells Wyatt, "We did it. We're rich." Wyatt profoundly thinks, "We blew it." "Go for the big money, you're free," differs Billy. "We blew it," Wyatt maintains.

On an open country highway in Florida, Wyatt and Billy encounter two redneck hunters in a pickup. The passenger tells Billy to get a haircut. Billy gives him the finger. The passenger fires his shotgun, knocking Billy off his bike. Horrified Wyatt tends to dying, delirious Billy. As he goes for help, the men turn around to silence Wyatt, who dies from another gun blast. Flying off the road into a field, his bike explodes, shattering into burning pieces.

Easy Rider was not a purely sixties lament to lost America. In cracker country, the bigoted and the tolerant are equally straightforward. Strangers may know unexpected courtesies, but also ride through a wilderness where safe areas can be few and far between. Where change is resisted with bloodied fingernails clinging fiercely to what must be protected, the "enemy" is a foreigner and the more exotic looking an easier target. When *Easy Rider* was made, Kids were the New Niggers and all Adult America was their Deep South. In their own consciences, they were pioneers, so Wyatt and Billy assumed the hippie look of martyrdom. Billy adopted full cowpoke gear while Wyatt signified his Captain America identity in copying Smiley France of *The Glory Stompers* by spreading Old Glory across his jacket back. The flag may have also been Peter Fonda's way of telling critics of *The Wild Angels* he wasn't a genuine Nazi. Wyatt and Billy sold dope to fund their trip, but were doomed by appearance.

Exercising their right of individuality, Wyatt and Billy became moving bulls-eyes with nothing more tangible for a compass than the belief that True America lay somewhere beneath its morass of crud. Most aspirations begin as something wishful but must be achieved by hard work. The vision was not something they labored to make happen like the dream of the hard-luck but determined communers. If they *had* found "America," what would they have done that they hadn't already done? Drugs are the same in Florida as they are in California, so they wouldn't have found any Peninsula Gold. No use itemizing the women since they were the least important of any diversion.

A homely flower in a garden of weeds, George Hanson was a reminder of an Old South that dominated slaves and had its own white underclass, but nevertheless did not actively promote an uncouth, unwashed image. Attached to the yoke of humdrum living like the nice rancher, George deserved a vacation. His travel agents, Wyatt and Billy, unlocked *his* cage after he sprung them from the one saved for potential scalpees (John Ashley's Army sergeant would have been much at home here). Once out of his coop, the fettered Bird Man could flap his wings. Ingesting the new "alcohol," George shed the rest of forced convention. Loosened up but still cognizant of his old insights, he repaid Wyatt and Billy by enlightening them to the reason for their persecution. Once with them, he came by associative guilt to be one of those free spirits the night riders wanted to snuff out. Wyatt and Billy gave George his happiest hours, but indirectly killed him for being in his company.

When Wyatt and Billy reached New Orleans, the predication for their marred journey fell out from within. Wyatt, who had a greater emotional stake, felt the fullest implications. Unintended by the film but coincidental, the shootings of him and Billy echoed the rings of the history-making gunshots fired in 1968. Justice reacted to those deaths. Wyatt and Billy were slain by a whole milieu in the shape of two yahoos.

Defying hidebound film rules, *Easy Rider* was a visual poem, a music video and a record of its creation. Marketable for the majors was a product that speeded the end of old Hollywood's senile notions of what it thought was "in"—woefully dated junk full of beads, Nehru suits, sitars and an attitude of amused contempt. The Buddy aspect of the film compared it with *Midnight Cowboy* (1969)—which also saw its characters head for Florida, ending with Ratso's death—and *Butch Cassidy and the Sundance Kid* (1960). But where the latter was a romanticized "normal" western and the former pretentiously flirted with underground faddism, *Easy Rider* was as liberating as the first popular works of minority and feminist filmmakers—proving a bit heavy even for the Hip. Troubled by the ending, Bob Dylan asked Fonda and Hopper to make it happy.

Easy Rider said something, but spoke in mumbles, murmurs and cryptic gestures. It didn't push in order to communicate and its de-evaluation of potential sleaze was charmingly offhanded. Cocaine was only a bundle of merchandise, pot was puffed like Marlboros and the acid trip was the first enactment of "LSDts" that wasn't a corny light show or amateurish pantomine. Sex was apathetic to register indifference. For the swimming hole scene, a hack director would have lowered his sights and a square would have ordered water immersion just above the bottom halves of the female pecs.

Fonda and Hopper weathered the worst physical and psychological tolls. Brooke Hayward had left Hopper during the location filming. During part of Mardi Gras, he and Fonda nearly fell out and Fonda had to hire a bodyguard to protect him from Hopper. The rednecks were from various towns and encouraged to ad-lib. For the café scene, they were incited to hate when told to react to the imaginary rape-murder of a girl outside of town and every venomous line they improvised was kept. Only one man, not in the film, caused trouble. In his Bourbon Street restaurant, the man's wife overhead Peter Fonda say "fuck" during a phone conversation. Incensed that the word was uttered within her delicate earshot, he menaced Fonda with a club until Dennis Hopper arrived with an ex-bouncer friend. The police came, but the man was in the wrong for intruding on Fonda's privacy.

The grass Fonda, Hopper and Nicholson smoked was real. Each take required a whole joint, putting them in a state of stuporous improvisation. Near Taos, Hopper and Nicholson dropped acid while relaxing by the tomb of D.H. Lawrence in a close approximation of the cemetery trip. The grass scenes were "hard-core," but since all film joints are perceived as hand-rolled tobacco masquerading as Killer Weed, the activity was unprosecutable. Taken by the right users under favorable conditions, drugs helped *make* rather than ruin a movie.

The commune scenes were shot in California. There, Fonda developed a hay fever allergy. The ailment settled in his lungs, but he ignored it until he was treated for bronchial pneumonia in New Mexico. The disease almost proved fatal.

Editing took a year. Hopper cut the film from two hundred forty minutes to two hundred twenty. His colleagues knew this and after Hopper's involvement ended, Fonda did some revising; ditto Jack Nicholson, who edited his scenes with Henry Jaglom under Bert Schneider's supervision. Bob Rafelson took a turn with the Movieola too. The ninety-five minute release version was shorn of a longer beginning where the police chased Wyatt and Billy across the Mexican border. During the "Born to Be Wild" road shots, billboards were to insert counterpoint reactions to the song lyrics. There were additional minutes to the café sequences, the campfire scenes and the "Blew It" ending.

Music was mostly pre-existent material by noted singers and bands. Steppenwolf and the Byrds contributed new numbers. "Born to Be Wild" became a Number Two Hit—*the* biker song—but "The Pusher" was banned by many radio stations. In the movie, but not the Dunhill album, was some music from *The Trip*.

Fonda and Hopper gave excellent personifications rather than real performances. Audiences were waiting to see a new Fonda feature and he owed them his physical presence, but the person audiences were talking about most was Jack Nicholson. He created instant empathy for George in the ad-libbed moment where George waved at the camera from the back of Wyatt's bike during "Do You Want to Be a Bird?" The gesture looked as unaffected as a greeting by someone in a home movie to its watchers. Giving over some portion of the spotlight to make a *character* stand out, Fonda and Hopper helped create a *Star*.

Karen Black saw her career take off from *Easy Rider*, but her potential was much more noticeable when she appeared with Nicholson in Bob Rafelson's *Five Easy Pieces* (1970) as Rayette. Sabrina Scharf married sitcom writer Bob Schiller in 1968. She studied law and became an eminent environmental activist, taking credit for passage of the Clean-Air Initiative. Scharf ran for Congress in 1972 and an episode of *Maude* Bob Schiller co-wrote concerning Maude's bid for the same office was based on Scharf's experience.

Toni Basil went on to choreograph *American Graffiti* (1973). Luke Askew, whose last name fit some of his many villains, was so peace-loving in real life that his opposition to football made him quit the University of Georgia. A coffeehouse singer in Greenwich Village, he got into films with *The Happening* (1967).

The Happening was one of Robert Walker's last major movies. Others cast as communers were Dan Haggerty, Michael Pataki and Walker's ex-wife Ellie. Cast as the drug connection, Phil Spector wanted to produce *The Last Movie* until he and Dennis Hopper had a falling out.

The marketing for *Easy Rider* meant the exploitation of some sure things—Peter Fonda and bikes—and a theme too fragile, too vague for average Biker copy. There were *no* bikes in the original poster art ... only a solitary Wyatt staring at a landscape. "A Man Went Looking for America and Couldn't Find It Anywhere" read the copy line. Fonda again became a pop poster figure and this one outsold his *Wild Angels* poster.

Jack Nicholson won the New York Critic's Award and the film was in the Oscar running for his Best Actor nomination and Best Original Screenplay. Dennis Hopper was awarded at Cannes as Best New Director.

Universal was so overwhelmed by *Easy Rider*'s success that it financed *The Last Movie* (1971) on blind faith. What Universal got back was an interesting but demented fart blast in the face of Hollywood. Jack Nicholson was loved for his star value, but when he directed *Drive, He Said* (1971), with Karen Black and Bruce Dern, he detoured into *Last Movie* straits. Peter Fonda's directorial mishaps, *The Hired Hand* and *Idaho Transfer* (1971) were not BBS pictures.

A Stanley Kramer for his time, Bert Schneider was more activist than Hollywoodite and motion pictures served his political ends. His anti–Vietnam documentary *Hearts and Minds* (1974) won an Oscar, but Columbia had turned on Schneider with the retirement of his father and sudden death of his brother and the film was released independently. BBS soon after was R.I.P.

Jack Nicholson was the only *Easy Rider* star who really thrived until Dennis Hopper cleaned up his substance abuse and auditioned for the role of Frank Booth in *Blue Velvet* (1986). Peter Fonda couldn't connect with his sister and father on-screen. He was left out of *On Golden Pond* (1981) and had hoped to star with every thespian Fonda in a screen adaptation of Howard Fast's novel *Conceived in Liberty* until Henry died in 1983.

That year, Fonda announced he would produce an *Easy Rider* sequel to star him and Dennis Hopper. Terry Southern, who regained interest in *Easy Rider*, collaborated with *Saturday Night Live* writer Michael O'Donoghue on the script of the hypothetical followup, *Biker's Heaven*. A century after nuclear war, various deviant subcultures rule the globe: sadistic lesbians, mutant bikers and black Nazis. An alien resurrects Wyatt and Billy, who try to save America by looking for the likeliest candidate for an honest president. Their only weapon is a "Don't Tread on Me" flag endowed with protective magic. The café scene from the first *Easy Rider* was recalled in a scene where some Punk versions of the redneck customers got to beat Wyatt and Billy up.

Bert Schneider and Bob Rafelson planned to put on video a three-hour long director's cut of *Easy Rider* and a video documentary with Wyatt and Billy traveling to different music. In 1990, they asked Columbia to return the *Easy Rider* negatives, but were told the negatives vanished. Columbia then discovered five hours' worth of prints in its underground storage vault. It was hoped that this material would be used to make colorized videotape for the director's cut. Without the negatives, no new prints could be made. A ten thousand dollar reward was offered for the return of them. Schneider and Rafelson charged Columbia with gross negligence, instituting a lawsuit.

The outtakes were desired for a more definite *Easy Rider* sequel. At Cannes, Howard Zucker announced *Easy Rider— The Next Generation*. He intended to take the part of the cemetery trip where Karen cried "Oh God, please help me conceive a child!" and use it to start the sequel—with Dennis Hopper playing Billy's grandfather. The function of his character was to tie the story threads together.

Easy Rider— The Next Generation was tentatively planned for release in 1994, when Dennis Hopper sued Peter Fonda for owed money. Twenty-five years earlier, they had agreed to split the profits from *Easy Rider* equally, but Hopper alleged that Fonda kept an extra thirty-three percent for himself when Hopper felt entitled to forty-four percent. Fonda denied the allegation. The suit was dropped and Fonda and Hopper became friends again.

An Oscar nomination for acting was finally accorded Peter for *Ulee's Gold* (1998). During the thirtieth anniversary of *Easy Rider*, he was back on the road ... riding *real* easy.

Five the Hard Way

Fantascope 1969. Re-released by Crown International as *The Sidehackers*. Executive Producer–Cinematography: John Hall; Producer: Ross Hagen; Director: Gus Trikonis; Screenplay: Tony Houston a/k/a Enrique Touceda III; Story: Larry Billman; Associate Producers: Pat Somerset, Jerry Brutsche; Film Editor: Pat Somerset; Music: Mike Curb, Jerry

Styner; Music Editor: Ed Norton; Assistant Director: Tony Lorea; Sound Editors: Norman Wallerstein, Billie Owens; Script Supervisor: Rosemary Johnston; Stunt Coordinator: Erik Cord; Music Performed by: The New Life. Fantascope and Eastmancolor; Produced by Fantascope Corp. Running Time: 82 minutes.

Cast: Ross Hagen (Rommel); Diane McBain (Rita); Mike a/k/a Michael Pataki (J.C.); Richard Merrifield (Luke); Claire Polan (Paisley); Michael Graham (Cooch); Hoke Howell (Crapout); Robert Tessier (Jake); Edward Parrish (Nero); Erik Lidberg (Tork); Erik Cord (Dirty John); Toni Moss (Lois); Diane Tessier (Debbie); Joey Tessier (Billy); Warren Hammack, Irve Ross (Mechanics); Tony Lorea (Announcer).

On *The Hellcats*, Ross Hagen made some friends who would work in his own productions. The first, *Five The Hard Way*, was about the European sport of sidehacking. Hagen's financial backer was ex–movie sex symbol John Hall, now a distinguished photographic inventor. Fantascope was the name of Hall's company and the 3-D process he used to lense *Hard Way*, the earliest film directed by *West Side Story* dancer-actor Gus Trikonis, a *Hellcats* player then married to Goldie Hawn.

Winning sidehack racer Rommel is on a picnic with his girl Rita; his thoughts are about their future. Those thoughts include a dream house to be filled with "a hundred kids." Racing only on weekends now, Rommel opens a sidehack construction and repair shop with his friend Luke. On Luke's advice, Rommel feels he should marry Rita.

A weird exhibition rider, J.C., travels with his old lady Paisley, Cooch, Dirty John and Nero. J.C. wants Rommel to fix his sidehack. Making Luke uncomfortable, J.C. and his gang watch Rommel partake in the new trial runs. Asked to join him on the competition circuit, Rommel turns J.C. down. Alienated by J.C.'s rage, Paisley and Nero desert him. Rommel hires Nero as a sidehack mechanic.

Paisley tries to seduce Rommel, who tells her to "grow up." She gets even by telling J.C. that Rommel attempted to rape her. Rommel and Rita are at their paradise ranch house. J.C. and the gang beat and tie up Rommel, who is made to watch as Rita is raped and murdered. Her bloody, nude corpse hangs from a rafter while Rommel is left for dead.

Going to Luke for help, Rommel will not heed Luke's suggestion that he tell the police. Nero helps vigilante Rommel find two hired henchmen, Jake and Crapout.

When J.C. learns of Rommel's revenge plans, he has Cooch infiltrate the Rommel band. Cooch leads them to the vicinity of J.C.'s hideout. Trying to sneak off and tell J.C. where they are, Cooch is spotted and stopped. Luke again urges Rommel to call the police and leaves to get them himself.

Diane McBain as Rita.

Rommel, Nero, Jake and Crapout surround the hideout, but Cooch breaks free to warn J.C., who mistakes Cooch for one of Rommel's men and shoots him. Responding to the shots, Rommel, Nero, Jake and Crapout attack. Jake and Crapout crash their sidehack into the gang's stronghold. Jake guns down a few members before he is shot. As he flees, J.C. fires a bullet, wounding Rommel in the shoulder.

Catching him, Rommel beats up J.C. He feels he has won and walks away before J.C. shoots him in the back. A last vision of Rita appears to dying Rommel as he falls backward into a pool of water.

Rommel was a bike version of Jeff Logan, the broncobuster of *The Mini-Skirt Mob* who could not shake off the people from his old world. Standard gang malice was the only kind of plot *Five the Hard Way* had confidence in. Sidehacking kept the professional scenes of cycling interesting, but it was a sport that never really caught on in America. Rape was a dual-edged subject. Paisley's lie made Rommel look like a rapist to J.C., who reacted by doing it to Rita ... violating a love nest that would never see those "hundred kids."

Spoiling so much for payback, Rommel bought a part of his own gang. When he finally nabbed J.C., he wimped out. The winner by a cowardly advantage: J.C. Yet if true love survives the end of flesh, death's facilitators can expedite reunion of spirits, lessening the time of bereavement for the lover who survived the first to go.

Ross Hagen, who gave his most brooding and sensitive performance as Rommel, cast wife Claire as the woman Rommel didn't want while Rita was Diane McBain, Hagen's on-screen ex-love and foe in *The Mini-Skirt Mob*. Michael Pataki first made himself known as the younger self of a Hollywood mogul portrayed in old age by Rod Steiger in *The Movie Maker* (1967),

Claire Polan as Paisley.

adapted from a two-part *Bob Hope Chrysler Theater* story. Besides Robert Tessier himself, two of his eight kids (ninety two fewer than a hundred), Diane and Joey, were also in the film.

Fantascope released *Five the Hard Way* by that name before selling it to Crown-International, which renamed it *The Sidehackers*. Only a bike fan would have understood that title.

The future lives of John Hall and Diane McBain weren't kind to either. In 1977, a burglar broke into McBain's then-home and woke her, but the intruder was harmless. Two years later, Hall developed terminal bladder cancer, underwent chemotherapy and cured the disease by shooting the sufferer.

A divorcée raising a nine year old son, McBain moved to an apartment complex in North Hollywood. After working as an executive secretary and a real estate agent, she was acting again, on *Days of our Lives*.

Christmas Eve of 1982, McBain was repeatedly raped in her apartment garage by two Latino men posing as police officers. Neither man was caught. Able to resume as normal a life as possible under the circumstances, McBain became acquainted with other victims of sexual assault and wrote about her ordeal for *People* magazine.

The Glory Stompers

American International 1968. Executive Producers: Maurice Smith, Arthur Gilbert; Producer: John Lawrence; Director: Anthony Lanza; Screenplay: James Gordon White, John Lawrence; Associate Producers: Mike Curb, Casey Kasem, Paul Stevenson; Cinematography: Mario Tossi; Film Editor: Len Miller; Musical Supervision: Sidewalk Productions; Assistant to Producer: Scylla Stancuff; Unit Manager: Philip Marx; Assistant Director: Rudolph Kaddo; Sound: Arthur Names; Camera Operator: Massimo Butera; Artwork: S.F. Stancliff & Associates. Ed Roth Colorscope by Pathé. A Norman T. Herman Production. Running Time: 85 minutes.

Cast: Dennis Hopper (Chino); Jody McCrea (Darryl); Chris Noel (Chris); Jock Mahoney (Smiley); Lindsay Crosby (Monk); Casey Kasem (Mouth); Jim Reader (Paul); Saundra Gayle (JoAnn); Robert Tessier (Magoo); Astrid Warner (Doreen); Gary Wood (Pony); Al Quick, Tony Acone, Paul Prokop, Ed Cook, Peter Fain.

While struggling to make ends meet, producer John Lawrence and writer James Gordon White each did favors for the other. When White needed quick rent money, he sold to Lawrence for fifty-seven dollars a script called *The Man with Two Heads*, which became Lawrence's 1971 feature *The Incredible Two-Headed Transplant*. Lawrence and Maurice Smith came up with the idea of a sixteen-millimeter TV pilot about five bikers, two of them girls, who visited troubled towns, were accused of causing the trouble and then straightened the problem out. The proposed series found no interested takers.

Readapting the heroic position of bikers, Lawrence and Smith decided to make *The Glory Stompers*, from a script by Lawrence and Jim White. Gary Crosby, whose brother Lindsay would appear in *Stompers*, put up the financing. The director was former film editor Anthony Lanza. Two of the three associate producers were Mike Curb and Casey Kasem. Kasem acted in *Stompers* as a biker named Mouth.

Chris (Chris Noel) tries to impart maturity to committed Stomper Darryl (Jody McCree).

The Stompers throw a party

The Glory Stompers

Magoo (Robert Tessier), JoAnn (Saundra Gayle), Mouth (Casey Kasem), Monk (Lindsay Crosby), Chris (Chris Noel) and Chino (Dennis Hopper) need for Mexico.

for president Darryl Hudson's moody old lady Chris. The Black Souls—Chino, Chino's girl JoAnn, Magoo, Paul, Monk and Mouth—crash the bash. Chino tries to hit on Chris until Darryl warns, "You'd better split, man!"

In a forest clearing, Chris expresses to Darryl her yearnings for a normal life. "I want something better than being a Stomper's girl." Happy with things as they are, Darryl asks, "See it my way." The Souls attack, encircling Darryl and Chris on their bikes. Magoo slugs Darryl with a crowbar, apparently killing him. Chino decides to take Chris to "Big M" (Mexico) to keep her from telling the law. Paul opposes the idea because "this is a death gig."

Darryl recovers and hunts for the Black Souls alone, passing their wooded canyon camp. Chino's overtures to Chris make jealous JoAnn flash her knife. Chris bolts away, but is caught by Magoo, who tries to rape her until Chino attacks him. Chino contacts a Mexican pimp who will buy Chris in a ghost town near Porta Rosarita, five hundred miles south.

During a roadside break, Darryl meets Smiley France, the legendary ex–vice prez of the San Berdoo Stompers. He saw the Souls with Chris late yesterday afternoon. They may be going to a big love-in at Dome. Smiley tells Darryl, "The Stompers are losers. I got tired of being a loser." Darryl recalls a certain someone who echoed that opinion ... "not too long ago."

All the Souls attend the love-in except Paul, left to guard Chris. Just-married Pony and Doreen, friends of Darryl and Chris, are there. Boozy Mouth tells Pony what the Souls have done, mentioning their destination. Shocked Pony hits Mouth before police try to break up the party. Chris plays on Paul's sympathy to get him to untie her. Paul yields to her wish and diversionary seduction until Magoo appears—ready to finish with Chris where he left off. Paul brawls with Magoo until Chino runs into camp shouting about the cops.

After the party, Darryl and Smiley join Pony and Doreen, who tell them about the ghost town. The Souls reach it and wait for Chris' buyer.

Chris is roused threateningly from her sleep by Magoo, who leads her away with a knife at her throat. Paul spots them. Armed with a chain, he challenges Magoo on his bike and knocks Magoo off of his. As Paul bears down, Magoo tosses a rock in the way of his front wheel and Paul is thrown to the ground. Wedged under his bike, Paul is murdercycled by gleeful Magoo. "Magoo!" shouts angry Chino. Magoo fearfully cries, "Chino!" before Chino pumps him full of lead.

Sprinting to a rise, Chris feels her spirits lift when she sees Darryl and his companions. Chino shakes off his grief for Paul to ride straight toward Darryl. Knocking each other down, they throw fists. JoAnn hurls her knife—hitting Chino in the back of the neck by mistake. Tearful JoAnn collapses on Chino's body as Darryl and Chris embrace.

Like a serial that third male lead Jock Mahoney had done, *The Glory Stompers* was set entirely outdoors. In excluding citizens almost completely, *Glory Stompers* created a parallel universe inhabited by "decent" and indecent outlaws. The plot was perfectly designed for economy, simplicity and directness: get some bad guys to beat up a good guy and grab his girl, then pad the pre-showdown time with scenic riding, acts of jeopardy to the girl and lots of party animalism. Here and there, insert words to the effect that running with a wolfpack leads to nowhere.

Darryl was a determined quest-seeker on a mission. Smiley was *Stompers'* equivalent of a venerable old trail scout helping the young seeker. The odyssey was Darryl's growing up process. Still outlaws, Pony and Doreen in their matrimonial state were halfway where Darryl and Chris would be once they quit the Stompers and got hitched. Smiley, who matured at a late age, was a piston-powered figure of providence who would probably do a quiet fade after fade-out.

Dennis Hopper was easy to come by when *The Glory Stompers* was being cast. He had just played Max in *The Trip* and with Peter Fonda, they shot the movie's hallucinatory desert scenes. Ex-Tarzan Jock Mahoney had been replaced by Mike Henry and lost the *Tarzan* TV series role to Ron Ely. Mahoney partook in *The Glory Stompers* when Gary Crosby offered him a piece of the profits. Money ran out in mid-filming and the deal was killed. When Anthony Lanza became indisposed, Dennis Hopper directed the rest of *Stompers*.

With the drug-heightened volatility that earned him the nickname "Grass," Hopper made his Chino anything but the harmless Lee Marvin version. Darryl was Joel McCrea's son Jody, Bone/Deadhead of the A.I.P. Beach movies. Chris Noel, who bikinied her way through some youth musicals, was a radio star for the Armed Forces.

The most memorable Stomper was Mahoney's Smiley; Bob Tessier kept the tension high as Magoo when Chino wasn't around. Casey Kasem and Lindsay Crosby were a pair of tag-team comics, Kasem the funnier one.

Done for just over one hundred thousand dollars, *The Glory Stompers* made over six million. The lettering of one promo blurb was off. The B and first S of the Black Souls were not capitalized. In small letters, the words seemed racial: "When the black souls become white slavers, all hell breaks loose!"

This was no skin off of John Lawrence's Caucasian keester. A little bit of a Biker, a bit of *The Trip*, his next film was *Free Grass* (1969), aka *Scream Free*. A hippie involved with pot pushers saw them kill two narcs and a third dealer gave him LSD. Peter Fonda, Dennis Hopper and

Jack Nicholson were to star, but backed out when they decided to do something else. Lawrence hired a pair of "Westies," Richard Beymer and Russ Tamblyn, and Natalie Wood's sister Lana. Jody McCrea, billed by his real name, Joel Dee McCrea, Lindsay Crosby and Casey Kasem were, respectively, the two narcs and one of their killers.

The other killer was played by Warren Finnerty, who also got to work in Fonda, Hopper and Nicholson's "something else." Shown only in Michigan, *Free Grass* wasn't box-office green like *The Glory Stompers* or the even more profitable "something else"—*Easy Rider*. John Lawrence called it "the dumbest thing" he ever heard!

The Hard Ride

American International 1971. Executive Producer–Director–Screenplay: Burt Topper; Producer: Charles Hanawalt; Associate Producer–Production Manager: Byron Roberts; Cinematography: Robert Sparks; Film Editor: Kenneth Crane; Music: Harley Hatcher a/k/a Paul Wibier; Assistant Director: Leo Pepin; Script Supervisor: Edward Knight; Special Cinematography: Jack Willoughby; Camera Operator: Gail Parker; Camera Assistants: Gerald McClain, John Pratt; Assistant Film Editor: George Eppich; Production Coordinator: Marshall Reed; Sound Mixer: All Overton; Sound Recorder: Richard Spelker; Lighting Gaffer: Norman McClay; Key Grip: Richard King; Property Master: Randall Berkley; Makeup: Robert Bau; Construction Supervisor: Ross Hahn; Assistant to Producer: Gloria Betrue; Production Secretary: Terri Edwards; Transportation: Cliff Bush, Paul Schuster, Bob Dinsmore, Dave Rupp; Technical Advisor: Frank Charolla; Motorcycles designed and built by Downey Custom Shop; Sound Effects: Edit International; Titles-Optical Effects: Pacific Title, Ryder Sound Services, Inc.; Music Credits: Songs in Sequence: "Swing Low Sweet Chariot" sung by Bill Medley; "Falling in Love with Baby" sung by Junction; "Be Nobody's Fool," "Let the Music Play," "Shannon's Hook Shop," "Another Kind of War" sung by Paul Wibier; "Grady's Bunch" sung by The Arrows; "Where Am I Going Today?" sung by Bob Moline; "Carry Me Home," "I Came Along to Be with You" sung by Thelma Camacho; Background Vocalists: Ginger Blaine, Ron Hicklin, Juli Tillman, Stan Farber, Maxine Willard, Gene Morfiro; Orchestrations: Emory Gordy, Dennis St. John, Spencer Oldham, Dave Allen. Movielab Color: A Burwalt Production. Running Time: 90 minutes.

Cast: Robert Fuller (Phil); Sherry Bain (Sheryl); Tony Russell (Big Red); William Bonner (Grady); Marshall Reed (Father Tom); Mikel Angel (Ralls); Albert Cole (Mooch); Biff Elliott (Mike); Phyllis Selznick (Rita); R.L. Armstrong (Jason); Robert Swan (Ted); Larry Eisley (Rice); Frank Charolla (Meyers); Herman Rudin (Little Horse); Alfonso Williams (Lenny); Ford Lile (Floyd); John Cestare (Al); Del Russell (Nico); Rachel English, John Loma, Ron Stokes, Robert Tessier, Joe Folino, Gus Peters, Tony DeCosta, Tony Haig, Doug Matheson, David Bradley.

Awed by Wyatt's superhog in *Easy Rider*, Burt Topper decided to build a whole film around the appeal of an even greater one. "Chopper" was the working title of Topper's *The Hard Ride*, about Lenny, a dead Nam vet whose legacy was "Baby"— the Rolls-Royce of movie-commissioned scooters. As the builder of a masterpiece, Lenny had created an object of jealousy. That jealousy was transferred to black Lenny's white comrade Phil Duncan, the new owner of "Baby." The matters concerning Lenny's color were an undertone. The heart of the film was his pride and joy.

Rushed to a Medivac copter, Lenny cries, "Don't leave me, babe!" "I'm right here, buddy!" Phil tells him, "I ain't leavin' ya!" Lenny dies from his wounds.

Phil escorts Lenny's flag-draped casket to the Victorville military depot. The driver of the hearse, Father Tom, owns the orphanage where Lenny grew up. En route to the mortuary, Father Tom gives Phil a sealed letter Lenny wrote asking Phil to find his ex-girl Sheryl. She may know the whereabouts of Big Red, the leader of Lenny's club. Lenny wanted them to attend his funeral. From the mortuary, Phil and Father Tom go to the garage where Phil sees his new possession, "Baby." "Instead of Lenny making it a hobby," Father Tom says of his bike fixation, "he made it a way of life."

Sheryl is a waitress at Mom's, the café owned by her late mother, now run by Mike. "Where did you get that bike?" unsettled Sheryl asks Phil, who introduces himself. Local outlaws Ralls and Mooch see "Baby," telling Phil they can take him to Big Red.

Their real leader is Grady. Phil arrives at the Grady gang's desert camp, whose only "building" is a derelict bus. Phil smells setup. Bearded—unlike real Indians—Grady ignorantly asks, "Who's Baby?" Phil walks away "to find Big Red!" Overpowered, he has the pink slip to "Baby" taken so Grady can have the bike. Phil grabs Grady's knife, forcing Grady to ride him to safety. "I'll cut your balls off!" Grady wails at departing Phil.

Cleaning up at Mom's, Phil tells Mike, "Looks like Lenny's bike is a desirable commodity around here." Sheryl lets Phil spend the night at her place.

Sheryl joins Phil on his quest for Big Red. In a cave they had visited, Sheryl momentarily sees Phil as Lenny. She softens, but still carries a chip on her shoulder. Phil befriended Lenny when he showed no qualms about drinking from a black man's canteen. "You trying to make a point?" asks Sheryl. "I don't like being accused of something I'm not guilty of," Phil answers.

When "Baby" breaks down, Phil and Sheryl have a brief romantic interlude. Some punks drawn to "Baby" want grass. Sheryl gives them her own. Roughing up Phil, the boys want her, but a trucker scares them away. Sheryl had tampered with "Baby" to expedite her seduction.

At a cycle race, Phil and Sheryl meet two of Big Red's pals, who take them to the camp of Big Red's father, Little Horse. Big Red is at a brothel. No real friend of Lenny's, he only wanted "Baby" and Sheryl. Phil bribes Big Red with the pink slip to ensure his presence at the funeral service.

The moment they are reunited, Big Red aggressively leads Sheryl away. "Sometimes he makes me curse the day he was born," Little Horse tells Phil, who gets into a knock down, drag out fight with Big Red. Exhausted, Big Red tells tired Phil, "No broad on earth is worth all this trouble." Sheryl apologizes to Phil for causing this fight and they make serious love.

Phil and Sheryl return to Mom's, where Phil makes a phone call to take care of final arrangements. Grady's gang is back. Intimidating Mike, they kidnap Phil. "Now we play *your* game," declares Ralls, holding his knife on Phil to make Phil take him and "Baby" to Grady. Mike stops Sheryl from calling the cops, afraid the gang will burn his place … "the only thing I got." "You got nothing! Nothing!" screams Sheryl. Outside, she flags down Big Red and his group.

Once at Grady's camp, Phil is hustled into the old bus. "Baby" is hidden from the Big Red gang. Big Red says all he came for is "Baby." Phil is needed to sign the pink slip. When he is led out of the bus, Big Red strikes Grady, starting a rumble. Mooch gets a shotgun from the bus, firing point-blank at somebody.

A military gun salute is held over two flag-draped coffins—Lenny's and one for Phil. Sheryl, Big Red, his club and Mike are present as Father Tom reads the eu-

Sherry Bain and Robert Fuller pose with "Baby."

logy. The battlefield voices of Phil and Lenny echo: "Don't leave me, babe!" "Hang on, buddy! I ain't leavin ya!"

Having used up the earlier wars he depicted, Burt Topper settled on the "Coming Home" format of Vietnam drama, shaping a story similar to the 1969 pilot film of *Then Came Bronson*. Both Phil and ex–San Francsico reporter Jim Bronson rode bikes bequeathed to them by friends who met untimely deaths. In the bargain, each man acquired a difficult, neurotic saddlemate who became a love interest. Since Phil's obligation to honor the memory of a dead man entailed dangerous opposition, he found himself in the shoes of crippled World War II vet John J. McCready of *Bad Day at Black Rock* (1954).

Racially, *The Hard Ride* was light years away from the lukewarm jungle fever of *Guess Who's Coming to Dinner?* (1967), treating the objectively remembered affair between Sheryl and Lenny as no big sexual thing. On the frontline, Lenny had suffered overt prejudice ... never knowing that "Baby" and Sheryl were all that allowed him into Big Red's circle. Himself an outsider in the bike world, Phil became the third beau of a woman who slept with men of different races, loving two war buddies who rode the same fantastic machine. Not many women attend burials for *two* boyfriends at the same time.

If Topper's *Devil's Angels* had put the depravity of *The Wild Angels* through a strainer, then *The Hard Ride* was an *Easy Rider* about fulsome, in some cases expanding, not imploded personalities. Keeping abreast of "trip" narrative styles, the hitherto linear-minded Topper abstracted all appearances of the living Lenny—even including a flash shot of *Father Tom* riding "Baby"! Topper embarrassed himself, however, when he staged the Phil–Big Red

Phil (Robert Fuller) and Sheryl (Sherry Bain) on the road.

fight in hokey slo-mo, punctuating the punches with pretentious war sounds. With Phil's turn to be an *Easy Rider*–type victim, Topper cut away from the discharge of Mooch's gun so his death could be clarified by the irony of a second casket next to Lenny's.

The Hard Ride made for a more topographically lush travelogue than *Easy Rider*, which traveled farther, but visited mostly armpit surroundings. *Hard Ride* showed the Colorado River, Yosemite National Park and the seventeen-mile drive of the Carmel Peninsula. Both films took in cemeteries and bordellos (a cliché dyke came with Shannon's).

"Baby" was created by technical advisor and bit player Frank Charolla at Downey Custom Cycle Shop in Downey, California—a place mentioned on-screen by a cop interested in making a hog. Downey is also the home of John Garwood.

Robert Fuller fit the identity of Phil by not being a regular exploitation star. A William Smith or Jeremy Slate would have been too overly at home on "Baby," the passport to a series of new experiences for Phil. Being a stranger to Bikers helped strengthen Fuller's believability. Daughter of the owners of the Sportsman's Lodge, Sherry Bain was discovered working as a clerk at the Farmer's Market by repertoire group head John Cestare, who had a small role.

Tony Russell, the wacko G.I. Keefer in Topper's *War Is Hell* (1963), the film playing at the Dallas theater when Lee Harvey Oswald was arrested there, had been a leading man in Italian action films. For the part of Big Red, he was made up to look like the mod Elvis ... even down to the same heavy-metal-framed sunglasses.

"Baby" appeared at various cycle shows to help promote *The Hard Ride*. Jack Webb saw the film and liked Bob Fuller so much that he cast him as Dr. Kelly Brackett on *Emergency*.

The Hellcats

Crown International 1968. Producer: Anthony Cardoza; Co-Producer: Herman Tomlin; Director: Robert F. Slatzer; Screenplay: Tony Houston a/k/a Enrique Touceda III; Story: James Gordon White, John Zila, Jr.; Cinematography: Gil Hubbs; Film Editor: Bud Hoffman; Music Supervisor: Jerry Roberts; Assistant Director: Tony Houston; Script Supervisor: Mary T. Laub; Sound Mixer: Dave Caudle; Art Director: Karen Teichman; Wardrobe: Misty Maring; Cameraman: Wilson S. Hong; Assistant Cameraman: Paul Prince; Motorcycles: Ford Puckett, San Pedro, California; Automobiles: Ford Motor Company; Dubbing-Mixing: Ryder Sound Service; Lear Jet: Pacific Lear Jet; Songs: "I Can't Take a Chance," "Hellcats," "Mass Confusion": Produced by Richard Podlor, Sung by Davy Jones and the Dolphins; "I'm Up," "Marionettes": Produced by Chance Halladay, Sung by Somebody's Children. Pathécolor; A Gemeni-American Production. Running Time: 90 minutes.

Cast: Ross Hagen (Monte); Dee Duffy (Linda); Sharyn Kinzie (Sheila); Bryan "Sonny" West (Snake); Bob Slatzer (Adrian); Eric Lidberg (Hiney); Shannon Summers (Rita); Bro Beck (David Chapman); Diane Ryder (Candy Cave); Nick Raymond (Pepper); Dick Merrifield (Dean); Hildegarde Wendt (Hildy); Tony Cardoza (Artist); Elena Engstrom (Model); Irene Martin (Dee); Frederic Downs (Moonfire); Noble "Kid" Chissell (Sheriff); Robert Strong (Deputy); Ed Sarquist (Zombie); Gus Tikonis (Scorpio); Lydia Goya (Betty); Tom Hanson (Moongoose); Ray Cantrell (Scab); Joe Coffey (Pete); Eric Tomlin (Policeman); Warren Hammack (Attorney); Jack Denton (First Detective); Walt Swanner, Bill Reese (Senators).

All three of the first Girl Biker movies were made and released at the same time. Showing a cycle sorority of purely Amazon bent, *She-Devils on Wheels* was the most authentic. The entire gang of *The Mini-Skirt Mob* was a combination of goons and dolls—only one Skirt, the leader, a real bitch. The sexes co-existed best among *The Hellcats*, whose dress and more natural toughness made them similar to the Man-Eaters of *She-Devils*.

Mini-Skirt Mob author James Gordon White thought up the story of *The Hellcats* with John Zila, Jr. Producer Anthony Cardoza, the producer of and an actor in three pictures *Motor Psycho* player Coleman Francis directed, let Tony Houston write the script, rather than White or helmer Robert F. Slatzer. The most experienced scribe of the three, Slatzer had done everything from radio drama and a syndicated column for the *New York Journal American* to western novels and screenplays, many of them westerns. Author of *The Marilyn Monroe Story* and her personal press agent Slatzer has kept his name alive in tabloid news by alleging he was Monroe's secret fourth husband.

About to fink on them, Hellcats leader Big Daddy is killed. Clandestine watchers of his gang funeral are two separate groups of men. In one are drug kingpin Mr. Adrian and his minions Dean and Pepper. The other witnesses are narcs, including David Chapman. Hellcat Snake confidently knows who the next prez will be. "Me, baby, me!"

Dave and his fiancée, Linda Martin, enjoy some rural romance—until stalking, telescopic rifle–armed Pepper assassinates Dave.

An Army sergeant on special leave,

A pushover Hellcat feels the full Monte (Ross Hagen).

Dave's brother Monte meets Linda. Dave left a confidential address book that mentions the Hellcats. Inspired to infiltrate the gang with Linda, Monte teaches her bike riding and judo.

Posing as outlaws from "up north," Monte and Linda mingle with the Hellcats at seedy Moonfire's rundown inn. Pepper shows up to give female leader Sheila a map of the next dope route, noticing Monte.

On a fun run, the Hellcats molest an artist and his model. Rival gang leader Zombie challenges Snake to a race. When they are about to fight, Monte intervenes. For an endurance test, he and Snake grip the rear axel of a trike while their feet are tied to the back of another. Snake is dragged away by the active trike, but Monte holds on for a count of fifteen seconds.

Linda is invited to join Sheila and Betty on the next Mexican drug pickup. Depraved contacts Pete and Scorpio keep pitiful junkie Dee a sex slave in their shack. The dope is stashed inside the headlights of the girls' bikes. Back in the U.S., the police give chase and Betty dies in an accident.

Angry Adrian demands the recovery of Betty's dope. Sneaking into the police impound lot to get it, Moongoose is busted. Linda follows Sheila to Adrian's office while Monte trails her.

Adrian enters, capturing Monte and Linda. Sheila is expendable too. Adrian decides to flee the country, assigning Pepper to kill his dumb mistress, Hilde.

Monte and Sheila are tied up in a tool shed while Linda is kept bound in Adrian's office. Monte and Sheila free themselves, but Adrian gets the draw on Monte. He and Linda are taken to the waterfront, where Adrian keeps his yacht. Escaping, Sheila calls the Hellcats. Exposed as an Adrian spy, Moonfire is eliminated by the gang, who head for the docks.

Meanwhile, Monte and Linda are dumped into a garbage barge. Engine trouble delays the yacht's launch until Pepper joins Adrian. The Hellcats storm the dock for a savage melee. Adrian shoots Snake and is killed. Monte and Linda are freed from the barge. Hands still tied, Monte jumps Pepper. Dean is also apprehended. Snake dies from his bullet wound.

For helping the law, the Hellcats get leniency. Monte's service discharge is due. Linda sits in her Corvette, about to leave, when she looks at his bike and asks, "What are you going to do with it?" "Keep it," Monte replies. "I like it."

The idea of the Hellcats working as mob drug runners was not that far out. A credible match were freelance undercover agents Monte and Linda. The girl who might have become his sister-in-law, she was no abused innocent but assertive thanks to Monte's survival instructions. Once we got to know the Hellcats, they didn't seem as bad as the Adrian organization. Finished with the military and done with the business at hand, Monte was ready for some R&R and the bike that had previously been a tool of his mission would help him achieve it.

Unfortunately, *The Hellcats* wasn't so much badly written as it was poorly produced and timid in its sensationalism. The erotic deficiencies would be rectified when Bob Slatzer went to work on the paperback adaptation, but the movie was ineptly sound-recorded, the set design amateurish, the wardrobe shoddy and the bubble gum rock a flaccid sugarless flavor. The unimaginative cinematography wouldn't even depict an actual race between Snake and Zombie ... just the spectators looking at something *like* a race past the camera.

With *The Hellcats*, *The Mini-Skirt Mob* and *Angels' Wild Women*, Ross Hagen became the actor most often seen in Girl Biker films. Linda was Matt Helm Slaygirl Dee Duffy. Snake was Bryan "Sonny" West, one of Elvis Presley's Memphis Mafia gofers. An airline hostess vacationing in L.A., Sharyn Kinzie was spotted by Tony Cardoza riding a bike down Hollywood Boulevard. Cast as Sheila, she was the cycle coach for the other actresses. When the actor who was to play Adrian got sick the night before filming, Bob Slatzer took over to passable effect.

The Hellcats take on Zombie (Ed Sarquist).

Nudie star Marsha Jordan never made it into the final cut. One topless and one nude photo of her in a *Hellcats* article in *Adam* were just publicity shots.

If *The Hellcats* revved weakly as cinema, its open-throttle promotion left lasting skidmarks on the consciousness. The Crown International ad art made eye-patch-wearing blonde Rita the central figure, her fierce facsimile waving a chain.

Adam Publishing's paperback company Holloway House printed the novel. In its prurient pages, Bob Slatzer's uncensored imagination—saying a lot about his dark fantasies—pigged out. Dave Chapman's shooting interrupted coitus with Linda. The art model was viciously gang-banged. Dee's degradation was much more explicit. Mocked by an intelligent, bitchy Hilde for being impotent, Adrian offed her himself and was finally able to gain an erection. He shaved Hilde's blonde pubic hair, flushed it down the toilet and balled her still-warm corpse. To destroy evidence of his crimes, Adrian torched his house, letting pubeless, necrophiled Hilde burn on her bed as if it was a Viking funeral pyre.

Arthur Miller never wrote prose quite like that.

Hell's Angels on Wheels

U.S. Films 1967. Producer: Joe Solomon; Director: Richard Rush; Screenplay: R. Wright Campbell; Cinematography: Leslie a/k/a Laszlo Kovacs; Film Editor: William Martin; Music: Stu Phillips; Production Manager: Paul Lewis; Post-Production Supervisor: Igo Kantor; Sound Effects Editor: John Post; First Assistant Director: Willard Kirkham; Second Assistant Director: Bruce Satterlee; Script Supervisor: Joyce King; Assistant Cameraman: Frank Ruttencutter; Still Man: Peter Sorel; Sound Mixer: Leroy Robbins; Boom Man: Sam Kopetzky; Gaffers: Don Carstensen, James Field; Key Grip: Bill Pecchi; Set Decorator: Wally Moon; Makeup: Louis Lane; Wardrobe: Roy Vanderleelie; Grips: Foster Denker, John Oliver; Stunt Coordinator: Gary Kent; Technical Advisors: Sonny Barger, Tommy Thomas; Production Secretary: Sheila Scott; Song: "Study in Motion No. 1" by Chuck Sedecca, Stu Phillips; Sung by The Poor. Eastmancolor; A Fanfare Production. Running Time: 95 minutes.

Cast: Adam Roarke (Buddy); Jack Nicholson (Poet); Sabrina Scharf (Shill); Jana Taylor (Abigail); Richard Anders (Bull); John Garwood (Jock); I.J. Jefferson a/k/a Mimi Machu (Pearl); James Oliver (Gypsy); Jack Starrett (Bingham); Bruno VeSota (Minister); Robert Kelljan (Artist); Kathryn Harrow (Lori); Bud a/k/a John Bud Cardos (Redneck); Tex Hall (Angel); the Hell's Angels of Oakland, San Francisco, Daly City, Richmond and the Nomads of Sacramento, California, and Sonny Barger, President of Hell's Angels.

A few of A.I.P.'s distributors created their own exploitation companies. One was San Francisco native Joe Solomon. The son of an immigrant Romanian printer, young Joe ushered at the St. Francis theater and helped his father in the creation and maintenance of theater apparatus. Joe was involved in such things as twenty-four sheet billboards, extra-large type, and the rayon marquee-bottom signs used to advertise air conditioning. Following nightclub work in Los Angeles during World War II, Solomon returned to San Francisco and devised the luminous black light poster. In Detroit, he ran the underfinanced Majestic Poster Company, selling it to National Screen Service.

Solomon worked the Radshow circuit, handling the notorious censorship-challenging childbirth opus *Mom and Dad* (1944) and the filmed-in-Oklahoma passion play *Prince of Peace* (1949). Solomon then became the Philadelphia distributor of A.I.P. As a sideline, he started a private releasing outfit, Associated Film Distributors. Solomon issued the nudist classic *Nature's Paradise* (1955) and imported prestigious foreign fare—coming up lucky with *La Dolce Vita* (1960) while bombing out with other movies.

Going back to L.A. permanently, Solomon started Fanfare Films. Its most provocative feature prior to *Hell's Angels on Wheels* was the Ted V. Mikels race melodrama *The Black Klansman* (1966), aka *I Crossed the Color Line*, with Solomon playing a nightclub owner. Its Negro bar set would turn up in *Hell's Angels*.

To surpass *The Wild Angels*, Solomon decided to make a Biker with the Oakland Hell's Angels, run by Ralph "Sonny" Barger (Ralph to his friends), the Maximum Leader of the club since 1959. Angels in San Francisco, Daly City and Richmond were also recruited, as were the Nomads, a Sacramento club. Robert Wright Campbell, co-author of the Oscar-nominated screenplay *Man of a Thousand Faces* (1957), wrote the script of *Hell's Angels on Wheels*, a production that joined a great cinematographer, Laszlo Kovacs, with a promising director, Richard Rush.

Graduates of the Academy of Theater and Film in Budapest, Kovacs and his friend Vilmos Zsigmond secretly photographed the 1956 Hungarian Revolution. Zsigmond's father begged him to go to America and Kovacs joined him. On the run with the smuggled film, they hid it from machine-gun armed border guards in a cornstalk. Captured, Kovacs and Zsigmond were taken to a camp but sacrificed valuables to bribe their way out. After an exhaustive search of the cornfield, they recovered the film. To escape the returning patrol, Kovacs and Zsigmond fled five miles nonstop to the border. They reached America safely, but the film was too old for the local media to be interested.

In Hollywood, Kovacs and Zsigmond survived as lab technicians and still photographers. His name adopted by the Jean-Paul Belmondo character in *Breathless* (1959), Kovacs even wanted to become an actor. While he and Zsigmond were struggling, Richard Rush wrote the first film he directed, *Too Soon to Love* (1960) with another Laszlo—Laszlo Gorog—and cast Jack Nicholson to play Buddy, the name given to a character in *Hell's Angels*.

Rush and Gorog wrote Rush's next film, *Of Love and Desire* (1963). Rush made several quickies in Spain, did *Thunder Alley* (1967) for A.I.P. and shot the 1968-released *A Man Called Dagger*, aka *Why Spy?* with Kovacs, then Leslie Kovacs, in their earliest collaboration.

The Wild Angels was over a year old, but *Hell's Angels on Wheels* found a promotional hook in the chronicle of Gonzo journalist Hunter S. Thompson's association with the Angels: *Hell's Angels: A Strange and Terrible Saga*. Ask people like Roger Corman, Peter Bogdanovich, Bruce Dern and Hunter Thompson—who was viciously stomped by five berserk, unprovoked Angels until a friendly sixth saved him—and they will describe vividly how Angels communicate harsh criticism. However, with *Hell's Angels on Wheels*, they partook in a picture that showed all to greater objectivity ... not depicting the Angels as ghoulish, incompetent, stumblebums the way *The Wild Angels* did.

Somewhere in San Francisco, a chopper sits idle until the owner's right boot kicks the engine to life. Twisting the throttle furiously, he roars away. On the back of his jacket are the familiar colors of the Hell's Angels.

An undefined urgency spreads contagiously as various Angels congregate. Through wisps of cooking steam at Fisherman's Wharf can be glimpsed Buddy, an Angel leader. He, his old lady Shill, Bull, Jock and others of their group join Sonny Barger's at a crossroads where Buddy and

Sonny share a customary greeting kiss. Over one hundred seventy-five strong, the Angels cross the San Francisco Bay Bridge.

In a small city, Buddy's pack disrupts traffic and pedestrian movement. They pull into a gas station where an attendant named Poet is servicing a rude, impatient customer. While Poet checks his oil, the man honks loudly, causing Poet to bump his head against the raised car hood. Waving a dipstick, Poet growls, "You're one quart down!" The station manager scolds Poet, who gets violent. Poet impresses Buddy, who says, "You tell 'em, man" as fired Poet splits on his stock Harley.

That evening, the Angels carouse in a parking lot. Poet arrives. Bull broadsides into his bike, breaking the headlight. "Where did you get that piece of garbage truck?" mockingly asks Bull, who kicks the bike over. Poet is about to trash pugnacious Bull until Buddy restrains them.

Poet tags along as the Angels enter a bar to settle a score with some rival bikers. Buddy instructs Poet to guard the front door. A failed peace negotiation with the rivals disintegrates into violence. One fleeing opponent is ambushed by Poet to Shill's sadistic cheers. Inexplicably, she nurses the hurt individual. Shill kisses Poet's cut lip. "It's not what it looks like," Shill tells Buddy, who now has go-go dancer Pearl. Shill is made to ride with Poet.

The Angels visit an amusement park, where Poet is given a new headlamp and dismissed like a kid. Poet bumps into four sailors who beat him up until a disturbed witness protests. Poet describes the sailors' uniform patches to Buddy, who sends Poet and Shill to Shill's pad while he and his fellow Angels canvas the park for the sailors.

At the apartment she shares with casual Lori, Shill sexually toys with smiling but uneasy Poet. "You're square aren't you? Nice middle-class morals."

Stepping off a ride, the sailors confront the Angels. Their fearless leader pulls a knife on Buddy, who inflicts a mortal chain blow. The sailor is dead. The Angels split.

For an alibi, the Angels throw a party at Shill's, where Poet is alarmed to hear what happened. Body-painted Shill lures Poet into her bedroom to spite Buddy, proclaiming, "I'm me and I'm not ashamed of anything I do." Sgt. Bingham, investigating the sailor's death, shows up and openly accuses Buddy. Lovers Gypsy and Abigail are so publicly affectionate that Buddy decides they should get married in Nevada this weekend.

The Nevada run is planned at a cycle repair shop where Buddy sponsors Poet's membership. Intruding upon the moment, Poet is issued probationary colors and ceremoniously bathed in jarred grease poured on his head. Poet packs Shill while Buddy takes Pearl.

The wedding for Gypsy and Abigail is held in front of a rural church. The bikes are lined up in procession. Jock gives the bride away. "It's a joke," chokes troubled Shill. "So funny you could cry," concurs Poet.

Gypsy and Abigail take a honeymoon suite at a motel near a bar whose redneck customers forbid Angel patronage and start a battle royal in the motel courtyard. Gypsy perturbs Abigail by parking his chopper next to their bed to prevent theft. Abigail emerges from the bathroom in a sexy black nightie. "If I leave you outside," feels aroused Gypsy, "somebody's gonna steal you!" Gypsy notices the fight, anxious to help his pals. "They're doing fine," dispassionately assures Abigail. In bed, the couple tenderly smooch as the bedlam continues. Several armed thugs trap Buddy in the deep end of an empty swimming pool. Poet jumps to his defense before police appear.

In a park, the Angels frolic. Dozing Poet is awakened by Shill's hair brushing

Motel mayhem: Jock (John Garwood) is ready to dive in.

against his face. What happened between them last night, she states, was insignificant. "Love 'em and leave 'em. Is that why you're hooked with the Angels?" Shill asks. Why does she stay, Poet wonders. "Maybe I'm a spy for the cops," Shill jokes. "Or maybe you're a broad who likes to get pushed around," Poet speculates. "You're learning," praises Shill, who moodily admits, "We're all running scared ... no responsibility." "I might take the responsibility for you," declares Poet.

"If everybody dressed like I did," Buddy tells Pearl, "or looked like I did, I'd clean up." "Why?" she asks. "Because," Buddy answers, "I like walking down the street and having people pointing to me and saying 'there goes the leader'." The sexism of the Angels turns Pearl off. Buddy gives her to Jock, reclaiming Shill from Poet. "You're a rat! A beautiful rat!" cries Shill. "The king rat, baby!" declares Buddy as the gang rides away.

Along an empty stretch of road, the Angels pass a pokey old man, yelling insults. Stoned Jock weaves his bike, scaring Pearl, and edges the old man's car toward a dangerous embankment. It tumbles down. Looking back, Pearl tells Jock—who doesn't care.

On their side of the California-Nevada border, the Angels encounter a Highway Patrol roadblock where Bingham, out of his jurisdiction, is waiting for them. The old man was killed. On the basis of an eyewitness report, Bingham charges Buddy, but Poet says Buddy always rides up front. "I don't want to owe him anything for the swabbies," Poet tells Shill in an aside. When Bingham proposes a group bust, Pearl protests her innocence, fingering violent Jock. Jock refuses leniency if he will fink on Buddy for the killing of the sailor and is arrested. Pearl accompanies the police.

Trailing the cops at a safe distance,

Poet (Jack Nicholson) and Buddy (Adam Roarke) finally have it out.

the Angels put into action a rescue plan. They free Jock, leaving the cops rolling in the dust.

In the ruins of an old mansion, the Angels party. Poet joins forlorn Shill, curled up in a second story corner. "I am the greatest putdown artist of all time!" she pathetically laughs, "I put down all of them! I am a walking talking cliché!" She is pregnant with Buddy's child. Poet makes an earnest matrimonial offer. "You'd marry me anyway?" touched Shill asks. "In a minute," Poet swears.

Buddy surprises Poet, insisting, "That's my property!" He is completely callous to Shill's condition. "What's the matter with you?" asks outraged Poet. "Don't you care about anything?" "I care about my own," Buddy self-righteously replies. "You're a fake!" vilifies Poet. "A goddamn fake!" "Butt out!" shrieks Buddy. "I'll tell you what to think and when to think it!" "Don't tell me anything, man!" retorts Poet. "I'm not a member of your private army!"

Coming to blows, Buddy and Poet plunge to the first floor. Still drawn to him, Shill throws Buddy a tire iron. Piqued Poet rips off his colors and walks away from Buddy, who snatches the nearest bike, angrily revving it up. Trying to run Poet down, Buddy fails to see a large plate glass window he crashes through. When startled Poet shoves Buddy off-balance, the bike overturns and explodes. Buddy dies in the flames. "Buddy!" screams horrified Shill—who turns to numb Poet.

Like its predecessors, *Hell's Angels on Wheels* worked up to a tragic finish, but only for three Angels struggling in conflict indigenous to their personalities. Poet was a square peg too hip for convention and too decent to lose his humanity in a scene that totally inures all whom it completely absorbs. A face-impression pal, Buddy was only a "buddy" to tune dancers ("I care about everybody—as long as they do what I tell them"). Shill was a basically sweet, rational girl who hobnobbed with the Angels for kicks until she got in too deep.

Bob Campbell probably saw *The Wild Angels* and wanted to improve certain things it did wrong or to excess. *Hell's Angels on Wheels* didn't glorify Citizenland, nor was it a surreal vacuum. The pissy gas station customer was just a suburban asshole, not an ideology crank like *The Wild Angels'* super-patriot hardhat. The Tavern gang fight wasn't a Day of Disaster like that Mecca rumble ... just a night-in-the-life brawl. The killing of the sailor put Buddy in a legal fix the way that the hospital rape in *Wild Angels* made Heavenly Blues a fugitive. Guilty of justifiable homicide, Buddy's real offense was being an Angel. The occasion a wedding and not a funeral, the church scene in *Hell's Angels* blasphemed only in the coarse frivolity of how the nuptials were arranged.

Jock's highway manslaughter, like *The Wild Angels'* hospital rape, was another act by a club member making the leader appear guilty in the eyes of the law, but Poet's stand-up act helped Buddy there. Heavenly Blues was the Wild Angel jolted into sobriety. Poet and Shill were the sobered rebels in *Hell's Angels on Wheels*. His dishonestly laid bare, Buddy went over the high side in not so glorious a blaze.

Cinematically, the film was a flowing stream of fluid continuity, perfecting the late-early sixties look of the Rush-Kovacs movies with its agile, probing, thoughtfully lingering examinations of hard conciseness and sensual softness. The most lyrically photographed cycle movement had a kind of floating, dreamy élan soon to be much imitated. For the final shot, Poet and Shill stood on opposite sides of the screen and their frozen, separated forms became silhouettes against a dramatic fade of the background to white.

Composer of many Columbia features, Stu Phillips was the TV music arranger for the Monkees. Becoming Fanfare's music maestro, he complemented the visuals in *Hell's Angels on Wheels* with music that could gently seduce or savagely overpower.

Feeling he was too old, John Ashley turned down the role of Poet. Jack Nicholson, only three years younger than Ashley, was not yet the most famous person from Neptune, New Jersey. Nicholson leaned on his standard mannerisms—his best-remembered performance for 1967 that of the croaky gunman in *The St. Valentine's Massacre* who rubbed garlic on his bullets.

A product of Bay Ridge in Brooklyn, Adam Roarke was born Richard Jordan Gerler. The reformed delinquent who became a 1954 Golden Gloves semi-finalist trained for drama under Brian Hutton and made his acting debut as a juvenile tough in *Thirteen West Street* (1962). At nineteen, he signed a contract at Universal. Roarke got his part in *Ensign Pulver* (1964) after being spotted by Joshua Logan. Concurrent with the release of *Hell's Angels* was the other '67 Roarke film, Howard Hawks' *El Dorado* (Roarke played Hawks in the 1978 *Hughes and Harlow: Angels in Hell*). Roarke was a blunt departure from moody Blues and romantic Cody of *Devil's Angels*, his Buddy a charismatic user with a mean bite when tongue silk didn't work.

Married in Ohio at age fifteen, Sabrina Scharf had worn New York bunny ears and been a Columbia starlet, stylishly eclipsing the inferior old lady performances of Nancy Sinatra in *The Wild Angels* and Beverly Adams of *Devil's Angels*. Starlet-model Mimi Machu, billed as I.J. Jefferson, was Jack Nicholson's girl at the time. With him at the Cannes showing of *Easy Rider*, Machu became the mother of actor Sean Machu, who for years was led to believe that his father was Sonny Bono.

Jack Starrett, who played Coach Jennings in *The Young Sinner*, was one of several people rescued from obscurity by Joe Solomon. Both Texans, he and his former wife, Valerie, met when they were drama students. Starrett was parking cars on Sunset Strip when Solomon discovered the right actor to play Bingham. Dark, lean, fish-eyed, mustached, speaking in a laconic drawl, the easily unforgettable Starrett was as recurrent an authority figure in Bikers as Russ Bender had been in the A.I.P. Delinquency films.

John Garwood and Richard Anders were as notable supports in *Hell's Angels* as Buck Taylor and Marc Cavell had been in *The Wild Angels* and would make their own repeat appearances in *The Savage Seven*.

An Our Gang alumnus, John Bud Cardos was experienced in many production capacities. He played the rival biker thrown across a bar mirror, turning up as the leader of the rednecks and the Buddy stand-in on Buddy's death bike. Gary Kent was a journalism major at the University of Washington who covered the exploits of the Blue Angels flying team while in the Navy. A graduate of Texas theater, Kent was a clean-shaven rival biker and a bearded redneck.

Eddie Donno, the rival club prez, Chuck Bail, the slain sailor, and Tex Hall, an Angel with an unusual way of meeting girls (sliding into a moving car through an open rear window) were stuntmen too. So was Hal Needham, who had worked with Bert Reynolds since being Reynolds' designated double on *Riverboat*. Gary Littlejohn would get into the game too.

The man who came to Poet's aide when the sailors were attacking him was a Joe named Solomon.

Past and future directors in the cast of *Hell's Angels on Wheels* were Burno VeSota, Jack Nicholson, Adam Roarke, John Cardos, Gary Kent, Jack Starrett, Chuck Bail, Bob Kelljan, John Garwood and Needham ... Needham the greatest commercial success.

Adam Roarke and John Garwood made junket appearances on behalf of *Hell's Angels* with Sonny Barger, its most enthusiastic supporter (he saw it ten times) and eleven other Angels. Despite his strong leadership, Barger was known for unpredictable, often violent mood swings. One of these hurt the promo tour at a hotel, where he attacked a young radio station intern. In Canada, Adam Roarke received above-the-title marquee billing.

Sonny Barger's first wife, Elsie, who rode with him in the credits sequence of *Hell's Angels on Wheels*, didn't get to see many more movies because she died from what Barger termed a legal abortion (about five years before *Roe vs. Wade*). Buddy might have imposed on Shill the back alley kind if he hadn't been minutes away from the glass-and-gas conversion of his ass into non-cannabis grass.

Hell's Angels '69

American International 1969. Executive Producer: Pat Rooney; Producer: Tom Stern; Director: Lee Madden; Screenplay: Don Tait; Story: Tom Stern, Jeremy Slate; Cinematography: Paul Lohman; Film Editor: Gene Ruggiero; Music: Tony Bruno; Arranger-Conductor: Tom D'Andrea; Sound Mixer: George Alch; Production Supervisor: Paul McKinney; Stills: Fran Noden; Makeup: Sonny Martin, Richard Scarso; Hair Stylist: Sonny Martin;

Doctor: Dr. Martin Carroll; Transportation: Frank McMichael; Stunt Gaffer: Bob Harris; Assistant Director: Cliff Coleman; Production Coordinators: Dudley Roseborough, Alvin Shapiro; Assistant to Producer: Alberta Kennedy; Assistant Cameraman: Otto Nemez, Mike Chevalier; Production Secretary: Judi Brown; Sound: Ryder Sound Services; Music-Effects: Edit-Rite International Ltd.; Songs: "Hang On Tight" by Tony Bruno, Sung by Tony Bruno; "Lazy" by Sonny Valdez, Lyrics, Frank Avianca; "Say Girl" sung by Wendy Cole; "What's His Is His" by Sonny Valdez; "Al and Alice," The Stream of Consciousness, Music, Lyrics, Frank Avianca, Sam Weatherly; Themes: "Goofin," "Bass Lake Run," "Chase of Death" by Tony Bruno; Titles-Color: CFI; a Tracom Production. Running Time: 97 minutes.

Cast: Tom Stern (Chuck); Jeremy Slate (Wes); Conny Van Dyke (Betsy); Steve Sandor (Apache); Sonny Barger, Terry the Tramp, Skip, Tiny, Magoo (Themselves), the Oakland Hell's Angels; G.D. Spradlin (Detective); Bobby Hall (Motorcycle Dealer); Bob Harris, Ray Renard, Ric Henry, Michael Michaelian, Danielle Corn. Stuntmen: Bud Ekins, Jerry Randall, Joe Hooker, Ed Muler. The Hell's Angels of San Francisco, Daly City, Nomads, Berdoo, Diego, Richmond.

Another hog-riding buddy pair following Wyatt and Billy were silver spoon siblings Chuck and Wes of *Hell's Angels '69*. Tom Stern had seen every Biker and felt that most were wanting, knowing also all of them made money. Like Peter Fonda, he conceived and produced a Biker made by two genre actors. Stern's co-star was fellow story author Jeremy Slate. Fanfare had beaten everyone to using the Oakland Angels first with *Hell's Angels on Wheels* and for his movie, Stern hoped to get more out of them by making the Angels active dramatic participants.

Even the Angels acknowledged how vulnerable they were to false accusations and Stern exploited that handicap by making the Angels the dupes of thrill heisters Chuck and Wes. Citizens of an unnamed East Coast metropolis, these playboys were the latest caper artists to challenge the gaming security in Sin City. (Slate had imagined a small town bank robbery, but Stern wanted a bolder plot.) Reno was out as an alternate gambling center because the Angel destruction of a tavern in 1960 during their Fourth of July run created a local law prohibiting more than two bike riders on a street. In Las Vegas, *Hell's Angels '69* could be more authentically beholden to *Ocean's Eleven* (1960). The more recent *Where It's At* (1969) had been a fawning plug for a new kid on the casino block, Caesar's Palace, scene of the disastrous 1968 Evil Knievel cycle jump, and Stern valued its fresh attraction.

After hiring Don Tait to write and Lee Madden to direct, Stern contacted a friend with the Oakland phone number of Sonny Barger. Barger approved the story, agreeing to recruit his chapter brothers for a piece of the profits. They included Terry the Tramp, Tiny, a rugged Sergeant at Arms who led the attack against Berkeley war protesters in 1966, an Angel named Skip and the engaging one-time physician Magoo, who supposedly started the Porterville riot. These Angels received billing with the lead players for the size of their parts.

Chuck arrives late at a swinging soiree in his and Wes' fancy bachelor pad. The early phases of the plan have been completed. "It's a mind bender! It's gonna be the upper to end all uppers!" predicts excited Chuck. "Or the downer to end all downers," fears Wes, "if we get caught." "*If* we get caught," says Chuck. "Don't worry about a thing. Baby brother'll take care you like he always has."

Chuck and Wes drive to their country home. Under dawn's first light, they head for Oakland on choppers, wearing the colors of the Salem Witches of Boston.

Outside of Oakland, Chuck and Wes watch an Angel party breaking up. To draw attention, they harass a convertible driver. When the car goes off the road,

Sonny Barger confronts Capt. Rhodes (G.D. Spradlin) on the farm of Tiny's aunt.

Chuck hurts his leg. Blamed for this, the driver is humiliated by the Angels. Tramp's old lady Betsy, digging Chuck, says "I'll look at his leg." "Why doesn't mama kiss it and make it better?" Chuck asks. Betsy is about to, but hostile Tramp preemptively kisses her.

After Chuck recovers, he and Wes ride with the Angels to show off their cycling skills. Tramp, demonstrating his, swerves around a turning car but broadsides a parked auto and flies over a hedge into someone's front yard. Tramp is offended by Betsy's amusement. "I don't need this broad no more!" he tells Chuck. "I'm selling! You buying?" Chuck offers a half-empty cigarette pack Tramp crumples up, giving Chuck Betsy. In Chuck and Wes' quarters, she offers herself as "room service" to Chuck, who accepts.

Expediently, Chuck suggests Vegas as a good place for an Angel run. The vote is positive. Chuck and Wes can come along. Ever-testy Tramp forces them to prove their fighting abilities in a wild brawl. Chuck and Wes are in.

The Angels visit the ranch of Tiny's aunt—who thought he was still matriculated at Stanford. Capt. Rhodes of the police stops by, warning the Angels to stay out of Vegas. Chuck refuses a swim with Betsy, who leads Wes to the pond. They dive in wearing clothes. Wes tells Betsy she can't spend her whole life with the Angels. "Can you see me with a cottage and picket fence?" asks Betsy. "Yes, I do," replies Wes. Betsy ran away from home at a young age. "I've been on the back of some dude's hog ever since."

Chuck and Wes are about to take in Vegas. Betsy has changed into a dress so she can accompany them, but they leave her. Touching her apparel, Tramp condescendingly asks, "What is this?" "It's a dress, Tramp," Betsy replies unhappily. Tramp is through with her for good.

In town, Chuck phones Caesar's to confirm reservations. He and Wes pick up a bundle of regular clothes. At the hotel front desk, they cause a stir in their bike duds. "Caesar's believes in informal dress, but this is really off-limits," insists the concierge until he is threatened with a discrimination suit. A bellboy carries Chuck and Wes' luggage in a saddlebag to their suite. Wes patronizingly tips him with a house coin. Betsy walks to Vegas, trying to hitch a ride.

Once they have changed into business suits and removed their longhair wigs, Wes calls the Angels, alleging he and Chuck are being hassled by the management. The Angels leave the ranch to help out. Betsy arrives at Caesar's.

As part of the plan, Wes tries to change a thousand dollar bill, producing insufficient ID and a stolen credit card. Wes is escorted into the outer cage while Chuck pulls a toy gun on the door guard. The guard is instructed to say that Rhodes is here to see Wes. This opens the door for Chuck. In special pouches under their jackets, Chuck and Wes take six hundred thousand dollars. Outside, they are spotted by Betsy.

The Angels arrive in force, but riot police hold them back. Chuck and Wes change back into their bike clothes, stashing money in the saddlebags. Capt. Rhodes arrives. Chuck and Wes tell the Angels the trouble really wasn't all that bad. Betsy, hinting at what she knows, tells Chuck and Wes, "You sure look cute in your square little suits and square little haircuts. Is that your real bag?"

Escorted across the county line, the Angels decide to make Chuck and Wes leave. Betsy divulges to Chuck and Wes her knowledge of their crime, forcing them to take her along.

To avoid roadblocks, Chuck and Wes go to a bike rental shop, trading in their hogs for scramblers. Betsy wants one. "There's no point in riding caboose when we can go first-class."

Rhodes sees the Angels, suspecting them of being robbery accomplices. Sonny tells him they sent Chuck and Wes on their

Wes (Jeremy Slate) and Chuck (Tom Stern) with Betsy (Conny Van Dyke) outside of Caesar's Palace.

way. "Maybe they sent you on *their* way," theorizes Rhodes. Showing the house coin they gave the bellboy, Rhodes says Chuck and Wes were monitored the entire time and were never near the slot machines. An accessory rap against the Angels may be filed. "We'll catch 'em." Sonny tells his boys, "The cops can have 'em when we're done—if there's anything left!"

At the bike shop, the Angels inquire about Chuck, Wes and Betsy. The best riders rent scramblers for the pursuit. Once Chuck and Wes reach Los Angeles, they plan to send the money back. "We did it just to prove we could do it," Wes tells Betsy, "for excitement."

Chuck, Wes and Betsy camp in a desert cave. Betsy wants Wes to tell her he likes her. "I've got to stay with Chuck," says Wes, who reveals they are half-brothers—the sons of different fathers who married a rich woman. "So Chuck holds the purse strings," understands Betsy, "and you do what Chuck says."

The police launch a morning helicopter search. Betsy antagonizes Chuck by scattering the money. In the next town, he decrees, she splits. "Is that official?" asks Wes, beginning to stand up to Chuck. Chuck insists Wes' life with him means "no strings." Wes sees the money as his bid for personal autonomy. "Maybe this makes me Wes Patterson instead of Wes Patterson dependent. It's drop dead money!" "It's all going back!" demands Chuck. Defending the part he feels entitled to, Wes declares, "Not this half!" Chuck tries to punch some sense into Wes, who knocks him out. Betsy wonders if Chuck should be left here. "He always comes up with all the answers," assures Wes.

Chuck comes to as Wes and Betsy start off and is frantic at the thought of losing Wes. "I don't care about the money!" he screams, throwing bills about. "*I need you!*" The Angels spot Wes and Betsy ... and Chuck trying to catch up to them. Pursuing him, the Angels trap Chuck—who leaps toward the opposite side of a deep canyon. His flying bike crashes against an outcropping and explodes. Chuck's fiery corpse plummets to the ground.

Wes and Betsy silently face punishment as Skip collects the scattered money, waving it around. Tramp mockingly strokes Betsy's hair. The money Wes holds is confiscated. Tramp takes his canteen. On Sonny's nod, he empties it. The Angels leave as Wes and Betsy abandon their useless bikes and hike for sanctuary.

Hell's Angels '69 played best as a character study of two jaded ne'er-do-wells out to outrage the establishment. This concept was borrowed from *The Jokers* (1967), a British farce about another pair of brothers wanting to steal and then return the Crown Jewels. There was a streak of unnatural brotherly love in Chuck's need to have around the more cautious, considerate and reflective Wes, a rewarded puppet whose shift of affection toward Betsy became stronger when she started to care more about Wes than misogynistic, egotistical Chuck. Both brothers were perfect gentlemen in comparison to Terry the Tramp, written as being the most hellish Angel in Sonny Barger's crew, and the writing was probably based on his real-life reputation (resulting in not one felony conviction). Besides being an abusive boyfriend to the fictitious Betsy, he was also her pimp.

Although the robbery plan was clever, *Hell's Angels '69* was nothing more than *Ocean's Eleven* reduced to two conspirators and one casino. Slack in down-to-the-wire crime tension, *Angels '69* was most dramatic in its Vegas scenes with the Angels staring down the cops in front of the Palace, whose night-lit Romanesque splendor made the Angels and the police look surrealistically out of place.

Of course, *real* jeopardy was supposed to happen in the aftermath of the robbery with Chuck, Wes and Betsy on the run from more formidable hunters than the police. The Angels would never have done the film had they not been allowed to exercise righteous menace. How much righteous is *too* righteous? If the Angels had killed Chuck directly, they would have been no better than the mindless mass murderers of *Satan's Sadists*. A fatal accident was the solution. Made sympathetic by falling in love, Wes and Betsy were granted a milder punishment they could hopefully walk out of.

Tom Stern's company, Tracom Productions, raised five hundred thousand dollars, pushing *Hell's Angels '69* as far as possible toward the appearance of a major movie. The apartment where Chuck and Wes lived, the opulent Caesar's surroundings ... these were not your average Biker surroundings. Except during stunt work, *Angels '69* wasn't adventurous technically. Only the Angel riding in Oakland gave off any *Hell's Angels on Wheels* spontaneity—*that* kind of spontaneity. Within its more routine photographic style, *Angels '69* exploded like a burning firecracker warehouse during the brawl at the Angels' place. Not the producer, not the director, the *Angels* were in control—and *out* of control inflicting real blows.

Several Angels got into a tiff with director Lee Madden, beating him up, but he reportedly took it very well. One Angel sprayed a building with machine-gun fire. When Magoo fell off his bike during the climactic chase, he rolled into the path of another that barely missed him. Jeremy Slate took a bike spill, breaking his right leg.

Stern and Slate were easily the most impressive professional actors. While waiting for his leg to heal, Slate, undergoing a period of personal reevaluation, took a long sabbatical at Sandstone Retreat, becoming one of its teachers. This chapter of Slate's life was covered in the Gay Talese book *Thy Neighbor's Wife*.

Ex–child model Conny Van Dyke had been Miss Teen U.S.A. of 1960 and the first white Motown recording artist. She did a part in *The Young Sinner* and some auto commercials Lee Madden directed. Working in the Universal mail room, Van Dyke started doing TV roles and Lee Madden got her the role of Betsy in *Hell's Angels 69*. Van Dyke entered country music in Nashville and campaigned for the Dixie part in *W.W. and the Dixie Dancekings* (1974), winning the approval of star Burt Reynolds. Van Dyke became Joe Don Baker's leading lady in *Framed* (1975) and continued her TV appearances.

Angel Apache was simmering, teeth-gnashing TV bad boy Steve Sandor. Texas oil millionaire turned actor G.D. Spradlin (Capt. Rhodes) later directed Sandor and Bo Hopkins in his bike movie *The Only Way Home* (1972).

Sonny Barger kept his temper in check on-screen to convey some measure of dignity as Prez. The Terry the Tramp that Conny Van Dyke knew was a sweet guy she hung out with. All the Angels loved Van Dyke, keeping the leather jacket she wore in *Angels '69* as a souvenir in the Oakland clubhouse.

A more profound drama than *Hell's Angels '69* happened that December in Altamont, California. The Rolling Stones' Hyde Park concert had been adequately policed by the British Angels. In America, Mick Jagger hoped to surpass Woodstock, hiring documentary filmmakers Albert and David Maysles to record the event. San Francisco's Golden Gate Park was the chosen concert site, but the nervous city denied a permit. Out too was the nearby Sears Point Raceway. An appendage of Filmways, Concert Associates wanted either the distribution rights of the film or one hundred twenty five thousand dollars in cash. The owner of the Altamont stock car raceway donated his track for free hoping it would help business. Recruited by

Jerry Garcia of the Grateful Dead, the Oakland Angels were paid in five hundred dollars worth of beer.

The chaos of Altamont on December 6, 1969, began when the most antagonistic Angels attacked the kids with weighted pool cues. When Jefferson Airplane performed, a black boy was assaulted and lead singer Marty Balin got whacked in the face with a cue while trying to urge calm. Arriving late, the Stones had underestimated the restlessness they aggravated, intending to make a more spectacular entrance.

Escorted on stage by several Angels, Mick Jagger sang "Sympathy for the Devil." Another black youth, eighteen-year-old Meredith Hunter, affronted some Angels because his girlfriend was white. One struck Hunter, five others chased him to the stage and Jagger spotted Hunter holding an unloaded gun. One Angel stabbed Hunter in the back. Killed by multiple injuries, he became in death the new focus of the documentary.

The Altamont disaster so affected Terry the Tramp emotionally that he committed suicide by taking pills the following March. Meant to beat the 1970 release of *Woodstock*, the Maysles documentary *Gimme Shelter* came out in 1971.

In 1971, Tom Stern produced and starred in the nightmarish underworld drama *Clay Pidgeon*. He was an ambitious comer, another Steve Ihnat, but his career seemed to lose impetus just as he was getting it all together. Stern divorced Samantha Eggar, accusing her of being an unfit mother. In the eighties, Stern did some minor TV roles and became a production associate on Clint Eastwood films.

Hell's Belles

American International 1969. Producer-Director: Maury Dexter; Screenplay: James Gordon White, R.G. McMullen; Associate Producer: Hank Tani; Cinematography: Ken Peach; Film Editor: John Schreyer; Music Supervision: Al Simms; Music: Lee Baxter: Assistant to Producer: Julie Foote; Set Decorator: Harry Reif; Men's Wardrobe: Dick Bruno; Women's Wardrobe: Sharon Thober; Property Master: Ted Berkley; Script Supervisor: Marshall Schlack; Special Effects: Roger George; Hairstylist: Wava Green; Makeup: Paul Malcolm; Chief Electrician: Lloyd L. Garnell; Sound: Brad Trask; Transportation: Alee Reed; Berkey Pathé Color; A Maury Dexter Production. Running Time: 95 minutes.

Cast: Jeremy Slate (Dan); Adam Roarke (Tampa); Jocelyn Lane (Cathy); Angelique Pettyjohn (Cherry); William Lucking (Gippo); Michael Walker (Tony); Jerry Randall (Crazy John); Kristen Van Buren (Zelda); Dick Bullock (Meatball); Astrid Warner (Piper); Eddie Hice (Mongoose); Jerry Brutsche (Rabbit); Elaine Everett (Big Sal); Fred Krone (Buzz); Ronn Dayton (Barney); Henry M. Kendrick (Gas Station Attendant); James Owens (Leo); Larry H. Lane (Charlie); Jackie Hummer (Girlfriend); Bill Thompson (L.G.); Michael Jones (Sonny).

Mini-Skirt Mob author James Gordon White looked at westerns on TV for plot inspiration. With Robert G. McMullen, he wrote the next Maury Dexter Biker, *Hell's Belles*, as *Winchester 73* (1950, remade as a 1967 television movie) and *The Appaloosa* (1966) with a motorcycle becoming their respective objects of great value. Hero Dan Holt was the victimized but resilient synthesis of Lin McAdam, winner of a stolen shooting-prize rifle, and Matt Fletcher, the stud horse owner who wanted to settle down to ranch life. *Hell's Belles* was even *The Bicycle Thief* (1960) set in America.

The cycle rustlers in *Hell's Belles* liked their women as passengers, no co-riders—meaning they were "average" outlaws—

but Dexter wanted to get a little more out of miniskirts, dressing his Hell Belles in same. The first title of *Hell's Belles*—the name of an incidental song in the film—had been *The Girl in the Leather Skirt*.

In a motocross race, Dan defeats Tony Carlyle, winning a medal and a new bike. Tony offers his bike and three hundred dollars, but Dan won't sell the bike for less than two grand.

After a date, Dan drives home, stopping his pickup to help an injured biker lying on the road. The "victim," Tony, slugs Dan. Tony and his cronies steal the prize bike, crippling the truck and the old bike. Coming to, Dan siphons some truck gas to make the bike run again.

Leaving a bar, Tony and his boys catch the Tampa gang admiring the prize bike. "Don't you be touching *my* sickle if you please," Tampa tells Tony, offering his own in trade. Tony's resistance precipitates a fight he and his guys lose. The gang leaves with the bike before Dan confronts Tony, punching him.

The gang camps at an arroyo, watched by Dan. After they go to sleep, he tries to take the bike, but has a violent altercation with stupid Gippo. Dan tries to ride off, but the gang surrounds him and Tampa clubs him. "Looks like we have a motorcycle thief," declares Tampa. Dan's claim of valid ownership is proved when Tampa's old lady Cherry produces his inscribed race medal. Tampa proposes a "swap." "I know just the thing." The "thing" is Tampa's former girl, Cathy. Tampa kicks Dan unconscious—alarming Cathy when he makes her realize she is staying with Dan while the others head for Nogales.

An hour into the gang's departure, Dan recovers, planning to leave Cathy in distant Mammoth. At the Mammoth gas station, Crazy John makes Gippo the butt of a fuel pump nozzle prank. Gippo attacks Crazy John, whose dropped cigarette starts a fire. The gang beats a fast retreat.

Arriving in Mammoth, Dan drops Cathy off, but when angry locals at the scene of the extinguished blaze see them, Cathy is forced to flee with Dan.

Two riders are buying food at a store where Dan and Cathy stop. Dan subdues them, learning the others are parked near a road cut-off. Cathy refuses to go with Dan until he reminds her she may be arrested by the Mammoth police for the station fire.

During mealtime, someone bugs Gippo by tossing a rock into his plate of pork and beans. Blaming Mongoose, Gippo gives him free lunch. Tampa quells their brawl before Dan calls from the top of a hill, holding Cathy. "A swap is a swap!" argues Tampa. As Dan kicks down shale, the gang scatters to avoid a slide. Cathy obstinately prefers to stay here until Dan scares her by describing, graphically, how poisonous desert reptiles kill.

Dan (Jeremy Slate) and wary Kathy (Jocelyn Lane).

Dan and Cathy watch the gang nearing a canyon. Dan knows the territory thoroughly. With a boulder, he impedes the gang, who push their bikes toward a ridge. Starting a slide, he injures a biker. "This is just the beginning—friend!" Dan tells Tampa.

In an old mine shack, Dan rummages around for useful items, finding a piece of rope and some dynamite.

Using the rope, Dan lays a trap for two guys as Cathy impulsively flees on his old bike. One downed rider hurts his arm. Dan catches Cathy so the two men will have a bike in order to get the injured one to a hospital. From the wrecked bike, Dan obtains a gas tank. "You live for a damn motorcycle!" exclaims perplexed Cathy. Its price is worth a year's payment on Dan's ranch. Dan's life wasn't going anywhere until he bought the land. "Now it's growing up and so am I." "What does that mean?" asks Cathy. "It means," replies Dan, "I can see both sides of the coin. I can't hate your friends." Cathy fell out of favor with Tampa thanks to Cherry's lie she was making it with another rider.

Dan concocts a plan with the gas tank while Crazy John rigs a snare, since Tampa expects Dan to sneak into camp and sabotage the bikes. By exploding the tank, Dan destroys the camp—and Crazy John is left dangling in his own trap.

Dan leaves Cathy to do some scouting. Absent from a war council, Gippo finds Cathy. When Dan returns, Gippo is holding a knife to her throat. Dan bluffs Gippo into discarding her protective body. During their combat, Gippo tumbles into a nest of rattlers. One kills him with its bite.

Dan delivers Gippo's corpse to the remaining riders and runs off. Accepting the tragedy as an accident, they turn against Tampa. Cherry offers the prize bike to Dan, but Tampa stops her. She and the others leave Tampa.

Cathy begs Dan to cease his vendetta. "Are you trying to protect Tampa or me?" He asks. "Up to now we've been fighting on your terms!" shouts Tampa, "Now it's my style!" The victor gets Cathy as well as the prize bike. "No sense wasting her," Tampa reasons. Tampa throws a chain to Dan, who accepts the challenge, brushing Cathy off. Tampa knocks Dan down. Dan hugs the ground as Tampa tries to run him over. Leaping over Dan's bike, Tampa is hurled off of his, breaking his shoulder against a sharp protrusion of rock.

Unable to rise, suffering Tampa begs Cathy not to leave him. "Sure, he needs you—he's alone!" Dan tells Cathy, "But how long is he gonna keep you this time?" Humbled into pleading for forgiveness, Tampa is abandoned until Cathy makes her choice and returns to him. Without a word, Dan exits.

Hell's Belles was almost a kinder, gentler film for Maury Dexter. His other A.I.P. movies contained drug addiction, anti-Mexican bias, gang bangs, arson, riots and torture—plus deaths from suicide, auto accident, fire, neck injury and falls, as well as attempted murder by junkyard wrecking machine. The sex tension that was so ugly in *The Mini-Skirt Mob* was here comical and sometimes sweet. Tampa dug Dan's bike more than any girl and Dan exercised uncommon mercy for a hunter, keeping a sense of humor. One of *Mini-Skirt Mob*'s more unpleasant scenes was Shayne's recall of the eating habits of snakes. *Hell's Belles* used a more grisly description of desert wildlife, but this talk was only tongue-in-cheek (the first thing Dan saw when he woke up from being robbed was a gila monster).

Slapped fannies, ruined food, a gas version of a water gag and a trap that trapped the trapper made for fun dumbness. If snake victim Gippo could have risen from the dead, everything would have been as okay as before. Dan already had a girl in town, so when Cathy reconciled with Tampa, the love particulars balanced out. In memory of a male *Mini-Skirt Mob* casualty, one of the minor characters was named L.G.

Some of *Hell's Belles* was made in the ghost town of Helvetia, a mining village that had once been Arizona's third largest community. Its founder was Swiss immigrant Ben Hefti, who was known as Old Man Golden, even though he had made his fortune extracting copper from the Santa Rita mountains southwest of Tucson. Hefti named Helvetia in honor of his native land. Once a wild, open place, Helvetia was where two candidates for the position of sheriff were tied and neither of them took office. Throughout its life, Helvetia never had a sheriff.

A few of the most memorable spots in Helvetia were where Maury Dexter staged his action scenes. Jocelyn Lane and Angelique Pettyjohn performed a catfight in the place where Ben Hefti, a volatile drunkard always ready to brawl, challenged comers on payday. Hefti fought until he dropped from exhaustion. Jeremy Slate and Adam Roarke acted out the chain fight scene where a Pima Indian stabbed Oscar One Leg Buckalew, causing him to lose a leg.

The Mammoth gas station was a station that had caught fire some weeks before. Maury Dexter's staff refurbished the charred structure for the beginning of the first scene, then set it ablaze.

Closed down in 1910, Helvetia was empty of the people who made it lively, but the *Hell's Belles* cast and crew were plagued by downpours, landslides, the ever-present rattlesnakes and the Hong Kong flu, which hit over half the company.

With the role of Dan, Jeremy Slate was able to move past the almost silent melodrama evil of Danny Carmody and the situational wickedness of *Mini-Skirt Mob*'s Lon. Adam Roarke, previously a ladies' man outlaw, went along well with the silliness of treating a motorcycle as a love object. The sister of British actress Mara, Jocelyn, formerly Jackie Lane, grew up in New York and collected international real estate.

Angelique Pettyjohn was the most heavenly body on *Star Trek* in its episode "The Gamesters of Triskelion." Success as a Las Vegas–based dancer paid Pettyjohn's bills more often than her occasional film roles, although she profited from marketing alternate posters of how she looked on *Star Trek*, one in full costume and one almost nude. When her luck was low, Pettyjohn got it up by getting guys up in two above-average XXX movies, *Body Talk* and *Titillation* (both 1982). The bisexual Pettyjohn died of cancer in 1992. The Elvis impersonator who claims to be his illegitimate son identified Pettyjohn as the mother.

Michael Walker was Robert's brother. William Lucking was John F. Kennedy in the play *Macbird* and Renny in the fizzled filmization of *Doc Savage* (1975). He returned to Tucson to play Mac on the flop Lindsay Wagner show *Jessie*.

Hell's Bloody Devils

Independent International 1970. Executive Producers: Rex Carlton, Fred Gebhardt; Producer-Director: Al Adamson; Screenplay: Jerry Evans; Associate Producers: Robert Kinoshita, Jerry Evans; Production Consultant: Samuel M. Sherman; Cinematography: Frank Ruttencutter, Leslie a/k/a Laszlo Kovacs; Film Editor: John Winfield; Music Composer: Don

McGinniss; Production Manager: Bud Cardos; Unit Manager: Rick Jackson; Sound Recording: Robert Dietz; Lighting: Aggie Aguilar, Brian Smith, Peter Wagner; Still Photography: Hedy Dietz; Script: Pat Cardos, Joyce King; Re-recording: Cinesound; Assistant to Producer: Mike Haggerty; Assistant Director: Greydon Clark; Second Unit Cameraman: Gary Graver; Makeup: Kent Osborne; Hair Stylist: Margaret Erman; Wardrobe: Nancy Gilmore; Title Design: Bob LeBar; Songs: "The Fakers": Music by Nelson Riddle, Lyrics by John Gabriel; "When Did the Sun Come Up": Music by Don McGinniss, Lyrics by David McKechnie; Sung by Debbie Stuart; Location Scenes filmed at Green Acres Studios, Roosevelt, Utah; DeLuxe Color; East-West Pictures and Four Crown presentation of an Al Adamson Production. Running Time: 92 minutes.

Cast: Broderick Crawford (Gavin); Scott Brady (Brand); Kent Taylor (Count Von Delberg); John Gabriel (Mark Adams); Keith Andes (Joe Bramonte); John Carradine (Pet Store Owner); Robert Dix (Cunk); William Bonner, Jerry Mills (Bloody Devils), Bambi Allen, Jill Woelfel (Pickup Girls); Erin O'Donnell (Leni Marvenga); Vicki Volante (Carol Bechtol); Anne Randall (Amanda Whitfield); Jack Starrett (Rocky); Emily Banks (Jill Harmon); Dan Kemp (Karl); Carol Brewster (Baroness Whitfield); Leslie McCrae (Maggie); Gene Shane (Dr. Ker); Arland Shubert (Doctor); Alyce Andrace, Rhae Andrace (Girls in Pet Store); Alice Wong (Receptionist); Jane Wald (Girl on Boat); Richard Brander (Lester); Brand Bell, Greydon Clark, Gary Kent, Sy Prescott, Sid Lawrence, John Cardos, Kent Osborne, Sheldon Lee, Philip Difermian, Hessians motorcycle club.

Nazi Germany's scheme to flood the U.S. with funny money was Operation Cicero. Based on this was Rex Carlton's last film, *Operation M*, from a story by Jerry Evans. *Operation M* was a merger between Paragon International and the Manhattan indie East-West Pictures. Al Adamson originally planned to film in New York and Germany with Stephen McNally and Carol Ohmart to star. The film renamed *The Fakers* got some early non-trade publicity from the star buildup given to Playmate player Anne Randall, Miss May 1967.

Thanks to the unreleased *The Fakers*, Adamson and Sam Sherman did not have to do a complete movie for their follow-up to *Satan's Sadists*. Outlaws were into their own Facist bag and the ex–*Fakers* became *Hell's Bloody Devils*, which showed bikers serving the people who invented their favorite decorations. Adamson and Sherman liked the word "Blood" because its irresistible scent was good for almost every exploitation genre.

Cunk, Weird and Curly lead the Bloody Devils, hired by Count Otto Von Delberg's New Nazi party to do its dirty work. Von Delberg's aide-lover is Carol Bechtol, an Israeli spy looking for Col. Bernhardt Kruger, the Auschwitz commandant who murdered her parents. Carol pays the Devils off for their last job and they are assigned to take care of two enemies of the organization.

The top boy of Las Vegas Mafia don Joe Bramonte, Mark Adams is an F.B.I. plant. Bramonte assigns Mark to broker a deal between Von Delberg and the Syndicate for circulation of vintage wartime German counterfeiting plates.

Cunk—who drapes a bra over a handlebar of his bike like a trophy—would like Carol to lose all her laundry, but she favors Mark. The Devils work over Mark, who escapes doom in a car fight that ends in a mountain crash. The Devils pick up two hitchhiking girls for an orgy. Arriving at the scene, Carol nearly gets raped by Cunk. She kills him, Weird and Curly with a hidden explosive device.

The F.B.I. closes in on the Nazis and the money is destroyed in an exploding hearse, but Von Delberg gets away. Meanwhile, Carol uncovers proof he is Kruger. Von Delberg finishes her with a switchblade.

Mark confronts Von Delberg and his ward Leni Marvenga—Von Delberg's daughter—in the underground print shop. Left in the burning cabin above, Mark is saved by rookie Fed Jill Harmon. Mark

hides a bomb in Von Delberg's escape helicopter, which explodes, killing him and Leni.

For the *Hell's Bloody Devils* footage, Robert Dix, Jerry Mills, Bambi Allen and Jill Woelfel were hired, John Gabriel and Vicki Volante of *The Fakers* rehired and the California Hessians were gang extras. Adamson shot these scenes at the Spahn Ranch. During the shoot, the local Highway Patrol busted the Hessians for illegal weapons possession. Not found were any drugs or conquest brassieres. A Nazi death camp battle cut from *The Fakers* would be resurrected in *Angels' Wild Women* as part of its movie set scene and the car wreck was in the opening of *Satan's Sadists*.

Publicity credit for the music went to Nelson Riddle, who only worked on the

Top: Ad for *Hell's Bloody Devils*.
Bottom: Tongue love among two Bloody Devils.

song "Faker"—lyrics by John Gabriel, sung by Shirley Bassey sound-alike Debbie Stuart.

Veteran actor Gabriel was "introduced" along with Anne Randall. Erin O'Donnell, Vicki Volante, Emily Banks, Bambi Allen and Jill Woelfel were "The Wild Rebellion Girls"—a title that seemed to trade on the Dodge Rebellion Girl and Regina Carroll's "Freak-Out Girl" status from *Satan's Sadists*.

Drawn and quartered for its revised *Satan's Sadists* campaign hyping the Manson murders, Independent-International took the discretion not to push *Hell's Bloody Devils* by a "From the Producers Of" tag. The claim "All Action! All New!" should have read "All Action! Half New!" The *real* fakers were the reel fakers who recycled—no—*be*cycled a film that originally had no bikers, then sold it to TV as it once was, adding the supplemental title *Smashing the Crime Syndicate*.

The return of *The Fakers* to its basic form may not have been planned. The disappearance of the biker scenes was allegedly due to the misplacement of the last reel, but the plot synopsis would indicate that the Devils figured in the story from its beginning to at least half its length or better. Much of the tale was a long flashback recounted by narrator Mark after his car crackup brush. No modern Bikers had yet aired on TV and the bloody deviltry may have been seen as a censorship liability. So too maybe the *Bloody Devils* name. I.I. made a point of changing the "Bloody" title in anticipation of both the objections of some newspaper advertising departments and video bluenoses.

Satan's Sadists was not the only I.I. link between fact and fiction. Art director Robert Kinoshita, an associate producer of *The Fakers*, was himself charged with counterfeiting during his job on the cursed espionage show *Cover-Up* in 1984.

Hell's Chosen Few

American General / Thunderbird-International 1968. Producer-Director: David L. Hewitt; Screenplay: John McCarthy, David Prentiss; Associate Producers: Titus Moody, Ewing Brown; Cinematography: Ewing Brown; Music: Charles Walden; Music Supervision: Commercial Sound Recorders; Sound: Movie Tech; Sound Effects Editor: Frank Coe; Sound Recording: Jean Mainferme; Lighting: John McNicholas, Fred McGee, Brian Smith; Set Continuity: Gary Eacock; Script Supervisor: Jean Hewitt; Makeup: Jean Lister; Re-recording: Cinesound Eastmancolor Borealis Enterprises; Running Time: 92 minutes.

Cast: Jody Daniel (Joe); Kelly Ross (Sharon); Bill Bonner (Jimbo); Vic McGee (Deacon); Joe Folino, Jr. (Sheriff Harris); Gary Kent (Willie); Mick Mehas (Mick); Titus Moody (Twichy); Jan Arlen, Shirley Cash, Mike Kannon, Megan Timothy, Ralph Campbell, Ron Draves.

In 1966, David L. Hewitt made *The Girls from Thunder Strip* where bikers from California encountered three bootlegger sisters down South. Until recently, the film was believed lost.

Discouraged by the effort needed to film a bike story by John K. McCarthy, Hewitt recalled *Teenage Bride*, a 1960 religious short about violent, alcoholic Dan Harris, his wife Hedda and their daughter Penny, whose beau, Brad Martin, Penny's father accidentally killed. He also saw actor-filmmaker–fringe rebel Titus Moody's 1967 documentary *Outlaw Motorcycles*. Claiming he put into Roger Corman's head the idea for *The Wild Angels*, Moody, owner of one of the early choppers, edited a like-named adult magazine centered on bike activity. Moody was sure to plug the movie.

Outlaw Motorcycles became part of the '68 biker crop as *Hell's Chosen Few*. Acquired in a percentage deal along with *Teenage Bride*, its scenes were interwoven with the now Christianity-free sermon saga. Hewitt hired *Teenage Bride* actor Joe Folino Jr. to play Harris in his scenes, making Harris a sheriff. John McCarthy received co-writing credit. Billed as an associate producer, Titus Moody appeared as a biker named Twichy.

Willie Grady and Sharon Smith ride with Willie's gang, Hell's Chosen Few, to a coastal town where hundreds of outlaws are rallying. While they hit the beach, the other Chosen head for the Cactus, a bar run by club treasurer Deacon Dafoe.

Penny goes out with Brad. Revolted by Harris' boozy passion, Hedda drives him to drink up at the Cactus. At the Tiki Club, Penny and Brad join more kids on the beach. Looking for her, Harris catches Penny in Brad's innocent embrace. Berserk Harris chases Brad, who dies in a fall from the rocks. Harris plucks wet, hysterical Penny out of the surf and drags her home. Uninformed of what Harris did, Hedda is made to think Penny is a "tramp."

Sans Sharon, drunk Willie is arrested for Brad's murder. Harris hopes to keep Penny sequestered until this blows over, but he meets Willie's long-estranged brother Joe, an Army lieutenant. Convinced Willie is no killer, Joe aims to clear him. Joe persuades dour Deacon to let him join Hell's Chosen Few. On the night a new girl is being initiated, Joe meets Sharon and antagonistic Jimbo, who makes Joe take part in the sex ritual.

Joe and Sharon slowly fall in love. Harris considers him a troublemaker. In an amusement park, Joe tangles with Jimbo over Sharon until the police come. Harris attempts to blame Joe for a gang fight fatality the previous evening.

Coming back from Mexico, bitter, intoxicated Penny angrily lashes out at her hypocritical father. She phones Joe at the gang's garage to incriminate Harris. Panicked, Harris tells Joe to leave town, pulling his gun. In a struggle, Harris shoots himself. Out of jail, Willie wants Sharon back, but Joe is her man now. Jealous Willie rapes Sharon.

Inebriated Willie celebrates his freedom in the closed amusement park. Vengeful phantom Joe calls for Willie, who stumbles around scared and disoriented until Joe fiendishly throttles him from behind. Later while Willie's casket is being loaded into a hearse across the street, imprisoned Joe watches from his cell window.

Conforming to the on-the-spot news feel of Titus Moody's material, *Hell's Chosen Few* got into the *Born Losers* atmosphere of an outlaw gang invading a beach city. The *Teenage Bride* scenes established how drink helped Harris to kill while in *Chosen Few* it put Willie in a fall guy position. More intrinsically dangerous was Joe, who held himself superior to Willie, Harris and the gang. In becoming a Chosen one, he lost the reins on his dark side except during his tender moments with Sharon. Vindicated of homicide but turning rapist, Willie shattered Joe's last vestiges of humanity—making Joe the Grady who would go up the river. Titus Moody filled most of the riding close-ups, twitching his head for effect. Prominently decorated with swastika flags, the Cactus also mounted an *Outlaw Motorcycles* poster. One biker extra was the funny fatso from *Devil's Angels* who rammed his helmet spike into the wrecked camper. The service for Willie was a real outlaw funeral.

Hewitt didn't do enough to hide all the cracks in his filmic fixer-upping. The bar where Harris was initially going to get bombed was mentioned in *Teenage Bride* as the Alibi. Willie's arrest, the sequestration of Penny, how she talked to Joe and confirmation of Harris' demise were all indicated by phone calls and awkwardly inserted newspaper headlines. Hewitt either didn't want to strain himself staging violence or felt the scant, static and rushed amount he showed was enough.

Texas rock star Jody Daniel blended

A new mama (Megan Timothy) cozies up to a "Chosen" one.

the looks and sass of prime Presley as Joe. He didn't sing here, but his mouth kept busy singing nail-tough, rat-a-tat dialogue. Gary Kent, Bill Bonner and Mick Mehas had appeared in *The Girls from Thunder Strip*. Kent and Bonner became Al Adamson regulars. Kent would break away from biker typecasting when he played the Nam vet hero in *Satan's Sadists*. Conversely, Jody Daniel would dodge the draft in *The Girl in Gold Boots* (1968)—where he did sing.

The Hot Angel

Paramount 1958. Producer-Screenplay: Stanley Kallis; Director: Joe Parker; Associate Producer: Kenrick Sweet; Cinematography: Karl Struss; Film Editors: Eda Warren, Leon Selditz; Music: Robert Drasnin, Richard Markowitz; Ariel Cinematography, Elmer G. Dryer; Sound, Clarence Peterson; A Paragon Production. Running Time: 73 minutes.

Cast: Jackie Loughery (Mandy Wilson); Edward Kemmer (Chuck Lawson); Mason Alan Dinehart (Joe Wilson); Emory Parnell (Judd Pfeiffer); Lyle Talbot (Van Richards); Zon Teller (Mick Pfeiffer); Heather Ames (Lynn Connors); Steffi Sydney (Myrna); John Nolan (Ray); Richard Stauffer (Monk); Kathi Thornton (Liz); Harold Mallett (Pilot).

A hot angel sounds like someone with wings, a harp and a halo who has somehow displeased God and been sent to a lower place with much higher room temperature. Seriously, *The Hot Angel* was written and produced for Paramount release by Stanley Kallis, the brother of A.I.P.'s brilliant ad designer Albert. From the Edmund Chevie production *Eighteen and Anxious* (1957), Stanley hired director Joe Parker and actress Jackie Loughery.

Forward in several aspects of its conception, *The Hot Angel* was the first film with bikers to have the word "angel" in its title (*Dragstrip Riot* had been the earliest movie to refer to cyclists as "bikers"). Hot Angels were light planes used to detect uranium ore from the air ... hot, of course, meaning the element. In *The Hot Angels*, we could see signs of the eventual westernization of Bikers. The Grand Canyon was its visual set-piece and uranium a substitute for gold, the resource most often sought by crooks in cowboy pics. Also endemic to Bikers would be a war vet protagonist.

Alive because of the sacrifice of a fellow Korean War pilot, flyer Chuck Lawson answers an urgent message from the man's sister, Mandy Wilson. She is the radio operator for an aerial uranium prospecting

The Mick Pfeiffer gang almost look like Norman Rockwell kids.

company owned by Van Richards. Hired to scan traces of ore in the Grand Canyon, Chuck meets Mandy's kid brother Joe. Joe and his girl, Lynn Connors, ride with a gang of cycle punks led by Mick Pfeiffer. Mick's father Judd is a friend of Van.

Mandy doesn't like the company Joe keeps, asking Chuck to help turn him around. When Chuck shows Joe how well he can maneuver a bike across rugged terrain, he succeeds. Chuck tells Joe that he is grateful to Joe's late brother for his valor. Convinced that Chuck is truly interested in him, Joe is willing to learn how to fly.

A claim-jumper only feigning friendship with Van, Judd is aided by Mick and his accomplice Monk. Mick warns gang defector Joe he will hurt Mandy if the law is brought into this matter. To get rid of liability Chuck, Mick sabotages his plane. Mandy and Joe find out, but are too lat to stop Chuck's takeoff. When the plane loses altitude, Chuck makes a forced landing in the bottom of the Grand Canyon. Appalled by Mick's willingness to attempt murder, Judd decides to turn Mick, Monk and himself over to the sheriff.

Putting his newfound aviation skills to the test, Joe lands in a perilously narrow part of the canyon and rescues Chuck. Chuck marries Mandy.

The more typical semi–Bikers, such as *Dragstrip Riot*, linked their opposing forces to share one thing: wheels. Taking to wings, *The Hot Angel* related to airpower as an industry tool, a device of pleasure and a facilitator for premeditated death. Planes were too unwieldly and specialized to be made vehicles for delinquent behavior (even with sky chicken). Hot rods or bikes were better and Stan Kallis probably picked bikes because rods had been overexploited. Bikes injected some color into the identities of the young felons and Joe's interest in them gave Chuck a way of breaking the ice so that once won over, Joe could adapt to another kind of nerve-testing machine in hot angels.

The Hot Angel confronted adult delinquents ... most often drug pushers, vice lords or junkyard owners fencing hot auto parts. Judd Pfeiffer's thing was acquisition of uranium. Like some opportunists who consort with young hellcats to make their plans materialize, anti–role model parent Judd had to reckon with unplanned, unexpected, unwanted overzeal on the part of his henchmen. Judd's problem helper was Mick, whose murder plan had two positive upshots: provoking Judd into shutting down his illegal operation at legal pain to all parties and allowing Joe to save mentor Chuck by use of his new talent. Twice in a lifetime, Chuck owed his ass to a Wilson.

Certain wild youth films separated themselves from town-bound movies by seeking exotic necks of the great outdoors. Benefiting from the aerial camerawork of Elmer G. Dyer, *The Hot Angels'* chosen backdrop, Arizona, would become a Biker setting favorite.

Miss U.S.A. of 1952, Jackie Loughery had been married to Jack Webb, who cast her in his production *The D.I.* (1957). Edward Kemmer had patrolled space as Comm. Buzz Corry. Mason Alan Dinehart III was Bat Masterson on *The Life and Legend of Wyatt Earp* and co-starred in the next Stanley Kallis picture, *Road Racers* (1959). Like his character, Judd Pfeiffer, Emory Parnell too was a tragic father—actor son James died at age thirty-eight in 1961.

The Grand Canyon would appear at the ending of *Evel Knievel* (1971) as a vision of the jump Knievel never made.

Ivy League Killers

Ivy League Films 1962. Alternate Title: *The Fast Ones*. Producers: Norman Klenman, William Davidson; Director: William Davidson; Screenplay: Norman Klenman; Cinematography: William H. Gimmi; Musical Score: John Bath; Art Director: Leif B. Pederson; Sound: A. James Willis; Camera Operator: W. Jackson Samuels; Assistant Cameraman: George Morita; Continuity: Diana Dorkin; Wardrobe: Thelma Timmins; Makeup: Kenneth Brook; Electrician: Harry Lake; Properties: Roy Culley; Production Assistant: Lindsay Shonteff; Songs: "Get Hep," "Easy Rider," Sung by Igors Gavon. Running Time: 72 minutes.

Cast: Don Borisenko (Don); Don Francks (Andy); Barbara Bricker (Susan); George Carron, Jean Templeton, Patrick Desmond, Barry Lavender, Igors Gavon, Art Jenoff, Marin Lager, John Ringham, John Paris, Walter Balay, Dianne Blaney, Gertrude Tyras, Jack Blacklock, Rolf Carron, Paul Firestone, Boyd Jackson, and the Black Diamond Riders.

Canada didn't become a viable exploitation film center until the seventies. A very early North of the Border entry, *Ivy League Killers*, a/k/a *The Fast Ones*, was a reverse *Dragstrip Riot*. Its cycle cutups were pawns of three educated sports car drivers rating a bigger zero for conduct. Ahead of American Bikers, *Ivy League* used a real-life club, the Black Diamonds of Toronto.

At a deserted airfield, Don Gibson and the rest of the Diamonds encounter unctuous college boys Andy, Charlie and Bert and Andy's girl, Susan. Harassed, the foursome leave. The Diamonds playfully buzz them, running Andy and Susan into a ditch. Susan accompanies Charlie as he leaves to get a tow truck for Andy.

Curious about the Diamonds, Susan goes to their hangout, where Don's girl Nancy picks a fight with her. Leadership tension between Don and Bruno gets them to brawl. Don offers Susan a ride home, where Andy is. She cancels their golf date. Don no longer loves Nancy.

Suspected of killing a girl in Florida, Andy plots a fun robbery—and who better to frame than the Diamonds, who will be partying near the heist spot, the Palace Pier dance hall. Andy, Charlie and Bert store their crime props in a lakeside barn.

The Diamonds visit the dance hall before going to Rock Beach. Dressed like them, masked Andy, Charlie and Bert pull their job, Andy accidentally shoots the manager. During the escape, Andy's bike stalls and he runs a parking lot attendant down.

Deciding to set up Don, Andy returns to the dance hall in his car and tells the manager where the Diamonds are before surreptitiously leaving Don's stolen saddlebags. Bruno announces his takeover bid to late arrival Don. They fight until police raid the party. Only Don escapes. Andy, Charlie and Bert burn the money.

The police think the Diamonds are covering for the robbers. When Bruno recognizes the saddlebags, he inadvertently implicates Don. At the golf course, unseen Susan notices Charlie flashing a fake Black Diamonds crest ... realizing what the boys have done.

Susan finds Don in hiding and they shake the law. Andy, Charlie and Bert look for them on their bikes at the airfield. Don and Susan find the barn. She stays while Don goes for the Diamonds.

Hidden in back of the truck carrying the bikes, Susan sees the damaged front end of Andy's. Exposed, she must go along with the robbery evidence. Don returns to the Diamonds, who are being held by the police, but they escape and follow Don to the barn. There, Don catches Charlie, who says Andy and Bert are going to dump Susan and the truck in the lake.

Andy and Bert are surprised by Don, who fights Andy below the cliffs before a distant cop shoots murderous Andy.

So much of Canada looks like the U.S., giving *Ivy League Killers* the gray aura of an East Coast quickie. Even farther away from sunny Hollywood is Great Britain, whose youth dramas often contained mild peculiarities of characterization and plot minituae like those found in *Ivy League* (what American teen movies ever showed young people playing golf?). Canadian films pandering to American topics could easily simulate America, dropping an occasional reference to some Yankee locale—like where the Florida girl Andy met mysteriously died.

Don was a fuzzy Johnny Strabler retread minus inner torment, Nancy his Britches and Bruno a Chinoesque troublemaker. Susan was an interesting outsider chick. Not a mopey Kathie, a cloying Janet Pearson or a flamboyant Terry Lindsay, she was her own woman without having to prove anything. She dug collecting oddballs—collecting in Don a rough jewel. A more slimy, multi-faceted heel than *Dragstrip Riot*'s cardboard Bart Thorson, Andy was a creepier psycho than grief-maddened Silva of *Dragstrip Riot*, lapsing into periodic childish tirades like Nick of *Motorcycle Gang*. Andy's sense of superiority and how it sought confirmation in the execution of a perfect crime were gleanings from the psychology of Leopold and Loeb.

Sung by a happy faced guy named Igors Gavon were two tunes, "Get Hep" and "Easy Rider"—the last a surprising title.

Don Borisenko looked like a young pompadoured Mel Gibson and spoke in lethargic Bruce Willis inflections. Sly, fox-featured and here, overly-mannered, Don Francks did some acting in the States, playing Woody Mahoney in *Finian's Rainbow* (1968).

Other people from *Ivy League Killers* who left Canada were production associate Lindsay Shonteff, who directed low-budget horror films and cheap spypix in England, and two more people who went to Hollywood. One was actor Art Jenoff, who appeared in *Naked Angels* and the other was music composer John Bath, who scored *Outlaw Riders*, a tale of real biker robbers.

J.C.

Avco Embassy 1972. Producer-Director: William F. McGaha; Screenplay: Joe Thirty, William F. McGaha; Cinematography: Gerald M. Crowder; Film Editor: Avrum Fine; Music Composter-Conductor: Paul Jarvis; Cameraman: Stan Boring; Associate Director: George Watkins; Production Supervisor–Script: Janet Caldwell; Sound: David Patterson; Boom: Joe Clayton; Mix: Manhattan Sound; Mixer: Sol Tabachnik; Music Mixer: Don Wagner; Chief Gaffer: Robert Vee; Gaffer: George Mooradian; Assistant Cameraman: John Tackwood; Grips: Eddie Williams, Larry Robertson, Charles Garris; Set Design: John Finley; Makeup: William Gammon; Wardrobe: Mike Hayes; Stills: Bill Fibben; Casting: Kerm Kelly; Driver: C.V. Hall; Effects: Frank Jenkins; Titles: B & O Film Effects; Dream Sequences: Atlanta Regency Hyatt House; Songs: "Man Who Doesn't Know Where He's Going," Paul Jarvis; "Walking on Down to See My Jesus," Kathy Burdick; "Fault of Every Man," Paul Jarvis; "Hey Mister," Jay Jacobs; "Cripple Creek" (Banjo), Ron Jarvis; A Wilmac Intercontinental Production. Running Time: 101 minutes.

Cast: Bill McGaha (J.C. Masters); Hannibal Penney (David Little); Joanna Moore (Miriam Wages); Burr DeBenning (Dan Martin); Slim Pickens (Grady Caldwell); Pat Delaney (Kim McCool); Judie Frazier (Rachel Myers); Max Payne (Mr. Clean); Conrad Peavy (Hunter); Matthew Garth (Carlton Wages); Brenda Sutton (Neffie); Carol Hall (Shirley "The Saint"); Byron Warner (Disciple); Bob Corley (D.J. Nabors); Bud Allen (Beaver); Simone Griffith (Harriet "The Hare"); Bill Chapman (Foreman); Beverly Littles (Panama Red); Gracia Dean (M.Y. Bird); Mike Vann (Ben Wages); Steve Brown (Charles); Howard Lynch (Von Wheelie).

Atlantean industrial filmmaker Bill McGaha wrote, produced, directed and acted in *The Speed Lovers* (1968), a stock car drama starring real-life champion Fred Lorenzen. His next movie, *J.C.*, cast him as a benign Manson type. McGaha compared J.C. Masters and his group to the early nomadic Christians ... radicals of *their* time. Son of an evangelist, J.C. stood for *Jesus Christ*. His ideological duality was not unique considering the flip-side morality of self-proclaimed God fearers into earthly pleasures.

J.C. Masters tells his girl, dropout sociologist Kim McCool, how he and his black pal, David Little, were fired from a construction job when the boss caught them smoking pot. Under the influence of grass, J.C. has a cosmic vision of "a giant winking eye." J.C. tells the club of his revelation, wanting them to spread love out West. First, he wants to visit his hometown of Mason, Alabama, "...just to let them know that J.C. Masters is back."

The club causes quite a stir as they rumble into Mason. One spectator is J.C.'s old high school sweetheart, Rachel Myers. J.C. greets his sister Miriam, wife of gas station owner Carlton Wages. Deputy Dan Martin reports the presence of the club to Sheriff Grady Caldwell. Grady and Carlton are both offended by the sight of black David.

David goes into town to buy beer. Grady and Dan arrest David and give him the third-degree, trumping up a drug charge. J.C. offers to take the club out of town if David is released in his custody, but Grady won't cooperate.

J.C. plans to bust David out of jail. The others raise hell down main street to lure Grady and Dan out front. Grady wants restraint, but shotgun-armed citi-

J.C. (Bill McGaha) gives his last sermon.

zens open fire and Grady is injured. Rachel helps J.C. free David, who is shot by Dan. J.C. slugs Dan with one of his boots, strangling Dan. Mourning David, J.C. puts on his headband.

Back at the Wages' home, J.C. sends his surviving comrades away, ignoring Miriam's plea to go too. J.C. delivers a sermon to the hostile villagers. As he rides off, a gun blast sends him to his maker—the "eye." Rachel repeatedly screams, "Why?"

Almost as bad as an evil messiah is an inept messiah. If McGaha's roiling indulgences were based on that idea, the danger-baiting quotient of J.C.'s actions were a baring of his defects, not his nonconformist virtues. Knowing the character of the town, a smart J.C. would have bypassed Mason, but he had to show the local yokels what life was like outside their protective bubble. In most Cycle Buddy situations, one of the two friends is weaker in judgment. With J.C., the pals were equally suicidal. J.C. and David both helped to kill David. J.C. did it by his dumb decision to return to a place with a low cuture shock threshold, making himself and most of the other club members loud, boorish, inconsiderate intruders.

David sealed his doom by going where his goofy guru went and venturing into town alone. If minority reaction to J.C.'s club had been included, some brother or sister would have said or visually suggested to David what a fool he was (ever see a German helmet on a black guy's head?). David was truly little and his girl Neffie even less, the pair letting grandiloquent ofay Kim speak for them ("This woman is a *black* woman! And her man is a *black* man!") when she PC-ed a racist storekeeper.

Miriam and Rachel loved J.C. in different ways, doing no worse to themselves than catch a little proprietal heat. Devotion to David ultimately destroyed J.C.'s dream of "loving" everyone from Alabama to California. His martyristic try at "converting" the mob did nothing but put him eye to "eye" in God's kingdom.

McGaha let it be known from the start of *J.C.* that he craved a big grandstand. Instead of during J.C.'s interminable ride home, lest they would have cluttered the narcissistic establishing travel shots of J.C., the credits were inserted fifteen minutes into the film. Before the club left Atlanta, J.C. perused bad new headlines, recounted the loss of his job (symbolically carpentry) and tuned into the "eye" in a dream sequence photographed against the backdrop of the Atlanta Regency Hyatt House (the house of the Lord?). J.C. even wore a bike helmet similar to Wyatt's and in donning David's headband adopted his own crown of thorns.

The way he performed J.C., McGaha was like a wiggy, somewhat bathetic Dan Haggerty. Pat Delaney, the wife of *Hellcats* co-writer and *Outlaw Riders* director Tony Houston, was capable as Kim and Hannibal Penney was good as David. The finest, most unforced player was Joanna Moore, ex-wife of Ryan O'Neal and mother of Tatum and Griffin. Too a victim of serious dysfunctions, her drug habit resulted in trouble with the law. She died of cancer in 1998.

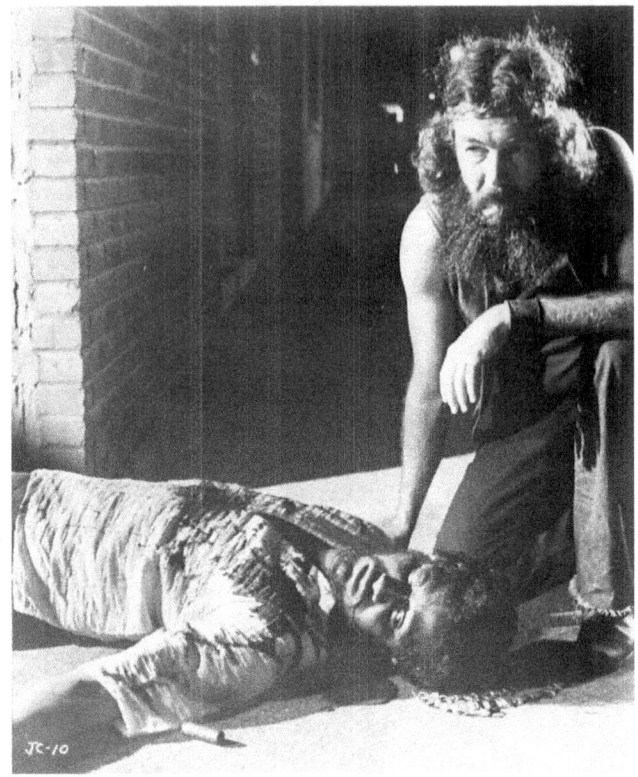

David (Hannibal Penney) is mourned by J.C. (Bill McGaha).

The grammatically flawed ads described J.C.'s club as comprising "broads, blacks and bikes." Since when are bikes people?

The Jesus Trip

EMCO 1971. Executive Producer: Saul Brandman; Producer: Joseph Feury; Director: Russ Mayberry; Screenplay: Richard Poston; Associate Producers: William Baker, Lisabeth Hush; Cinematography: Flemming Olsen; Film Editors: Peter Parasheles, David Berlatsky; Music: Bernardo Segall; Art Director: James Eric; Visual Design: David Berlatsky; Assistant to Producer: Lisabeth Hush; Production Manager: William Baker; Assistant Director–Assistant Film Editor: William Wilson; Key Grip: Leo Behar; Gaffer: John Murray; Sound Mixer: Art Names; Makeup: Dennis Marsh; Wardrobe: Hudson Costume Rental; Special Wardrobe: Tomboy of California; Second Unit Director: Robert Tessier; Production Assistant: Tod Spence; Script Supervisor: Peg Robert Smith; Special Effects: William Bailes; Second Unit Cameraman: David Worth; Sound Effects Editing: Edit-Rite, Inc.; Re-recording: Producers' Sound Service; Supervising Sound Editor: Gordon Daniel; Supervising Music Editor: Bob Simard; Optical Effects: Modern Film Effects; Title Song: Lyrics, Bryan Ryman, Sung by Lee Dresser; A Joseph Feury–Saul Brandman Production; DeLuxe Color. Running Time: 84 minutes.

Cast: Tippy a/k/a Elizabeth Walker (Sister Anna); Robert Porter (Waco); Billy Green Bush (Clay Tarboro); Diana Ivarson (Casey); Virgil Frye (Folsom); Carmen Argenziano (Pinole); Wally Strauss (Jasper); Hanna Hertelandy (Elder Nun); Bebe Louie (Dragon Lady); Jenny Hecht (Folsom's Girl); Frank Orsatti, Robert Tessier, Alan Gibbs (Vigilantes).

The Playmate of June 1955, Russ Meyer's second wife, Eve, had been his associate producer during and after the end of their marriage. Out of their divorce settlement, Eve acquired the distribution rights to all the films Russ had then made. She and David Baughn ran EMCO, which handled other movies. One of them was *The Jesus Trip*—a name not alluding to acid (even though some users have claimed to see Christ or thought they *were* him).

Eve Meyer's second involvement with a Biker, *The Jesus Trip* was directed by another Russ—Russ Mayberry. Despite the vigilante drive of a main character, this was no *Motor Psycho*. One supporting actress had done a bit part for Russ Meyer. Its heroine a professional virgin, *Jesus Trip* was a nunsploitation movie.

Waco, Pinole, Casey, Folsom, Jasper, Dragon Lady and Lola are dubiously detained at an Arizona-Mexico border station on their return to the States. Asked to pull over, they split. One cop shoots Waco in the side. Pinole spots a mystery helicopter trailing the group.

Avoiding state trooper Clay Tarboro's roadblock, the group nears a convent whose nuns are moving. Waco accosts one staying behind, novice Anna, telling her, "I need your help, sister." The other nun, older Sister Charlotte, asks Pinole, "What crime have you commited?" "Sister, we didn't do a damn thing," he answers. Found hidden in the bikes are packets of heroin—what the helicopter people are after.

Tarboro arrives at the convent alone, seeing a parked bike. Told to get rid of him, Anna claims it belongs to a priest. Tarboro is about to examine the bike when Pinole ambushes him. He is tied up and his car driven into the convent. Sister Charlotte is caught making a radio call to the police.

Anna and Tarboro are taken hostage to make the cops back off. Left on the road, Tarboro swears revenge. Anna wants to be a missionary. "Why don't you stay home and save me?" Waco asks. At first, Anna desires her freedom. A change of clothes is followed by a change of heart when she sees how close the group is. They head for the ruins of Pinole's deserted hometown.

When the "big bird" attacks, Pinole shoots the copter down. A dilapidated mission affords shelter.

Sent for supplies, Casey, Folsom and Jasper go to a bar. Folsom is too drunk to travel and they spend the night in a motel, where the trio are caught by Tarboro and his deputy bike pals. In a lonely spot, Casey, Folsom and Jasper are buried in sand up to their necks. Folsom cracks under torture, leading the posse to the village. Jasper and Casey dig themselves out. Folsom is dumped on the village road.

Tarboro grabs Anna by a water well, handcuffing her to a tree branch. Anna's screams alert the others in the mission.

The start of a bad trip.

Shooting begins. The group play dead using smeared ketchup. From atop a cross, Waco holds his gun on Tarboro. Freeing herself, Anna interrupts their brawl when she fires a rifle shot into the air. She tells Tarboro that she went with the group willingly. "We're not in the smack business," declares Waco, who proves it by burning the heroin in a fireplace. "I don't need a badge to solve my problems," says Tarboro—seemingly amenable to letting bygones be bygones.

Alone with each other, Waco and Anna turn to a fallen plaster Madonna lying on the floor. Anna warms to Waco's gesture of putting it back on its shelf. Suddenly, four shots ring out, killing Waco. Anna stands over his grave at sunset, unsure about tomorrow.

Pushing the humanization of Bikers in a direction tolerant of old-fashioned religion, *The Jesus Trip* also took the romance out of drug dealing. The unknowing mules of *Jesus Trip* included an escaped con (Folsom of course) and a dropout executive. These loosely allied nomads rode *rented* bikes. The real motorcycle "gang" was the Tarboro crew. Viewed in the abstract form of a propellered vulture, the helicopter was present mainly to help the Waco group understand their situation. The rental bikes helped to establish their frame.

Once convinced that spiritual challenges for her lay in Third World lands, Anna had less practical effect on the group than they had on her—their tight loyalty the spiritual element. Kept to meaningful expressions and kind words, the growing love between Waco and Anna posed no danger to her career chastity. Just as the crisis at hand had run its course, that affection had to reach some resolution. A fashionable knee-jerk cliché, *Easy Rider*'s assassination was probably the *only* ending to go with. Tarboro's phony goodbye was simply too suspect to be true.

Tippy Walker was one of the girls who made *The World of Henry Orient* (1964)

Tarboro (Billy Green Bush) is forced to pilot Pinole's (Carmen Argenziano) bike.

a nightmare for the Peter Sellers character. Elton in *Five Easy Pieces*, Billy Green Bush fathered Lindsay and Sidney, the twins on *Little House on the Prairie*. Virgil Frye, who joined Marlon Brando, Paul Newman and Tony Franciosa on the Gadsen, Alabama, freedom protest, had been the make-up man for *Easy Rider* and is the father of Soleil Moon.

Bob Tessier, one of the vigilantes, was second-unit director and appeared in *Jesus Trip*'s semi-remake *Outlaw Riders* on his usual side of the law ... the wrong side.

The Limit

Cannon/New Era Communications 1972. Alternate Title: *Speed Limit 65*. Producer-Director-Story: Yaphet Kotto; Screenplay: Sean Cameron; Associate Producer: Frank Roh; Cinematography: Fenton Hamilton; Film Editor: Norman Schwartz; Music: Wayne Henderson; Assistant to Producer: Douglas Forward; Production Coordinator: Kelly White; Camera Operators: Manny Whittaker, James Edwards; Camera Assistants: Franko Guerri, William Forte; Assistant Film Editor: Freeman Davies, Jr.; Sound Technician: Jack Reed; Script Supervisor: Patricia Motyka; Lighting Gaffer: George Rumales; Lighting Assistant: Carlton McMillan; Best Boy: Skip Troutman; Key Grips: William Raleigh, Bud Schindler; Coordinators: Gary Littlejohn, Troy Melton; Automobiles: Chrysler Automobiles courtesy of Chrysler Corp., BMW courtesy of Ocean View Motors, Santa Monica, California; Wardrobe: Mr. Kotto's wardrobe furnished by Gazebo, Beverly Hills; Hospital sequence made possible through the cooperation of Parkwood Community Hospital; Metrocolor. Running Time: 90 minutes.

Cast: Yaphet Kotto (Mark Johnson); Quinn Redeker (Jeff McMillan); Virgil Frye (Kenny); Corinne Cole (Judy); Ted Cassidy (Big Donnie); Pamela Jones (Margaret); Gary Littlejohn (Pete); Irene Forrest (Delores); Nancy Ashe (Waitress); John Bellan (Pickup Truck Driver); Frank Belt (Man in Restaurant); Ed Cambridge (Police Captain); Vic Canupe (Bartender); Bobby Clark (Man in Bar Fight); Douglas Forward (BMW Driver); Richard Hale (Man in Park); Stuart Hirschman (Messenger on Beach); Joyce Hutton (Girl in Park); Peaches Jones (Woman in Station Wagon); Richard Kennedy (Man in Bar Fight); Natascha Kotto (Carol Southern); Fred Krone (First Drunk); Buddy Pantsari (Gas Station Attendant); Jack Perkins (Second Drunk); Frank Roh (John Woods / Mr. America); John Roh (Boy with Kite); Diane Regis (First Virgin Girlfriend); Nina Tresoff (Second Virgin Girlfriend).

Yaphet Kotto, who declined to play Shaft, and Christopher St. John, who took the part of Shaft's militant friend Ben Buford, were both kin to cops. St. John was the brother of one and Kotto was the nephew of an officer slain in the line of duty. Both actors wrote, directed (Kotto producing his film), and starred in movies about black lawmen. Earlier in 1972, there was St. John's surreal, depressing *Top of the Heap*, about George Latimer, an unhappy Washington, D.C., patrolman who fantasized himself as a jungle warrior and an Afro-naut. *Top of the Heap* did fair box-office, but the dying Fanfare Corporation failed to match in Blaxploitation the success it had known with Bikers (St. John blamed Joe Solomon for wrong-headed editing changes on his work).

The Limit, formerly *Speed Limit 65*, was made by Yaphet Kotto's New Era Communications, created to boost minority hiring in Hollywood. Both a Blaxploiter and a Biker, *The Limit* was the film Fanfare should have released and would have allowed Solomon's sinking empire to go out with a black Biker to its credit.

Mark Johnson can make errant drivers quake in their shoes just by walking in their direction. His white partner, Jeff McMillan, and girlfriend Margaret know another Mark the public doesn't see ... until Mark encounters the Virgins motorcycle club. Leader Big Donnie is intrigued when Mark shows concern for his pregnant girl Judy. Mark feels Judy deserves a more stable life and should stay off bikes until after the baby is born. Donnie's lieutenant, Kenny, hates Mark for his authority and would like to take over the gang. Donnie takes Mark's no-riding advice to heart, wanting Judy to do so. He openly admits that he wants to go straight.

Donnie doesn't know how to go about settling down. For more advice, he badgers Mark endlessly by phone and in person.

Believing a display of power will enable him to replace Donnie, Kenny goes with some Virgins to Mark's place to beat up Mark. Mark is absent and Kenny does his number on Margaret. Leaving her in a state that maddens Mark, Kenny offers Judy a ride on his hog. Foolishly, she climbs aboard. Kenny races at top speed, colliding with a car. The accident seriously injures Judy, threatening the baby too.

On his own bike, Mark sees Kenny escaping. Mark's frenzied pursuit is blocked by another auto and his bike is wrecked. A short way up ahead, Kenny takes a second spill and his bike is damaged. Mark chases Kenny on foot. Several times, they brawl. Each time, Kenny escapes. Mark finally catches Kenny, who slashes his throat with a knife, but Mark manages to throttle Kenny and cuff one of Kenny's hands to his wrist.

At Parkwood Community Hospital, Mark clings precariously to life. A cardiologist's labors are rewarded when a nurse says Mark will live. Mark returns to duty.

Not the beaten-down, paranoid George Latimer, Mark refrigerated his potentially hot emotions in the benefit of

The black cop who went the limit with the storm-troopers of hell's highway.

Ad for the film *The Limit*.

personal sanity and job expedience. The living thing Judy carried inside her brought out a spot of rare on-duty warmth. Feeling a part of Mark normally reserved for friends, Donnie found a practical incentive for losing his Virgin-ity. Rigid cop-hater Kenny reacted to Mark the badge, needing to prove himself by knocking down a monolith.

A hopeful fountain of wisdom for

guidance-hungry Donnie, Mark had *two* stalkers working at cross-purposes. No precision heat-seeking missile, Kenny expended his campaign brawn on substitute Margaret—unleashing on his own ass ballistic Mark. Entitled by his knife wound to kill Kenny if only on injury reflex, Mark took the high vigilante road. For his superhuman restraint, Mark was owed survival.

Yaphet Kotto continued tracking bad guys in other cop roles, doing it weekly as Det. Al Giardella on *Homicide: Life on the Street*. Lurch on *The Addams Family*, towering Ted Cassidy made Donnie's hog look like a kid's bicycle under his monstrous frame. His size and Judy's swollen belly made Donnie and Judy a peculiar bike couple. Also a writer, Cassidy died of a heart ailment in 1979.

Quinn Redeker, who played Jeff, used to make film shorts and helped write one of the most monumental pictures of the late seventies, *The Deer Hunter* (1978).

The Loners

Fanfare 1972. Executive Producer: Sam Katzman; Producer: Jerry a/k/a Jerome Katzman; Director: Sutton Rolley; Screenplay: John Lawrence, Barry Sandler; Story: John Lawrence; Cinematography: Irving Lippman; Film Editor: John Woetz; Music: Fred Karger; Production Manager: Robert Stone; Assistant Director: Gary Grillo; Script Supervisor: Ray Quiroz; Makeup: Douglas Kelly; Sound Effects: Marvin Kerner; Post-Production Supervisor: William Martin; Titles: Metro-Goldwyn-Mayer, Inc., Metrocolor, A Four Leaf Production in association with Cinemobile Systems, Inc. Running Time: 80 minutes.

Cast: Dean Stockwell (Stein); Pat Stich (Julio); Todd Susman (Alan); Scott Brady (Hearn); Gloria Grahame (Annabelle); Alex Dreier (Chief Peters); Tim Rooney (Howie); Ward Wood (Sheriff); Hortense Petra (Mrs. Anderson); Richard O'Brien (Driver); Hal Jon Norman (Father); Duane Grey (Man in Diner); Jean Dorl (Woman in Diner); Stuart Nisbet (Bridegroom); Larry O'Leno (Policeman).

Following *The Glory Stompers* and *Free Grass*, John Lawrence planned another romantic opus called *Juliet and Stein*. Delayed in production for nearly three years, the script was revised by him and Barry Sandler and finally brought to the screen by producer Jerome Katzman and his executive dad, the legendary Sam Katzman. Sam wanted to get out of exploitation and named his new company Four Leaf, as in turning over a new leaf ... but the profitability of old clover cast its corrupting aroma. Also, Sam's serious youth drama *Angel, Angel, Down We Go* (1969) had plunged to earth so resoundingly that its distributor, A.I.P., re-cut and renamed it *Cult of the Damned* to make it seem like a Manson movie.

Juliet and Stein became *The Loners*, a co-production between Four Leaf and Cinemobile Systems Inc. Like the Seymour Robbie–helmed *C.C. and Company*, it was directed by a TV vet, Sutton Rolley. Fanfare picked up *The Loners*, resulting in an even stranger alliance ... a Sam Katzman–backed film handled by Joe Solomon.

On a New Mexico highway, a driver hails down Sgt. Joe Hearn and his son-in-law partner Kelly to tell them how he was forced off the road. In what really happened, Stein was en route to River Park to join a motocross race when the driver viciously tailgated him. Stein threw a rock, breaking the man's windshield. The biased story of the driver is believed.

Hearn and Kelly chase Stein to an abandoned mine, where a huge pit swallows their car. Kelly is killed. Stein turns back to view the accident and Hearn's crazed shooting scares him away.

In River Park, Stein joins his halfwit friend Alan. At home, young Annabelle Carter Jr. is being hassled by her shrewish mother. She meets Stein and Alan at a rock concert she attends with her boyfriend, Howie Rudd. After Stein gets into a fight with Howie, Annabelle splits with him and Alan. Stein renames Annabelle Julio after an old girlfriend.

Stein, Julio and Alan break into a closed general store. The owner surprises Stein and Alan. To keep him from shooting them, Julio bashes a shovel over the owner's head, killing him. Later, they surprise a honeymooning couple having outdoor sex and take their wedding clothes.

So he can get Stein, Hearn turns to fascistic Chief Peters for help. Acting on a description of Julio, the police trace her, Stein and Alan to a motel. Stein and Julio escape by crashing through a window on Stein's bike. The trio embarrasses Peters by robbing a country club political rally for him. While they are spending the night in a junkyard, Julio has a frightening vision of death.

When Alan goes to a diner to buy food, a flirtatious wife winks at him. Alan requites the wink. When the woman's jealous husband attacks him, panicky Alan shoots up the place, leaving some people injured and dead. Hiding in a mission, Stein and Julio put on the stolen wedding clothes so monkishly garbed Alan can "marry" them in mock ceremony. Stein hopes his father, a retired crop-duster, will fly them to Brazil in his plane. Using stolen dynamite, Stein, Julio and Alan blast their way around a police roadblock.

Once Stein, Julio and Alan reach Stein's Indian hometown of Garatse, a cop spots them. The elder Stein, who has been estranged from his son for years, cannot help because his hands are severely crippled by arthritis and he sold his plane. The police surround Garatse. Sighting their cars, Alan tries to warn Stein and Julio, who hear the shots that kill him. Hand in hand, they flee to Stein's bike. Stein loudly proclaims his innocence—but he and Julio are mercilessly cut down.

Part-Navajo, part-Irish, Stein must have had some Yiddish blood to explain his name. If this was *Rebel Without a Cause*, his name would have been Jim Stark since the trouble circumstances of *Rebel* and *The Loners* both began with car wreck disasters each of them was blamed for. Plato counterpart Alan was introduced next, then topless bedroom window figure Annabelle, whose own name was odd since so few females are named after their mothers (Nancy Sinatra is one).

Meant to be Shakespearean in its misfortune, *The Loners* missed on the point of young love being impeded by the class differences between rival families. Stein and Julio had walked out on their respective relatives *before* coming together. And with Alan making them part of a trio, it wasn't about just two people. Stein thought so much of his last girl that he named Annabelle after her—but why masculine-sounding Julio instead of Julia or the more symbolically fitting Juliet? The world was threatening to this couple because they were on the Wanted List ... no one outside the three knowing or caring that they were in love. Their "marriage" was just as much secret.

The Loners had more of a sense of being like *Bonnie and Clyde* than it was another *Easy Rider* swipe. Even the *Jesus Trip* fugitives were pleasure riders. Stein, Julio and Alan were put in motion by fear beginning with Stein's run-in with Hearn. Dying was only about when.

Stein was Dean Stockwell. Julio was Pat Stich, the white student ceremoniously

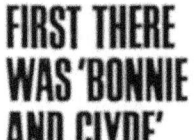

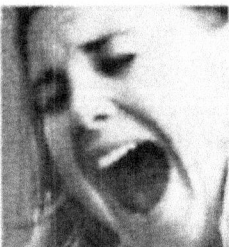

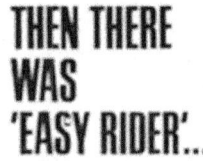

A movie poster for the movie *The Loners.*

stripped of her clothes by a gang of black girls in *Halls of Anger* (1970). Alan was Todd Susman, once a script reader at A.I.P. for sixty dollars a week. A faded Gloria Grahame was now part of the schlock scene which Scott Brady had been ensconced in for some time. Alex Dreier was a former radio newscaster.

The Loners was Sam Katzman's last film. Survived by son Jerry and actress wife Hortense Petra, Mrs. Anderson of *The Loners*, he died in 1973.

John Lawrence then produced and directed a psuedo–Biker psycho thriller originally called *The Savage Slaying of Sara Ridelander*. Adam West was sought for the role of Sara's attorney husband Dick and Burt Ward for Harvey, the maniac Dick hired to kill Sara. The roles went instead to Tom Drake and Joseph Turkel. *Savage Abduction* was the most common title (others were *Numbered Days* and *Cycle Psycho*) of Lawrence's sickest, most unromantic story.

The Losers

Fanfare 1970. Producer: Joe Solomon; Director: Jack Starrett; Screenplay: Alan Caillou; Associate Producer–Production Supervisor: Vincente Nayve; Cinematography: Nonong Rasca; Film Editors: James Moore, Richard Brockway; Music: Stu Phillips; Camera Operator: Erno Santos; Sound Mixer: Levy Principe; Assistant Director: Herman Robles; Casting Director: Pearl Kempton; Script Supervisor: Tom Moore; Boom Man: Tiny Corpuz; Cable Man: Jose Nides, Jr.; Key Grip: Mario Carnona; Makeup: Ricardo Vallamin; Wardrobe: Vicente Cabrera; Hair Stylist: Carmelita Sloson; Gaffer: Julian Baltanado; Property Master: Eduardo Urbano; Special Effects: Roger George & Joe Zoomar; Chief Armory Dept: Maj. Lopencino Juban; Bike Stunts: Gary McLarty, Paul Nuckles; Re-Recording: Producers Sound Service; Post-Production: Synchrofilm, Inc.; Sound Effects: Edit-Rite, Inc.; Titles: Cinefx/Phil Norman; Songs: "The Losers" written by Stu Phillips, sung by Clover Ann Courtney, "Sweet Little Lady" written by Stu Phillips, Bob Storn. Eastmancolor. Running Time: 96 minutes.

Cast: William Smith (Link); Bernie Hamilton (Capt. Jackson); Adam Roarke (Duke); Houston Savage (Dirty Denny); Gene Cornelius (Speed); Paul Koslo (Limpy); John Garwood (Sgt. Winston); Daniel Kemp (Maj. Thomas); Ana Korita (Kim Sue); Lillian Margarego (Suriya); Paraluman (Mama-San); Paul Nuckles (Kowalski); Ronnie Ross (Lt. Hayworth); Armando Locero (Screw); Fran Dihn Hy (Charlie); Vic Diaz (Diem-Nuz); Alan Caillou (Albanian); Paquito Salcedo (Tac Houn); Von Deming (Shillick); Herman Robles (Inspector); Jack Starrett (Chet Davis); Monica Phillips (Negro Baby).

In 1967, Sonny Barger had sent a telegram to Washington volunteering the services of the Hell's Angels for special combat duty in Vietnam. The offer wasn't accepted, so the Angels had to console themselves with harassing anti-war demonstrators.

Outside of several early-in-the-conflict quickies and John Wayne's embarrassing Green Berets movie tribute, the war belonged to documentary films and the nightly news. The last popular World War II epic, Robert Aldrich's *The Dirty Dozen* (1967), had made heroes out of Army stockade misfits and showed the depths of desperation to which the government would try to accomplish an urgent mission.

Written by Alan Caillou, *Nam's Angels* was a Fanfare property that visited the current war during the escalated protests. Representative of the Nixon administration was presidential advisor Chet Davis, once an anti-biker politico in the Thomas Lynch mold. The story was less "Us vs.

Them" between Americans and Asians than it was the Generation Gap fought on the soil of the Killing Fields. The main sparrers were Davis and Link Thomas, leader of another Fanfare bike gang called the Devil's Advocates (same club logo from *Run, Angel, Run*). There was supposed to be grim irony in the fact that those who didn't fit Davis' idea of acceptable Americans were recruited to save a staunch enemy of liberalism.

Robert Aldrich, meanwhile, was in the Philippines making his own anti-war film, *Too Late the Hero* (1970), safely set in World War II. Most of the same crew worked under the direction of Jack Starrett for *The Losers*—a name Joe Solomon felt would appeal to kids and sounded far less patriotic. Starrett also played Davis.

In an idyllic Vietnamese hamlet, natives go about their daily business while some G.I.s relax. From an ox cart Trojan horse, Charley opens fire, cutting the defenseless men down. More G.I.s storm out of a hut, blasting the assassins. One man nearly kills an innocent, cowering peasant girl. Moved by her tears, he lowers his rifle in shame and weeps.

Later, the enemy ambushes an Army convoy led by Sgt. John Winston. A slain grunt is avenged by his hurled grenade. "Get that truck moving!" Winston screams, as he jumps aboard the most important vehicle. It leaves a muddy road strewn with corpses.

At a nearby command post, the truck's human cargo climbs out of the back: Link, Duke, Dirty Denny, Speed and Limpy. Duke and Denny are vets. Neither Winston or the other soldiers know what to make of them. A Jeep brings Link's brother, Maj. Matt Thomas, who conceived the C.I.A.-sponsored mission. Thomas greets Link. "Oh," laughs Link, "I forgot to salute." Duke bumps into Capt. Lincoln Jackson, the officer who will be giving the orders. In a tent, Thomas briefs the team over a model of Dang Huk, the neutral zone Cambodian border village where Chet Davis is being held. "Speed's all ya got goin' for ya," says Thomas. "Fast in—out faster!" "We'll get 'im," determines Link ... nursing a personal agenda.

Jackson and Winston will escort the team to their headquarters in the "safe" city of Loc Sai. To be made weapons within three days, their bikes are Yamahas. "It's a broad's bike!" yelps Limpy, reeling from one. Privately, Thomas tells Link he knows how Link feels about Davis, but wants him back safely. Link promises to do his part.

On the scenic highway to Loc Sai, Link, Duke, Denny, Speed and Limpy vex Jackson by breaking out of formation. The Loc Sai populace immediately takes notice of these strange Americans who carry on rowdily in their marketplace. Duke heads for the jungle to see someone.

Going to Mama-San's brothel in search of Denny, Jackson sees some street urchins stripping his bike. In an opium den, Jackson glimpses the Albanian, an unsavory black marketer. Serviced by three topless girls, Denny says to Jackson, "Welcome to my place." Mama-San's used to be his until his dishonorable discharge. Jackson tells Denny about his bike. Freaking out, Denny chases the kids, strikes one, hits his angry mother and battles half the neighborhood until Jackson routs Denny's attackers. "You're not such a bad spook after all," Denny tells Jackson—who returns the racist compliment with a slap.

Conversion of the bikes will be done at the garage of a trusted mechanic, Diem-Nuz. "If you're waitin's on the bikes, man, you're waitin' up," Link tells Jackson. "Chet Davis is waitin'," says Jackson. "I'm glad I'm not in his boots." "Let me tell ya somethin' about Chet Davis and his boots," rages Link. "He uses those boots for stompin' on people like you and me. I guess you wouldn't know about that,

Cambodia is about to be invaded by (left to right): Limpy (Paul Koslo), Duke (Adam Roarke), Link (William Smith), and Speed (Gene Cornelius).

would you captain? Those bars beat you out, don't they?" "That's right," sardonically replies Jackson. "They make you colorless." "You really believe that, man?" questions Link. "Yeah, man," declares straight-faced Jackson. "I believe it."

Duke reaches Tac Houn's farm, where his girl, Suriya, has been staying. Duke rushes to Suriya, who hears his call, and the passionate lovers meet each other halfway. Duke wants to take Suriya back to the States tomorrow, but she must wait a few days for the return of her soldier brother.

At Mama-San's, Denny cheats her out of a gambling sum and she swears to fix him. On the discothèque dance floor, Limpy is drawn to a pretty hostess smiling at him from her table. Instantly in deep like, they dance gaze to gaze and go up to her room. After sex, they make introductions. She is Kim Sue, mother of a crying black infant. Her father, Kim Sue wistfully remembers, was "A good man ... a good officer—only he don't need me no more ... so, here I am." Limpy empathizes with Kim Sue. Gently enfolding Kim Sue and the baby in his arms, he starts a "family."

Mama-San calls in the M.P.s who demand the money Denny "stole" from her. Wildly brandishing a sawed-off shotgun, Denny wreaks havoc as Winston enters. Speed and Limpy get caught up in the bedlam. Limpy runs outside, but the M.P.'s Kim Sue warns Limpy of catch him. Denny is billyclubbed into submission.

Denny, Speed and Limpy are jailed on charges that carry seven years maximum. They are dropped in return for full cooperation with Jackson.

Once the bikes are finished, the team prepares to ride back to the command post in a truck. Limpy exasperates Link by bringing Kim Sue and her baby. Seeing the love Limpy has for them, Link manages a smile of approval. Jackson pays off Diem-Nuz. Duke jumps ship in the middle of the road, promising to catch up.

At the command post, Link covers for Duke. He arrives with Suriya and her brother. Kim Sue has a brief, painful reunion with her ex-lover ... Jackson. Turning to Limpy, holding his daughter, Jackson asks Kim Sue, "Is that your man now?" They exchange muted goodbyes. Link shows Thomas the battle bikes—the most spectacular hog wagon Speed dubs "The Gook Flattener." Duke tells Suriya about his decision to desert. "It's just a question of loyalty. And if so, to whom?"

The next morning, Duke and Suriya prepare to leave. Link tries to catch them. Jackson says to Denny, "He'll be here—right?" Crossing a booby-trapped bridge, Duke and Suriya are thrown into the water. Dazed Duke carries injured Suriya to shore, looking up into the squinted eyes of merciless Cong who machine-gun them.

The bodies are brought back to the command post. "Now why the hell would he want to do a stupid thing like that?" wonders Thomas. "I guess he only wanted to live a little," assumes Link.

At 4:55 a.m., Link, Denny, Speed and Limpy start out. For cover, the Army launches a mock battle. Limpy crashes the hog wagon through the front gate of Dang Huk, detonating a fuel dump. One soldier knocks Denny off his bike. Denny shoots him, but is pinned down by gunfire from a rooftop rifleman. Link tears up the roof, lobbing a saddlebag grenade. Scrambling for his bike, Denny is cornered and executed where he stands.

Speed and Limpy are captured. Link bursts into the hut holding startled Davis, who tries to run away. Link tackles Davis who, in contemptuous recognition, says, "You stupid bastard." Link is restrained and taken along with Davis, Speed and Limpy to a prison hut.

Locked up with his would-be rescuers, Davis frantically demands release until Link assaults him. "Still an animal," accuses Davis, who convicted Link of alleged rape. "If somebody's different," con-

Dang Huk troops take Speed (Gene Cornelius).

demns Link, "you squash 'em or you turn your back on 'em or you kill 'em!" "Every newspaper in the world," predicts Davis, "is gonna read something like this: 'Three Doped-Up Freaked Out Motorcycle Tramps Tried to Fight the Red Chinese Army.' Isn't that a little bit ridiculous?" "They started as five," informs Link, "and you ain't worth a pimple on their ass!" Davis slaps him. Davis didn't just happen into captivity because he has been negotiating with the Reds to get them out of Cambodia. "Now," Davis asks acidly, "Is there some other way you would like to deprecate the United States of America and its representative—or maybe you'd like to hit me again?"

The Albanian enters wearing a Red uniform, bringing cigarettes for Davis and "something stronger" for Link, Speed and Limpy. "We have a long trip tomorrow," he says. "Have you ever been to Red China before, Mister Davis?"

To lure the Albanian and the guards, Link, Speed and Limpy fake a noisy group high. Link stabs the Albanian while Speed kills his companion and Limpy thrusts a sharpened bamboo pole into a guard outside. Davis is forced to join Limpy. As the Americans crash out, the other guards rally.

Across the border, the Army hears Dang Huk gunfire and mobilizes swiftly. Falling off his bike, Speed hides in the jungle. A barbed wire fence overturns the hog wagon, throwing Davis and trapping Limpy. Jackson and Winston engage enemy troops while Thomas orders a tank cover barrage. Link holds dying Limpy, telling Davis to help, but sniveling, spiteful Davis cries, "I hope they kill you!" Jackson tries to effect a one-man rescue—but dies in an explosion.

Link chases Davis and collars him before bullets spray his back. Suddenly, knife-armed Speed confronts Davis. "I'm gonna cut your guts out!" In mortal flight, Davis beseeches Winston, "Shoot! Shoot!" Winston shoots Speed. In remorse, he chucks his rifle.

Thomas bends over dead Link to shut his eyes. "Well, Major," sneers Davis, "you did something right. Now get me back to Washington so I can straighten out this mess." Thomas glares at him.

Since the high echelons were to blame for everything, the G.I.s were treated with a modicum of understanding—for they too were losers. The most unfortunate characters carried some ethnic outcast status. Despite his rank, Jackson was a part of the black oppressed who made excellent cannon fodder. Duke and Limpy were gang anomalies because their affections for Suriya and Kim Sue evinced longings for sexual commitment. The women were marked because they were Gooks and Kim Sue's Amerasian bastard was the baggage of racial complications. Jackson was the dark corner of a romantic triangle, having contributed to a ready-made family he had no place in.

Link's vendetta against Davis should have disqualified him from the mission as it was known why he was so eager to find the man who railroaded him into jail. Denny returned to Nam for profit. Only the profiteers were real winners.

Politically, the big pay-off was Link and Davis locking horns over their violently opposite standards. Nationally chauvinistic, cravenly deferent to his captors, Davis caused unnecessary death through his cowardice and malice—then turned around sarcastically to thank the Army for its unorthodoxy.

Unusual spectacle was automatically built into the storyline. Even if Yamahas were beneath their taste, the gang lost none of its home-cultivated bravado and penchant for destruction. Their looks and demeanor added to the surrealism of a primitive culture living off the fringes of Yankee consumerism. It was only a few steps from an outdoor New Year's pageant to go-go dancing Vietnamese girls or from the opium den to grass.

The Gook Flattener was christened in publicity as Leapin' Lena. Built on location, it boasted Volkswagen power, machine guns, rocket launchers and quarter-inch armor plating. Printed on one plate was an incongruous white peace sign. Also armored, the other bikes had detachable nine-millimeter Swedish machine guns and grenade pouches that released the unpinned grenades when they were pulled out. Battle conditions required regulation safety helmets (no German helmets in a place where everything from dope to girls was for the buying). As if to bring their wearers luck, Limpy painted three of the helmets in wild psychedelic schemes. Baddest ass Denny wore a dark helmet.

To extract the most war gore, Jack Starrett used Peckinpah-style slow-mo and generous squib squirting. *Two* bloody battles occurred before the main title—the effect to acclimate one to where death rattles were as common as breathing. Other than a few tricky *Run, Angel, Run*–ish shots, Starrett didn't try to make the stock Yamahas look more than what they actually were. Some combat shots were lensed from another special bike by a cinematographer wearing a fifteen-pound camera helmet.

During the third week of the six-week production, the cast learned that Joe Solomon was holding back their money. Bill Smith encouraged a strike from the location site and their agency came through with the funds.

In the Philippines, Smith maintained, lived some of the greatest Biker fans. A few may have been souvenir hunters. After *The Losers* wrapped, Leapin' Lena (did anyone get its peace sign?) was stolen!

Playing a leader figure in Link prepared Bill Smith for his most typical Biker roles. Adam Roarke, an old hand at leading, seemed very comfortable in a softer role as Duke. Paul Koslo, a great find among lowlife specialist actors of the seventies, was refreshingly different as Limpy. Gene Cornelius was an antic one-dimensional as Speed.

The animal one-dimensional Denny was real-life Vietnam vet Houston Savage. Born Giuseppe DeBlasio, he was an engineering graduate of the University of West Virginia who pro footballed with the San Francisco Forty-Niners. Savage joined the Green Berets. Attached to the One Hundred First Airborne Division in Vietnam, he won the Congressional Medal of Honor in 1965. After his discharge, he was an engineer for the Aerojet General Company in Sacramento for five years.

Bernie Hamilton was a filmic credit to his race in *One Potato, Two Potato* (1964) as Frank, the black half of a mixed couple. This time playing a former partner of such a union that ended, Hamilton imbued Capt. Jackson with a quiet dignity that stood up to war but cracked when he was reminded of lost love.

John Garwood and Dan Kemp were solid in the smaller roles of Winston and Thomas. Jack Starrett, more vulnerable here than in any of his other parts, scathingly etched the personality of a Capitol Hill creep who belonged in the Nixon White House.

Bill Smith's last Biker with heart as well as muscle, *The Losers* was no popularity poll winner. It was accused of celebrating the violence it condemned—a common criticism leveled at *Born Losers*—and some found the concept of motorcycle guerrilla fighters as implausible. Even Ed "Big Daddy" Roth took an editorial swipe at *The Losers*, comparing it unfavorably to *Easy Rider*. At the New Jersey premiere of *The Losers*, Bill Smith fought with some bikers who accused Link of being a "sell out." Five more outlaws in a bar attacked the martial arts–trained Smith, who injured three.

Smith's Biker roles so endeared him to the Filipinos that he made a number of bike films in that country. Paul Koslo was able to get a little iconography value from the Limpy role on *Crazy Like a Fox* as an outlaw who uttered the "broad's bike" line.

Jack Starrett became much in demand for directing action features. Each of the first films with the Blaxploitation characters Slaughter and Cleopatra Jones were among them. So was the final Buford Pusser story. Starrett and Joe Solomon renewed ties on the last movie Joe Solomon produced, *A Small Town in Texas* (1976). Moving into TV, Starrett directed episodes of *Starsky and Hutch*, where Bernie Hamilton played Capt. Dobey. He continued to act, playing the brutal Deputy Galt—a recollection of his *Born Losers* lawman Fred—in *First Blood* (1982) and took the first lead in *Nightwish* (1989) before his death from kidney failure the year it was released.

Not only did Starrett and *Nightwish* co-star Bob Tessier die early, so did Adam Roarke, whom Frank Perry cast as Carter, a director of Bikers, in *Play It as It Lays* (1972) after seeing Roarke in *Hell's Angels on Wheels*. Roarke teamed with Peter Fonda in *Dirty Mary, Crazy Larry* (1973), done before Jack Starrett directed Fonda's *Race with the Devil* (1975). Roarke did Dick Rush's *The Stunt Man* (1980), featuring John Garwood and Chuck Bail, and moved to Texas. He taught drama and co-directed *Trespass* (1983) before a heart attack took him in 1996.

During his time on *The Losers*, John Garwood thought up the story of *A Taste of Hell* (1973), the Garwood production co-starring William Smith. Co-director Basil Bradbury had been the associate producer of *Dragstrip Riot*, whose editor, John Bushelman, worked on *Violent Zone* (1988), produced and directed by Garwood.

A 1988 "remake" of *The Losers* was filmed using a variation of its original name. Done by Filipino director Cirio Santiago and set in the Johnson era, *Nam Angels* was about four Angels suckered into a mission to rescue some M.I.A.s. Unflattered by *Nam Angels*, the Hell's Angels tried to sue the producers, claiming they were misrepresented. Joe Solomon once considered doing a legitimate remake of *The Losers* and Quentin Tarantino included footage of the original in *Pulp Fiction* (1994).

The Mini-Skirt Mob

American International 1968. Producer-Director: Maury Dexter; Screenplay: James Gordon White; Associate Producer: Hank Tani; Cinematography: Arch R. Dalzell; Film Editor: Sidney Levin; Music Supervision: Al Simms; Music: Les Baxter; Production Supervisor–Assistant Director: Jack Voglin; Assistant Producer: Ted Berkeley; Script Supervisor: Bonnie Prendergast; Men's Wardrobe: Dick Bruno; Women's Wardrobe: Sharon Thober; Chief Electrician: Lloyd L. Garnell; Markep: Ted Coodley; Hair Stylist: Wava Green; Sound: Bard Trask; Sound Facilities: Ryder Sound Service; Title Song: Lyrics; Guy Hemric, Music; Valjean Johns, Sung by; Patty McCormick; A Maury Dexter Production; Perfect Color. Running Time: 82 minutes.

Cast: Jeremy Slate (Lon); Diane McBain (Shayne); Sherry Jackson (Connie); Patty McCormick (Edie); Ross Hagen (Jeff); Harry Dean Stanton (Spook); Ronnie Rondell (L.G.); Barbro Hedström (Bea); Saundra Marshall (Fran); Steve Balats (Hank); Robert Shelton (Carl).

All of Maury Dexter's A.I.P. programmers except *Maryjane* (1968) were

Connie (Sherry Jackson) feels the hostile hands of Shayne (Diane McBain).

done in Tucson. One was *The Mini-Skirt Mob*. Dexter couldn't think of any other way to exploit the mini-skirt than by putting such impractical but photogenic road apparel on female bikers. Accompanied by three male rodeo bums, the Mini-Skirts (what they actually called themselves) did no serious wrong until the leader, Shayne, sought revenge on her ex-beau Jeff Logan, who dumped Shayne to marry Connie, a shy bank teller.

Jeff and Connie are parked by a peaceful lake, ready to make love as man and wife in their trailer when unexpected revelers show for a wild shivaree. Among Jeff's former rodeo buddies are Lon, Spook and L.G., the companions of Shayne, her sister Edie, Fran and Bea. Jeff agrees to have one drink with romantically persistent Shayne, who wonders why he picked Connie. "Does she own that bank you found her working in? You need a woman, Jeff ... not a ... mouse." The party moves to another spot while Jeff and Connie get back to where they were so rudely interrupted.

The next morning, Shayne comes back with her "grievance committee." Jeff and Lon mix it as Shayne viciously musses up Connie. Slugged by Lon, Jeff wakes up and gets his rifle, forcing the gang to split.

Down the highway, the gang chases Jeff and Connie's convertible. When the trailer jackknifes on the next turn, L.G. is knocked off the road. Unaware of this, Jeff and Connie keep going. Three Boy Scouts see the gang standing over L.G.'s body. Shayne blames Jeff and Connie for the accident.

Jeff and Connie park in open desert. While he surveys it, she is accosted in the trailer by Lon and Spook. Jeff comes back to find Connie tied up and the rifle stolen. The car's tires are slashed. While the police investigate L.G.'s death, the Boys Scouts come forward.

Lon (Jeremy Slate) takes aim at distant Jeff (Ross Hagen) and Connie (Sherry Jackson) as Shayne (Diane McBain) watches approvingly.

Shayne tells Lon and Edie a gruesome story about a snakehouse reptile that devoured a live rodent. "Ever see a snake eat? He swallows his prey alive and whole—but not all at once—just a little bit at a time. He has to dislocate his jaw so he can eat it. And that mouse ... he just cries and cries all the way down." Jeff turns up the trailer's propane gas, pushing the trailer away from the car before Lon fires a shot at him from a high perch.

Jeff is converting the trailer stove into a makeshift flamethrower to fry anyone who enters. Edie tries to coax Lon into a ride to get him away from there, but Shayne still controls him. Edie attempts to seduce Spook in order to grab the rifle so she can return it to Jeff and split. Unconvinced that Shayne is using him, Lon overpowers Edie.

Connie tells Jeff about a restaurant waiter she met as a child. He seemed so debonair—until she saw his brown socks. "Brown socks with black pants. Is that you, Jeff? Are you that waiter? What are you *really* like underneath?" Jealous of the allure Shayne once held, Connie wonders, "How was she, Jeff? Was she better than me?" Straight out, she asks, "Did you love her?" Jeff denies that he did, insisting, "Rodeo people are no different than any others. They're good ones, bad ones—just like in your fancy restaurant!"

Spook guards hog-tied Edie, who cuts her hands free, slugs Spook and takes the rifle, telling Jeff and Connie about L.G. Jeff and Connie sneak out the back of the trailer while Edie impersonates Connie. Lon wonders if Shayne really is taking advantage of him to reclaim Jeff. "I don't want Jeff back," she giddily explains. "I just want to make him and that little bank teller squirm." Lon tries to force himself on Shayne before Spook alerts them to Edie's escape.

Taken in by Edie's deception, Lon

and Spook throw beer bottle molotovs at the trailer as she fires rifle shots from a window. One explodes the propane. Edie runs out of the burning trailer on fire and drops dead. Discovering who actually died, Spook tries to tell Shayne, "We didn't know … we just didn't know!" Shayne screams at Len, "You killed her!" Shayne is more determined than ever to get Jeff and Connie, but Spook, Fran and Bea want out and leave.

Jeff and Connie reach a dirt road where Jeff waves at a pickup driver who callously races by. A patrolman running down leads on L.G.'s death stops Spook, Fran and Bea.

Shayne chases Connie toward a cliff while Lon pursues Jeff through brush. With a heavy stick, Jeff breaks Lon's neck. Shayne corners Connie by the edge of the cliff, but her back wheel slips on the crumbling edge. Tumbling over the side, Shayne clings to the precipice for dear life. Connie extends a helping hand—but when overjoyed Shayne sees Jeff coming, Connie calmly loosens her grip and lets Shayne fall.

Maury Dexter absurdly, yet dramatically, perverted both the biker and rodeo cultures. The Mini-Skirts first appeared in a rodeo parade on horseback and in a remarkable jump-cut, Lon's stirruped boot became the same foot starting up his bike. Dexter could only trust Shayne to be a menacing Mini-Skirt, making the guys dangerous, sometimes on their own. Well-realized was how the grinding ordeal wore down Jeff and Connie's marital devotion. Jeff was paying for his past relationship while demure Connie—wearing Edie's gang uniform instead of any spare personal clothes—became another Shayne at the end in a surprising act of quasi-murder.

Mini-Skirt Mob "skirted" the Hell's Angels look of outlaw bikers by reaching for very self-conscious individuality in the look of the women and career cowboys as their partners. Once it all came down to escalating mayhem, Dexter stilled any titters by daring to show physical destruction tolerated in only a few film genres, like horror pictures and war movies. Edie's fire scars left a half-charred face and dead Lon's head was twisted as grotesquely as that of someone who had been hanged (worse, his eyes were open).

Even Dexter felt some qualms about the controversial ending until he weighed budget over revision. If Jeff had made Shayne the ultimate "fallen women" and not his once-mousy bride, the decency worry-warts might not have griped. Female vigilantism was more gender-provocative—like the early sixties case of a New York secretary who fended off a rapist with a switchblade or the more documented Inez Garcia murder trial of the seventies.

Shayne was played by Diane McBain, the spectacular blonde model who acted at Warner Bros. and once roomed with former *Make Room for Daddy* star Sherry Jackson. Grown-up Jackson had shown her svelte pelt in a *Playboy* spread tied to *Gunn* (1967). Ex–Bad Seed Patty McCormack was the third woman in the cast who had worked for Maury Dexter. She sang the title song for *The Mini-Skirt Mob*, backed by the American Revolution.

Harry Dean Stanton had appeared with Jack Nicholson in *Rebel Rousers*, due for 1970 release. Blonde, gravel-voiced Ross Hagen was born Leland Lando Lilly in Williams, Arizona, in 1938. The Oregon-raised Hagen married at age nineteen, divorced four years later and wed his soulmate, actress-writer Claire Lynn Polan, in 1963. Hagen at this time was a regular on *Daktari* as Bart Jason.

Jeremy Slate and Maury Dexter teamed again for *Hell's Belles* while Diane McBain revereted to her more ladylike roles in *Five the Hard Way* with Ross Hagen its producer.

Motorcycle Gang

American International 1957. Presenters: James H. Nicholson, Samuel Z. Arkoff; Producer: Alex Gordon; Director: Edward L. Cahn; Story-Screenplay: Lou Rusoff; Cinematography: Frederick E. West; Film Editor: Richard C. Meyer; Music: Albert Glasser; Music Editor: Charles Clements; Production Supervisor–Assistant Director: Bartlett A. Carre; Art Director: Don Ament; Set Decorator: Harry Reif; Property Master: Karl Brainard; Sound Editor: Henry Adams; Wardrobe: Marjorie Corso; Hair Stylist: Edith Keon; Makeup: Ernie Young; Sound: Ben Winkler; Technical Advisor: George Dockstader; A Golden State Production. Running Time: 78 minutes.

Cast: Anne Neyland (Terry); Steve Terrell (Randy); John Ashley (Nick); Carl Switzer (Speed); Raymond Hatton (Uncle Ed); Russ Bender (Joe); Jean Moorehead (Marilyn); Scott Peters (Hank); Eddie Kafafian (Jack); Shirley Falls (Darlene); Aki Alelong (Cyrus Wong); Wayne Taylor (Phil); Hal Bogart (Walt); Phyllis Cole (Mary); Suzzanne Sydney (Birdie); Edmund Cobb (Bill); Paul Blaisdell (Don); Zon Murray (Hal); Felice Richmond (Hal's Wife).

Produced by Alex Gordon, directed by Edward L. Cahn and written by Lou Rusoff, *Motorcycle Gang* was a remake of their 1957 *Dragstrip Girl*, where poor Dudley-Do-Right Jim Donaldson and rich rival Fred Armstrong vied for the love of a Stickshift Sally named Louise Blake. Fred killed a man while testing Jim's borrowed hot rod, letting him take the rap until Louise pinch-hit for Jim during a race and found a piece of plaster from the leg cast of Fred's companion. Fred was caught and Jim cleared.

A.I.P. wanted Steve Terrell and John Ashley to repeat their hero and villain roles in *Motorcycle Gang*, but Ashley had been drafted and reported to Fort Ord for basic training. *Motorcycle Gang*, then titled *Motorcycle Girl*, had to be shot during a two-week furlough. After an indoctrinary haircut, Ashley was allowed by a lieutenant to grow his hair back. A mean sergeant who wanted Ashley reskinned hoped to justify it as a field inspection shearing for his whole company. At the base barbershop, Ashley bribed a newsboy with ten bucks to take his place in line while Ashley sneaked off the opposite way carrying the newsboy's papers. A.I.P. wouldn't have to get a wig for *Motorcycle Gang*'s second male lead.

Visiting L.A. from her home in Chicago, biker Terry Lindsay meets Randy Smith of the Sky Riders at a traffic stop. With him are Speed, Darlene and Marilyn. The five play cop tag and hide in the hills, where a rock throws Terry off her bike head-first. Randy attends to Terry, feeling friendly. "Burning rubber is my one big vice," huffs Terry, who is invited to join the Pacific Motorcycle Group at the Blue Moon. She is staying with her Uncle Ed, a rancher.

Two sinister bikers join the Sky Riders. One is Hank. The other reminds the Riders who he is, "Rogers—Nick Rogers!" Randy's ex-pal is back from a fifteen-month jail stretch. Randy tells him to forget it. "Here's how I forgot it!" yells Nick, who hits Randy, menacing him with a piece of broken glass. Randy has a reason for not taking on Nick.

Terry attends the next meeting for the P.M.G. race, as do club overseer Sgt. Joe Watson of the police and Nick. Randy is their entrant. Nick decries this "lousy nursery school," preferring "things the way they used to be."

Randy and Nick were street racing when Nick hit an old man who later died. Randy, who wouldn't protect Nick, drew a two-year suspension. Terry dates Nick, who asks her, "Is Randy beating your time?" "I'm a free agent," Terry answers.

During a picnic with Randy, Terry caresses her bike, telling him, "To you this is a symbol of a future careerist. To me it's a hell-raiser. I say 'go faster' and it does. I say 'take a turn' and it does. Ever since I remember, someone has been telling me what to do ... and this is the one thing I control!" Recalling the dead old man, Randy warns, "Beyond a certain point, the machine's the boss." "Some arguments can only be settled out of court," implies Terry. "You mean Nick," understands Randy, who admits, "I need a good manager."

Ineligible for the P.M.G. race, Nick wants to set the practice trial pace and tries to kick Randy off the track. During a victory party at Uncle Ed's, he formally challenges Randy. Sensing the game Terry is supposedly

Top: Nasty Nick (John Ashley) rips into Randy (Steve Terrell).

Bottom: Randy (Steve Terrell) and Terry (Anne Neyland) on Uncle Ed's spread.

playing, Randy snipes, "Anything to please the queen! She's got to have her kicks!"

A scramble run leads to Nick daring Randy to a dangerous ride across a railroad trestle. Leaking oil, Nick's bike makes it. Setting the time, Terry spots the oil and tries to warn Randy, but Nick gags her. Randy slips on the oil and plunges off the trestle. Terry is blamed.

Nick pays a late night visit to Terry, insisting, "We're the same kind!" Resisting his paws, she bites his hand and runs indoors.

Terry is coaxed into seeing recuperated Randy, who now realizes she was concerned for his safety. Mitigating circumstances put to board review save Randy's race qualification.

One town the racers pass through is the hamlet of Attville, where Nick, Hank, Jack and Phil go. Nick becomes troublesome during lunch at a café. Held prisoner, the owner and his wife are joined by more captive citizens. Outside, they are subjected to cruel Harley sport. Sent back to the café for more booze, the wife calls the police before Jack rips out the wall phone.

Joe receives the message over his bike radio. Flagged down, sure winner Randy is needed. When he accedes, Joe tells him, "You've won yourself more than a race." Joe and the Sky Riders break up Nick's party. Randy catches Nick. "One thing, folks," says Joe, "These aren't P.M.G. men. They're alleycats on motorcycles. There's a big difference."

Randy broods at the after-race party for not finishing first. "You've won everything in sight," thinks Terry. "Everything?" asks Randy. "With reservations of course," Terry says. Speed's former girl Birdie tempts him with a custard pie. Darlene tells him to pick between them. "A little brainwork and you can have it both ways," thinks Speed before incensed Birdie pies him.

In the intervening years since *The Wild One*, cycling, along with hot-rodding, had become more respectable. A.I.P. felt it was promoting these sports positively once audiences got past the lurid titles and lobby ads of these films. Any surrenders to recklessness undertaken by the heroes were small infractions or big trouble they could get out of once it was proven their enemies incited it. According to *Motorcycle Gang*, outlaws were the past except for a few nostalgic punks like Nick.

Terry, like *Dragstrip Girl* Louise, was a rebel for competing with men and in her fickle affections for Randy and Nick was the conscience of those who want hard kicks without a painful price. True love put Terry on the right track after Nick's rogue charm faded. They and Randy were all susceptible to vanity. Randy could usually regulate his. Terry was impressionable. Nick considered her a kindred spirit who needed his influence to feel all her rebelliousness. Mortal jeopardy to Randy dispelled Nick's power. Randy lost the race, but there were other consolations.

Motorcycle Gang made its ninety-nine percenters more human and appealing than the stuffed shirts in *The Wild One* and there was much more racing. For the cast, most of it was bad process photography using street shots from *Dragstrip Girl*. Another flaw the films shared was cheap ethnic humor. The mini-town takeover in *Motorcycle Gang* was underwhelming, but suitably called to a four-man gang. Attville was at least a *real* town.

Alex Gordon and his wife saw Anne Neyland in an English-dialogue Danish film and heard she was doing *Jailhouse Rock* (1957), borrowing her from MGM for *Motorcycle Gang*. Off-screen, she got involved with "bad boy" John Ashley, who got into *Dragstrip Girl* because he was dating another girl up for a role. After the Army, Ashley became a rock singer, starred on *Straightaway*, acted in *Hud* (1963), became a beach movie support, managed a movie theater chain in Oklahoma, produced and starred in numerous Filipino exploitation films and was a producer of various TV movies and series. Ashley returned to acting, but on the set of a New York production died of a heart attack in 1998. Steve Terrell became a minister.

A has-been since his early teens, Carl "Alfalfa" Switzer became a drunken Big Rascal who was shot at by an unknown gunman outside a bar. Things looked up for him with a good role as Angus in *The Defiant Ones* (1958). Then in the winter of 1959, Switzer and a drinking buddy crashed into the home of a mutual friend who owed him fifty dollars. A heated argument led to Switzer pulling a knife on the man, who fatally shot him in self-defense.

HBO "remade" a number of fifties A.I.P. drive-in titles, altering the plots. Two of these were *Dragstrip Girl* and *Motorcycle Gang*. The 1993 cable version of the latter starred Gerald McRaney as an ex-soldier fighting to save his teenage daughter from a pack of drug-dealing desert bikers.

Motor Psycho

Eve 1965. Alternate Title: *Motor Mods and Rockers*. Released in Canada as *Les Enrages de la Moto*. Released in Germany as *Motor Psycho—Die Wilde Hengate*. Released in Belgium as *La Gang Sauvage*. Producer-Director-Cinematography: Russ Meyer; Screenplay: W.E. Sprague, Russ Meyer; Story: Russ Meyer, James Griffith, Hal Hopper; Associate Producer: Eve Meyer; Film Editor: Charles G. Schelling; Special Photographic Effects: Orville Hallberg; Sound Recordist: Carl G. Sheldon a/k/a Charles G. Shelling; Production Manager: Fred Owens; Assistant Director: George Costello; Production Assistant: Richard Brummer. Toyota Land Cruisers furnished through the courtesy of Toyota Distributors of Hollywood, California and Chief Samuelson and Associates Public Relations. Running Time: 74 minutes

Cast: Haji (Ruby Bonner); Holle K. Winters (Gail Maddox); Sharon Lee (Jessica Fannin); Arshalouis Aivazian (Frank's Wife); Alex Rocco (Cory Maddox); Stephen Oliver (Brahmin); Joseph Cellini (Dante); Thomas a/k/a Timothy Scott (Slick); Coleman Francis (Harry Bonner); Steve Masters (Frank); E.E. a/k/a Russ Meyer (Sheriff); George Costello (Doctor); F. Rufus a/k/a Fred Owens (Rufus); Richard Brummer (Ambulance Driver).

The Hell's Angels were little-known outside of California until politicians, police and the press jumped on the implications of two incidents. The first was the Angels' Hollister-like Porterville run in 1963. They caroused for awhile, left and came back. Police armed with dogs and fire hoses forced the Angels to move South. Several chapter leaders were held for questioning. When a few Angels tried to free their busted buddies, they were threatened with arrest and impoundment of their bikes.

Kenneth "Country" Beamer, an Angel from North Carolina, was the San Bernardino chapter vice-president. Just before Labor Day, he died in a collision with a truck. So his body could be sent home to his mother for burial, the Angels decided to make this holiday a fund-raising venture. Extending atypical sympathy, the police let them rally in an isolated sand dune between Monterey and Fort Ord.

Allegedly, twenty Angels kidnapped a fourteen year old black girl, five black boys and a pregnant fifteen year old white girl. A deputy sheriff summoned to the camp found the girls scared and disheveled. One wore a torn sweater. The other was nude. Arrested for rape were Terry the

Tramp, Moldy Marvin, Crazy Cross and Sacramento chapter prez Mother Miles. According to them, the Angels met the youths in a bar. For about three hours, they socialized and the kids went to the camp willingly. Accepting pot, the girls voluntarily screwed some Angels until they had enough. Fearful, the boys called the cops.

Claiming he had been abstinent for three days, Terry the Tramp was denied a medical test to prove his innocence. Examination of the girls showed no signs of sexual assault. The rape suspects were freed on the surprisingly low bail of eleven hundred dollars. State troopers forced the other Angels to leave the area. The next month, all rape charges were dropped. State Senator Fred Farr was so incensed that he demanded an immediate investigation.

All this raised the dander of Senator George Murphy and new state attorney general Thomas Lynch, who launched a full-scale Angel report. Compiling data from various prejudiced sources, his investigation amassed information on the Angels dating back ten years. Sex crime cases were especially interesting. In 1962, in a North Sacramento bar, a menstruating nineteen year old woman was held down on the floor while Terry the Tramp performed cunnilingus on her. Angel parlance called the act "Red Wings" ("Black Wings" for black women). In 1964, eight Oakland Angels broke into another woman's house, made her boyfriend leave at gunpoint and raped the woman in front of her three children. Later, two Angel mamas threatened to razor scar the woman if she testified.

The Lynch report described all known Angel customs, showing a few discrepancies. "Mamas," for example, were referred to as "sheep." Information was quoted in *The New York Times*, followed by a contest between *Time* and *Newsweek* to see who could dish up the juiciest dirt. This surge of yellow journalism actually rejuvenated the life of the ailing club.

From winter 1962 into early 1965, the Angels were hit by unrelenting police harassment. There were only eighty-five California members and only in Oakland could they publicly wear colors. Gossip witch Hedda Hopper dropped the biggest bomb of all when she accused *The Wild One* of contributing to this trouble.

Although Roger Corman's *The Wild Angels* started modern Biker films in earnest, Russ Meyer borrowed the handwriting first with a movie whose horse operatic working title *Rio Vengeance* became *Motor Psycho*. Rape being such hot outlaw news copy, Meyer found something within his commercial capabilities to play up. The lead heavy Brahmin, a Section Eight ex-Marine, was the screen's first Vietnam kook. Serial gangbangs were the m.o. for the Brahmin bunch, but the women of *Motor Psycho* seemed to invite it by their lust-inflaming non-dress and bodies made for recreation rather than procreation.

Riding east to Las Vegas, Brahmin, Dante and radio-junkie Slick are diverted by something more interesting than slot machines: a napping girl in a striped bikini. She doesn't know that Brahmin is the one kissing her. "Real poetry," smirks Dante. The spell breaks when the girl opens her eyes, screaming her husband's name, "Frank!" There like a shot, fisherman Frank yells, "Everybody out!" "We get your message, dad," pretends Brahmin, who abruptly karate kicks Frank and attacks the wife.

In Blythe, veterinarian Cory Maddox leaves his wife Gail, who gets out of their Land Cruiser before the cyclists harass her and Cory does a Frank intervention. Brahmin kicks Cory's medical bag out of his hand and Cory punches him to the ground. Brahmin sees Cory's name on the back of the Cruiser as he and Gail leave.

Duty calls Cory to the ranch of rich,

amorous, married horsewoman Jessica Fannin. At home, Gail is being molested by dancing Dante while sullen Brahmin watches and Slick phones his mother in Hoboken to tell her about his new friends, particularly Brahmin. "He thinks about his mother a lot. And mom, he called *me* mother!" Cory surrenders to Jessica's hot kisses, but stops because Gail is more filly than he can handle. "Well, some gals have it made," sighs Jessica. Gail knees Brahmin who's trying to "make" her. Throwing Gail onto a couch, Brahmin shouts as a prelude to rape, "The Viet Cong don't believe in courting traditions!"

Cory gets gas from Rufus, who rages as Brahmin, Dante and Slick whiz through his property. Cory comes home to find the Sheriff investigating Gail's sexual assault. "Nothing happened to her that a woman ain't built for," tactlessly comments the sheriff, who thinks Gail may have invited this. Not tolerant of lazy police work, Cory vows, "They won't get away with it, angel!"

The ambulance passes a truck en route to Los Angeles. Its bickering occupants are World War I vet Harry Bonner and his young, tempestuous Cajun wife Ruby. They get a flat. While Ruby answers nature, Harry works on the wheel, meeting Brahmin, Dante and Slick. Brahmin shows his respect for the old soldier by pummeling him. Playing with Harry's carbine, Slick almost shoots Brahmin in the foot. Ruby wants to leave Harry, but then Dante paws her bristles. Expressing pleasure if Ruby goes, Harry provokes her into clawing his face. When Harry attempts to grab the rifle away from Slick, it goes off, killing Harry. Brahmin fires at fleeing Ruby, grazing her head.

Brahmin, Dante and Slick steal Harry's truck before Cory finds Ruby alive, administering first aid. Ascertaining the direction his quarry went, Cory follows with reluctant Ruby. Low on gas, Brahmin, Dante and Slick double back to Rufus' station. He vaguely recognizes the trio before a distant highway patrol car siren scares them away.

Fortuitously, Cory and Ruby spot the gang, who race to stay ahead. Up the road, Brahmin shoots one of Cory's tires. He and Ruby run for cover. Cory is confident the gang can't get far because they are heading for a box canyon, the Cauldron. A rattlesnake bites Cory, who makes Ruby cut open his leg and suck out the venom.

The parched pickup stalls. Brahmin gives Slick permission to split—then shoots him in the back and blasts his transistor radio. Out of fear, Dante stays with Brahmin. At the Cauldron, Brahmin patiently awaits Cory. Dante feels they should move on, but Brahmin ... his mind back in Vietnam ... orders, "We wait for the chopper."

At the first chance, Dante runs away. Ruby nurses Cory for delirium. She falls asleep and awakens to see Dante trying to repair the Land Cruiser so he can take it. Dante begs Ruby to tell the cops he didn't kill Harry. Cory hallucinates while Ruby wildly seduces Dante. As Dante responds with expected violence, Ruby jabs a hunting knife between his shoulder blades, killing him.

Fully recovered, Cory fixes the Cruiser. Near the Cauldron, he and Ruby view Slick's body. "Two down, one to go," counts Cory.

Brahmin fires at Cory and Ruby, wounding Ruby. Cory carries her to a blocked mine entrance, begging Brahmin to let him take her to a hospital. "You Commies think I was born yesterday?" shouts mad Brahmin, who asks, "Pulled a pin on a grenade yet?" "Grenade...," mumbles Cory as he turns to a dynamite box. He lights two sticks, tossing them toward the feet of approaching Brahmin. Aiming the rifle at Cory's head, Brahmin giggles, "I'm gonna retire you! Kind of a permanent discharge." Brahmin blows up. Cory helps Ruby back to the Land Cruiser. "You'll be all right," he assures her. "In L.A.?" Ruby asks. Smiling Cory answers, "Anywhere."

Today, *Motor Psycho* looks rather weak as a Biker, using dinky little Hondas—probably because Meyer got a rental deal on them like he did for the Toyota vehicles (only Toyota received screen credit). It was like seeing desperadoes riding Shetland ponies. By stripping all criminality down to bodily harm, *Motor Psycho* got to the real fear that outlaws engendered.

More than women, the Brahmin gang violated marital unions. Being Russ Meyer wives, the ladies, with the exception of Ruby, had nothing on their minds but sex. Only the most wanton woman, Jessica, existing as Cory's test of faithfulness to Gail, escaped tragedy. Ruby and Harry were the kind of grousing couple so common in Meyer drama. Cory got the "ideal" mate, vapid Gail, the only compliant one and sole wife with an on-screen spouse close to her age. The worthiest husband, vigilante Cory made up with Ruby a rare Meyer pair: a man-woman team. When Cory was sick, Ruby used her body and Cory's knife as instruments of healing and killing.

Once he had enough bike shots, Meyer wisely heave-hoed the Hondas (shot by Brahmin as if he was killing horses) and developed Brahmin's Nam-induced dementia, unleashing it on an ex-doughboy in some sort of irony clash between warriors of then and now. It was after Brahmin, Dante and Slick went truckin' that civilian Brahmin went "Over the Top" his way in the continued Southeast Asia war he was imagining. The jungle recaptured Brahmin's brain almost supernaturally because the Cauldron, so the Indians believed, could cloud the minds of men. Brahmin's "cloud" was a psychic rice paddy. His articulated delusion that Cory and Ruby were Reds gave Cory his inspiration for the TNT fragging.

A danger to the people who made *Angel Unchained* and *Hell's Belles*, snakes were a hazard on the Mohave Desert *Motor Psycho* set. Sound man and editor Charles Schelling kept at the ready a long-barreled Colt .45. Schelling's "anti-venom" couldn't help cameraman and special photographics effects technician Orville Hallberg, who was struck by a bike while filming a road scene and hospitalized.

Born Stephen John Welzia in Philadelphia, Stephen Oliver was a real-life hero of the war. More unique than most James Dean twins, he sustained his Wild One image on *Peyton Place* as Lee Webber. One morning, Oliver met Lana Wood, who played Lee's wife Sandy, and they wed that afternoon. The marriage was annulled almost as quickly (Lana never mentioned Oliver in her Natalie tell-all that told as much about Lana). After dying in his one hundred eighth *Peyton Place* episode, Oliver joined the cast of *Bracken's World* as Dean-type actor Tom Hutson, riding a chopper to work.

Variety noted Oliver's promise, seeing some potential in Alex Rocco, Joseph Cellini and Thomas Scott. Losing the role of Albert De Salvo to Tony Curtis was just a temporary setback for Boston son Rocco. Cellini's only other part was "Man-Flowered Pants" in *Beyond the Valley of the Dolls* (1970, with Haji and Coleman Francis of *Motor Psycho*). Thomas Scott found steady support work after becoming Timothy, playing characters with names like Shagbag and Gore.

Often requiring his Army buddy helpers to take roles, Meyer couldn't get one of them to give a good performance as the sexist sheriff and cast his chauvinist self.

Motor Psycho clearly pitched its promotion to primal fears about marauding cyclepaths. In the ad art, sneering Steve Oliver crashed through a collage of lurid biker press clippings ... astride a Triumph. An "X" scratched by the blurb "The Most Adult Film You Will Ever See!" made Russ Meyer a ratings classification pioneer.

Naked Angels

Goldstone 1969. Producer: David N. Dawdy; Director-Screenplay: Bruce Clark; Additional Dialogue–Assistant Director: Marc Seig; Associate Producer: James Schaeffer; Cinematography: Robert Eberlein; Film Editor: Johanna Bryant; Music: Bizarre Productions; Randy Sterling; Jeff Simmons; Art Director: Michael Levrsque; Second Unit Cinematography: William Kaplan; Script Supervisor: Jacqueline Masciola; Still Photography: Karl Metzeberg; Production Assistant: Adrienne Levesque; Earl Sampson; Makeup: Dean Cundy; Key Grip: Charles McCoy; Gaffer: Don Clark; Sound Recorder: Jon Michael Hall; Wardrobe Properties: Derek Hicks; Motorcycles: Dean's Custom Service. Pathecolor. A Rio Rialto Production. Running Time: 89 minutes.

Cast: Michael Greene (Mother); Jennifer Gan (Marlene); Richard Rust (Fingers); Bruce James (Animal); Glenn Lee (Moldy); Tedd King (Mighty Mouse); Leonard Coates (Sweaty Jesus); Joe Kasey (Cockroach); Elaine Guy (Ginny); Penelope Spheeris (Shirley); Michael Perrotta (Prospector); Frank Whiteman (Hotdogger); Art Jenoff, Felicia Guy, Steven Ader, Barbara Eaton, Sahn Berti, Corey Fischer, Jules Garrison, Franco (aka Frank) Cuva, Dick Daddazio, Carol Ries, Earl Sampson, Howard Lester, Patrick McCrystle, Marvin Vanderventer, Milton Moses.

Written and directed by New Zealand–born U.C.L.A. graduate Bruce Clark, *Naked Angels* purveyed in its sex and skin the most saleable commodities that would be found in the films of production supervisor Roger Corman's forthcoming independent company New World. Replacing the sea with land—*very* dry land—*Naked Angels* combined the revenge mania of Capt. Ahab with the tyranny-provoked mutinies aboard the Bounty and the Caine.

In a dark alley, Mother, president of the Los Angeles Angels, steals a rival club member's bike. The pursuing bikers are led into an ambush on the Angels' front doorstep. Reclaiming his old lady Marlene and his president's colors from vice-prez Fingers, interim leader Mother can't forget the beating he suffered at the hands of the Las Vegas Hotdoggers, who put him in the hospital for four months. Only by wasting them can he erase the trauma.

In a Vegas topless bar, the Angels find a lone Hotdogger who says they went to Devil's Head, an old desert mine. Mother allows the Angels some relaxation time. He attracts a showgirl riding in a gangster's convertible. Mother jumps into the car and takes the girl to a room at the Mint Hotel casino. The gangster and his cronies break in, chasing Mother to the roof. The Angels rescue Mother, but the cops kick them out of town.

The Angels camp outside a deserted barn, where Mother violently renews his ownership of Marlene in twisted love that becomes near rape.

The town of Good Springs offers hospitality, but Mother pushes the Angels on. The harsh environment gets on everyone's nerves. Moldy falls off his bike from heat exhaustion. Mother tells him to leave the bike for now and pack with someone else. Losing it, angry Marlene excoriates Mother for his cruel recklessness. Mother demotes Marlene to mama—proposing a gangbang right here. A couple of Angels are half-willing, but Fingers takes over. With some sadness, he expels Mother, giving him enough gas to leave.

Lost, the Angels are out of gas until a tanker truck comes their way. Mother, however, is denied gas by a crazy gun-waving station owner upset about Angel crimes—particularly sex crimes. Mother swipes some gas from a parked camper. When his bike goes dry, he wanders off ... losing himself in a hallucination where he guns down cowboy-dressed Angels in a sa-

Fingers (Richard Rust), Marlene (Jennifer Gen) and Mother (Michael Greene).

loon. Mother wakes up in the shack of a strange old prospector who found him.

Separately, Mother and Angels converge on the mine, where the Hotdoggers are sleeping in a building. A fired gun wounds one of the Angel mamas. Animal drops lit dynamite down a vent. The blast forces the Hotdoggers outside. Mother leaps into the battle and he and Fingers turn to each other momentarily. The top Dog steals one of the Angels' bikes. Mother chases him across the salt flats and kills him. Fingers wars with Mother, who wins, but the taste of victory is sour and he splits.

Bruce Clark must have boned up on outlaw culture very thoroughly, picking so many character names belonging to real Angels: Mother, Moldy, Animal, etc. Before and during Mother's solitary adventures, *Naked Angels* pitted outlaws against a worse enemy than cops or rival gangs: a mother called nature. The desert dwellers were all eccentrics or worse, withering in an arid frame of too-easily accepted stupefaction. Only the gas man so sensitive about rape was touched by urban paranoia. The desert got to Mother by filling his head with familiarly faced frontier specters his dream gun killed in Man-With-No-Name–like wrath.

The Angels were honor-bound to avenge a man no longer acceptable to them. Mother's own quest for revenge was what brought them into the desert. He couldn't fight all the Hotdoggers alone and by their fulfilled code obligation, the Angels did what Mother wanted them to do all along. Despite excommunication, Mother found closure for the Hotdoggers' attack.

Marlene (Jennifer Gan) is threatened with a gangbang by Mother (Michael Greene).

The Las Vegas scenes were difficult to film because of an anti-chopper city ordinance. Since the script called for Metro to get tough with the Angels, the city agreed to a concession and the cop extras obviously enjoyed their work. The desert scenes were shot in California at the Big Butte Mining and Milling Company of Randsburg and the Ballarat Salt Flats, once a California mountain lake.

Praised for the cinematography of Robert Eberlein and Bill Kaplan, *Naked Angels* used an adroit, creative acid score by Jeffry Simmons, formerly of Frank Zappa's The Mothers of Invention (mothers everywhere!). Zappa's record label, Straight, issued the soundtrack album.

Six-foot four Michael Greene lacked the overpowering vocal resonance of William Smith, but his whiny, petulant voice captured Mother's irritability and impatience. Greene made wooden flutes, one of which Mother carried as a club as well as a musical instrument. Six-foot Jennifer Gan, an ex–Vegas showgirl, designed her open-sided, criss-cross laced pants. Greene and Richard Rust were two of the many actors with Biker credits who appeared in *The Last Movie*.

Like makeup man Dean Cundey, who became a cinematographer, Penelope Spheeris, playing Mama Shirley, changed her career course when she became a director. Spheeris' musician brother, Jimmy, died in a 1984 motorcycle accident.

Jack Hill, the writer-director of *Naked Angels*' black and white 1967 co-feature *Pit Stop*, created an integrated ad campaign emphasizing *Naked Angels* (very magnanimous of him). The ad mat showed a topless blonde seen from a rear three-quarter left angle wearing panties that slid down part of her left buttock. On it was tattooed "Property of the Angels." A retouched censored ad gave the girl black panties and a matching bra strap across the back. The teaser copy screamed "Mad Dogs from Hell! Hunting Down Their Prey with a Quarter Ton of Hot Steel Between Their Legs!" So much weight in that part of the body should have made it impossible for them to even move—let alone hunt!

Outlaw Riders

Ace-International 1971. Presenter–Executive Producer: Robert G. Gyger; Producer–Assistant Editor: Anthony Cardoza; Director–Assistant Film Editor: Anthony Houston a/k/a Enrique Touceda III; Screenplay: John Zila, Jr.; Associate Producer: Bill Reardon; Cinematography: Frank Ruttencutter; Film Editor: Michael Lynch; Music Sound Effects: John Bath; Script Consultant: Mary McCabe; Property Master: Ray Centrell; Sound: Carl Davenport; Boom Operator: Tony Gary; Makeup: Tony DeMarca; Lab Processing: FotoKem; Cycle Stunts: Jim Barrington, Randy Cheyney, Kathy Adam; Camera Operator: Jerry McClain; Assistant Camera: David Minton; Still Photography: Joe Correl; Production Manager: Ronald Cardoza; Production Board: Jill Murphy; Negative Cutter: Howard Moore; Camera Supervisor: Bob Raven / F&B Cecci, Optical-Tiles; Film Effects: Hollywood Sound Transfers, Audio Tran; Automobiles: Ford Motor Company; Dubbing/Mixing: Ryder Sound Services, Inc.; Songs: "Mexican Riding Theme," "Waco's Walking Blues," Bob Correl; "Ride On Angel," "Where Are You Going?," "You've Been In," "Which Way," Simon Stokes & the Nighthawks; "Outlaw Riders," Michael Lynch; "Nothing to Talk About" sung by Lenny McDaniel, Produced by Michael Lloyd for MGM Records. Color. Running Time: 83 minutes.

Cast: Bryan "Sonny" West (Waco); Darlene Duralia (Sharon); Bambi Allen (Linda); William Bonner (Chuck); Lindsay Crosby (Lee); Jenifer Bishop (Maria); Rafael Campos (Pedro); Ray Cantrell (Manuel); Ed Sarquist (Juan); Tim Brown (Ramon); Robert Tessier (Beans); Randy Cheyney (Smitty); Jerry Maren (Bartender); Warren Hammack (Clerk); Valda Hanson (Sister Ann); Karen O'Callaghan (Sister Julia); Jacqueline Johnson (Barmaid); Don Raven (Jose); Terry Lynn (Dancer); Candy Carte (Bill Clerk); Bob Strong (Sheriff); Marge Eckhart (Bill Clerk); Kim Cardoza (Little Girl); Bob Linder (Bill Guard); Joe Correl, Craig Carter (Deputies).

If willful felons, the Jesus trippers would have been the *Outlaw Riders* of this film made by some of the team behind *The Hellcats*. As bank robbers, these guys were *Wild Rebels*, their Mexican enemies behaved like *Cycle Savages* and—*Hell's Belles* —the Mexican thieves who stole from other thieves. Determined to get their possessions back—the money and their women—the outlaws hunted the Mexicans down like a couple of *Glory Stompers*.

Waco, Chuck, Lee, Beans and Smitty rob a mill payroll office, getting only one grand in petty cash. Waco and Chuck pick up their waiting girls Sharon and Linda. The attempted heist of a bank goes completely awry. The police shoot Lee, Beans and Smitty, wounding Waco, who is treated by two nuns, Sister Ann and Sister Julia. Grateful Waco gives them a portion of the mill money.

In a border cantina, Waco and Chuck clash with anti-gringo outlaw Pedro and his henchmen, Manuel, Juan and Ramon. Fugitive Pedro takes the mill money, along with Sharon and Linda, so he can sell them to his cousin. Pedro's girl Maria resents the attractive hostages. When he takes a fall, Chuck breaks his leg and his bike. Waco's bike runs out of gas, but he and Chuck take another parked by a farmhouse.

Pedro wants Sharon to be his new old lady—willing to sell Maria instead. Incensed Maria strikes Pedro, who grabs her arm, pressing her down to her knees to demand an apology. Maria spits in his face and he stabs her.

Above the pass that the gang is expected to cross, Waco and Chuck create a landslide, crushing advance rider Manuel. Pedro threatens to kill Sharon and Linda unless Waco and Chuck show themselves. When Pedro knifes Sharon, enraged Waco charges down the hill with Chuck. Juan stabs Chuck. Waco kills Ramon and looks for Pedro, who bullwhips Waco's feet, shoving him off a cliff. Pedro flashes the money in Linda's face—but she pushes both of them to their deaths.

Waco ... where have we heard *that* name before? And with an extra "a," Sister Ann's name could have been Sister Anna. The only way *Outlaw Riders* topped *The Jesus Trip* was by including *two* young nuns. Otherwise, it was a long, dreary pursuit of criminals by other criminals (Waco committed a postal crime by dropping a lit cigarette into a mailbox near the bank). Everyone in the two factions died and who would miss them?

Early interments befell five of the cast. Bambi Allen died of silicone poisoning in 1973. Rafael Campos, who gave a terrific performance as Pedro, was taken by cancer in 1986. Lindsay Crosby shot himself in 1989. Baldness made Robert Tessier's appearance more distinctive as he moved into big pictures, creating Stunts Unlimited with Hal Needham. Born in Pawtucket, Massachusetts, he was raised in Lowell and there made an honorary police officer. The new commercial Mr. Clean, Tessier died of cancer in Lowell in 1990. Valda Hanson, the ex-girlfriend of *Outlaw Riders*' producer Anthony Cardoza, was also sent to Valhalla by cancer in 1993.

The Peace Killers

Transvue 1971. Producer: Joel B. Michaels; Director-Cinematography–Film Editor: Douglas Schwartz; Screenplay: Michael Berk; Story: Diana Maddox, Joel B. Michaels; Associate Producer-Script Editor–Editing Consultant: Diana Maddox; Music: Kenneth Wannberg; Camera-Lighting: David Smith, Steven Katz; Production Manager–First Assistant Director–Assistant Film Editor: R.J. Louis; Production Manager: Carl Randall; Sound–Special Effects: William Munns; Production Assistant: Brenda Poole; Gaffer: Jack Fisk; Wardrobe: Pat Walter; Key Grip: John Peipens; Set Decorator: Stephen Oliker; Property Master: Jim Jermias; Assistant Production Manager: William Mackey; First Assistant Cameraman: Ed Witcher; Second Assistant Cameraman: John Swain; Makeup: John Elliot; Negative Assembly: Colliers Editorial Service; Titles-Opticals: CFI Production Equipment, Cinemobile Systems Inc.; Motorcycles: Bud Ekins Motorcycles; Songs: "White Dove," "Rebel" composed and sung by Ruthann Friedman. DeLuxe Color, a Damocles Production. Running Time: 88 minutes

Cast: Clint Ritchie (Rebel); Jess Walton (Kristy); Paul Prokop (Alex); Michael Ontkean (Jeff); Lavelle Roby (Black Widow); Nino Candido (Snatch); John Hill (Whitey); Gary Morgan (Gadget); John Raymond Taylor (Cowboy); Robert Cornthwaite (Ben); Kres Mersky (Carol); Albert Popwell (Blackjack); Milt Gold (Hippie).

With an endangered bike gang dropout, hippies forced to fight, an outlaw club helping the hippies and rivalry between two clubs, *The Peace Killers* was *Run, Angel, Run, Angel Unchained* and *Angels—Hard as They Come* all rolled into one potent speedball of a film on constant crisis mode. It had its quiet interludes, but they were drowned out by a flood of fear generated by the seekers of an ex–old lady who wanted to make her old before her time and, psychologically, she had more than a few gray hairs.

Gadget, Cowboy and Whitey of Death Row Motorcycle Club gas up at a country store where Kristy and her brother Jeff, members of a neighborhood commune, are buying supplies from Ben the owner. Spotting the gang's colors, alarmed Jeff makes Kristy sneak out the back. Atop the roof of their van, Cowboy glares down in recognition of horrified Kristy. She and Jeff shake him off in their escape. To learn where they live, Cowboy tries to garrote the information out of Ben.

Once with Death Row, Kristy tells Jeff about the gang rape of Whitey's ex–old lady. This drove Kristy from president Rebel, who threatened to kill her if she ever split. Rebel rides to Ben's with Gadget, Cowboy, Whitey and Snatch. Panicked Ben fires a shotgun at Rebel, who furiously drags him to the gas pumps. Since Ben still won't divulge the location of the commune, Rebel jams a pencil into his palm and waves a lit flare in his face.

Kristy's lover Alex, the commune's leader, holds a dining room conference to discuss the problem of Death Row. Rebel makes a thunderous, crashing cycle entrance. Jeff urges Kristy to hide in the barn. Gun-toting Gadget forces Jeff's girl Carol to defiantly bare her breasts. Jeff lunges with a knife, but is shot in the arm. Alex is tied to a large gateway peace sign and stoned.

Black Widow (Lavelle Roby) has Rebel (Clint Ritchie) where she wants him.

Kristy is seen fleeing on horseback and caught in the woods. She will be formally punished when all the gang is together. Sedated Kristy is bound in a blanket.

While the gang stops for beers, Kristy awakens and inches into the highway, catching the attention of the Branded Banshees. Leader Black Widow yearns to pay Rebel back for scarring her face. As a rumble invite, she slashes Death Row's tires.

The Banshees take Kristy back to the commune. All the hippies join forces with them except devoutly non-violent Alex, who takes a long, soul-searching walk in the hills.

On new rubber, Death Row returns with reinforcements. Kristy lures Rebel into the barn. Its doors slam shut and Black Widow ambushes Rebel so she can gleefully cut him—but Cowboy forces the barn doors down with his bike. Gadget kills one Banshee. Manipulating his revolver hand, Rebel shoots Black Widow in the head. Her lieutenant, Blackjack, vents his rage by pitchforking cornered Gadget. Rebel chases Kristy across a field in sight of Alex—moved to murderously defend her until Kristy screams at Alex to stop.

Police and paramedics clean up after. A departing detective throws Alex one of the makeshift battle spear peace emblems. Painfully squeezing its sharp sides, he draws blood. "Peace."

The *Angel Unchained* and *Angels—Hard as They Come* hippies roughed it out in the desert. Kristy's commune were L.A. county tenderfeet. Less *legally* justified to be vigilantes, they could have just called the cops. Which ones? Death Row detail? Death Row was always ahead of them in nips and tucks. This rock-hard pestilence had to be pulverized ... not merely broken. Acting against a leader whose unyielding pacifism held firm until philosophy lost to love-spurred chivalry, the hippies received silent gratitude from a constabulary happy to close this book.

Director–cinematographer–film editor Douglas Schwartz photographed in runny watercolor tones that made everything look unvarnished, setting the mood

Gadget (Gary Morgan) observes the commune carnage.

for tranquility about to be trampled with soft-focus nature shots. The rape flashback jolted with the suddenness of what it is like to be thrown from bright light into a dark room. Shot in wild angles, the nude, shrieking, outstretched victim struggled in a pitch black void that reduced her world to slimy pawing hands and sadistically poured, golden shower–like streams of beer.

Schwartz pushed the Christ symbolism of the peace sign continuously like he was beating a rug ... even attaching the symbol to blacksmith tooled weapons (remember the Gook Flattener in *The Losers*?). He also drained the dairy milking the horse-against-horsepower chase scene.

Semi-chopper looking, the unglittery, scuffed-up Death Row bikes were interestingly personalized. Rebel's flew a Confederate flag, Cowboy's was trimmed in cow hide and Snatch's boasted a pair of tits on the gas tank.

As Rebel, Clint Ritchie affected sudden, jagged eruptions of temper when Rebel spoke and uttered some scary rape implications. Ritchie was terrifying throughout, but in mid-story he paled against the supernova theatricality of shrill, androgynous-looking Lavelle Roby as Black Widow. His only recurring black actress, Roby was one of the few Russ Meyer women who has had a career outside of his silicone valley. The smaller the breasts of Meyer starlets, the bigger their talent and Roby was no bra-breaking vixen.

Ritchie and Jess Walton found their fortune in soap opera while Michael Ontkean became Officer Willie Gillis on *The Rookies*. A Canadian who played hockey, Ontkean went on to a film career that utilized that skill in *Slap Shot* (1977). He returned to TV as Sheriff Truman on *Twin Peaks*.

Doug Schwartz and *Peace Killers*' scriptwriter Michael Berk would show a lot of those—twin peaks—as two of the co-creators and producers of the Russ Meyer–oriented *Baywatch*.

The Pink Angels

Crown International 1971. Producers: Gary Radzat, Patrick J. Murphy; Director–Associate Producer: Lawrence Brown; Screenplay: Margaret McPherson; Cinematography: Mike Namin; Additional Cinematography: John Koester; Film Editor: Grant O'Hoag; Music: Mike Settles; Art Director: Mike Minor; Production Manager: Harry Goldfarb; Sound: Audio Services; Key Grip: Lester Kahn; Gaffer: Larry Gould; Script Supervisor: Elissa Gilbert; Makeup: Tony DeMarco; Sound Mixer: Bill Oliver; Stills: Gary Radzat; Songs: "Thought," "I See America" composed and sung by Mike Settles; Eastmancolor; A Plateau Production. Running Time: 81 minutes.

Cast: John Alderman (Michael); Tom Basham (David); Bob Bihiller (Henry); Bruce Kimball (Arnold); Henry Olek (Eddie); Maurice Warfield (Ronnie); George T. Marshall (General); Dan Haggerty, Joe Hansen, Michael Pataki, Steve Pue (Bikers); Melody Santangelo a/k/a Melody Patterson (Hotel Waitress).

The D.W. Griffith of homoerotic celluloid, Kenneth Anger made his 1963 *Scorpio Rising* as a short, surrealistic tour of bike life as dictated by the gay sensibility. Returning to America after living in Europe for twelve years, Anger saw a bike club in Coney Island and decided to use it for a documentary. He took the common impression that bikers are latently gay to satirize pop culture, a factory for litmus marks that become full entities in the fetishistic mind when those signs solidify private obsessions. Crossing kitsch and the sacrosanct—comparing Christ to Hitler and depicting his life through snippets of an inept religious film intercut with a gay orgy—*Scorpio* intrigued and insulted the taste buds like an experimental meal.

Few tongues savored the taste of *The Pink Angels*. From the double-entendre color reference in the title, you knew *these* guys were not into Red Wings. Fanfare had tried limp-wrist levity in *The Gay Deceivers* (1969), about two AC youths who faked DC to evade the draft. The entire Army, the unartful dodgers learned, was made up of gays—who regarded straights as "that kind." Weirdoes in their own movie, the Cupcakes would have made good G.I. material according to *The Gay Deceivers*—but this wasn't *The Gay Deceivers*.

The Cupcakes are six San Francisco hairdressers en route to a drag ball in Hollywood. Their bikes are sidecar-equipped and three of the "gang" are passengers. Michael, David, Henry, Arnold, Eddie and Ronnie cover few miles without causing some sort of an uproar. Lurking in the background is a homophobic Army general planning an infiltration maneuver.

A hitchhiker gets a ride with the Cupcakes. At a roadside café, they compete to see who gets him first and throw a mustard-flying hot dog food fight. The intended "dessert" runs away. State troopers roust the Cupcakes for an ID check, finding in the sidecars transvestite gear instead of weapons or drugs. In a hotel, a topless, bottomless waitress fails to turn the Cupcakes on.

In the woods, the Cupcakes prepare a lavish candlelit wine-and-cheese banquet interrupted by a pack of roaming Hell's Angels. The Angels want women and David goes into town to pick the hookers up. They are a "piece offering." The Cupcakes get the Angels drunk in order to feminize the intoxicated macho men. When the Angels wake up, the Cupcakes are gone and the Angels find themselves lipsticked, beribboned and wigged.

The Angels catch the Cupcakes all dolled up in a motel and the Cupcakes end up in the Army maneuvers area. The Gen-

A movie poster for the film *The Pink Angels*.

eral thinks they are real women—until Henry doffs his wig.

That the Cupcakes were gay was about all that the humor was predicated on ... that and the real military's official position on sexual deviancy. Contrary to the leather look of actual gay bikers, the Cupcakes wore standard Angel garb. They couldn't be made to look swishy-washy at first glance or else the gags wouldn't have had any spring in their board. By now, the Hell's Angels—the *real* Hell's Angels—must have been pretty used to derogatory treatments of them on film. Two possibilities for a more sophisticated title than *The Pink Angels* would have been *Chrome and Hot Lavender* or *Scorpio Sinking*.

Pink Angels was yet another Biker film involving porn people. One was director-associate producer Lawrence Brown, a maker of gay films. Brown certainly wasn't the man to tap any camp flair from the script, imposing a stilted seriousness on how the Cupcakes were supposed to act.

The other x-rated luminary was John Alderman, who played Michael. Alderman's *Pink Angels* bio left out any mention of this, but claimed he liked grunion hunting and his favorite actors were Francis X. Bushman and Theda Bara. Tom Basham starred in Larry Brown's *An Eye for an Eye* (1975), a/k/a *The Psychopath*, a better Brown credit for Basham's acclaimed portrayal of Mr. Rabbey. The unlikeliest actor cast as a Cupcake was Bruce Kimball, who aspired to produce family entertainment.

Someone in *The Pink Angels* who did make his mark in that field for Grizzly Adams was Dan Haggerty, mostly a prop biker figure. The other familiar face from the Hell's Angels was Michael Pataki.

Henry Olek wrote *A Different Story* (1978), about a gay man and a lesbian who fell in love—a development that would have been lost on the stunted imaginations responsible for *The Pink Angels*. Conceiving a ripe absurdity and wasting it, the film didn't do much for motorcycle sales in its "Think Pink" promo gimmick of dealers wrapping showroom bikes with pink streamers.

Rebel Rousers

Four-Star Excelsior 1970. Executive Producer: Rex Carlton; Producer-Director: Martin B. Cohen; Screenplay: Abe Polsky, Michael Kars, Martin B. Cohen; Associate Producer: Dascha Auerbach; Cinematography: Leslie Kouvacs a/k/a Leslie Kovacs, Glen Smith; Film Editor: Thor Brooks; Music Supervision: Igo Kantor; Music: William Loose; Production Manager: John Cardos; Assistant Production Manager: Rick Jackson; Sound Recorder: Robert Dietz; Gaffer: Richard Aguilar; Assistant Cameraman: Peter Sorel; Boom Man: Ken Carlson; Still Photography: Hedy Dietz; Key Grip: John Murray; Script Supervisor: Joyce King; Hair-Wardrobe: Lee Davis; Costumes: Shannon; Makeup: Kent Osborne; Assistant Film Editor: Sam Annis. Paragon International Pictures. Eastmancolor. Running Time: 77 minutes.

Cast: Cameron Mitchell (Paul Collier); Bruce Dern (J.J.); Diane Ladd (Karen); Jack Nicholson (Bunny); Dean a/k/a Harry Dean Stanton, Lou Procopio, Neil Burstyn, Earl Finn, Phil Carey (Rebels); Robert Dix (Miguel); Bud Cardos, Sid Lawrence, Jim Logan, Helena Clayton, Frankie O'Brien, Rita Reinhardt, Candee Earle, Maria Cove and the Townspeople of Chloride, Arizona.

Before *The Fakers* became *Hell's Bloody Devils*, Rex Carlton executive produced *Rebel Rousers*, co-written, produced and directed by Martin B. Cohen. Bruce Dern, Diane Ladd and Lou Procopio of *The Wild Angels* worked with Jack Nicholson and John Cardos of *Hell's Angels on Wheels*. More like an expanded TV anthology drama, *Rebel Rousers* was a tale of bittersweet reunions between ex-lovers and old high school pals. One of the lovers and one of the pals was Paul Collier, played by Cameron Mitchell in a rare exploitation performance drawn from his sensitive side.

The Rebels, their two mamas and Paul arrive in a small Mexican village at the same time. J.J. Weston, the Rebels' leader, recognizes Paul from their school

Jack Nicholson taking five.

football days. While the Rebels crowd into the local cantina, Paul registers at the hotel where he and his mistress Karen used to stay together. A baby crib in her room indicates she is pregnant.

Sheriff Rico Alvarez and his lazy, pudgy deputy Pancho are called to the cantina to run the rowdy Rebels out of town. Paul had been away on business when Karen learned of her condition, coming here to have the baby away from him and the prying eyes of her family. Abortion was an option Karen would not consider. Paul wants to marry Karen, but she turns him down. The Rebels camp on an isolated beach.

Paul and Karen drive to the beach to discuss their problem further. Three prankish Rebels harass them in Paul's car until J.J. appears. The Rebels feign civility until further, more violent misbehavior ensues. J.J. tries to head off more trouble, but psycho Bunny instigates the brutal gang stomping of Paul. Rico, meanwhile, leaves town with a prisoner. Pancho is in charge. Karen's fate depends on who wins a drag race along the shore and gets to keep her for the night. Regaining consciousness, Paul scrambles to his car, evading two Rebels in pursuit. J.J. tells Karen he is stalling for time so Paul can get help.

Paul joins Pancho and the village priest at Rico's office, but neither of them have the guts to give him any aid. J.J. loses the race to Bunny, who wins Karen. Neither the hotel manager nor the cantina people will help Paul. Wailing his frustration on the street, he meets Ninyo, a boy who knows who Paul can turn to.

Miguel, a fisherman, is hosting a birthday party at his home. His daughter, Marguerite, leaves with a tray of tacos. She goes down to the beach, where the Rebels grab her. As a further stall, J.J. "marries" Bunny and Karen—his Bible an innuendo-filled copy of the Harley-Davidson maintenance manual.

Armed with pitchforks, Miguel and his people join Paul and confront the Rebels. Marguerite breaks away, but Cowboy holds a gun on Karen. Bunny demands more game playing and J.J. fights Bunny, who falls on his knife and dies. Paul and Karen reconcile. J.J. stays on the beach to ponder his own future.

Rebel Rousers was forced by its limited scope and mostly tame violence to emphasize the troubles of Paul and Karen, an older than usual pair of unwed parents-to-be. He was an architect and she an interior decorator. Both made their livings designing homes. With the dilemma of an unplanned baby on the way, they had to consider starting a real home for all three. Until Karen became imperiled, J.J. did not know that *he* had a problem: owning a bright mind gone to waste on holding together a group which, like the clubs of Heavenly Blues and Cody, had become too unmanageable for its leader.

Through its maternal condition,

Karen's own body was her major impediment to freedom. The thought of possible rape on a woman this far pregnant was passed over for the juxtapositional elements of J.J. trying to control the Rebels while Paul looked for help in a village with only one pocket of concerned citizens.

Technically, *Rebel Rousers* had nearly as many defects in production style as it had smart casting. The Rebel costumes were quite tacky, though Bunny's striped jailbird pants were amusing and one Rebel wore an armband with Hebrew writing on it instead of the customary swastika. The streets of Chloride, location of the Arizona scenes, were so blandly forgettable that the Spahn Ranch could have done just as well. Paul's stomping was viscerally intense, but when he fled, his car and the Rebel bikes chasing him moved at the speed of a broken wheelbarrow.

Laszlo (Leslie) Kovacs helped on cinematography, but showed very little of his usual panache except in one moody high-angle long shot of Karen staring at the ocean near the hotel. The tinny but lively music, featuring the *Wild Angels* "Bongo Party" theme, was reprised in *Lassiter*, a 1968 Burt Reynolds TV pilot with Cameron Mitchell.

Mitchell's sniffly, high-strung acting topped all the other histrionics for sound and fury, but didn't shut out the resonances in the work of Bruce Dern and Diane Ladd. Laura Dern was about eight months along at the time of *Rebel Rousers'* filming and made what might be called a prenatal cameo.

Rebel Rousers actually benefited from its late release because of Jack Nicholson's *Easy Rider* Oscar nod. Heralding his name and face in the ads, Four Star Excelsior ran it on a twin bill with another 1967 film, Samuel Fuller's *Shark!*, starring Burt Reynolds.

Ride Hard, Ride Wild

Phoenix-International 1970. Re-released in 1972. Presenters: Elov Peterssons, B.T. Kobenhaven; Producers: B.T. Kobenhaven; Director: Elov Peterssons; Screenplay: Lenhart Nielsen; Based on the novel *Korsor 500* by Dahl Kristensen; Cinematography: Torvald Nyquist; Music Composer–Conductor: Daniel Sydow; Editing Supervision: Stig Salstrom; Production Manager: Eric Malmso; Assistant Director: Lars Nyberg; Sound: Gert Hoberg; English Version: International Film Associates; Hollywood Dubbing Supervision: R.L. a/k/a Lee Frost Color Kobenhaven Films. Running Time: 68 minutes.

Cast: Brigit Kroyer (Annelise); Helger Stroybe (Leif Vederin); Nickie Burstrom (Karl Borsch); Dahl Kullenberg (Ruhl); Vera Ryssen (Orla).

Phoenix International was a company that tried to look truly international in passing three of its skinflicks off as Danish. The first two were based on books. *Fire* was made into *The Captives* (1970), starring Brigit Kroyer, who played Annelise in *Ride Hard, Ride Wild*, from Dahl Kristensen's novel *Korsor 500*.

Traveling with hippies Ruhl and Orla, bike racer Karl Borsch dreams of the Le Mans accident that scarred his face. By chance, Karl spots Leif Vederin, the competitor he blames for this condition, and Leif's fiancée Annelise, who see him as they pass in their camper en route to the cross-country Korsor Five Hundred event. Karl goes after them, warning, "This time, Leif, things will be different."

Karl's attempt to kill Leif gets him eliminated from the race and Leif wins.

Leif is financially free to marry Annelise, but Karl, Ruhl and Orla waylay them. Leif is incapacitated. Karl rapes Annelise upon a motorcycle and his companions take turns molesting her. Leif tells Annelise there is a shotgun in back of the camper. Karl wields a flare to disfigure Leif, aiming it at shotgun-armed Annelise, who blows his head off. Ruhl and Orla follow departing Leif and Annelise—but wave amiably at them and ride on.

Ride Hard's villain had the same name as the man credited with directing *The Captives*. Its dirt-riding scenes and the vendetta of a maimed biker made it a pre–*Dirt Gang* with most of the debauchery staged in a smaller tent. More merciful to its victims than other Phoenix pornos, *Ride Hard* had a certain amount of *loving* sex. An amusing twist was how Karl's accomplices, Ruhl and Orla, after his death, suddenly became nice. Whether to be perverse or pleasant, everything for them was a condition of the moment.

The well-known California racetrack in *Ride Hard* also appeared in Phoenix's other porn Biker, the distinctly American-set *Sleazy Rider*. Both pictures were probably made around the same time, so similar they were in content, environs and technical execution. Released sooner in 1970, *Ride Hard, Ride Wild* provided *Sleazy Rider* and the 1974 Phoenix bondage tale *Slaves in Cages* with the same R & B music. *Ride Hard* also contained a fifties Danish pop song.

Slaves in Cages was also directed by Karl Borsch and the leading lady once again was Brigit Kroyer.

Run, Angel, Run

Fanfare 1969. Producer: Joe Solomon; Director: Jack Starrett; Screenplay: Jerome Wish, V.A. Furlong a/k/a Valerie Starrett; Story: Richard Compton; Associate Producer: Paul Rapp; Cinematography: John Stephens; Film Editor: Renn Reynolds; Music: Stu Phillips; Art Director: Paul Silas; Production Supervisor: Peter Fain; Assistant Director: Dave Marks; Camera Operator: Don Birchkrant; Property Master: Walter Starkey; Wardrobe: Frank Tauss; Makeup: Harry Thomas; Gaffer: Bobby Petzolot; Key Grip: John Murray; Mixer: Bud Alper; Set Dresser: Ray Boltz; Stunt Action Coordinator: Bill Catching; Assistant to Producer: Pearl Kempton; Script Supervisor: Marie Messenger; Recording Producers: Sound Service; Post Production: Synchrofilm, Inc.; Sound Effects: Edit-Rite, Inc.; Song: "Run, Angel, Run" by Billy Sherrill, Stu Phillips, Sung by Tammy Wynette; Other Songs: Byron Cole, James East, Stu Phillips, Performed by the Windows. Eastmancolor. Running Time: 95 minutes.

Cast: William Smith (Angel); Valerie Starrett (Laurie); Daniel Kemp (Dan Felton); Gene Shane (Ron); Lee DeBroux (Pappy); Eugene Cornelius (Space); Paul Harper (Chic); Margaret Markov (Meg Felton); Ann Fry (Flo Felton); Brian Rapp, Jennifer Starrett, Jeb Adams (Felton Children); Lou Robb (Roger); Homer Thurman (Elmo); Austin Roberts (Harry); Stanford Morgan (Stan); Richard Compton (Richie); Rachel Romen (Maggy); Joy Wilkerson (Estelle); Wally Berns (Doctor).

In 1969, Bikers reached the peak of their media attention. Four years earlier, ex–Hell's Angel Skip Von Buegening, supermarket clerk, part-time rock musician and transient outlaw, posed with a mama for the cover of the *Saturday Evening Post* with the Angels piece. Curtly, the Angels dismissed Von Buegening as a phony exhibitionist. Such grandstanding had more dire consequences for the hero of Joe Solomon's third Biker, *Run, Angel, Run*—the only Biker of its season other than *Easy Rider* with an appreciated sense of integrity. Since its bracket was programmer, the good reviews it would receive would be all the more surprising.

Run, Angel, Run was a Starrett family project based on the Richard Compton story "Angel's Flight." It was turned over to Mrs. Jack Starrett and Jerome Wish, who wrote the script. She was credited as V.A. Furlong after her maiden name. Jack Starrett would direct.

"Angel's Flight," the prerelease title, gave its protagonist the name Angelo so his nickname Angel could exploit the biker significance of the word. Angel betrayed his gang, the Devil's Advocates, by exposing them in *Like* magazine for ten thousand dollars. Angel's old lady Laurie, a topless joint waitress and part-time hooker, was played by Valerie Starrett—doing an Elizabeth James by being the second authoress star of a Biker credited under two versions of her name.

While Angel rides to San Francisco, where a bank is holding his check, the *Like* issue with his story and cover photo hits the newsstands. One magazine rack display is smashed and copies are flung across a pool table where Duke, president of the Advocates' L.A. chapter, sees them. "Our Angel baby burned us real bad!" declares the unseen deliverer. Angel is also recognized by one of the Pismo Beach cops who busts him for speeding in a school zone.

Angel phones Laurie at her work place so she can bail him out. While she arranges a sex transaction to raise money, Ron, Pappy, Space and Chic hear Duke give the word from Oakland about Angel, "Waste him!" Leaving the go-go club, Laurie joins a frisky middle-aged client waiting for her in a taxi. Watchful Space steps out of the shadows of the club.

Joining Angel, Laurie leaves Pismo Beach with him. Ron, Pappy, Space and Chic are traveling in their Northward direction. Ron phones their chapter so the other clubs will be alerted to Angel's route. Menacingly, he murmurs, "I want him!"

At a hamburger stand in La Puente, curious Laurie asks Angel, "Why did you do it?" "For the bread," he bluntly replies. "To burn your own people...," Laurie remarks with concern. "I ain't got no people!" declares embittered Angel, "All I got is me!" "What about me?" asks hurt Laurie. Angel plans to buy a boat and "split this whole crummy scene." Two passing bikers spot alarmed Angel and inform their club.

Angel and Laurie head out of town with the gang in hot pursuit. Luckily, Angel spots a motorcycle cop, urging Laurie to say something that will get the gang off their tail. Responding to a sexual harassment claim, the cop pulls the gang over. At a train station, Angel berates Laurie for letting them be seen. "Why not?" she retorts, "You're a big celebrity now, aren't you?"

Abandoned Laurie takes a seat in the waiting room of the station. Her ears pick up the roar of the gang's bikes. Panicking, Laurie runs down the tracks, calling for Angel, who rescues her. Angel rides alongside a moving Southern Pacific freight and pushes Laurie into an open boxcar. Zooming ahead of the train, Angel leaps off a loading ramp into a flat car.

The train rumbles through the night. Asleep in a corner of the boxcar, Angel and Laurie are awakened by the communal laughter of three hoboes: leader Harry, black Elmo and neurotic Roger. The trio seem friendly—but the mood becomes dark. Their unwritten law decrees "sharing" ... they want Laurie. Knife wielding Harry edges Angel to the open door, ordering him to jump out. As Elmo mauls struggling Laurie, racist Roger screams, "*Take your filthy black hands off that white woman!*" Angel wrests Harry's knife, shoving him into railside darkness. With the knife, he makes Roger jump. Relaxed Elmo offers a truce. Angel is chagrined to hear that the train is Oregon-bound, but it has one more California stop.

At the stop, Angel and Elmo trade jackets. Inspecting the La Puente train yard, Ron, Pappy, Space and Chic discover Angel's tire marks on the ramp. "Question is," muses Ron, "where did he come down?" The Advocates find Elmo at a hobo camp and demand some answers.

Now in Napa Valley, Angel and Laurie crash in an empty old schoolhouse. They frolic and lie on the straw-strewn floor, where Angel wildly articulates his fantasy plans over pot.

In a country roadhouse, travel-weary Ron, Pappy, Space and Chic drink beer. Space perversely takes a fancy to an old barfly at the end of the counter. Loud Stan, fey Richie and their dates Maggy and Estelle are noticed by Ron, who imposes himself on the four at their table. Insulting the women, Ron yells that Stan defamed every female here and the incensed men start a brawl. Space sits it out with the barfly. The melee continues as the Advocates sneak out.

Angel wakes up the next morning to find Laurie gone from the schoolhouse. Calling frantically, he finds her sitting placidly in the woods. Angel's show of worry embarrasses him.

On the property of sheep rancher Dan Felton is a small cottage for rent. Angel and Laurie move in. Angel lights the stove to disastrous results. Laurie's cooking is more disastrous. Childishly, Angel storms out but comes back coasting his bike. "It's out of gas," he sheepishly tells forgiving Laurie.

Dan meets Angel, who hires on as a handyman. Dan admires Angel's chopper. In the barn, Dan keeps the 1917 Harley he once raced at county fairs. A little work and it can be as good as new. The oldest of Dan and wife Flo's children is pretty teenaged Meg. Angel and Dan become after-work riding buddies while lonely Laurie slaves to improve the cottage.

The search for Angel is getting on the Advocates' nerves. Chic gripes that Ron has "flipped out." Offended Ron "flips out" on Chic until cool-headed Pappy restrains him.

Angel cannot fathom Dan's decision to raise sheep. Dan sees a difference between "moving" and "running away." "Sheep work," he says, "is part of a bigger scene I *do* dig—this farm and my family." "Not for me," feels Angel, "I gotta be free, man. I gotta fly," indicating a bird in flight. "Yeah, I see what you mean," observes Dan, "but I bet if ya follow that bird, he's got a nest to fly home to."

For some hooking money, Laurie propositions a suave passing stranger. Conditions aren't right, however, and nothing comes of it. Laurie's small shopping spree angers Angel. She envies his close rapport with Dan. "He's a right guy and I can talk to him," blurts Angel, "and he's got an old lady who knows where it's at!" "You don't care about anything or anybody!" wails deeply wounded Laurie. "I'm trying," Angel piteously asserts. When he admits that he loves her, they make up.

Meg attends a snack bar dance with her friend Sally, where the Advocates are. Admiring his bike, Meg is surprised by Ron, who asks solicitously, "You dig choppers, honey?" She tells him about Angel and his bike. Sally sees Meg going off with the Advocates.

Angel and Laurie are entwined in their deepest sexual passion while chit-chatting, innocent Meg sits with Ron, Pappy, Space and Chic at their camp. Ron instigates her rape as Angel and Laurie reach orgasm.

At dawn, Ron frees mute, violated Meg, threatening to hurt her mother if she talks. Flo discovers Meg staring comatose in her bed. Through a bedroom window of

Brother Hoods: Space (Eugene Cornelius), Ron (Gene Shane), Chic (Paul Harper) and Pappy (Lee DeBroux).

the cottage, Space spies on sleeping Laurie.

In Dan's borrowed pickup, Angel goes to the San Francisco bank. The family doctor tells Dan about Meg's rape. A slight fender-bender on the way home delays Angel, who dials Dan's number but Sally is on the line with Flo, mentioning she saw Meg with a chopper rider. Dan ponderously sits vigil by unimproved Meg—realizing the *Like* cover Angel is his employee.

After dark, Angel returns with the money and a repair bill. As he starts his bike, its exhaust roar makes Meg sit up in bed and scream. Blood in his eyes, Dan storms downstairs past worried Flo.

Bringing the money home, Angel shows it to semi-conscious Laurie. He kisses her lips and tastes blood. She has been raped too. Stunned Angel recoils as unseen Ron tells him things will be even if he forks over the money. Taunted by nocturnal hoots, quivering, rage-wracked Angel bursts outside, snatching a garden hoe. Raising it combatively, he bellow, "*Come on, you yellow bastards! Let's get it on!*"

In answer, shining headlights blind Angel. Ron leads the charge. Angel gets knocked down but rises, wielding the hoe like a club. Bathrobed Laurie throws out the money case so the gang will take it and leave. "No, man, no!" shouts frantic Angel as Laurie collapses. Ron stops Space from killing crouched Angel, who holds scattered bills in his fingers because "He's all mine!" Raising a piece of the hoe, Ron hoarsely asks, "Well, man, was it worth it?" "Yeah, man," unrepentant Angels sobs. As Ron swings the hoe, a fired shotgun blows him off his feet. Coldly, Dan approaches grateful Angel, "Thanks, man." Dan cocks the weapon—ready to execute Angel until Laurie crawls into his arms and Dan relents.

Run, Angel, Run had been told before as *The Informer* (1935) and a year earlier as the Black Revolution drama *Uptight!* Beginning after his sell-out, *Run, Angel, Run* treated Angel's reason as the least important concern. How many in the Devil's Advocates wouldn't have done the same thing? His defection for dollars made them targets, but without the need to hide, Angel and Laurie might not have discovered "upscale" living.

Negative about gangs, *Run, Angel, Run* said there was nothing wrong about bikes as long as the amount of interest is not disproportionately consuming. For a change, square society—represented by the homespun Feltons—wasn't a hotbed of conservative meanness, crediting Angel's reformation to a family man who was once in the bike life. Away from the corruptiveness of the city, Angel and Laurie underwent a purifying relationship rebirth—their tumultuous romance going from simpatico lust to spiritual love.

With his money, Angel could start anew without that boat he had been dreaming about. Unfortunately, he left too many land impressions of his movements, drawing his designated executioners ever closer. Angel had to know some comeuppance for betraying the Advocates since nobody likes a snitch. Meg's rape made Dan believe that Angel was behaving according to outlaw stereotypes he read about in journalistic information supplied by Angel! The rapes of Meg and Laurie were both devastating ... would Meg ever recover from hers? ... and cathartic ... the impetus for a showdown whose aftermath, with the appearance of Laurie to Dan, convinced Dan that he had misjudged Angel.

For its most immediate impact, the film employed split screen, put to striking use by cinematographer John Stephens. An ex–Navy cameraman who photographed parachute jumps, Stephens had shot parts of *Grand Prix* (1966) and the aerial work in *Stay Away, Joe* and *Ice Station Zebra* (both 1968). Stephens' work on *Run, Angel, Run* was complemented by the sharp flash-cut editing of Renn Reynolds.

With split-screen, the premise was compressed into quick, informative vignettes while the railroad yard chase was a heart-stopping cliffhanger. Some riding scenes were done in anamorphic, rhythmic depths of focus other bikers would copy. However, it appeared that all the Coastal highway riding the Advocates did was pass the same row of beachfront apartments in Malibu. Stephens couldn't hide the artificiality of the soundstage set campgrounds, but his shadowy lighting counted for some of the tension in the cramped, dingy boxcar.

Jack Starrett did an audial cameo as the dispatcher voice on a police car radio. The title tune of *Run, Angel, Run*, co-written by Stu Phillips and Billy Sherill, was sung by Tammy Wynette.

Joe Solomon had found good leading men in Adam Roarke and Tom Stern, but true luck smiled on William Emmett Smith III. Born in 1932 to a Columbia, Missouri, cattle ranching family, he spent his Depression childhood living in California. Afflicted with severe but temporary asthma and a hernia that barred him from high school football, Smith wanted to become a doctor. A bodybuilder, he spent a year at Glendale College, joined the Air Force, received a bachelor's degree in Russian and won the Air Force weightlifting championship. Smith became a Korean War intelligence spy and after his discharge in Germany studied German for a year at the University of Munich. He mastered French at the University of Nice and the Sorbonne. Fulfilling his language studies at U.C.L.A., he received a master's degree.

Smith was about to join the C.I.A. as an interpreter when he married French actress Michelle Marley, losing his government clearance because of her Gallic citizenship. Smith taught Russian at U.C.L.A. while earning a doctorate. Tired of instructing students more knowledgeable than he, Smith quit. On the advice of his actress sister Joy Windsor, Smith did an MGM screen test, won a contract and made his film debut in *The Mating Game* (1958). Smith also did stunt work in TV westerns.

Fully committing himself to drama, Smith enrolled at the Actors' Workshop at Studio West. He played Det. Sgt. Danny Keller on *The Asphalt Jungle*, co-starred on the British TV series *Zerocone* as airline investigator Jimmy Delaney, and on a segment of *Stoney Burke* was cast as Lt. Joe Cardiff on the unsold pilot "Border Patrol."

Smith graduated to the stage in the Los Angeles play *Down to Earth*. At the Players Ring, he was Chief Bromden in *One Flew Over the Cuckoo's Nest*, becoming Randall P. McMurphy when Warren Oates left the show. Universal hired Smith for *The Streets of Laredo*, a pilot that led to him playing Texas Ranger Joe Riley on *Laredo*. After its cancellation, he did more Universal vidfare, rejecting the lead in the *Tarzan* series. Long a biker, Smith lived with the Banditos Motorcycle Club, wanting to do a documentary on them.

Figuratively, Smith became a "movie" star when Universal re-edited some *Laredo* episodes and passed them off as features. In the 1968 TV movie *The Manhunter*, Smith played his first major heavy, Clel Bocock, but the film was unaired until 1978. Then came *Run, Angel, Run*.

The pairing of Smith and Valerie Starrett was a superlative matchup. Though they sometimes stumbled in their tender moments, Angel and Laurie each had a physical counterpoint to some conditions. Big, brawny Angel was like a confused kid at times while Laurie's good grooming couldn't conceal the fact she

William Smith's greatest character between Joe Riley and Arthur Falconetti: the embittered fugitive bike gang dropout and traitor Angel.

was getting a bit old for whoring or gypsy travel on a hog.

Daniel Kemp judiciously sprinkled the earthy salt of Dan's warmth and wisdom, and Margaret Markov, a ballet dancer who performed at the Civic Auditorium in her hometown of Pasadena, brought convincing body motion to the raped Meg. Gene Shane, an actor who resembled Adam Roarke, Lee DeBroux, Eugene Cornelius and Paul Harper were satisfactory villains. Mentionable too were Austin Roberts, Lou Robb and Homer Thurman as the hoboes. Bill Bonner looked right as Duke, but a deeper voice had to be dubbed into his mouth. Unbilled Robert Tessier was one of the La Puente bikers.

The Felton kids were played by associate producer Paul Rapp's son Brian, Jack and Valerie Starrett's daughter Jennifer and Jeb Adams, son of the late Nick Adams.

The trailer for *Run, Angel, Run* began with the jarring scene of Meg's post-rape hysterics, but audiences and critics were to discover that *Run, Angel, Run* was better than its lurid advertising. Auspiciously presented at the Cinerama in Times Square, *Run, Angel, Run* received a quotable hyperbolic rave from Archer Winsten of *The New York Post*. Even *Time* gave it mixed praise, lauding the railroad scene as a marvel of split-screen that shamed the hollow flash of the original *Thomas Crown Affair* (1968). Most of all, the unexpected sensitivity of the film got to people—even those who normally disparaged Bikers.

The careers of Bill Smith and Jack Starrett, divorced from Valerie, thrived in the seventies. In William Smith, Joe Solomon not only helped advance the career of a solid general purpose actor, but one of the few truly bankable stars of seventies drive-in cinema.

Satan's Sadists

Independent International 1969; Re-issued as *Nightmare Blood Bath*. Executive Producer: Dan Q. Kennis (A. Meteor); Producer-Director: Al Adamson; Screenplay: Dennis Wayne; Associate Producer: Sid Frazier; Production Consultant: Samuel M. Sherman; Cinematography–Film Editor: Gary Graver; Music: Harley Hatcher a/k/a Paul Wibier; Unit Manager: Bud a/k/a John Bud Cardos; Sound: Robert Dietz; Script Clerk: Sandy Portelli; Makeup: Susan Arnold; Negative Cutter: Howard Moore; Assistant to the Producer: Denver Dixon a/k/a Victor Adamson; Stills: Hedy Dietz; Key Grip: Forest Carpenter; Re-Recording: Tele-Sound; Dune Buggies: Jim Rotta; Bodies: Poty; Technical Advisor: John Gregoire; Title Design: Bob LeBar; Songs: "Satan (Theme)," "Gotta Stop That Feeling," "I Like the Way You Work," "I'm on My Way Out," "Is It Better to Have Loved and Lost?" "Baby, How I Fell for You," written by Harley Hatcher, Recorded by The Nightriders. DeLuxe Color; Kennis-Frazier Films Presentation of an Al Adamson Production; Running Time: 86 minutes.

Cast: Russ Tamblyn (Anchor); Scott Brady (Baldwin); Kent Taylor (Lew); John Cardos (Firewater); Robert Dix (Willie); Gary Kent (Johnny Martin); Greydon Clark (Acid); Regina Carroll (Gina); Jackie Taylor a/k/a Jacqueline Cole (Tracy Stewart); William Bonner (Muscle); Bobby Clark (Romeo); Evelyn Frank (Nora Baldwin); Yvonne Stewart (Carol); Cheryl Anne (Jan); Randee Lynn (Rita); Bambi Allen (Lois); Breck Warwick (Ben).

Al Adamson and his future partner Sam Sherman met when Sherman was working as a distributor for Adamson's father Victor. Together, they hooked up with Rex Carlton and Martin B. Cohen, who ran Paragon International. Carlton wrote the Cohen picture *Nightmare in Wax*. Adamson produced with Carlton *Blood of Dracula's Castle*, directing it and *The Fakers*, a Carlton movie that gave Adamson sole producer credit.

Blood of Dracula's Castle and *Nightmare in Wax* were foreclosed by their processing lab in New York, where Sherman told a horrified Carlton. Some blame Martin Cohen's deal-making practices, but Carlton allegedly secured mob money. Back in Los Angeles, he checked into the Sunset Towers, got drunk, wrote a note to his brother citing health problems and shot himself in a bathtub.

Rex Carlton may have been afraid of dying in a syndicate hit, but Al Adamson *needed* a hit … the success kind. His career had been productive but paradoxically inert, making films that didn't see light until years later and rarely by their original names or initial content. Flat broke, Adamson was living in Manhattan's Edison Hotel on money Sam Sherman loaned him. In his possession was an Oliver Drake screenplay, *The Unavenged*. Rewritten by Sherman's sister Ruth and Greydon Clark as *The Last of the Commacheroes*, ABC wanted to make it a Movie of the Week, but the lung cancer death of tentative star Robert Taylor and financial problems with the Spanish co-producers killed that venture. Dan Q. Kennis, a distributor friend, was willing to bankroll a feature if Adamson could devise a good story.

Angry at Hollywood, at all of violent 1968, Adamson borrowed a title Sherman was saving for something else and wrote the twenty-five page treatment of a Biker that would set back the genre respectability achieved by *Easy Rider* and *Run, Angel, Run*. That life-changing quagmire escape, *Satan's Sadists*, established the gutter showmanship of Adamson, Sherman and Kennis' bantam company Independent International.

Anchor, his old lady Gina, half-breed Firewater, one-eyed moron Willie, acidhead Acid, Romeo and Muscle are the Satans, who roar down California Interstate One.

"Oh, Ben," sighs Lois as her lover attempts to undress her as they lie on a blanket. "Want me to help you, baby?" asks leering Romeo as unwanted company approaches. Defensively, Ben jumps to his feet and tells the Satans to "run along," but laughing Muscle catches him in a vice-like grip. Acid offers cowering Lois some pot. Willie wants to take her first. Acid prefers to be last. "Take your stinking hands off her!" shouts restrained Ben before Muscle punches him out. Helping to strip feebly protesting Lois, Gina tells her, "You'll learn to enjoy it." Inwardly repelled, Gina distances herself as Willie rapes Lois to Muscle's sick, clucking laugh of pleasure.

Force-fed Firewater's booze, Lois and Ben are put in the front seat of their car. Shoved down a mountainside, it explodes.

Along the Interstate, Pittsburgh vacationers Charlie and Nora Baldwin pick up hitchhiking Vietnam vet Johnny Mar-

Lew (Kent Taylor), Gina (Regina Carroll), Charlie (Scott Brady) and Willie (Robert Dix).

tin. Charlie is a cop. Nora worries about their son, a Nam Infantryman.

A coed at Clifford Junior College, dune buggy driver Tracy Stewart drops off a pair of jeans for classmate Rita, who is going on a desert field geology trip with Jan and Carol. En route to L.A., the Baldwin's destination, Johnny notes, "Everyone seems to be having lots of problems. I'm kinda tired of problems." Charlie feels former M.P. Johnny should join the police department. "We need kids like you and good, level-headed honest cops. You've got to have law and order."

Tracy pulls into Lew's café, where she works as a waitress. Johnny and the Baldwins stop for gas and lunch. Johnny sits at the counter and meets Tracy. Lew warns the Baldwins how dangerous the desert is in this part of California. Tracy wants to be "somebody." "You're a person, aren't you?" asks supportive Johnny.

The Satans boisterously enter. Craving love from ungenerous Anchor, Gina complains, "I do anything he wants me to. I sleep with anyone he wants me to. Doesn't he know how much I dig him?" Their life, feels Firewater, "ain't much, but it's better than nothin' ... and I've had a whole lot of nothin'." Gina does a sexy tabletop dance to arouse Anchor until Lew unplugs the jukebox. Romeo sneaks up on Nora while she is drinking coffee and titty-cops her with both hands. She throws the hot coffee in his face and Charlie hits him. Drawing his gun, Charlie orders the Satans to leave, but Firewater pins Charlie's arms. Johnny is struck as he dives for the gun. Anchor takes it, wanting Charlie, Lew and Nora taken out back.

While Tracy nurses scalded Romeo and Muscle guards Johnny, Charlie, Lew and Nora are tied to an overturned junked car. Producing Charlie's badge, laughing Anchor rapes Nora. Enraged Charlie calls him a rotten bastard. Anchor agrees, "You're right. I am a rotten bastard. I admit it. But, I'll tell you something—even though I have a lot of hate inside, I have some friends who ain't got hate inside—they're filled with nothing but love. Their only crime is growing their hair long and smoking a little grass and writing poetry in the sand. And what do you do? You bust down their doors, man! You dumb-ass cop! You bust down their doors and you bust down their heads, and you put 'em behind bars. And you know something funny? They forgive you!" Anchor abruptly head shoots his hostages, "I don't!"

Tracy and Johnny treat Romeo in the café bathroom while Muscle waits outside with a switchblade. Johnny slams an open medicine cabinet door mirror into Romeo's face, throws severely cut Romeo into a bathtub and breaks his neck. Reacting to the noise, Muscle pulls the knife on Johnny, who drowns him in the toilet bowl.

As they flee in her dune buggy, Johnny and Tracy back over two bikes. Anchor leads the remaining Satans after them. The buggy's tank was damaged and loses gas. Johnny and Tracy head for the hills on foot.

Not built for mountains, the Satans' bikes break down. Firewater elects to scout the territory ahead. Acid only wants to get stoned. Firewater spots Carol, Jan and Rita's camper. Anchor sends him for topless sunbathing Rita while he and Willie visit wary Carol and Jan. Gina and Acid are summoned. Firewater and Willie go off to find Johnny and Tracy.

Firewater and Willie split up. Acid makes Jan eat a spoonful of stew while Anchor offers some to more cooperative Carol. Gina wants to leave. Anchor crams stew down her gullet, shoving her aside.

Johnny and Tracy discover a cave. While Johnny explores it, Tracy screams at a rattler. Johnny sends her into the cave, sighting Willie, who heard the scream. Willie pulls out his switchblade. With a stick, Johnny throws the snake around

Willie (Robert Dix) succumbs to snakebite.

Willie's neck. Bitten, he frantically takes off while Johnny collects the dropped knife. Willie dies of venom poisoning.

Firewater returns to camp, asking for absent Willie. He wants to split and bring Willie along. Acid puts some LSD into a coffee pot. Gina begs Anchor to leave for his sake. "You ain't nothing, man…," Anchor tells her, "a piece of dead meat." He socks Gina in the stomach.

Exiting on a spare bike, Gina mentally reviews all of the sordid events while Anchor, Acid and the girls trip out. Eyes turned skyward, Gina lets herself crash down a ravine. Longingly, dying Gina gasps, "Anchor."

Firewater finds Willie's body and tells Anchor as he and Acid play Russian Roulette. When Firewater asks where the girls are, Anchor gleefully throws back a blanket covering their shot, face-down bodies and bursts into demented laughter. "You sadist bastard!" cries shocked Firewater. He turns to desert Anchor, who lunges at Firewater for a sprawling brawl. Anchor takes a short ledge drop and Firewater leaves him for dead. Acid has shot himself.

Johnny and Tracy near the outskirts of Clifford. Firewater is coming and Johnny sends Tracy ahead. Jumping Firewater, Johnny shoves him down a hill. Loose rock avalanches on Firewater, who before dying tells Johnny, "Don't worry about Anchor. He ain't gonna bother you no more." "Oh Christ!" rues Johnny, "In Vietnam, they at least paid me when I killed someone."

Closer to town, Johnny and Tracy hear the engine of Anchor's bike and barely discern his sun-obscured form. Pistol drawn, Anchor dismounts as Johnny shields Tracy. Behind his back, he flicks open the knife. "You thought you could get away from old Satan," laughs Anchor, "I've paid my dues, man. Now it's your turn." Anchor takes aim at Johnny, but lowers his head to cough. Johnny hurls the knife into Anchor's throat as Anchor shoots his leg. Still ambulant, Johnny rides off with Tracy.

Career desperation drove Al Adamson to write *Satan's Sadists*, but an unconscious psychic force seemed to shape its eerily prophetic elements. The Manson gang were not yet hippie versions of the Satans and parts of *Satan's Sadists* were like a drill for Helter-Skelter. Charlie and Nora could have been Leno and Rosemary LaBianca. Anchor referred to himself by Charles Manson's nickname. The Mansonites occasionally entertained the Straight Satans Motorcycle Club, the second word in their name identical to the Satans. Acid died from Russian Roulette, the assumed demise for Manson member Phillip John Haught, a/k/a Zero.

Satan's Sadists developed its good people as rationally as it was perverse in the depravity of the Satans, who killed as if it was purely second nature to them. A cop killing and the rape of a nice middle-aged woman helped secure *Satan's Sadists'* reputation for violence that was generic Adamson. Pausing only for rape and psychedelic party games, *Satan's Sadists* would spare only two of its seventeen characters.

The conservative streak in Adamson's personality may have inspired Johnny. Left without family, scarred by war, noble nomad Johnny came back to an America he didn't recognize anymore, articulating the cruelty of combat in plain, simple language ("It's pretty rough out there."). Ingeniously, Johnny dispatched the Satans who were not yet ready for the Hell-after. His showdown with Anchor—growing crazier as he lost more followers, like Brahmin—reversed the weaponry Billy Jack and Danny Carmody turned on each other with Johnny the one who caught a slug.

Technical and budget limitations created some glaring gaffes. The clacky-sounding Satan bikes, one with yellow paint peeling off the gas tank, looked ready for the glue factory. Firewater's Mohawk was a cheap skullcap with the real hair of the wearer protruding through a middle slit. The deaths of Lois and Ben was the car crash from *The Fakers*. The acid trip was blurry, delirious, pulsating focus-pocus. Some of the fighting between Anchor and Firewater was foolishly sped up.

Reaction shots were often striking: Gina's disgust when Lois was raped, her bloody-mouthed, luminous lipstick smeared death face, laughing, insane Anchor's head backlit by the blinding sun, his mug shoved into a dirty waterhole and Anchor furiously pounding his fist into the camera from Firewater's P.O.V.

A dancer since childhood, Regina Carroll led a nightclub revue, penned a newspaper entertainment column, and hosted a TV variety show in Las Vegas. In Hollywood, while helping her coffee shop owner father, Barney Gelfan, Carroll spilled some hot java on customer Al Adamson. He asked Carroll to read for the role of Gina, naming Gina after her. While *their* love story was going on, Greydon Clark, who started working for Adamson as an actor on *The Fakers*, fell for drama classmate Jacqueline Cole. Chuck Connors' secretary, she had done a bit in *West Side Story* with *Satan's Sadists* star Russ Tamblyn. Clark felt Cole was the perfect Tracy.

Scenes from *Satan's Sadists* were done at the Spahn Movie Ranch because Victor Adamson knew blind, elderly owner George Spahn. Manson himself repaired the dune buggy in the film. In Indio, the site of Lew's café, the escape of the Satans looked too realistic for witnesses, who called the police. Only when they recognized Scott Brady and Kent Taylor did the cops realize it was only a movie. Filming aerial shots of the Satans on the Interstate, John Cardos was forced to make an emergency landing. The police could have ticketed him for blocking the road, but didn't.

A bachelor until 1967, Scott Brady became the father of a son at this time.

Not only did the bikes look bad, their motors kept stalling and Adamson changed the desert trackdown to mostly foot pursuit. So he would look decent for a court appearance, Robert Dix shaved his chin stubble and regrizzled himself afterward by gluing to his cheeks snippets of Greydon Clark's hair.

The distributor of *Free Grass*, Sam Sherman persuaded friend Russ Tamblyn to star. Since the Army, Tamblyn had become a Bohemian, delving in art, poetry (not in the sand) and short films. He lived off residuals and "Take It and Run" money earned by exploitation roles. Wearing his *Free Grass* hillbilly hat and round purple shades, Tamblyn was a scary, yet impish evildoer who could be the nicest guy around when he wasn't killing dumb-ass cops or mistreating female meat.

Scott Brady and Kent Taylor furnished acceptable sanity ballast. Brady's career was actually revitalized by *Satan's Sadists*. Taylor, an early sixties Maury Dexter regular, stayed active a few years more thanks to Al Adamson. Gary Kent made a fine Johnny, displaying Billy Jack–like capability without pretentious Tom Laughlinisms.

Regina Carroll really looked and acted like a girl who had been on a few million miles of bad road. John Cardos' Firewater was a low-key illustration of the deprived red man who fared little better in the white world.

Under the newly-formed M.P.A.A. system, *Satan's Sadists* was threatened with an "X" until a few mild cuts. Despite fierce competition from pre-booked summer films, Sam Sherman managed to impress exhibitors who fit it into their schedules. Advised to sell *Satan's Sadists* to A.I.P., he went for complete autonomy. Through the I.I. label, he acquired over five hundred playdates.

The sales blitz of *Satan's Sadists* didn't miss a thing—except maybe T-shirts, a paperback adaptation and a *Satan's Sadists* drink (equal parts blood, booze and LSD). All exploiting Regina Carroll and Bambi Allen, ads came in four approaches. The first three showed Willie and Acid holding the arms of Lois while Gina unbuttoned her dark blouse, revealing Allen's left breast in a black lace bra cup.

Non–Motorcycle Approach, the Cool ads, offered the optional substitute title *The Satans*. "Wild Beyond Belief!" and "Helling It Like It Is!" read the catchlines.

Sex–General Release Approach magnified the rape scene: "She Said 'Let Me Have It' and The Sadists Socked It to Her!"; "When They Sock It to a Girl, She Feels It!" and "Human Garbage in the Sickest Love Parties!"

Sex–Art Approach was a closeup of Willie raping topless Lois while her bent arm partially hid her right breast: "Depraved Beyond Description: They Experimented with Cruel Acts of Sensual Stimulation!"

Sex–Motorcycle Approach—the most versatile design—played up both sex and action: "They Start Where All the Motorcycle Ganges Leave Off!"; "Wild Men and Warped Women in a Cruel Rebellion!"; "They Get Their Kicks from Cruelty!"; "A Sick Story of Savage Lust!"; "Sick! Savage! Sensual!" An extra-large ad featured a box with the lascivious, lip-licking face of Gina and a tentative caption announcing that Regina Carroll, "The Freaked-Out Girl," would appear in person at a given theater.

For advance publicity, newspaper teaser lines would announce the coming of *Satan's Sadists*, a ban and the revocation of the ban. Promo buttons that read "I'm Helling It Like It Is, Baby—With Satan's Sadists" were to be given to the first few hundred patrons under twenty-five.

The most artistic gimmick was the

Harley Hatcher score on a stereo LP smash soundtrack album and a hit single. Pendulum issued another hit single with a promo jacket. The singles were for limited audience giveaways.

The smash album proceeded the release of the movie, whose trailer began with a lengthy black and white scene indicating by words it was done at the Spahn Ranch. Anchor appeared, doing his legendary "rotten bastard" speech. A bold title read "Starring Russ Tamblyn — In His Greatest Role Since West Side Story."

Regina Carroll went on the personal appearance circuit for sex goddess interest. A guest of the Shriner's Club Convention, she was formally welcomed in Birmingham, Alabama, and, along with chaperone Sam Sherman, traveled the historic road where the Civil Rights marchers walked.

The most aggressively — and tastelessly — promoted Biker, *Satan's Sadists* roared through theaters like Santa Ana wind. On August 9, 1969, the air of Los Angeles' Benedict Canyon carried screams from the Roman Polanski home. In Los Feliz, the LaBiancas found that drama happening to them. When Regina Carroll heard about Charles Manson's arrest, she remembered him as the guy who fixed the dune buggy in *Satan's Sadists* and phoned Sam Sherman. Taking into consideration all the ominous parallels between the film and the Manson case, I.I. solicited the help of *Box-Office*, whose tepid review was the most lenient, to reballyhoo *Satan's Sadists* as "The Real Story of California's Sadistic Tate-Murder Movie Cult!"

Engagements for *Satan's Sadists* continued past fall and it did well even in Boston drive-ins during cold December. No amount of critical frostbite would spoil the early spring of I.I. On the profits of *Satan's Sadists*, "The company that helps the exhibitor to make money" was able to finance several new films.

The Savage Seven

American International 1968. Presenters: James H. Nicholson, Samuel Z. Arkoff; Producer: Dick Clark; Director: Richard Rush; Screenplay: Michael Fisher; Story: Rosalind Ross; Cinematography: Laszlo Kovacs; Film Editor: Renn Reynolds; Music: Mike Curb, Jerry Styner; Art Director: Leon Erickson; Production Manager: Jack Bohrer; Assistant Director: Gene H. DeRuelle; Second Assistant Director: Wally Jones; Assistant Film Editor: Herb Steinore; Production Secretary: Sheila Scott; Chief Electrician: Aggie Aguilar; Still Photography: Peter Sorel; Script Supervisor: Joyce King; Wardrobe: Dick Bruno; Key Grip: Tom Ramsey; Assistant Grip: Bill Pecchi; Assistant Grip: Ross Kelsay; Assistant Camera: Peter Heiser; Mixer Recordist: Leroy Robbins; Sound Boom: James Contreras; Electrical Grip: Foster Denker; Production Assistant: Beach Dickerson; Best Boy: Mel Maxwell; Property Master: Robert O'Neill; Assistant Property Master: Dick Compton; Makeup: Louis Lane; Second Unit Director: Chuck Bail; Second Unit Camera: Frank Ruttencutter; Sound Effects: Edit-Rite, Inc.; Music Editor: Eddie North Music Company; Titles-Effects: Cinefx; Songs: "The Savage Seven Theme (Anyone for Tennis)" by Cream; "The Iron Butterfly Theme," "Unconscious Power" by Iron Butterfly; "Ballad of the Savage Seven" by Valjean Johns, Guy Hemric, Performed by Bobby and the Braves. Color by Perfect; A Dick Clark Production; Running Time: 96 minutes.

Cast: Robert Walker (Johnnie Little Hawk); Adam Roarke (Kisum); Larry Bishop (Joint); Joanna Frank (Maria Little Hawk); John Garwood (Stud); Max Julien (Gray Wolf); Richard Anders (Bull); Duane Eddy (Eddie); Chuck Bail (Taggart); Mel Berger (Fillmore); Billy Bush a/k/a Billy Green Bush (Seely); John Cardos (Running Buck); Susannah Darrow (Nancy); Beach Dickerson (Bruno); Eddy Donno (Fat Jack); Alan Gibbs (Stunt Man); Fabian Gregory (Tommy); Gary Kent

(Rodeo); Gary Littlejohn (Dogface); Penny Marshall (Tina); Walt Robles (Walt).

The urge that drove outlaws to ravage small towns disappeared like a destructive but passing virus. In movie reality, outlaws were still dangerous to entire communities, but the communities themselves became more diversified. Dick Clark made the first Terrorized Town Biker with an unusual category of population.

Clark produced three A.I.P. pictures of 1968. The first and most critically successful was *Psych-Out*, a hippie drama directed by Richard Rush who, with Laszlo Kovacs, recreated some of the lively flourishes from *Hell's Angels on Wheels* (even bringing back the same creep motorist missing a quart). Rush, Kovacs, Adam Roarke, John Garwood, Richard Anders, Gary Kent, Gary Littlejohn, John Cardos, Chuck Bail and Eddy Donno grouped again in *The Savage Seven*, which also brought back Max Julien, Elton of *Psych-Out*. Garwood and Anders were essentially Jock and Bull from *Hell's Angels*, except now Jock was called Stud.

A Biker remake of *The Magnificent Seven* (1960), *The Savage Seven* was filmed on the cusp of Hollywood's revised attitudes toward Indians, whose poverty, reverence for ecology and sometimes drug-oriented mysticism endeared them to the hippies. Replacing the oppressed Mexicans of *The Magnificent Seven*, the Indians did not hire their dubious defenders and the bandits from *Savage Seven*'s model were corrupt whites who operated within the law.

On a fringe-of-desert Shacktown, the arid serenity is broken when Running Buck emits a piercing war whoop. He and another brave settle a dispute with their hands until Running Buck holds a knife to his opponent's throat. "Will you guys quit screwin' around?" asks amused referee Johnnie Little Hawk.

As the braves head back to Shacktown in a truck, Grey Wolf anticipates a land development enterprise that means wealth for the tribe. "And the buffalo and the wild horses will return and everything will be as it was before the white man came," snidely remarks Johnnie. Suddenly, the braves see a bike gang coming down the highway. Bull shouts "Indians!" to leader Kisum, who says, "Don't worry. They only attack wagon trains."

The bikers destructively and noisily invade Shacktown, where Johnnie's little brother Tommy is drawn to Kisum's parked bike. Ignoring Kisum's warning, he touches the hot pipes and burns his fingers. Bull winces at the squalid living conditions. "These Indians—they got it bad." "I don't know," admits Kisum, "They did all right against Custer."

The braves line up for payday at the village store. Manager Seely is assisted by Taggart, karate enthusiast and bully. In the tavern, Bull taunts proprietor Fat Jack by attacking him with large deer antlers pulled down from a wall. Jack complains to Seely, who refuses to call the sheriff. Twenty-five dollars has been docked from Johnnie's pay for tractor repairs.

Kisum is attracted to Johnnie's beautiful sister Maria, a substitute tavern waitress. Rankled about the tractor bill, Johnnie goes looking for Fillmore, the businessman who runs Shacktown. Stud menacingly points a revolver at Johnnie's head—making him flinch when he pulls the trigger of the empty gun.

Fillmore arrives on the scene. Johnnie interferes when Kisum hits on Maria again. "Got any dirty pictures of her? Kisum asks, offering to sell some of his own before Johnnie punches him. Fillmore's men attack Johnnie, who asks Fillmore for the twenty-five dollars. Kisum makes Fillmore hand it over. "You're a regular Robin Hood," says Fillmore. "Not really," Kisum tells him—then wallops

Johnnie (Robert Walker) attacks Kisum (Adam Roarke).

Johnnie to finish their business. "If you waited your turn," Kisum tells Fillmore, "you could have saved yourself twenty-five bucks."

Johnnie and his friends talk over ways to deal with the bikers. Johnnie has an idea. "These bastards want to play cowboys and Indians. Let's give 'em a game."

The bikers camp near Shacktown. Suddenly, the war-painted braves raid the camp, causing a loud commotion. Johnnie holds a knife on Kisum and the Indians steal a keg of beer. "Pretty scary, huh?" mischievous Johnnie asks Kisum, who lets the Indians go.

Maria is mad at Kisum because Johnnie got fired from his job. Taggart refuses to give the Little Hawks any more credit. He catches Tommy trying to snitch some penny candy from a jar and slams his hand down on Tommy's. Kisum tells Tommy to sneak the candy away. Alert Taggart makes Tommy put it back. Taggart slides the jar over to Kisum as a challenge. Kisum violently overturns the counter. Taggart dares Kisum to fight until he is backed by the whole gang. Kisum belts Taggart and Bull heaves him upside down into a flour barrel and beats him with sticks. Johnnie tells Seely he talked to Fillmore over the phone and the credit has been renewed.

Kisum decides to liberate the store, letting the Indians take everything. Maria considers this stealing until she sees Tommy join in. The police are coming and Kisum forces Maria to come with him as the bikers flee.

At the resting place of some desert auto junk, Kisum tells Maria, "Everybody sells out if they have a price." She penetrates his macho by discovering he has feelings. Kisum acts on them—from a sweet kiss to rough pawing on the ground until Maria breaks away.

Johnnie, some other Indians, Bull and Rodeo have been arrested. Fillmore wants

Ad for the film *The Savage Seven*.

to see Kisum. The charges against Bull and Rodeo will be dropped if the gang levels Shacktown so Fillmore can take the land. Fifty bucks a man, all the beer they can drink and dismissal of charges against the Indians are Kisum's terms.

The bikers and the Indians celebrate with a big outdoor party where Grey Wolf awards Bull a hunter's medal. Maria invites Kisum to the Little Hawk home to thank him for fixing everything up. Things will improve, she claims, once a dam is built over the Shacktown ground. As he begins foreplay with Maria on her bed, Kisum is gripped with conscience. Knowing what he must do, he tells himself, "I've got to do this thing right. If it's a bear, it might as well be a grizzly." Kisum tells Fillmore the deal is off. Kisum and Maria spend the rest of the night making love.

Johnnie comes home during breakfast and attacks Kisum because he learned of the deal. Unable to convince Johnnie or Maria that he canceled it, Kisum storms out in a huff. A threatening crowd of armed braves demand the whereabouts of Bull. One man's daughter was found raped and murdered near missing Bull's bike. Kisum denies knowing where Bull is and the man swats his face with a chain. The bikers and the braves tussle until Taggart fires a shotgun to get their attention. Fillmore says he has called the police.

Led by Eddie, the main body of the gang joins Kisum's contingent. The police and the Indians are searching the desert for Bull. If anything has happened to him, warns Eddie, the deal is on again.

Bull is found dead and the hunting medal he wore is gone. The bikers work themselves into a massacre mood.

Early the next day, the bikers and the

Indians gird for war. Shacktown is barricaded as the bikers form a long column along the brow of a hill. Kisum leads some riders through the barricade. Blood flows freely. Johnnie fights Taggart and sees Bull's stolen medal around his neck. Fillmore had Seely commit the murders to turn the groups against each other. Johnnie shows Kisum the medal. Kisum tells Eddie the Indians are innocent. With the dead making his point, Eddie says, "Well, it don't make no difference ... not now."

At the tavern, Fillmore decides to clear out. He orders bloodied Taggart to go back to the fighting, but frightened Taggart refuses. Fillmore shoots Taggart, figuring either the bikers or the Indians will be blamed. "What about me, Fillmore?" yells Kisum, breaking in with Johnnie. Fillmore wounds both with his gun, then sadistically uses a raised tabletop to press Kisum against some narrow pillars. Seely grabs a mounted Indian spear, hurling it through a gap into the table—and groaning Fillmore's heart. Incapacitated Johnnie begs Kisum to find Maria.

Kisum locates Maria amidst the carnage and burning buildings. "I'm sorry," he tells her.

An analogy could be drawn between the Indians and similarly exploited inner-city blacks. White America largely ignored the Indian because it was more afraid of urban uprisings by the largest minority percent ... those whose ancestors passed Plymouth Rock in chains. Most of the people at the bottom of the ethnic totem pole lived in boondock ghettoes, making Native-Americans the North American counterpart of the black South Africans of Soweto. The Shacktown Indians were on the brink of economic freedom ... the only ointment spoiler a fat fly named Fillmore.

In its dancing, kinetic, wall-to-wall brutality, *The Savage Seven* not only reinterpreted *The Magnificent Seven* but achieved the level of apocalyptic violence that would distinguish *The Wild Bunch* (1969) and *Soldier Blue* (1970). Fillmore's dominance was a condition of dwindling months as Shacktown itself would soon become an artificial lake. The slaughter he engineered simply hastened its eventual demolition. The land remained intact and, in time, the surviving Indians would get rich. The media would surely make something of the riot, but since those who took part were scooter trash and poor Indians, most white Americans knotting their pants over the broader, more socially explosive black problem probably wouldn't care. Shacktown's bloodbath didn't happen in *their* territory.

Again, Dick Rush and Laszlo Kovacs catered a rich buffet of interesting observations worked into practical situations. Property was more than just something to be stolen or destroyed as its possession and use were power play tools, like the business with the broken tractor or the candy. The flour he was dunked in made Taggart a literal "white" man. Joint carried a box of planted pot on his bike and the substance of his mobile garden became an item in cultural exchange when grass-smoking Joint and peace pipe-puffing Grey Wolf traded what each was inhaling. In the Little Hawk residence, Kisum complained to Maria, "Who does your decorating? Sergent Shriver?"

Some bikers going to war effected the look of the Indians. One was consigned to a trash can by two braves and in another reference to Johnson's White House, it was labeled "Lady Bird Says Put It Here." Bull's stolen medal helped identify his killer. When the riot left him bleeding, Taggart became a "red" man. Fillmore was slain by an ancestral weapon of the people he kept down by his weapon of discriminatory economics.

Filmed in Nevada, *The Savage Seven* chalked up some of the most injurious stunts for a Biker ever. For the battle, John

Cardos played an Indian who jumped a bareback horse over the barricade and also played a biker who leaped across it. When Cardos went down, other cyclists were to jump over him. His bike engine wouldn't shut off and to keep the rest of the bikes from hitting him, Cardos peeled off his stomach padding, unable to move. For several days, he was pretty sore.

During a road scene, stuntman Alan Gibbs lost control of his bike and fell. Gary Kent, traveling behind him, was knocked off his bike and run over by actor Larry Bishop. Suffering a few cracked ribs, Kent was rushed to a hospital and it was reported that Chuck Bail got hurt. Psychically, Max Julien knew it was Kent.

Almost as unlikely an Indian was Robert Walker as Johnnie. Generally seen as an inferior carbon of his late father, the son of Walker Sr. and Jennifer Jones was hired by Dick Clark to play Johnny Ward in his next production, *Killers Three* (1968). Ellis in Richard Rush's *Getting Straight* (1970), Max Julien played Goldie in *The Mack* (1973) and wrote *Cleopatra Jones* (1973) as a vehicle for his then-companion, Vonetta McGee. She didn't get the part, but did co-star with Julien in *Thomasine and Bushrod* (1975).

The sister of Steven Bochco, Joanna Frank trained under Lee Strasberg, whose wife Anna recommended her to Elia Kazan for the role of Vartuni in *America, America* (1964). Frank later married Alan Rachins of Steven's show *L.A. Law*, epitomizing the worst of the Me generation as bitchy Shiela Brackman. Joey's son, Larry Bishop, belonged to the comedy troupe the Session. After playing hook-handed trombonist Abraham Salteen in *Wild in the Streets* (1968), he stayed with A.I.P. to do *The Devil's Eight* (1969), *Angel Unchained* and *Chrome and Hot Leather*.

Eddie was twang guitar legend Duane Eddy, who strummed the title tune in Clark's starring film *Because They're Young* (1961). Tina was Penny Marshall. She and ex-husband Rob Reiner worked with Larry Bishop, Adam Roarke and John Garwood in the obscure *How Come Nobody's on Our Side* (1975).

Released around the time of the King-Kennedy assassinations, *The Savage Seven* was cited as an example of Hollywood's alleged role in fostering the national climate of violence. In response to this charge, the industry pledged to curtail excess mayhem—but the promised purge was about as lasting as a New Year's resolution.

The only TV show Richard Rush directed was "The Guru" episode of *The Mod Squad* with Adam Roarke, Max Julien and Mimi Machu. *Getting Straight* and *Freebie and the Bean* (1974) were reportedly the biggest hits for Columbia and Warner Bros. the years they came out. Unable to produce *One Flew Over the Cuckoo's Nest*, Rush spent most of the remainder of the seventies getting Paul Brodeur's novel, *The Stunt Man* on the screen—the price of that accomplishment a minor heart attack. Rush's critical success did little box-office and he was inactive until he co-wrote *Air America* (1990). Unable to direct that, Rush made a middling directorial comeback with *The Color of Night* (1994).

Savages from Hell

Trans International 1968. Alternate Title: *Big Enough 'N Old Enough*. Producer: K. Gordon Murray; Director-Screenplay: Joseph a/k/a Jose Prieto; Story: K. Gordon Murray, Reuben Guberman; Cinematography: J. Ralph a/k/a Rafael Remy; Film Editors: Manny a/k/a Manuel

Sanfernando, J. Ralph Remy; Music: Frank Linali, K. Gordon Murray; Assistant Film Editor: Ralph Remy Jr.; Colorscope Prints by Perfect. Running Time: 79 minutes.

Cast: Bobbie Byers (Lucy); Pete Parsons a/k/a William P. Kelley (High Test); Vi a/k/a Viola Lloyd (Teresa); Diwaldo Morales (Marco); Cyril Poitier (Reuben); Manuel Sanfernando (Claudio); Marci a/k/a Marcia Bichette (Olivia); Velia Martinez (Maria); William Read (Bingo); Delores Carlos (Redhead); Ricky Carpenter, "Fuzzy" Miller, "Bones" Cockoshell (Outlaws Motorcycle Club).

Imported kidfilm titan K. Gordon Murray, once a circus man and roadshow distributor, also handled horror pictures from Mexico, the country that made most of his children's movies. Based in Florida, Murray retained his Latin connection when he produced films through his later company Trans International, whose technicians were low-paid Cuban refugees. Murray dealt with racism before Laurence Merrick, the bikers in Murray's *Savages from Hell*, a white club actually named the Black Angels. About discrimination toward Latinos, *Savages from Hell* had one black character who was significant only because of who played him—and that person's stature was entirely because of a famous relative.

Teresa and her brother, Marco, are tired of the migrant labor life. Marco sees a future for them, their mother Maria and strict patriarch father Claudio, by working at a gas station with his black friend Reuben. At the café adjoining the station, Teresa meets High Test, the Black Angels' leader. Unable to forget her, restless High Test chills on his old lady Lucy.

Spitefully, Lucy makes a bold play for Reuben at the gas station. When High Test sees this, Lucy claims that Reuben made a pass. Unconvinced, High Test hits Lucy. Reuben interferes, getting into a fight with High Test. Marco saves Reuben. High Test vows to get both of them.

High Test invites Teresa to a swamp

The Black Angels get serviced by Reuben (Cyrill Poitier).

buggy race Marco competes in. He doesn't take her rejection of a date well and Marco slugs him again. High Test is out to get everyone. About to leave the Black Angels' camp, Lucy overhears him planning to kidnap Teresa.

Unsuccessfully, Lucy tries to warn Marco at work, alerting Teresa, Claudio and Maria. High Test, Bingo and Ernie catch Lucy leaving their house and hold her. High Test says that Marco is hurt and Teresa is needed. Claudio attacks High Test, who accidentally shoots Claudio and wounds Lucy. Teresa is whisked away in a hot rod. Lucy ignores her injury to help Marco and Reuben save Teresa.

High Test and Bingo airboat Teresa to an Everglades party shack where High Test rapes her. Marco and Reuben confront him and Bingo. Dying Lucy runs High Test down with Marco's swamp buggy. A deputy sheriff arriving on the scene arrests Bingo.

In its passions derailed by class differences, *Savages from Hell* harkened back to *The Wild One*, making the flawed father a tyrant. Teresa and Marco, like Johnnie and Maria of *The Savage Seven*, were siblings living in a special minority enclave. Like Johnny Strabler in the grizzled skin of Chino, High Test was a conditioned bigot who was able to find one "beanpicker" appealing when her innocent sensuality touched his most alien erogenous zone: his heart. The only Black Angelette who owned a bike, Lucy was a more assertive Britches. He deranged by pride, she sick with love, High Test and Lucy had been perfect for each other until they got involved with people outside their race.

Bill Kelley had been the bank teller in *The Wild Rebels* and Bobbie Byers was Linda of that film. Sidney's older brother, the late Cyril Poitier, left their Caribbean home, found handyman work in Miami and was urged by their father to give young Sidney an American upbringing. Sidney Poitier had reached the peak of his box-office success in 1967 and K. Gordon Murray shrewdly magnified "Poitier" in Cyril's large-letter screen billing, hoping familial fame would rub off.

Most of the Black Angels were the Outlaws Motorcycle Club, who had their day of infamy when three members crucified an eighteen year old girl by nailing her hands to a tree.

She-Devils on Wheels

Mayflower 1968. Executive Producer–Story: Fred M. Sandy; Producer-Director: Herschell Gordon Lewis; Screenplay: Allison Louise Downe; Editorial Supervision: Richard Brinkman; Background Music: Larry Wellington; Assistant to Producer: J.G. a/k/a Pat Patterson, Jr.; Camera Operator: Roy Collodi; Sound Recorder: Spyridon Horiatus; Unit Cameraman: Eskindar Ameripoor; Set Design: Robert Enrietto; Assistant to Production Manager: Ralph Mullin, Steve White, Paul Jensen, Robert Morrison; Costumes: Alma Kamp, Miriam Jones; Assistant Editors: Robert Lewis, Rick Williams; Song: "Get Off the Road," Words: Sheldon Seymour a/k/a Herschell Gordon Lewis; Music: Robert Lewis. Eastmancolor; Running Time: 83 minutes.

Cast: Betty Connell (Queen); Nancy Lee Noble (Honey-Pot); Christie Wagner (Karen); Rodney Bedell (Ted); Pat Poston (Whitey); Ruby Tuesday (Terry); John Weymer (Joe-Boy); Joani Kramer (Russian); Donna Stelzer (Poodle); Roz Cohen (Camila); Donna Testa (Mac); Laura Platz (Supergirl); Sharon Brown (Ginger Scaggs); Robert Wood, David Harris (Bill); Steve White (Doodie); Leslie Sharoff, John Shackleford, John Chaffin (Police); Rick Williams (Outlaw); Roy Collodi (Bartender) Robert Lennard, Robert Morrison, James Madila, Rocky Williams, Lourdes Artique, Toni

Newshome, Maria E. Arrequi, Jim Pindras, Paul Jensen, Rosalind Leva, Joseph Smith, Ana Arteaoa, John Nagar, Martin Wade Lewis, William C. Read, Vernon Herbert, Randall Woodbury, Albert G. Dawe, Barry Whitmore, Anita Martin, Kathy Cole, Richard Laird, Ken Trager, John Vardamis, Ray Welden.

Andy Warhol, who featured Valerie Solanis in *Bike Boy* (1967), once entertained the idea of making a Girl Biker film. If Solanis herself had provided one, it would have probably been something like Herschell Gordon Lewis' *She-Devils on Wheels*.

Lewis' partner in Mayflower Pictures was Fred Sandy, whose son Jerome ran the A.I.P. exchange in Washington, D.C. Fred conceived the idea of the Man-Eaters—Mini-Skirts in pants who rode without men ... keeping their horny male harem in line—the stud line. Employing many of the cast and crew from Lewis' teen vandalism movie *Just for the Hell of It* (1968), *She-Devils* was made in Medley, Florida, at the deserted Amelia Earhart Field near Miami.

An ex–probation officer, Lewis writer Allison Louise Downe took her screenplay's dialogue from actual case histories. Lewis put a casting call ad in the *Miami Herald* for attractive women cyclists who owned bikes, securing the Female Cutthroats division of the Iron Cross Motorcycle Club. The members who possessed the best acting skills were blimpy blonde Pat Poston as big Whitey and pretty brunette Betty Connell as Queen, the Man-Eaters' leader. Connell got so drunk at one time that she tried to slice a piece of skin from another girl's arm, mistakenly cutting *her* arm—and didn't notice for three days.

The roles of soft kittens Karen and Honey-Pot went to non–Cutthroats Christie Wagner and Nancy Lee Noble, Bitsy of *Just for the Hell of It*. The only Man-Eater who saw men other than slabs of meat, Karen was meant to show in her conflicted character the high cost of fidelity to a group whose motto was "Sex! Guts! Blood! and all men are muthas!"

Karen drives from her mother's home to a garage and exits on her new bike a Man-Eater. Every weekend, the Man-Eaters hold races down the airstrip runway. Keeping time, beloved mascot Honey-Pot is judge. The victor chooses her favorite stud.

On a winning streak, Karen too often picks Bill, a boy she likes. Intimacy between Man-Eaters and studs is a grave demerit. Suspicious Queen calls a meeting without Karen to discuss this.

Summoned to the airfield that night by Honey-Pot, Karen will take his place unless she drags beaten, tied-up Bill behind her bike up and down the strip. Tearfully, Karen complies. Half-dead Bill is reduced to shreds.

For her initiation, Honey-Pot undergoes a blood-sharing ritual before she is bathed in honey and chocolate. The studs enjoy "a taste of honey." Destructively celebrating, the Man-Eaters raise hell all over town. Without brave witnesses, police threats are empty.

The next Saturday, the Man-Eaters catch Joe-Boy's hot rod gang using the track. Whipping out her chain, Queen starts a rumble the Man-Eaters win. Brother of a Joe-Boy crony, Karen's former boyfriend Ted warns of reprisal. He asks her to quit the Man-Eaters even if she won't take him back. Karen feels she is in too deep.

Persistent Ted infiltrates the Man-Eaters' clubhouse by becoming a stud. Winning the current race, Karen selects Ted. In the bedroom, he reveals Joe-Boy plans a raid while the girls are drunk. Secretly, Karen leaves with Ted during the orgy. Joe-Boy now decides to pick off individual Man-Eaters. When she steps out for some air, the hot rodders grab Honey-Pot. Karen returns to the house.

Late in the morning, the hot rodders deposit a blanketed, viciously assaulted Honey-Pot for shocked Queen to find. A

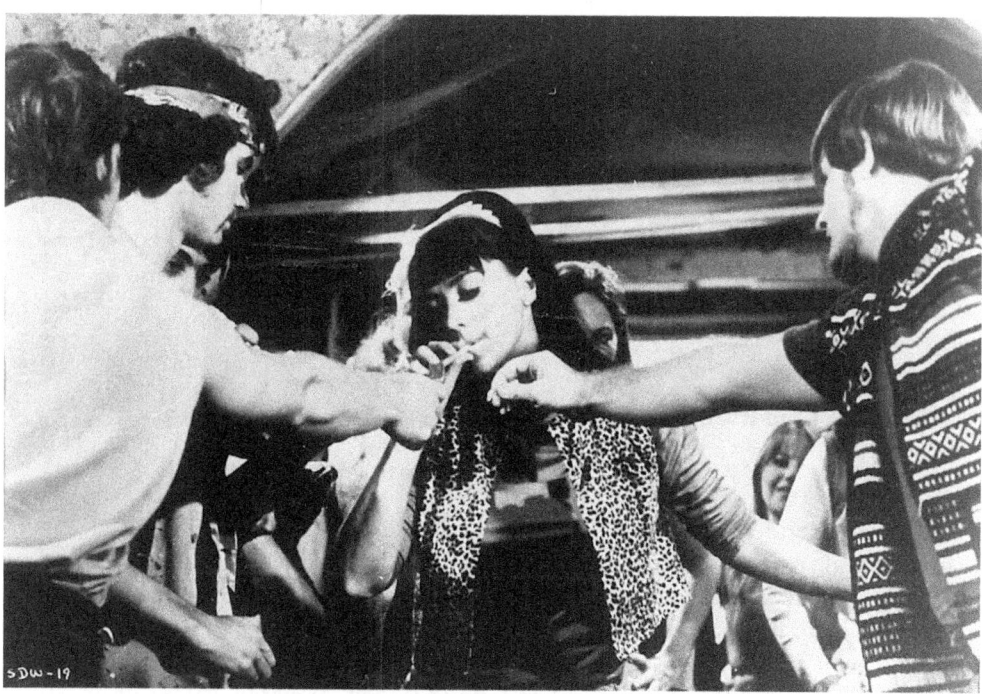

Studs eagerly light up their smokin' Queen (Betty Connell).

note stuck to a nose ring reads, "This little *Pig* went to market … the other little *Pigs* stayed home … the third little *Pig* got all carved up … but the Queen'll get burned to the bone."

Preemptively, the mad Man-Eaters visit Joe-Boy's usual bartender, who says he hasn't been around. Queen chains his face. She hatches a booby-trap plan.

The Man-Eaters stretch a neck-high piano wire on two poles across a dirt road near the restaurant where Whitey and Terry locate Joe-Boy and friends. Whitey slashes Joe-Boy's car tires to get his attention. She sprays insecticide in his eyes. Terry takes off with Whitey on the back of her bike so Joe-Boy will chase them on Terry's. Beyond the wire, the Man-Eaters taunt charging Joe-Boy—who sees the wire just before he is beheaded. Ceremoniously kicking his body, Queen drops her chain.

In the field near the clubhouse, Ted begs Karen one more time to accompany him. Under silent, reproachful persuasion stares, she can only kiss Ted good-bye. Dejected Ted watches the Man-Eaters depart. They help Queen look for the missing chain at the scene of Joe-Boy's murder. The police, who found it, have been waiting for them and make their arrest.

The evidence is circumstantial and the Man-Eaters walk. In poetry, Queen declares, "We don't owe nobody nothing. And we don't make no deals. We're swinging chicks on motors. And we're Man-eaters on wheels."

She-Devils on Wheels both glamorized the Man-Eaters and demystified them. What they made Karen do to Bill was like an execution performed by a loved one of the condemned. Their only true omnipotence was their hold over Karen—somehow giving Karen a need for belonging that Ted couldn't overcome or understand. If the Man-Eaters really wanted to master the opposite sex, they should have raped guys—not acquired them as trophies.

A new Stud race begins.

The hot rodders forced the Man-Eaters to deal with men who could also play rough. They could have been male bikers, but casting the Iron Cross might not have been smart, as on-screen they would had been required to lose out to their Cutthroat sisters. In revenge and counter-revenge, the Man-Eaters and the rodders were equally cowardly, targeting isolated people in each group. Only luck was why the Man-Eaters got away with murder.

Lewis' goofy stylisms were in full farce. The spirit of the Man-Eaters infused the film in a spinning scene-break card showing a growling Man-Eater kicking up her heels on a Honda Club that roared like a Harley. The no-nudity orgy was like clothed wrestling in molasses. Instead of piss and shit, Honey-Pot was baptized in same-colored edibles. One city rampage crime was the theft of a little girl's Coke. Outside the bar was a poster reading "Keep Steve Clark for Mayor." The customers who watched the bartender's beating were chair lumps completely devoid of reaction who sat frozen well after the Man-Eaters had left. Their dubious legal triumph was hinted by a caption: "Whoever Calls This 'The End' Doesn't Know the Man-Eaters."

If documentary cameras had been around, they would have recorded some mirthful mishaps. Like when the Kaopectate blood-stained paper mache head of Joe-Boy landed on cameraman Lewis' new white Levis, temporarily staining them. Or when Agi Gynes of *Just for the Hell of It* auditioned for a Man-Eater role on a borrowed Cutthroats bike, sending it and herself into a motel swimming pool.

Not the sexiest Lewis starlet, Nancy Lee Noble got to appear in several Hollywood films like *Medium Cool* (1969), portraying Lola in *Jackson County Jail* (1976) and its made-for-TV sequel *Outside Chance* (1978).

Herschell Lewis was willing to let Jerry Gross of Cinemation Industries release *She-Devils on Wheels* in certain territories, but Fred Sandy strongly favored A.I.P. In some areas, A.I.P. ran *She-Devils*. Lewis and Sandy controlled the others. *She-Devils* played in saturation bookings with the flat fee *Born Losers*. Mayflower Pictures finally wilted when Fred and Jerry Sandy took from Lewis the rights to some of its films, including *She-Devils on Wheels*. Roger Corman offered Lewis a chance to work for him, but the arrangement, due to things they couldn't agree on, came to naught.

The only memento of *She-Devils* still available is a preserved part of Betty Connell's Cutthroat—or rather cut arm.

Sinner's Blood

Cinema-International 1971. Executive Producer: Joe W. Grace, Jr.; Producers: Walter Robles, Michael Rae; Director: Neil Douglas; Screenplay: Lee Stone; Story–Associate Producer: Buddy Arett; Cinematography: Greg Lewis; Assistant Camera: Bradley Lane; Assistant Director: Peter C.J. Deyell; Sound Mixer: Bill Munns; Boom Man: Mike Burk; Key Grip: Mark Robles; Gaffer: Wendell Hall; Script Girl: Caroline Davis; Assistant Director–Stunt Coordinator: Michael Rae; Makeup: William Munns, Peter C.J. Deyell; Still Photographer: Linda Howard; Assistants to Producer: Linda Grosswirth, Val Jensen, Pam Poulson. DeLuxe Color; Running Time: 80 minutes.

Cast: Stephen Jacques (Zack); Nanci Sheldon (Pat); Christy Beal (Penny); John Talt (Aubrey); Parker Harriott (Gentry); Julie Connors (Edwina); Dennis McKenna (Chip); John Fisher (Clarence); Drucilla Hoy (Grace); Walter Robles (Monster); Buddy Arett, Justin Wells, Joe Steed.

Castration was a movie shock trend of the seventies. Mammary mutilation is a far less common effect. In *Sinner's Blood*, one of the "sinners" was metaphorically "castrated" via the latter. Standard castration usually happens south of the camera. *Sinner's Blood*, reveling in its mode, dared to bare.

Recently orphaned sisters Penny and Pat are taken in by their Aunt Grace and Uncle Clarence. At the train station, they meet Zack, a preacher's son. Grace and Clarence's children are geeky, repressed Aubrey and friendly lesbian Edwina. Aubrey spies on Penny through a bedroom wall peep hole. He is viciously teased by Zack's pal Gentry. Zack and Pat feel a reserved attraction. Penny makes it with Gentry.

Zack and Gentry join a bike gang Gentry's fond friend Chip belongs to. To spite his dad, Zack takes part in some hell at a church social that leaves the minister hurt. Aubrey watches Pat and Edwina as Edwina tries to seduce Pat, who freaks. Shamed Edwina flees. Aubrey thinks Pat was trying to steal Edwina's love and mauls her. Overcome by remorse, he does his own guilt run.

Aubrey sees the bikers having an orgy. Participant Penny spots Gentry and Chip having secret gay sex. Zack wants to make amends to his father. Penny gives Gentry a drink spiked with LSD. Wanting desperately to talk to Zack, Gentry follows him, taking Penny along. Gentry trips out and sails over a high bank to his death as Penny is thrown clear.

Stumbling back to the orgy, hysterical Penny admits she drugged Gentry. Coldly abandoned by the rest of the gang, Penny receives comfort from Aubrey. Chip, hurting because he "loved" Gentry, stabs Aubrey and proceeds to mutilate Penny's breasts. Aubrey alerts Zack and Pat to her peril. They go to save Penny.

In a hallucinatory operating room, one doctor says Penny can't be helped. "I think I can fix her," says another—Chip—who requests a scalpel.

Sinner's Blood came down hard on male homosexuality while showing some sympathy for nice Edwina. Voyeur nut Aubrey, once turned on by centerfolds, posed sex danger to his two cousins, but the most seriously dysfunctional character was Chip. Zack broke away from the gang in time and Aubrey got past passion dementia in his treatment of Pat. Chip acted out the stereotype that some fags are latent lunatics waiting to psychotically break and Penny's torture was the price for her irresponsible trick on Gentry.

Starting with a flash-forward taste of its distinguishing outrage, *Sinner's Blood* was influenced by Norman Bates' peek at

Marion Crane in copy-angle close-ups of Aubrey's curious eye. Not presenting any credible aftermath, *Sinner's* imagination blood ran dry as the ending disintegrated into a dumb abstraction that equated psycho cutting with the medical.

A bad bike movie, a downbeat youth movie and a morbid sex movie, *Sinner's Blood* invested some sensitivity in characterization—so blowing its chance to be flawlessly awful.

Sisters in Leather

Sack Amusement Enterprises 1969; Alternate Title: *Sisters in Leatherette*. Producer: Manuel S. Conde a/k/a Zoltan G. Spencer; Director: Spence Crilly a/k/a Zoltan G. Spencer; Cinematography: Manuel S. Conde; Film Editor–Sound: W.G. Meadows; Production Manager: Wallace Dare; Satyr IX Productions; Running Time: 64 minutes.

Characters: Husband Joe; Wife Mary; Leather Girls: Butch, Dolly, Billie; Bike Gang: Mike, Eddie, Turk; Bar Dancer: Tasha.

Sisters in Leather was the first lesbian Biker film. The Mini-Skirts and the Man-Eaters preferred "swordfish" (Man-Eater for cock) because their stories needed to play off of hormonal heat from hetero female libidos. General Bikers flaunted only mild suggestions of male homosexuality, disguising it as outrageous male camaraderie. Only softcore films could be candid about women who liked "oysters." The bike dykes of *Sisters in Leather* did not concern themselves with DC passion alone. As blackmailers, they traded on the social stigma of adultery and one sister violated club etiquette by enjoying her tryst with a mister.

Said sister, Dolly, plants herself in the convertible of Joe, a young executive. Their sex is interrupted at knifepoint by leader Butch, who demands two thousand dollars. Joe sees the lightning bolt emblem on her glove. Joe's wife Mary gets mad when he is unable to have sex with her. Joe brings the money to Dolly at the seduction spot. She makes it with Joe for kicks this time. Jealous Butch slugs Joe, vowing to fix him.

Mary receives a call from Butch hinting of Joe's infidelity. Joe goes to the hangout of the male Motorcycle Studs, meeting their prez, Mike. Joe says that the girl gang has the same lightning bolt symbol.

Butch (Bambi Allen) makes Mary (Kathy Williams).

The girls lure Mary to a picnic, where Butch tries to alienate her from all men. Mary wants to go home, requesting the photos of Joe and Dolly. Joe comes home to find Mary gone, but she left the photos as a message of indignation. On a notepad is a faint impression of the girl gang's address.

In their pad, the girls throw a lesbian orgy. Joe tips off the Motorcycle Studs. Mary realizes what the girls are. The Studs break in and aggressively administer their kind of loving. Joe and Mary reconcile and the girls now groove with the Studs.

Adhering to a porno dramaturgy standard, *Sisters in Leather* depicted lesbianism as some kind of innate female weakness brought out by sexual depravation or the influence of women who actively embrace it. Subjugation of the Sisters by the Studs perpetuated the myth that rape is a turn-on—and did so in the temerity of a mass gangbang that not only "cured" lesbians but helped save a marriage!

Mary was Kathy Williams and Butch was Bambi Allen. Williams' softcore career was at its height while Allen was just starting her career in both adult and non-softcore exploitation. Allen would do more Bikers than any other actress, becoming a favorite component in cinematic train pulls with her large, upside down cupcake-like breasts created by silicone.

Sleazy Rider

Phoenix International 1972. Executive Producer: Armond Atamian; Producer: Marland Proctor; Director-Screenplay: Roger Gentry; Cinematography: Rod Williamson; Sound: Veldor Sound of Hollywood; Electrician: Franklyn Torres; Key Grip: Ted Mills. Color; Running Time: 80 minutes.

Cast: Jody Bishop (Fry); Jim a/k/a Roger Gentry (Sheriff); Penny Boran, Starlyn Simone, Becky Perlman, Dalana Bissonette, Sandra Henderson, Sandra Casselman, Greg Peters.

Made by softcore actors Marland Proctor and Roger Gentry, who shared a few earlier x-credits, *Sleazy Rider* was *Ride Hard, Ride Wild* without Brigit Kroyer, any allusions to Denmark and the only adult Biker that didn't end with the comeuppance of a gang. "Justice" in *Sleazy Rider* was a Karl Borsche–like response to what a motorcycle gang would consider a sex crime ... the violation of one of their own.

Sheriff Sam and Deputy Roger decide to roust the visiting Conchos. Leader Fry needles Sam, who says, "You keep your fuckin' mouth shut!" "Hey man," Fry retorts, "We don't say *that* word in front of the ladies! I mean, we say cock, cunt, shit, piss and asshole and cocksucker ... but we don't say *that* word in front of the ladies!" "It takes a lot of guts to call any of these shit bitches ladies!" Sam fires back. Resisting a group frisk, scrappy Hannah spits in Sam's face. In the back seat of his car, he makes her undress and sadistically probes her vagina for hidden dope.

Fry assigns a man to tail Sam. At their camp, the Conchos meet Cathy, a desperate teenage runaway. Fry will make her a mama if she passes two initiation rites. First, she must ask someone to fuck her. No male accepts. "*I'll* fuck you," offers brazen Barbi. Their lesbian show stimulates an orgy. Fry learns that Sam and his family are moving out of their old home.

While Sam and his wife are packing the last of their things, their teenaged daughter, watched by two Conchos, masturbates to a muscle magazine in the bath-

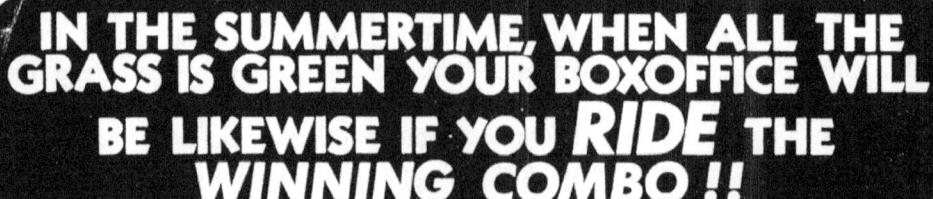

room. Sam answers the front door ... turning white when he sees smiling Fry, who says, "Hi, Sheriff. Remember me?" Fry punches Sam in front of Sam's screaming wife.

Tied up, Sam is put on trial. Hannah tells Fry what Sam did to her. As Sam's screaming, struggling daughter has her legs pulled apart, Fry shoves two gloved fingers up her vagina. Her mother is also made an orgy participant. For the next part of her initiation, Cathy smothers Sam's face with her crotch and administers fellatio. Hannah pays Sam back personally by pissing all over him.

The morning after, the Conchos prepare to leave, taking Sam's wife and daughter along. "Someday, when you tell this story—and you will—," lectures Fry, "and someday, when another bike gang happens to be passin' through—and they will—*be gentle!*" "*I'll get you myself,*" threatens Sam.

Cutting his hands free, Sam races madly to catch the Conchos, but his car goes out of control and crashes down a steep embankment. The Conchos view the burning wreckage.

Sleazy Rider eased extremely close to hardcore in its gynecological focus on the vagina as something brutal men can hurt even without phallic trespass. Nearly all of it was about those controlling and being controlled. Power perversion was Sam's duty-rationalized sexual battery on Hannah, Fry's manipulation of fresh "shit" Cathy and the defilement of Sam's loved ones for his crime. The only "innocuous" sex scene was the well-remembered masturbation sequence, playing on the fear onanists have of being discovered. Never getting their wicks wet, Fry and Sam seemed to be above groin-interaction on *their* part ... letting their fingers do their "fucking."

The actor billed as Jody Bishop seems to be Bill McKinney of *Angel Unchained*— just as Fred Bush of *The Takers* may be Josh Bryant. Dan Haggerty was the in-joke named Hag. Receiving no screen credit (or perhaps not wanting it), he was the only male Concho other than Bishop to keep his clothes on.

With the re-issued *Ride Hard, Ride Wild, Sleazy Rider* made up the first and only porn Biker double bill. *Sleazy Rider's* name was so catchy that other pornmakers couldn't pass it up. The *Sleazy Rider* of 1988 was an *Easy Rider* satire full of bike movie clips—including footage of Karen Black from the *Easy Rider* cemetery scene.

The Takers

Box-Office International 1971. Presenter: Harry Novak; Producers: Gary Troy, John Galyon; Director: Carlos Monsoya a/k/a Carl Monson; Screenplay: Dash Freemont; Cinematography: Gary Troy; Film Editor: C.C. Evers; Art Director: Pete Jay; Lighting Director: Peter Saxby; Second Unit Director: Sid Zieble; Stunt Gaffer: Dennis Troy; Best Boy: John Kauppi; Key Grip: John Key; Eastmancolor; Running Time: 81 minutes.

Cast: Susan Apple; Deborah Borroli; Fred Bush; Dennis Troy; Coe Bart; Rulo Thumb; Kim Kiya; Tony Zeno; Louise Douglas; Nosrom Lrak a/k/a Carl Monson.

The Jesus Trip and *Outlaw Riders* were not the only bookend Bikers of 1971. *The Takers* was a clone of *Wild Riders*, the work of softcore pros trying for something better. The only things *The Takers* had were more flesh and a "surprise" ending.

E.J. clobbers a rival biker and with friend Wil celebrates by picking up two girls for a drug and sex party. Needing more dope money, they rob a gas station. E.J. shoots the attendant. He and Wil move in on Laura and her out-of-town friend Barbara, who violently snub them.

Laura's husband Jack is away on a business trip. E.J. and Wil break into their suburban home. Jack calls Laura to say he will be delayed one week. Barbara comes on to Wil while E.J. molests helpless Laura. The foursome sleep together with Laura and Barbara's legs chained to the bed.

E.J. holds a sexual power over Laura, who tries to intimidate him with an empty gun and carefully dismisses a cop investigating a noise complaint. Barbara tries to talk Wil into letting her out of the house.

Returning early, Jack sees E.J. and Wil's bikes parked in the garage. Arming himself with a shotgun, he finds them in bed with Laura and Barbara. Jack tells Barbara to call the police. When E.J. tries to make Laura give him his gun, she shoots him. Jack shoots Wil. "The moral to be learned here," Jack tells us, "Thou shalt not covet another man's wife." Just an actor, "Jack" laughs in stage embarrassment. "Jesus Christ! That was terrible!" "Cut! Cut!" yells the director. Everybody gathers on the set for a big yuk.

Dropping any real pretense of narrative once the clothes came off at Laura's, *The Takers* was good feature-length gratuitous porn when the camera closely pressed the flesh. Out of some curious oversight, it missed any opportunities to show lesbianism between the women. Thankfully, *The Takers* didn't try to develop its relationship into anything truly significant. Raising the apochryphal dramatics beyond the level of erotic lead-ins might have dignified a picture that ended mooning the face of its audience with a manufactured blooper end—that "big surprise."

Laura was played by a 1963 Playmate who is one of the best-connected centerfold graduates cashing in on nostalgia. She has been open about her personal misfortunes and affair with Hef, but never discusses her skinflick career. Victoria's secret?

These Are the Damned

Columbia 1965. Released in England in 1963 as *The Damned*. Executive Producer: Michael Carreras; Producer: Anthony Hinds; Director: Joseph Losey; Screenplay: Evan Jones; Based on the novel *The Children of Light* by H.L. Lawrence; Associate Producer: Anthony Nelson-Keys; Cinematography: Arthur Grant; Film Editor: James Needs; Music: James Bernard; Music Director: John Hollingsworth; Art Directors: Bernard Robinson, Don Mingaye; Sound: Jock May; Assistant Film Editor: Reginald Mills; Production Manager: Richard MacDonald; Assistant Director: John Peverall; Sculptures: Elizabeth Frink; Camera Operator: Len Harris; Costumes: Molly Arbuthnot; Continuity: Pamela Davies; Makeup: Roy Ashton; Hair Stylist: Frieda Steiger; Casting: Stuart Lyons; Production Manager: Don Weeks; Songs: "Black Leather Rock" by Evan Jones, James Bernard. A Hammer-Swallow Production. British Running Time: 87 minutes; American Running Time: 77 minutes.

Cast: MacDonald Carey (Simon Wells); Shirley Anne Field (Joan); Viveca Lindfors (Freya); Oliver Reed (King); Alexander Knox (Bernard); Walter Gotell (Maj. Holland); James Villiers (Capt. Gregory); Kenneth Cope (Sid); Thomas Kempinski (Ted); Brian Oulton (Mr. Dingle); Barbara Everest (Miss Lamont); Alan McClelland (Mr. Stuart); James Maxwell (Mr. Talbot); Rachel Clay (Victoria); Caroline Sheldon (Elizabeth); Rebecca Dignam (Anne); Siobnan Taylor (Mary); Nicholas Clay (Richard); Kit Williams (Henry); Christopher Witty (William); David Palmer (George); John Thompson (Charles); David Gregory, Anthony Valentine, Larry Martyn, Leon Garcia, Jeremy Phillips (Teddy Boys); Edward Harvey, Neil Wilson, Fiona Duncan, Tommy Trinder, Victor Gorf.

Despite its ban on *The Wild One*, all the things that Britain feared about American teens were showing up in the ways of U.K. youth. Expatriate American director Joseph Losey, once he got commercial footing in London, turned to the H.L. Lawrence novel *The Children of Light*, a story that would have been appreciated by those who wanted to ban bombs—not movies.

Losey's screen adaptation of the book, *The Damned*, kept its allegory about the slow decay of known civilization and a secret government experiment to breed atomically immune offspring. Created by artificial insemination, the cold-blooded (temperature-wise) children lived in automated isolation. Where they were genetically made Frankenspawns meant to continue humanity in the event of H-war poisoning the air, the bikers of coastal Weymouth were existing human pollution. These youngsters happened because of a current order resigned to sleaze.

A weary American tourist, businessman Simon Wells docks in Weymouth aboard his boat the *La Dolce Vita*. Promenade predator Joan lures receptive Simon into a mugging carried out by her brother King and his gang.

Lovers turned friends, sculptress Freya Nielson and tutor Bernard are at a tea shop where Freya unveils her new creation, "graveyard bird." She lives in a studio on the cliff above a secret Army project Bernard oversees. Freya calls him "the only servant who hides secrets from his masters." Some soldiers bring in Simon and he meets Bernard, who says, "the age of senseless violence has caught up with us too."

Under Freya's stone house is the hidden bunker occupied by mutant children conceived for their planned role in dealing with "The Day of Megadeaths." Over closed-circuit TV, Bernard educates them to Western civilization, but not their key function. The one adult who is more than a radiation-suited keeper, only Bernard holds an altruistic view of the program.

Though incest-minded King thinks of all sex as dirty, Joan is tired of aiding him and being "protected" from all men. She takes refuge on the *La Dolce Vita* and Simon forgives her for her part in the mugging. Together, they sail off for Freya's studio.

After Simon and Joan make love, they are menaced by the gang and run away. An installation Army patrol spots them. Fleeing Simon, Joan and King fall into the ocean.

Rescued by the children, Simon, Joan and King find themselves in a cave and meet Bernard's pupils. This is their sole sanctuary from the constant video surveillance. King dislikes the children, who wonder if the above-ground strangers came to rescue them. Unknowingly, the kids spread their contamination to the visitors. At a loss for understanding the situation, Simon and Joan gain an ally in King.

When Simon, Joan and King bring the children into the sunlight, they encounter radiation-suited soldiers waiting for them. Horrified Freya and King cohort Sid watch their capture. Fatally contaminated King takes a child and escapes in a sports car, plunging off a bridge.

Still fond of Freya, Bernard promises she will be spared if she tells no one about the project. She spurns the offer and Bernard is forced to shoot her. Doomed Simon and Joan sail away as vigilant helicopters trail after them ... patiently waiting for the couple to die of radiation sickness. The voices of the children beg, "Help us, please!"

Freakish control in *The Damned* was not all the doing of the authorities who occupied Weymouth, letting hooligans get away with anything as long as it did not hinder the project. Wearing a snazzy sport coat over his leathers in a pose of elegance, anal anarchist King was pretty tight-assed in his sex hygiene hang-ups, but like many analists, he needed some kind of erotic safety valve. For money, he made Joan tug the zippers of enticed wallet-holders. And what was Joan supposed to get out of this except enforced, unwanted celibacy thrust upon her by a sibling sex-negative with tainted intentions.

Simon, Joan and the children all sought escape hatches: Simon via a vacation, Joan passage on his love boat and the kids, a way to the surface. Physically fit only to be part of a population made up of their kind, the strontium-unfriendly children wouldn't have had much of a life in a world where every warmblood they came near would die. The tomorrow they were created for was too many days away. The King gang were undesirables who nonetheless held a secure place in a part of pre–World War III earth composed of faded elegance. The only vitality in Weymouth was in its residents, who took rather than gave back.

Original producer Anthony Hinds hated Joseph Losey and quit, forcing Michael Carreras, son of Hammer founder Sir James, to take over. Hammer found the relationship between King and Joan too diffuse and wanted a clarifying scene. Losey's way of killing Freya off was to have her shot by an Army helicopter. Michael and Sir James Carreras didn't get along and after *The Damned*, Michael left Hammer.

MacDonald Carey was Losey's leading man choice, not Hammer's because Carey had starred in Losey's *The Lawless* (1958). Hammer helped the career of Oliver Reed immeasurably, but it was

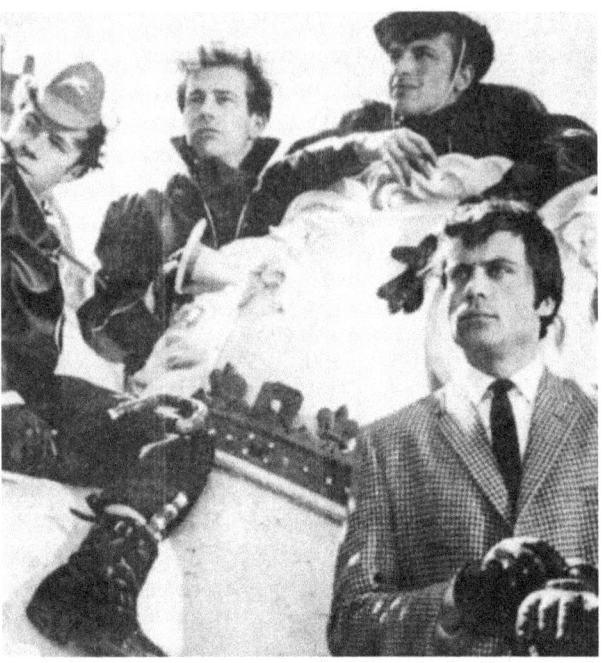

The wild ones of Weymouth and their leader King (Oliver Reed).

Shirley Ann Field, one of Reed's co-players in *Beat Girl* (1961) a/k/a *Wild for Kicks*, who got America's attention first in *The Entertainer* (1960) and *Saturday Night and Sunday Morning* (1961).

It was the bomb paranoia, not the cycle violence, that disturbed Hammer, and the British release of *The Damned* was delayed for eighteen months. Cut from one hundred minutes to eighty-seven, it went out as a second feature. Unsure of how to market the film, Hammer hyped it as a Biker, omitting all sci-fi references. The ads showed King and his gang harassing Joan while King's face all but shouted lust ... the censors not knowing or caring that this guy had the hots for his own sister.

The Damned was a title Warner Bros. owned, later the name of Luschino Visconti's 1969 picture, so American distributor Columbia added *These Are*. Columbia stressed the sci-fi, making the children seem like little Midwich monsters before shelving the film. Added to the praise of English critics was Hollywood columnist Shielah Graham's strong endorsement of *The Damned*, which in 1964 became the second recipient of the Golden Asteroid Award at the Trieste Science Fiction Film Festival.

In 1965, Columbia picked *The Damned* to back up *Genghis Khan*. To tighten the double bill length, it cut another ten minutes. Various New York critics hailed the mutilated but still potent movie. *These Are the Damned* was damned to box office failure, but it was revived periodically at the New Yorker Theater and an uncut copy was included in the horror films at the Museum of Modern Art.

Werewolves on Wheels

Fanfare 1971. Producer: Paul Lewis; Director: Michel Levesque; Screenplay: David M. Kaufman, Michel Levesque; Associate Producer: Stewart Fleming; Cinematography: Isadore Mankofsky; Film Editor: Peter Parasheles; Music: Don Gere; Art Director: Allan Jones; Script: Joyce King; Props: James Dunn; Camera Assistant: Steven Wolper; Stills: Joanne Lee; Key Grip: William Clausse; Assistant Art Director: Gil Valle; Production Assistant: Stuart Ganong; Production Secretary: Meryle Selinger; Sound Mixer: Leroy Robbins; Boom: James Contreras; Assistant Editor: James Eric; Stunt Coordinator: Chuck Bail; Post-Production: Edit-Rite; Sound: Producers Sound Service; Equipment: Leonetti; DeLuxe Color; A South Street Production; Running Time: 84 minutes.

Cast: Stephen Oliver (Adam); Severn Darden (One); D.J. a/k/a Donna Anderson (Helen); William Gray (Bill); Gray Johnson (Movie); Deuce Berry (Tarot); Barry McGuire (Scarf); Owen Orr (Mouse); Anna Lynn Brown (Shirley); Leonard Rogel (Gas Station Owner); Tex Hall, Dan Kopp, Ingrid Grunewald, Keith Guthrie, John Hull, Carl Lee, Marilyn Munger, N.A. Palmisano, Bart Smith.

Growing into a large-small pond frog, Joe Solomon made Fanfare the Fanfare Corporation. Its big film for 1971 was *Evel Knievel*, starring George Hamilton, who co-produced with Solomon. Bruce Kessler, meanwhile, was shooting *Simon—King of the Witches*, a Hippie occult piece. Just in case *Simon* was a hit—and it was—Solomon was ready to okay a Satanic bike story called *Devil's Advocate* and *Demon Angels*. Describable in one sentence—devil worshippers turn bikers into werewolves—even *he* didn't fully understand the plot. With his other Bikers, Solomon had a clear grasp of things. Here, he was too caught up in profit, hiring a skilled but overly esoteric director, Michel Levesque.

Near a gas station–general store, the Devil's Advocates encounter two redneck truckers who force a member off the road. The offenders are summarily dealt with. In the store, the Advocates make the owner ogle the goodies of topless Shirley. Mystical Tarot sees death in the cards for leader Adam's old lady Helen. "We're gonna crash and burn," is Adam's pat prophecy for everyone. He dares Tarot to validate his notion.

Obliging Adam, Tarot guides the Advocates to a secluded monastery. Relaxing in the garden, they meet a group of monks led by nefarious One who serves bread and drugged wine.

While the Advocates are asleep, One snips off a lock of Helen's hair—luring entranced Helen into a nude snake dance altar ceremony ... so that she may become Satan's bride. Adam wakes up first, finds Helen gone and hears the incantation chants. With his comrades, Adam violently disrupts the ritual. They take Helen and go into the desert.

Only Tarot realizes the occult significance of what has happened. During sex, Helen bites Adam's throat, drawing blood. Mouse and Shirley carnally cavort beyond camp and are slain by two werewolves. Their deaths are blamed on a fall and hungry wolves supposedly fed off them. Mouse and Shirley are buried.

The next camp is an auto graveyard where Adam sets up an all-night watch and the cars are burned to create a huge bonfire. Bill takes first watch, but Movie casually replaces him. One of the werewolves tosses Movie into the fire.

Lovers and lycanthropes-to-be Adam (Stephen Oliver) and Helen (D.J. Anderson).

Some of them now spooked, the Advocates decide to bash the monks. On the way back to the monastery, a strange fog looms up ahead, placing the Advocates in a dune valley. The fog was meant to delay them. Sick of Tarot's ideas, Adam leaves him behind. When Tarot catches up, they fight.

At a third camp, Adam and Helen suddenly go into wild convulsions—simultaneously becoming the werewolves. Tarot grabs a flaming brand, spurring the others to do likewise. Helen is burned while Adam makes a fast escape on his bike. The rest go after him. His colors set ablaze, Adam plunges off a cliff.

Tarot leads the remaining Advocates back to the monastery for revenge—but the cult turns them into new members.

Different in its transmission of lycanthropy, *Werewolves on Wheels* wasn't a very satisfying horror film. Its only real sense of danger was in the dread of anomic, superstitious Tarot. With such a high-concept title, a whole kennel of hairy Harley riders was expected. Until their last scene, the Adam and Helen wolves were practically subliminal and even their exposure was a partial letdown. Helen immolated almost as quickly as flash paper and Adam preferred flight over fight. This paid off so far as showing one wheeled wolf. By his death, Adam fulfilled the prediction of "crash and burn" for himself.

Devil cults, like vampires, depend on new members for their life blood. Were the Devil's Advocates monk marks because they spoiled the "marriage" ceremony or was this an elaborate conversion scheme? The Advocate who led the gang to the monastery twice, Tarot was possibly a cat's-paw. Those who had taken Lucifer's name in vain—either for retribution or because they were needed—were taken to a higher (or maybe make that lower) level of decadence.

Steve Oliver had just come off of *Bracken's World* and his third recurring character would be the creampuff tough Dugan Hicks in *The Van* (1977) and *Malibu Beach* (1978). D.J. Anderson was the former Donna Anderson of Stanley Kramer's *On the Beach* (1959) and *Inherit the Wind* (1960). Mostly a baleful, staring,

Adam (Stephen Oliver) wolfs down a fellow biker.

ash-covered face, Severn Darden helped form the Compass Theater, which later became the St. Louis improv group Second City. A role in Second City's Broadway show won Darden a Tony nomination.

Bill Gray of *Father Knows Best* was a professional bike racer and heavy doper seen as a dealer in the drugumentary *Dusty and Sweets McGee* (1971). The singer of "Eve of Destruction," Barry McGuire got carried away in a funny parody of used car advertising, imitating a mutt high on PCP. McGuire kicked his own drug habit to become a Christian vocalist.

The ad art of *Werewolves on Wheels* showed a fierce wolfman on a bike slinging an upside down, scantily clad girl over his left shoulder. The girl held a skull while a fat serpent was coiled around the werewolf's neck like a scarf. The pressbook mentioned a sequel to be called *I Married a Teenage Werewolf Who Rode a Chopper*. Fanfare was kidding, of course.

People who liked plain Bikers found *Werewolves* too fuzzy while fright fans wanted less hogs and more canines.

The Wild Angels

American International 1966. Presenters: James J. Nicholson, Samuel Z. Arkoff; Producer-Director: Roger Corman; Screenplay–Assistant to Director: Peter Bogdanovich (screenplay credited to Charles Griffith); Associate Producer: Lawrence Cruikshank; Cinematography: Richard Moore; Film Editor: Monte Hellman; Music Producer: G.P. IV Productions; Written–Arranged by Mike Curb, Performed by the Arrows; Art Director: Leon Erickson; Production Manager: Sharon Compton; Production Designer: Rick Beck-Meyer; Wardrobe: Glen Wright; properties: Richard M. Rubin; Assistant Director: Paul Rapp; Makeup: Jack Obringer; Hair Stylist: Suzzanne Germain; Script Supervisor: Bonnie Prendergast; Sound: Phil Mitchell; Pathecolor and Panavision; a Roger Corman Production; Running Times: 82, 83, 85 and 90 minutes.

Cast: Peter Fonda (Heavenly Blues); Nancy Sinatra (Mike); Bruce Dern (Loser); Diane Ladd (Gaysh); Buck Taylor (Dear John); Lou Procopio (Joint); Coby Denton (Bull Puckey); Marc Cavell (Frankenstein); Norman Alden (Medic); Michael J. Pollard (Pigmy); Joan Shawlee (Mama Monahan); Gayle Hunnicutt (Suzie); Art Baker (Thomas); Frank Maxwell (Preacher); Kim Hamilton (Nurse); Dick Miller (Hardhat); Frank Gerstle (Hospital Policeman); Gina Grant, Hal Bokar, Jack Bernardi, Members of Hell's Angels of Venice, California.

Roger Corman accepted an offer from Columbia to leave A.I.P. and work there. Promised big-budget assignments, the only thing he would realize would be 1967's *A Time for Killing*, from the novel *The Long Ride Home*, finishing up for credited director Phil Karlson. A.I.P. President James Nicholson knew Columbia chief Mike Frankovich and until he could sever his Columbia contract, Corman was granted a leave of absence to produce and direct for A.I.P.

In January 1966, Mother Miles was traveling to Berkeley when a truck ran a red light and smashed into his bike head-on. Hospitalized for two broken legs and a skull fracture, Miles—born James—lingered in a coma and died six days later, one short of his thirtieth birthday. Miles left a wife, two children, a mistress and his mother. On the mother's arrangement, he was interred in Sacramento. Though the body was shaved and laid out in a conservative suit, the funeral otherwise was an Angels service, attracting other clubs—some rival groups—and a number of "barebacks" (unaffiliated riders). The service, however, was soured by the sermonizing of a stern minister who warned all bikers present that someday they would have to answer to God.

Roger Corman saw a *Life* photo of the funeral, claiming *this* was the inspiration for *The Wild Angels* while A.I.P. employees Milt Moritz and Al Kallis alleged they had shown vice-president Samuel Arkoff a *Saturday Evening Post* spread of the Angels. Corman assigned his best writer, Charles B. Griffith, to the job.

Griffith befriended a Venice Angel and set up a meeting with some at a Hawthorne dive, the Gunk Shop. Corman paid each Angel who brought his own bike and more to those who furnished their old ladies. Using pot and liquor as bribery, Corman attended an Angels party in Venice, recording accounts of some of their exploits. One girl mentioned an Angel felon who was shot by the police and hijacked from a Tijuana hospital to keep him from going to jail. And there was the church defilement at Bass Lake.

Corman and A.I.P. agreed on the title *The Hell's Angels*, but A.I.P. wanted to repeat *The Wild One*'s design of identifying with victimized villagers until Corman recommended the Angel viewpoint. Writing with extremely minimal dialogue, Charles Griffith contrasted their lifestyle with that of a motorcycle cop. Sometimes, he indulged in unusable esoterica, such as fixating on a roadside frog that saw the Angels from a frog's eye view. A cop protagonist wasn't sound exploitation sense to Corman, who wanted to tie the Mother Miles funeral to the hospital story and make the funeral a reenactment. Griffith submitted a rewrite that focused on an overestimated sense of power the Angels felt they had.

At a screening, Corman met Peter Bogdanovich, an *Esquire* movie critic, and his wife, Polly Platt. Not registered with the Writers' Guild, Bogdanovich couldn't receive credit for the final draft script Platt helped him on. Griffith was the "official" scribe while Bogdanovich was billed by his other function as Assistant to Director.

Angel liaison Big Otto Friendly, of the San Bernardino chapter, okayed the script, but Corman was too stingy to pay them for their copyrighted name. In prerelease news, *All the Fallen Angels* was picked and *The Wild Angels* was finally chosen so the word "wild" could capitalize on *The Wild One*.

The leader in *The Wild Angels* was at first named Blackjack and James Nicholson wanted George Chakiris, who won an Oscar for his stunning portrayal of Bernardo in *West Side Story*. A Chakaris portrayal of a biker may have been interesting given his excellent physical credentials, but at probable cost to the career future of Peter Fonda, still dwarfed by the combined shadows of his father Henry and sister Jane.

Fonda met Dennis Hopper when Hopper was married to Brooke Hayward, the daughter of Margaret Sullavan, Henry's first wife, and Leland Hayward, Henry's agent and producer. At the time *The Wild Angels* was being cast, Fonda and Hopper were writing a screenplay, *The Yin and the Yang*. In New York to raise money for financing, Fonda was contacted by agent Jack Gilardi to play the secondary role of Loser. For total realism, Roger Corman was going to eschew process-screen riding. George Chakiris was scared shitless of bikes and when refused a double for his riding scenes, he bowed out.

One of the longer-haired actors then, Fonda arrived at Corman's office wearing hexagonal shades with mirrored upper quarters (a gift from Rolling Stone Brian Jones) and a Sheriff's badge proclaiming he belonged to the Chicago branch of Navy Intelligence (an epithet meant to ambiguously shock Corman). Chakiris' replacement, Fonda considered Blackjack a hokey handle, suggesting Heavenly Blues after the hallucinogenic Heavenly Blue morning glory seeds crushed down and mixed with water. Even wanting the seeds to decorate his chopper's gas tank, Fonda thought of playing Blues with a beard and spirit gum gaps in his teeth, but A.I.P. preferred a handsome hero. As a concession to funk, he wore orange aviator shades in almost every scene.

Nancy Sinatra was picked to play Blues' girl Mike (nicknamed "Monkey" by the Blues) because the oldest child of Frank was riding high on "These Boots Are Made for Walking," a tune that outsold every Old Blue Eyes song.

Some prints began with the caption "The Picture You Are About to See Will Shock You, Perhaps Anger You. Although the Events and Characters are Ficticious, the Story Is a Reflection of Our Times."

A Venice tot tricycles out of his fenced front yard, alarming his mother, who catches the boy as Heavenly Blues briskly brakes before them. Blues drags on a joint and slowly rumbles away. Opening up his chopper, he zooms past street traffic. Down the freeway, he turns into the San Pedro oilfield.

Climbing up a rig, Blues tells fellow Angel Loser that his stolen hog is in the desert town of Mecca. A gruff co-worker objects to Blues' Iron Cross pendant. "If you guys had been at Anzio, you'd know what that junk means!" Insulted Blues grabs the hardhat and Loser taunts him with a wrench. Below, the foreman reprimands Loser, who throws the wrench at him and is fired. "We used to kill guys who wore that kind of garbage!" the emotional hardhat yells at departing Blues and Loser.

Blues takes Loser home to his old lady Gaysh. Storming inside, Loser grumbles, "I don't like nobody gettin' uptight with me, man!" He comes out with beer for himself and Blues and a bag of heroin

Heavenly Blues (Peter Fonda) strikes a pro–Protest pose.

powder. "You never get a straight deal around here," Loser bitches over a sniff. Gaysh chides Loser because he can't hold a job. "How are we gonna fix this place up?" "Who cares?" huffs Loser. "*I* care!" Gaysh retorts. The thought of recovering his bike puts Loser in a happier disposition.

The Angels travel to Mecca on the San Bernardino road, passing a Highway Patrol motorcycle cop who turns around and follows them, calling backup. The cops trail the Angels to a canyon where Loser starts a race for the favors of blowzy housemother Mama Monahan.

Blues, Loser, Dear John, Pigmy, Medic, Joint and Bull Puckey sneak off to quiet Mecca and march to the garage of the Mecca Muscle Men. Sympathetic Loser unties a hitched horse that won't budge. "Most pitiful thing I ever saw," Loser tells Blues, "He's free and he won't even go." "Yeah, you've made a friend for life," sourly remarks Blues.

Working on their bikes, the Muscle Men nervously face the Angels. "Which one of you taco benders stole an Angel's machine?" Blues demands to know. The Angels look around and Loser finds a brake pedal he identifies as his. "One of you beaners told a lie," he accuses. A rumble ensues. The two motorcycle cops are outside, drawn by the whinnies of the horse to the gang fight, which they break up. Separated from the other fleeing Angels, Loser steals a police cycle.

During a high-speed mountain chase, the pursuit cop shoots Loser in the back before he skids off the highway. Weakened Loser nears a roadblock ahead and cracks up. The roadblock cops slowly converge as grimacing Loser stiffly rises and collapses, clutching the medal of his Maltese necklace as he blacks out.

Blues' party returns to the wild canyon festivities. Flushed with victory over whipping the Muscle Men, Blues brags, "We've got the power!" Gaysh is worried aobut Loser. "Think he's all right?" asks Mike. "Now how the hell would I know?" Blues replies—deep down very concerned. Frankenstein tries to make it with Gaysh, who knees him and runs to Blues for protection. Blues spots Dear John inhaling something in a carton and bolts his way, shouting, "I warned you about horse!" They brawl in a stream until the police intervene and send the Angels off.

Meanwhile, in a Palm Springs Hospital, critically injured Loser is being readied for emergency surgery.

The Angels hold a beer parlor summit meeting. Gaysh fears Loser's next stop will be prison and begs Blues to do something. Dear John says knock the hospital over. Frankenstein feels it can't be done. "It *can* be done," hints clever Blues, "if you're smart!"

After normal visiting hours, Mike goes to the hospital desk nurse posing as Loser's sister. The nurse summons his police guard. Permitted to see comatose Loser, Mike feigns distress and secretly unlocks a sliding glass door. Blues, Dear John, Joint and Pigmy sneak in a moment later. While getting a sedative for Mike, the nurse hears Loser groaning and sees him being carried off to a waiting station wagon. Stationed behind the door, Joint assaults the nurse.

When Pigmy drops Loser's plasma bottle, the guard reacts to the sound of breaking glass. Blues pulls Joint off the raped nurse. Charging into the room, the guard glimpses her unconscious form and fires at the escaping wagon. Hearing the shots, Mike runs out front, where driver Blues lurches to a halt and she jumps in.

Brought to Mama Monahan's, Loser is placed on a bed and wakes up, glad to be with his comrades. "You sprung me … you're beautiful!" He turns his necklace. "I broke my medal … ain't it pitiful?" "You want anything?" asks Gaysh. "I want to get high," says Loser. Medic takes Loser's fading pulse. Dragging on a joint, he convulses and dies. "He's wasted," solemnly whispers Mike. Gaysh breaks down in tears while Blues carries his silent grief outside, followed by Mike.

The nurse sees a mug shot of Blues, identifying him as her attacker. Loser's body is taken to a shady mortician who accepts a patently fake death certificate. Loser will be sent to his hometown, Sequoia Groves.

Detectives are looking for Blues, who ducks for cover. He arranges a club meeting on Medic's fishing boat. Dear John favors a gaudy funeral procession, but arriving Blues disapproves. The other Angels will go to Sequoia Groves while Blues remains on the boat with Mike. "It's all my fault," regrets Blues, "the whole thing." "It's like you went with him or something," Mike tells Blues. "What if *I* died?" She tries another question. "Is it still you and me?" "I don't know," ponders Blues, who decides to attend the funeral.

Summoned to his church, the Sequoia Groves minister approaches Loser, lying in an open coffin in full colors under a Nazi flag draped across the altar. Painfully, the minister recognizes him. As he begins his eulogy, Blues and Mike dramatically enter.

The word "Lord" offends Blues. "The Lord gives life," says the minister, "and Man can make of it what he will. Why, this young man could have made any number of things." "Let me tell you what life made of him," shouts Blues, "About how life never let him do what he wanted to, and how life always made him be good, always pay the rent and shovel it. We're not children of God—but Hell's Angels!" "Woe unto them that call evil good and good evil thus sayeth Isaiah," quotes the sad minister. "We don't want nobody telling us what to do," Blues rants, "We don't want nobody pushing us around!" "Just what is it you want to do?" asks the minister. "Well, we want to be free," answers Blues, "to do what we want to do. We want to be free to rise. We want to be free to ride our machines without being hassled by The Man. We want to get loaded. And we want to have a good time. We're going to have a good time … we're going to have a party!"

Almost on cue, the Angels tear up the pews and begin a sacrilegious orgy. The minister bolts to the door, but Blues and Medic obstruct him. "He was my son!" the minister cries before Medic socks him in the stomach and Blues administers a neck karate chop. Blues makes love to Mike while Gaysh violently shrugs off lecherous Frankenstein and runs over to Loser's coffin. "Why don't you say we put her out of her misery?" Frankenstein suggests to Dear John. They drag hysterical, struggling Gaysh behind the altar and drug her preparatory to rape.

The trussed-up minister begins to rouse. "Intepreting" Loser, Medic reports, "He says the preacher belongs here." Loser is removed from the coffin and the minister is deposited. Propped in a corner, Loser is fussed over by "friends" who put dark glasses on his face and stick a joint in his mouth. Done with Mike, Blues is dumbstruck by what he started, grabbing Dear John's heroin to snort some. Unrelieved, he tells cuddlesome Mike, "Beat It! I don't want you!" She finds physical consolation in the arms of Dear John.

Blues takes Mama Monahan and goes off to screw her while tattered gangbang discard Gaysh tells Loser she wasn't responsible. "I couldn't help it ... honest ... you aren't angry at me, are you?" After doing Mama Monahan, Blues punches Dear John, throwing a look at Mike that says "It's over." He removes the minister from the casket. Waking up, the minister cuts his hands free with a broken bottleneck. Loser is returned to the coffin. "What do we do now?" asks Pigmy. "Bury him!" proclaims Blues. After the Angels leave, the minister calls the police.

Gawking locals follow the Angels to Loser's open marked grave near the cemetery gate. "Don't you think you should say something?" Mike urges Blues, who numbly declares, "Nothing to say." The bolder townsmen rush forward, then suddenly halt in menacing postures ... waiting for the Angels to make the first move. A young boy throws a rock at Pigmy, knocking him into the grave. "Let's get 'em!" shouts Dear John. Blues wants to bury Loser first, but the cemetery erupts in mob violence. Police sirens send the Angels scurrying to their bikes. Mike implores Blues to run, but he tells her, "There's nowhere to go!" She flees with Dear John. Shovel in hand, Blues throws dirt into Loser's grave.

The way Peter Bogdanovich wrote them, the Angels were pretty dismal company—as was everyone else. Citizens showed up just long enough to represent undesirable types. The police were uniformed or plainclothed androids, their voices usually emotionless and disembodied. Contact with the Latino bikers, the Muscle Men, revealed a tinge of Angel racism and various Angels couldn't get along with each other. Mike and Gaysh were merely supportive chattel.

The once Pleasantville-like America of *The Wild One* was a wasteland of dead-end industrial neighborhoods, enclosed spaces and congested traffic. Roger Corman saw the Angels as throwbacks in a high-tech society, making its ugliest facets dreary enough to show why the Angels wanted no part of it. To be a person in *The Wild Angels* was to be someone lobotomized by middle-class mediocrity or an individual straining to defy it. The real "love" in *Wild Angels* was not between Blues and Mike but the unstated closeness between Blues and Loser reading like the singular intimacy between Peter Fonda and Eugene "Stormy" McDonald III, the college pal and heir to the Zenith radio fortune who died mysteriously in 1965.

Blues had set himself up for losing Loser, first with the Mecca run, then the hospital mission. Blues wrecked Loser's chance for a dignified service with the protest party that became a profane wake. However, through this spectacle, Blues discovered his own capacity to be shocked. During the moments before his arrest, he was able to extend to a dead friend the nobility of sacrificing his liberty to ensure proper symbolic closure.

The Wild Angels had even more anecdotal nightmares than the average Roger Corman production. A few Angels stole a semi-truck loaded with bikes belonging to other Angels. To deter further heists, ex–C.I.A. man Paul Rapp hired a couple of guard Angels. Worried about daughter Nancy's safety, Frank Sinatra made him personally responsible for that. In a restaurant scene, an Angel was to slide out a chair Nancy would sit in, but he made her fall too hard. Rapp attacked the Angel and two more dragged him outside and beat him up.

Because one was an alleged cop killer, the San Berdoo Angels were watched over by over one hundred fifty police agents who photographed them, the cast and the crew. They tested bugging equipment by taping Paul Rapp and his girlfriend in a motel room. An elderly female extra was a paid intelligence spy. The accused killer and his chapter were going to rumble with the Venice Angels, but evening snow halted their procession. When the cops followed the company to Mecca, production manager Jack Bohrer begged them to delay the arrests of the Angels on sundry outstanding warrants until they finished their work (no Angel hung around for the entire shooting and those who left were replaced by more). Corman then warned the Angels about the law, buying them escape time.

While the cast and crew stayed in a motel, the Angels camped out in the parking lot and in the grove, where all partying was their actual entertainment. The beer and pot Corman donated were both to pacify their violent tendencies *and* keep the blast lively.

Nearby, brother Gene Corman was producing the World War Two epic *Tobruk* (1966). As a gag, he launched a surprise "raid" on *The Wild Angels* set. During the Mecca mayhem, Wehrmacht troops rolled in on sidecar bikes and in tanks and halftracks. Firing blank weapons ammo, they scared away the extras and "kidnapped" Peter Fonda and Bruce Dern. The amazing spectacle inspired Corman and cinematographer Richard Moore to keep shooting.

On the highway where Loser rode the stolen police bike, Bruce Dern was spotted by an armed civilian who thought he was a real fugitive and pointed a double-barreled shotgun out of his car window, threatening to fire. The intervention of highway patrolmen supervising the scene

Nancy Sinatra in her first big movie role, as Mike.

saved Dern. The stuntman playing the cop after Loser nearly lost a leg when his bike toppled on him. While chasing a rabbit out in the desert, Peter Fonda took a fall.

The interior of the Sequoia Groves chapel was actually Hollywood's Little Country Church on North Argyle. Some of its members objected to the Angels being there. Although Bruce Dern was "dead" for much of the movie, two Angels told him to remove his costume colors, believing only real Angels should wear them. Not giving Dern enough time to comply, the Angels clobbered him cold right in front of the church. Its pews were both church property and breakaway sets. Glass, wall panels and the seats were severely damaged during the orgy. The moment where Loser was made the "life" of the party was improvised and an Angel instructed to carve a swastika into the coffin could only manage Z with a center line.

The Sequoia Groves exteriors were shot in Idlewyld. Cold weather hampered the chopper engines, requiring personnel to raise their motel room heat. Actor Coby

Denton almost died from carbon monoxide poisoning due to a faulty heater. Corman wanted to resume filming while Denton spent two days in intensive care in Hemet, making everyone upset, but the show had to go on. An artificial arch and some fake headstones turned Idlewyld's park into a "cemetery" covered by traces of late-March snow. Pissed off by Corman's hard-driving, the Angels vented their anger on Peter Bogdanovich when Corman recruited him to play a Sequoia brawler (Bogdanovich later found it in his heart to treat outlaws sympathetically in his 1985 picture *Mask*).

Cut from the final print was a scene Peter Fonda had written for himself as a way of dealing with the suicide of his mother, Frances Seymour Brokaw. In the cemetery, Blues turned to a grave and asked, "Why did you do it, mother?"

The music was scored by Mike Curb and performed by Davie Allen and the Arrows. They had worked on the Oscar-winning 1965 short *Skaterdater*. Done with Fuzztone instruments, its main tune, "Blues' Theme" was a tangy chart-buster and Tower Records issued two soundtrack albums.

While proving himself an expert biker as he weaved through traffic in the fast credits scene, Peter Fonda was a little too mellow, often a fey zombie with an unconvincing tough guy sneer. He and Nancy Sinatra, the worst Corman actress, displayed no working on-screen chemistry and her few shows of emotion were pathetic.

Far better was Bruce Dern as Loser, who was married at the time to Diane Ladd, cast as Gaysh. Also headed for better things was Michael J. Pollard when he played C.W. Moss in *Bonnie and Clyde* (1967). The most attractive of the Angel old ladies, Gayle Hunnicutt was a Roger Corman girlfriend. The son of Dub, Buck Taylor became Newly O'Brien on *Gunsmoke*.

Much of the negativism *The Wild Angels* generated fell on Peter Fonda like a dump truck load of manure. A.I.P. sent him to New York to attend the sneak preview screening at the 1966 Theater Owner's Association Convention. While he was gone, California police raided a Tarzana home rented by Fonda's Man Friday John Haberlin III, where they found nine pounds of grass, issuing an arrest warrant for Fonda. With Fonda in New York were Henry and Henry's current wife Shirlee. Henry was doing a Broadway play and could not attend the preview. Some Jewish, many distributors were so revolted by *The Wild Angels* that they refused to book it. Going to his limo, Fonda was attacked by an enraged woman who had seen his stage work, calling him a Nazi. Fonda joined Henry at the Lincoln Center, where the theater exhibitors showed up and roundly booed him. Some Canadian exhibitors, sensing the profitability of *The Wild Angels*, applauded it.

Upon his return to Los Angeles, Fonda was arrested. Capitalizing on the notoriety of *The Wild Angels*, the prosecutor brought in as a star witness one Marilyn Casky, who claimed that Fonda and two other defendants, John Robischon and Steven Alsberg, held pot parties at the Tarzana address and got her high.

An entrant in the Venice Film Festival, *The Wild Angels* worried the State Department because of its unfavorable view of American life. Fonda went to Italy with Jim Nicholson, Sam Arkoff and Roger Corman, who felt he should not attend a special screening on the island of Lido due to his legal problems. Fonda got even by telling the captain of a charter ferry that Arkoff was already on the island and wanted the boat taken there. Temporarily everyone on Lido was stranded.

At Cannes, *The Wild Angels* won an award and was hailed by Fonda's then brother-in-law, French director Roger

Vadim, as one of the most important American films of the decade. U.S. critics razzed the picture. Since the film and soundtrack album exploited her name, Nancy Sinatra sued A.I.P. When the Hell's Angels felt defamed, A.I.P. was hit with a four million dollar lawsuit. Big Otto Friendly repeatedly threatened to kill Roger Corman, once on TV, but since the threats were open, he couldn't afford to harm the uninsured Corman. The Angels settled for the suit.

U.S. Senator Thomas Dodd, investigating the root causes of juvenile delinquency, subpoenaed Corman to appear at his committee. Thanks to the character witness testimony of Henry, the disappearance of questionable Marilyn Casky and no proof that he had ever paid rent or stayed at the drug house, Fonda was acquitted of the marijuana charge.

Fonda was arrested again—but this time for something minor. He was picked up during the Sunset Strip riots and claimed he was there to film a documentary about them.

Roger Corman finally terminated his Columbia contract and for A.I.P. prepared to make his LSD odyssey *The Trip* (1967), which was to reteam Peter Fonda with Bruce Dern and Nancy Sinatra until Corman fired Sinatra, casting Susan Strasberg. Corman was only the executive producer for *Devil's Angels*, set for filming in Tucson and Patagonia, Arizona, the next January. Although Charles Griffith hated *The Wild Angels'* rewrite and came to detest every Biker, he signed on to do the script.

The Wild One

Columbia 1954. Producer: Stanley Kramer; Director: Laslo Benedek; Screenplay: John Paxton; Based on a story by Frank Rooney; Cinematography: Hal Mohr; Filmed with Garutso Balanced Lens; Film Editor: Al Clark; Musical Director: Morris Stoloff; Musical Score: Leith Stevens; Production Designer: Rudolph Sternad; Art Director: Walter Holscher; Set Decorator: Louis Diage; Assistant Director: Paul Donnelly; Sound Engineer: George Cooper; A Stanley Kramer Production; Running Time: 79 minutes.

Cast: Marlon Brando (Johnny); Mary Murphy (Kathie); Robert Keith (Harry); Lee Marvin (Chino); Jay C. Flippen (Sheriff Singer); Peggy Maley (Mildred); Hugh Sanders (Charlie Thomas); Ray Teal (Frank Bleeker); John Brown (Bill Hannegan); Will Wright (Art Kleiner); Robert Osterloh (Ben); William Vedder (Jimmy); Yvonne Doughty (Britches).

On July 4, 1947, Hollister, California, held its latest annual hill-climbing and racing competition. Among the several thousand cyclists present were the first "outlaw" gang, the Booze Fighters. Mostly rootless war vets, they brought unanticipated fireworks. High on excess spirits, the Boozers conducted street races, committed vandalism and brawled among themselves. After thirty-six hours of turmoil, police managed to restore order by the following noon. Over fifty people were injured. Penalities ranged from traffic fines to jail time. The Hollister authorities claimed that some of them had been locked in their own jail while the Booze Fighters insisted they only threw the cops into trash cans and stacked their bikes on top of them.

Less documented was a 1948 disturbance farther south in Riverside, where hordes of partying bikers caused similar trouble. When an Air Force officer driving through the area honked his horn at them, the bikers got angry, terrorizing him and his wife. The town Sheriff tried to disperse the gang, who attacked him, tearing his uniform and ripping off his badge. Again, police had to pull out the riot control stops.

Hollister and Riverside were as circumstantial as the later Fort Lauderdale youth riots and the 1969 college invasion of Zap, North Dakota, but exaggerated rumors, lasting trauma and the innate scariness of large groups of unruly men on motorcycles had raped several sets of collectives. The wanton spectacle besmirched cycling, dealing a severe groin kick to confidence in the ability of police to handle civil riots. Outlaw clubs were not yet a viable entity or earlier, sterner steps might have been taken against them. The Booze Fighters, meanwhile, evaporated like phantoms of a bad hangover.

Some Boozers became the Hell's Angels, named after the World War One bomber squadron that cycled for recreation or the 1930 Howard Hughes film about them. Mostly factory and steel mill hands, they spent their nights building bikes to their specifications. The first Angels chapter began in 1948 in the California steel town of Fontana.

Author Frank Rooney used Hollister to spin an anti–Facism polemic in his 1951 *Harper's* story "The Cyclist's Raid." A band of outlaws led by Simpson invaded the town of hotel bar owner Joel Bleeker. Sequestering his teenaged daughter Kathie for her own safety, Bleeker learned from Simpson that the politically subversive gang—whose number was increasing—justified its carousing as "relaxation." A lieutenant-colonel in the war, Bleeker compared the gang's oneness to the rigidity among his own former troops. When two drunken bikers crashed through the hotel doors, the noise brought Kathie, who was run over and killed. The gang escaped, but one remorseful rider returned, seeking Bleeker's forgiveness. Bleeker attacked the man, realizing afterward he had violated his own moral principles.

Rooney may have written "Cyclist's Raid" to express alarm over the burgeoning beat scene and juvenile delinquency. Delinquency was almost a complement to bike gangs, being first to achieve a mythological level of disrepute. Actually a valuable piece of safety equipment for fall-prone cyclists, the leather jacket engendered the same unease as brown shirts.

Despite the thriving climate of McCarthyism, Stanley Kramer was an active cinematic liberal. Unfortunately, the profit ledgers from his Columbia movies ran red—matching the shade of president Harry Cohn's temper. When Kramer read "Cyclist's Raid," he correlated the anarchy of its gang to a famous photo of a Booze Fighter living it up on his bike. This gave him pegs on which to hang ideas about restless youth.

In 1953, Kramer hired writer Ben Maddow and Hungarian director Laslo Benedek to do a screen adaptation of "Cyclist's Raid." Benedek himself had been menaced in his car at Malibu by bikers who circled his vehicle, shouting threats before they left. Subpoenaed by the House Un-American Activities Committee, Maddow wrote a poor first draft script and John Paxton replaced him. Marlon Brando, who made his screen debut in Kramer's *The Men* (1950), had worked with him and Benedek on *Death of a Salesman* (1951), respected both and agreed to star. Kramer, Benedek, Paxton, and Brando, traveling on his bike, went to Hollister and spent three weeks interviewing ex–Booze Fighters, using some of their taped conversations in the dialogue. The working title for *The Wild One* was *Hot Blood*.

The plot concentrated most of the trouble on two factions of the Black Rebels motorcycle club. Into mindless merriment, the Rebels worked only to pay for their fun, meeting on weekends to go just anywhere. What was merely a pastime for regular riders was their life. By instilling established hatred in the citizens, *The Wild One* gave the Rebels a preexistent notoriety. What only started something in Hollister would be their downfall.

A regression to Marlon Brando's Stanley Kowalski–type characters was new hero Johnny Strabler. His "dark" counterpart was a colorful lout named Chino. Brando could only be accepted as a romanticized figure. The son of a brutal father, surly to authority, Johnny was almost an autobiographical character for Brando. In such films as *Viva Zapata!* (1952) and *Julius Caesar* (1953), he attained higher brow roles, but Johnny provided catharsis for some of his personal violence, caused by the abuse of alcoholic, womanizing Marlon Sr., a likely contributor to the terminal alcoholism of Marlon Jr.'s mother Dorothy.

The besieged town of *The Wild One* was called Wrightsville. Joe Bleeker became Kathie's uncle Frank, whose business greed was a catalyst for some of the misbehavior of the Black Rebels. New father Harry was a weak problem drinker sheriff. Made a few years older, Kathie was Frank's waitress. What killed her literary self—ambulant indoor bikes—was reduced to a minor stunt with only one rider. Set outside, the fatal bike accident claimed an old dishwasher named Jimmy.

Censor Jack Viszard of the Breen Office was appalled by the first draft script, feeling that hoodlum conquest of Anytown, U.S.A. glorified Communism. The villainy of the Wrightsville fold had to be limited so more blame would rest on the Rebels. Also sensitive was a scene where Johnny told Kathie their trips were a relief from the humdrum grind of nine to five because it insulted the work ethic. A gang-bang attempt on Kathie was turned into mild sexual harassment. Viszard also wanted an opening prologue stating that Wrightsville could never happen again, although Brando felt it could.

As a rushed production start date drew near, Brando tried to save the script with some eleventh hour writing of his own. Kramer and Benedek decided on all-location work, but Harry Cohn demanded the familiar Columbia backlot town at its San Fernando ranch. Putting his bike skills through a refresher course, Brando picked his own wardrobe and rode his personal bike. From some real bikers he brought in as technical advisors, he absorbed their slang and mannerisms.

Over an empty country highway, a bold caption warns, "This Is a Shocking Story. It Couldn't Take Place in Most American Towns, But It Did in This One. It Is a Public Challenge Not to Let It Happen Again."

In his vague, post-aftermath narrative, Johnny says, "It begins for me here on this road. How the whole mess happened, I don't know, but I know it couldn't happen again in a million years. Once trouble was on its way and I was just goin' with it. Mostly, I remember the girl. I can't explain it, but something changed me. She got to me. But that's later anyway. This is where it all begins for me ... right here on this road." Two columns abreast, Johnny's Rebels roar past—one rider skidding sharply to the left for a second.

At a scramble track meet, the Rebels ceremoniously cross the track on foot, obstructing contestants. Johnny challenges one who labels him "outlaw." Denny swipes a second place trophy ("First place was over two feet high") and gives it to Johnny, who considers the award credit for a race he knows he would have won. A tough security cop orders the Rebels to hit the road. "Where did that bunch come from?" he asks the race manager. "Everywhere," the manager replies, "I don't even think they know where they're goin'. What are they tryin' to prove anyway?" "Beats me," answers the cop, "Looking for somebody to push 'em around so they can get sore and show how tough they are. They usually find it somewhere sooner or later."

Johnny rides with the trophy tied to his headlight. En route to a dance in another town, the Rebels gas up in Wrightsville, then drag for beers. Their antics cause elderly Model A owner Art Kleiner to bump into a post. Skidding against the side of the coupe, Crazy breaks his leg. The Rebels hassle Kleiner, who demands payment for damages, but Johnny tells Harry the accident was his fault. Jimmy thinks everyone is "overstimulated." Spotting Kathie, Johnny follows her into Bleeker's café, orders a beer and plays jukebox bebop. Irate Kleiner is supported by town bully Charlie Thomas.

Johnny offers Kathie the unengraved trophy as a present. She naively thinks the Rebels enjoy things like picnics. "You don't go to any one special place—," Johnny says, "That's cornball style. You just go. Now, if you're gonna stay cool, you've got to wail. You gotta put something down. You gotta make some noise. Don't you know what I'm talking about?" This makes Kathie regret a Canadian fishing trip she and Harry never made.

Johnny decides the club will leave after Crazy is patched up. Frank Bleeker solicits their patronage. Johnny wants a date with Kathie, but she is busy. Mildred, a brassy beautician, asks Johnny, "What are you rebelling against?" Sullenly, he asks, "What've you got?" Gently, Harry asks him to control the gang, but he refuses. On back of another bike, Crazy returns with his injured leg in a cast.

Chino and his gang—once part of the same club—rumble down main street. Johnny wants to split, seeing that Chino has moved the trophy to his bike. "Johnny, I love ya," laughs Chino. When Chino refuses to return the trophy, Johnny knocks him down. Chino infers it was stolen and hands it to Kathie, then hits Johnny, who attacks him. Still cheerful, bested Chino

A defining image: Johnny (Marlon Brando) and his unearned award.

reiterates, "Johnny, I love ya." In his car, Thomas irritates Chino with his loud horn and collides with Meatball. Removing Thomas, the Rebels try to overturn the car. Thomas wants Chino arrested for assault. Harry will free Chino if Johnny makes the Rebels leave, but he still smarts from a bad deal he made with another cop.

Looking for Kathie, Johnny encounters Britches, an ex-girlfriend who has missed them. Ashamed of Harry, Kathie tells Johnny, "The town joke and I'm stuck with him. He's a fake—just like you!" Knowing he didn't win it, she returns the trophy to Johnny. "You've impressed everybody now, big motorcycle racer. Why don't you take that back so they can give it to somebody who really won it?" Johnny takes the putdown hard.

That evening, the Rebels become restless and bored. Those parked outside the jail honk their bike horns in unison to protest Chino's imprisonment. Harry asks the switchboard operator to call County Sheriff Singer, but some Rebels take over her office. Others shine their lights on Thomas' front door. When he indignantly emerges, they jail him with slumbering Chino. Unable to call anyone, Frank sends Kathie for Harry. Lonely, frustrated Britches throws herself at Johnny, who snubs her flat. After some citizens free him, Thomas forms an armed vigilante group with Frank opposed by Bill Hannegan and his friends. Once they exit, Chino wakes up and leaves the unlocked cell.

Some Rebels sight Kathie, chasing her into a dark alley, where they lasciviously encircle her on their bikes until Johnny appears on his, telling Kathie, "Get on!"

Shaken Kathie clings to Johnny as they ride to an empty park. To scare her off, Johnny mauls Kathie, who declares, "I'm not afraid of you. You're afraid of me." She wanted their relationship to be the way she hoped love would be, thinking Johnny was born to give her the trophy. "I wish I was going someplace. I wish you were going someplace. I wish we could go together." Telling Johnny she loves him, Kathie runs away as Kleiner watches. Johnny catches Kathie, who slaps him. Joining Chino, Johnny tells him to get everybody to leave. The vigilantes yank Johnny off his bike and spirit him away by car.

Kathie turns to soused, self-pitying Harry, who asks, "What can I do?" Badly beaten, Johnny tells the vigilantes, "My old man hit harder than that." His courage up, Harry tries to take him into custody. Johnny flees on his bike, but more people block his path. A hurled tire iron strikes him on the back of the head. As Johnny falls off, the careening bike kills Jimmy. Sheriff Singer and his men arrive. Johnny is arrested.

Kathie (Mary Murphy) and her knight in shining leather, Johnny (Marlon Brando).

Accused of manslaughter, Johnny is emotionally defended by Kathie. "You haven't fallen for this fella, have you?" asks puzzled Singer. "No, I couldn't," answers Kathie, making Frank and Kleiner inform Singer of the tire iron. Singer tells Johnny to thank the people for helping him. "That's all right," excuses Kathie, "He doesn't know now." Singer tongue-lashes Johnny. "I think you're stupid—real stupid. Last night you scraped by ... just barely. But a man is dead because of something you let get started even though you didn't start it. I don't know if there's any good in you ... if there's anything. But I'm going to take a big fat chance. I'm going to let you go." Singer gives the Rebels ten minutes to leave, warning them never to return to the county.

Johnny is at Bleeker's. As Harry leaves, he silently returns the trophy to Kathie with sincerity. Johnny's warm smile elicits hers before he mounts his bike and rides away.

Dated and compromised, *The Wild One* remains an excellent craft piece despite its archaic, blurred sociology, giving Johnny's background the kind of past that a delinquency character could have been built upon. Like street kids, he was exaggeratedly masculine to compensate for old pains and assurances of his own manliness. Antisocial to shield his virility, he permitted some rowdiness in his gang to keep them happy and look cool. Closer to the real outlaw image, Chino's troops had gone overboard and Johnny left with his pack figuring rule over half a club was better than none. His and Chino's semi-friendly rivalry would be recreated by Jim Stark and Buzz Gunderson in *Rebel Without a Cause* (1955).

In their sanitized guise, the people of Wrightsville found the Rebels exciting at first. Those whom they clashed with early like Thomas and Kleiner were uptight party poopers. The Rebels were the sexiest guys the local girls had ever seen and they must have been pretty starved for affection since there were no young men present. Extroverted Mildred was the only chick who would be called forward. Until this day, Harry had gotten away with his limp law enforcing because only a caretaker cop was needed. Johnny had been brutalized by his dad while Kathie bemoaned the passivity of hers.

When Chino's gang arrived, Johnny found himself surrounded by the people he wanted to forget. Frank Bleeker caused the Rebels to lose their few inhibitions through his avarice while Thomas gave them a hate focus. Johnny saved Kathie from implied rape only to find her "raping" him through her effort to show he was her white knight in black. The vigilantes felt *they* had been raped by their guests. To belittle them, Johnny cited the roughness of his father—another Charlie Thomas—who might have been an abused child too. This assault sobered up Harry, but led to the death of likeable Jimmy ... the only person who tried to keep his head through his willful rejection of anything too stimulating. If Johnny had struck Jimmy while still on his bike, that would have been second-degree murder. A fortuitous head bonk absolved him of any direct complicity.

The closing scenes allowed Johnny to grow up dramatically, first through a death he triggered many domino topples ago and later the impassioned defense of Kathie. Offended parties became his saviors while ultimate authoritarian Singer delivered a requisite sermon. The last scene, the most stirring and genuine, was a bittersweet relief from all the castor oil of indignation mixed with the brew of frothy hellraising.

The best cycle scene, the park ride, was simultaneously wistful and sexy, placing Johnny and Kathie in the only physical closeness they could enjoy. Cruising past tree branches, the camera caught the moving headlight of Johnny's bike—what resembled a passing moon. The ambiguity of the shot considered romance both celestially and in the power of a machine.

Various props were also imaginative. Putting on his dark glasses with ritualistic deliberation was Johnny's silent Up Yours to the racetrack cop. When Johnny took it off his bike, the trophy was bandied about like a billyclub. Kleiner's Model A symbolized his staid, obsolete generation while the TV and jukebox in Bleeker's café were hints of "overstimulation." (Jimmy on television: "Everything these days is pictures. Pictures with a lot of noise. People don't know how to talk.") Some of Chino's boys looked like mountain men. One sported a pre–Davy Crockett coonskin cap and another wore a false beard, connoting the fakery of their masquerade.

Many sexual suggestions were prop-telegraphed. Stung by Kathie's rebuff regarding the trophy, Johnny slammed a beer bottle against the counter, the geyser of suds the ejaculation of his frustration. The Rebel bikes that trapped Kathie circled like Indians hovering around covered wagons. They also recalled Laszlo Benedek's Malibu ordeal. Johnny's mobile phallus pierced the circle like a lance of chivalry. During the vandalism of Mildred's beauty parlor, intimations of drag saw a Rebel wearing a wig-like mop while others covered their heads with steel hairdryers. Their leather jackets and the bullet-shaped dryers made them look like caricatures of Commando Cody.

When Mary Murphy met Brando, she didn't know who he was. With the charisma that appealed to every woman he encountered, Brando put Murphy at ease. Production began with Johnny's speech about work. Brando knew that Murphy didn't care for the John Paxton dialogue either and ad-libbed, using dense jargon so only implication would register.

Brando took Murphy on bike rides that made her uncomfortable. On her way home from the set one evening in her British automobile, Murphy heard a peculiar rattling noise from the car's right front wheel, asking a crew member to investigate. Unscrewing the hubcap, he found large pieces of stone placed inside. Brando confessed to the gag.

Married at the time to the Mexican movie actress Movita, Brando inspired a crush in Mary Murphy. Lee Marvin and Laslo Benedek felt no love for Brando—at least some of the time. Marvin improved the ending of the brawl between Johnny and Chino by raising his fist like a defeated gladiator. For the scene where Johnny learned that Kathie was Harry's daughter, Brando annoyed Benedek by scratching his nose.

Benedek was hard on Murphy for wanting the bike harassment of Kathie to be as realistic as possible. The riders came at her closer than she anticipated. One bike even raised her skirt. The tears shed by Kathie were those of greatly distressed Murphy's.

For where Kathie thanked Johnny for saving her, Brando was supposed to lack an appreciative response. The writing didn't work and the scene was shot at five a.m. on the last day with Brando again improvising—but Johnny spoke *too* eloquently and Brando's intelligence overrode the emotions of Johnny.

Brando also couldn't abide Johnny's goodbye to Kathie, but did it as written to please Laslo Benedek. At the recording session for the unwanted prologue, Brando displayed his contempt by using a fake Southern accent, making faces all the while.

Composed by Leith Stevens and conducted by Morris Stoloff, the bebop score of *The Wild One* competed with the oft-inpenetrable jive talk for ear color. A toe-tapper in scenes of gay abandon, the music took on a mewling Mancini-ish din as a chilly, night-air portent of dread. Sadly sensual was the tune for the park ride, melancholy at first, then gearing up for potential amours in a slinky hippety-hop riff. *The Wild One* score made it to soundtrack album.

Nobody could deny the magnetism of Brando's performance, although the method frilled it with signs of him working too consciously to deliver the next emotion. An avoider of pretense, Lee Marvin made his Chino upfront, uncomplicatedly melodramatic. His dress, features and behavior were closer to what early outlaws were really like. The only shots of him riding a bike were live motion, with no rear-projection phoniness like Brando's vehicular close-ups.

Mary Murphy photographed exquisitely in pensive moods and acted best in the unworded profundities. The father of Brian, Robert Keith was a specialist in father roles. Jay C. Flippen was forceful as Harry's opposite in police effectiveness.

The most recognizable Rebels were Alvy Moore, actor-director Jerry Paris, Harry Landers and tombstone clammy badster Timothy Carey, a memorable Stanley Kubrick support in *The Killing* (1956) and *Paths of Glory* (1957) who appeared in Marlon Brando's only directorial effort, *One-Eyed Jacks* (1961) and played South Dakota Slim in two of the Beach Party movies. Also cast was Darren Dublin, an old actor friend of Brando's from New York.

Stanley Kramer and his staff believed *The Wild One* was moral, but familiarity with their product gave them advantaged vision. Kramer had wished the story had been an original idea—not a study of what he perceived to be a tear in the fabric of society. In the pit of his stomach, Harry Cohn loathed *The Wild One* but released it on the strength of Brando's name. Ads had been devised to exploit the movie under the Kramer-preferred *Hot Blood* title. The word "Hot!" was printed above Brando's face and a catch-phrase read, "Marlon Brando! Driven Too Far By His Own Hot Blood!" The ads were withdrawn, though the face of Brando was still the key promo illustration. *The Wild One* was actually a better title—referring to Johnny—and by implication describing Brando.

Some state censorship boards wouldn't pass a film unless there was clear proof that criminals were punished. *Wild One* prints for these areas came with an end statement alleging that all the Black Rebels were prosecuted. On the grounds it would incite violence, Britain banned *The Wild One* until 1968.

Marlon Brando considered *The Wild One* to be a tree-sized thorn in his side. He was so disappointed with it that he considered retirement at his Penny Poke farm in Broken Bow, Nebraska ... but the farm was a financial failure. Brando was also unhappy about the way Montgomery Clift and especially James Dean were trying to emulate his style. Moved to do so after seeing *The Wild One*, Dean haunted Brando's telephone. Showing some concern for Dean, Brando introduced him to a psychiatrist.

Another commercial flop for Stanley Kramer, *The Wild One* became part of the reality of millions of young people. At a Hollywood auction, a Hell's Angel named Frank bought Lee Marvin's sweatshirt. Marvin's star rose in the sixties as Brando's fell, but a reminder of the glory Brando years was a pop poster of him as Johnny. There was talk that Brando had finally come to terms with *The Wild One* and would do a tentative sequel exploring the middle-aged life of Johnny Strabler.

Hollister—the Pearl Harbor of biker violence—was hit by another riot in March 1987. This one was an organized rebellion of high schoolers protesting their grading system.

The Wild Rebels

Crown International 1967. Director-Screenplay: William Grefe; Associate Producer: Joseph Fink; Cinematography: Clifford H. Poland, Jr., Harry Walsh; Film Editors: Julio C. Chavez, Robert Woodburn; Music: Henry Stone; Songs-Music: Al Jacobs; First Assistant Director: Daniel Karoff; Second Assistant Director: Charles W. Persons; Camera Operator: William J. Walsh, Jr.; Sound: John Barry, Bernie Blynder; Boom Man: Nat Ragland; Lighting: Bill Swan; Head Grip: Jack Clark; Props: Charles Guanci; Makeup: Marie DelRusso; Script Supervisor: Betty Kerwin; Still Photos: Tony Gulliver; Set Designer: Patrick Nielsen; Technicolor; A Comet Pictures, Inc. Production; Running time: 90 minutes.

Cast: Steve Alaimo (Rod); Willie Pastrano (Banjo); John Vella (Jeeter); Bobbie Byers (Linda); Jeff Gillen (Fats); Walter R. Philbin (Lt. Dorn); Robert Freund (Detective); Seymour A. Eisenfeld (Walt Simpson); Phil Longo (First Man); Milton Smith (Bartender); Kurt Negler, Steve Geller, Chris Martell (College Boys); Nora Alonzo (Nori); Birdwatchers (Band); Dutch Holland (Driver); Art Barker (Gunshop Owner); William P. Kelley (Bank Teller); Cosmo Lloyd (Bank Guard); Tom Frysinger, Emil Deaton (Sheriffs); Jamie Hickson, Aaron Deaton, Nick Bontempo, Edward Waniski, Dennis French, Bob Sparks (Policemen).

With a Sebring auto rally picture already under his belt Miami filmmaker William Grefe was preparing a Daytona Beach stock car movie when *The Wild Angels* came out and he convinced his investors that a Biker would be more profitable. Ill-equipped to do a Hollywood-style Biker, Grefe retained stock car racing in his alternative film *The Wild Rebels* to establish the identity of hero Rod Tillman. To justify the film's continued emphasis on autos, Grefe used a bank robbery situation.

Swerving to avoid a wreck, Rod totals his car on the track. His career up in smoke too, Rod immediately auctions off all his possessions except a guitar.

Now a drifter, Rod enters a teen nightspot meeting Jeeter, Banjo, Linda and mute Fats of Satan's Angels. They have a proposition for him. Linda takes Rod to their shack, trying to make nervous Rod overly comfortable before the others arrive. For kicks, the gang plans to rob a bank and they need a skilled wheelman. Rod refuses the deal. Leaving, he encounters a police stakeout team led by Lt. Dorn. The Satan's Angels are suspects in a series of recent unsolved robberies. Dorn asks Rod to go undercover to help the authorities get a conviction.

On Dorn's arrangement, Rod returns to racing in a staged accident so the gang will approach him again. This time, he accepts their offer.

While Rod waits in the getaway car, the Satan's Angels knock over a gun store for weapons. Helped by Fats, Banjo kills the unconscious owner with a football kick to the head. Excluded from the confidential strategy meeting, Rod slips a note under a tree to cops monitoring the shack about the situation. Linda seduces a more willing Rod. Jealous Banjo catches them together and fights Rod, who beats Banjo.

Detectives trail Rod and the gang as they drive to Citrusville. Linda sedates the guard with a hypo and the money is taken. Blinking his car headlights, Rod signals two deputy sheriffs, tipping them off to the holdup in progress. Banjo shotguns the officers, killing one. Hostage Rod is forced to smash through roadblocks.

Bullets fired into the gas tank disable the getaway car near an old lighthouse where the gang makes its stand. Banjo flees on a police bike, but is shot before he can clear the beach area. Fats fires his pistol from a tower window until Dorn puts a slug in his brain. When Fats' falling beret flutters down his way, Rod impulsively dashes upstairs to grab the gun. Down the steps, Jeeter takes aim at Rod, but Linda shoots Jeeter in the back and he plunges over the stair railing. Linda is arrested.

Both limited and resourceful, *The Wild Rebels* was about as good as an afterthought film can be. Unable to develop big-scale biker violence, Grefe could have gone for sex crime activity. Instead, he made Satan's Angels stickup men. Carefully, he rationalized their tiny size by indicating they were visitors from California. This gave each member a distinct personality: Jeeter the pseudo-urbane brains; Linda the latently decent moll; Banjo the paranoid hothead; and mute Fats the comic. Stock car story heroes were sometimes men who fell on hard times, a workable circumstance for Rod meeting up with Satan's Angels.

Cautious about transportation but obvious in personal appearance, these Bonnie and Clyde–type bikers were as blithely suicidal as they were daring in their goal. Until *Motor Psycho*, outlaw bikers never used guns. Until *Motor Psycho*, no outlaw had ever been shown killing anyone on purpose. And until *The Wild Rebels*, outlaws were not multiple murderers. Being more comfortable with cars, Grefe didn't want to bother with bikes any more than he had to. Stock car fans, at least, got a fair portion of their like.

Copied from *The Wild Angels* were such things as constant police presence, a gang girl setting up felonies in respectable clothes (even drinking from a water fountain as *Wild Angels*' Mike did) and attempted flight on a cop Harley. The lighthouse was the most interesting set and every opportunity for visual impact on and around the concentrically-tiered steps was extracted.

Jeeter (John Vella) admires robbery hardware as Linda (Bobbie Bers) shows interest.

Steve Alaimo was a high school football and swimming champion from Rochester who enrolled at the University of Miami with his band the Red Coats to study pre-med. Guesting on "American Bandstand," he signed with Chess Records, becoming a popular face on *Where the Action Is*. Not bad for an untrained actor. Alaimo co-starred with Willie Pastrano, the light heavyweight boxing champ of 1963 who trained Muhammed Ali. Pastrano and Alaimo worked in to other Grefe films, *The Hooked Generation* (1969), starring Jeremy Slate, and *The Naked Zoo* (1970), co-starring Stephen Oliver. Pastrano died of cancer in 1998.

Pastrano, Grefe regular John Vella, Bobbie Byers and Jeff Gillen flexed a lot of individuality in their colorfully-drawn gang roles. A bit too excessive was Byers' main prop, a long cigarette holder. Making some funny Curly-like sounds, Gillen did an amusing pantomime routine in the gun shop when Fats tried on a British army helmet.

Crown International co-billed *The Wild Rebels* with *Hell on Wheels*, a routine stock car movie with Marty Robbins and John Ashley who, having rejected *Hell's Angels*, lent himself to a different *On Wheels*.

Wild Riders

Crown International 1971. Producers: John Burrows, Edward Paramore III; Director-Screenplay: Richard Kanter; Story: Sal Comstock; Associate Producer: Murray Perlstein; Cinematography: Paul Hipp; Film Editor: Marco Meyer; Music Composer–Conductor: Alan Alper; Additional Cinematography: Bob Maxwell, Scott Lloyd Davies, Bob Eisenber; Production Manager: Jax Carroll; Sound: Hollywood Sound Records; Assistant Cameraman: Henning Schellerup; Still Photography: Elliott Gilbert; Set Decorator: Lee Fisher; Script Supervisor: Jim Kelly; Head Grip: Jim Feazel; Head Electrician: Bob McVay; Makeup: Ron Kenney; Title-Optical Effects: Modern Film Effects; Re-recording: TV Recorders; Motorcycles: Frank Charolla; Song: "He's My Family" by Arell Blanton, Bill Matchum; DeLuxe Color; A Tudor Production; Running Time: 91 minutes.

Cast: Alex Rocco (Stick); Arell Blanton (Pete); Elizabeth Knowles (Rona); Sherry Bain (Laure); Ted Hayden (Will); Jax Carroll (Stud); Steve Vincent (Perry); Bill Collins (Kelly); Gail Liddle (Gemeni); Ray Galvin (Tom); Linda Johanson (Crucified Girl); Diana Jones (Samantha); Frank Charolla (Biker); Dirty Denney a/k/a Dennis Art (Gang Leader); Marc Rocco.

Yale graduate John Burrows, softcore producer Edward (Ted) Paramore and adult film director Richard Kanter presented a blacker side of *Easy Rider* in *Wild Riders*. Like *Angels Die Hard*, it put a later element of *Easy Rider* into an early part of its own story. The place where *Easy Rider* ended, Florida, was *Wild Riders'* start-off point. A Florida simulated in Hollywood, it was the backdrop to a variation of the Outlaws crucifixion atrocity.

While Pete holds her, Stick hatchets a spike through the hand of Pete's ex-girl as she is held against a tree. Suspended there, the girl dies.

"What would you do if you caught your broad with a black guy?" Pete asks gang leader Dirty Denney. Pete picks a fight with black Charlie and Stick rescues him. "I'd like to see how slick you'd be when he's not around," Frank tells Pete, "You're shallow." Denney fears a police investigation and decides the gang will split up. Pete and Stick are on their own.

In L.A., Pete and Stick wind up at

Misogynists crucify a miscegenist.

Griffith Park, hungry, broke and low on gas. Through a telescope, Pete sees two attractive women lounging around the pool of a nearby house. The house is home to Rona, with her ex-sorority sister Laure. Rona is unhappily married to Will, a concert pianist on tour.

To gain entry to the house, Pete seduces Rona with his bike. Looking at the sumptuous abode, he promises, "You share that with us and I'll share this with you. It's faster than you've ever been. No limits at all...."

Laure feels uncomfortable with Stick and hides in her guest room while Rona, Stick and Pete romp in the pool. Stick plays with Laure's panties until Pete makes him stop. Rona tries to break Laure out of her shell of artificial virginity. "It's time you found out, little sister, you can't turn around and go back."

Rona balls Pete while Stick accuses Laure of pulling a prank on her with a toy frog. "Do I look like that?" he howls, "*Do I look like that?*" In a sick game of hide and seek, Stick rapes Laure. "We're a lot alike," he comments afterward. Laure tells Pete and Rona what happened.

Pete berates Stick. Holding court on Rona and Laure, Pete mentions the Florida murder and proposes a game called "trade," asking Rona, "How does it feel to be a guest?" To her, he's "nothing" without Stick. Stick vividly relives Florida by hammering a knife into a wall poster. "Every hustler has to pay," Pete tells Rona as they lie together, "I've been paying a long time … Now it's your turn. That just the way the shitty world is. From now on, this house is ours. I'll take every drop I can bleed out of it."

Songwriter Perry, a former Rona playmate, calls to complain of noise. Rona carefully dismisses him. Pete decides to go to Mexico and fence some goods while Stick stays with the tied-up women.

Some of the Florida gang are in town. Girl member Gemeni tells Pete about Samantha, the daughter of a fence antique dealer. Frank wants to finish his feud with Pete, who leads Frank into the Hollywood hills and knocks him off his bike.

The fence will pay only one hundred dollars for the merchandise. Rona and Laure free themselves and run to Rona's car in the garage while Stick snoozes. Rona drives through the stuck door as Pete returns, and tries to run him down. "I figure a fall from a bike should be the same as your car crashin' down on me," threatens enraged Pete—who takes terrified Rona on a wild bike ride. Temper spent, Pete makes tender love to her in the woods.

In bed, Rona overhears as Pete talks over the phone to Samantha, who will split the loot with Pete to escape her father. Pete mentions Stud and Kelly, the guys he wants to accompany him to Mexico. Noticing the smashed garage door, Perry visits, bearing wine to celebrate with Rona the completion of his new score. Before she can send him away, Pete attacks Perry, who chokes Pete before Stick strangles Perry.

Pete goes to the double-crossing fence, who reaches for a gun, but Pete beats him to death with its handle.

Rona tells Stick about Pete's plans, warning he will be left to take the rap for Perry. "He can't do that!" argues Stick, "I'm the only one who knows!" What he means is that Pete killed his father as a boy. Rona pretends she can help Stick reach Mexico.

Stick, Rona and Laure are about to leave in Rona's car when Will suddenly comes home. Stick hustles the women back into the house, subduing Will. "We were invited," just-returned Pete tells "the fiddler." Believing the set-up story, Stick tears into Pete until Pete convinces him it is untrue. Pete wants Will to perform a

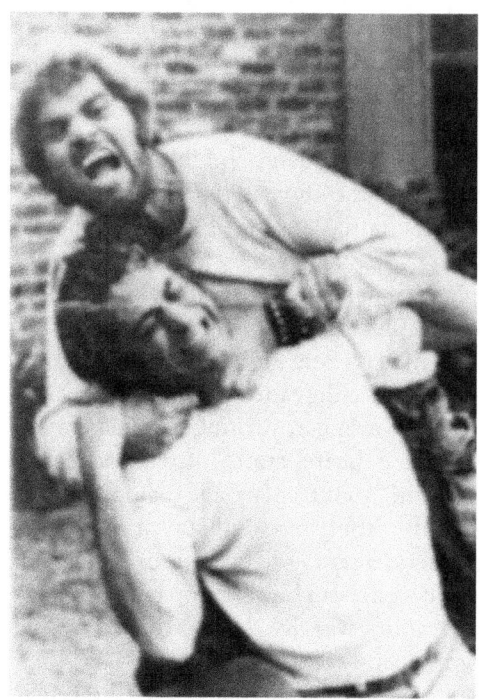

Thanks to Stick (Alex Rocco), songwriter Perry (Steve Vincent) is on the Shit Parade.

"farewell concert." "Your old man's not worried about your head," Pete insinuates to Rona, "He's only worried about that money-making fiddle of his." "That's nothing new," informs Rona, "I've known it for years."

Will works the cello, drawing Pete to the intricate movement of his sensitive fingers. Suddenly, Will jabs the bow into Pete's left eye and smashes the cello into lunging Stick, who crashes through a window. With the sharp metal stand, Will impales Stick, who falls into the swimming pool. Rona feels bad for dead Pete. She and Will can barely look at each other.

Chuck and Wes of *Hell's Angels '69* were rich, but the Angels' grievance was not about their wealth. *Wild Riders* unleashed Harley have-nots on the haves who flaunt it, tearing down their ostentaciously upholstered comfort walls as the pleasures contained therein were sucked up. The story put its two heroines through some *Desperate Hours* on *Private Property* with more than one *Lady in a Cage*, Rona, a seventies Ann Carlyle, the lonely wife of the third film.

Stick's challenge, inhibited Laure, was the conquest who had to be cracked open. Charismatic Pete inveigled his way into Rona's itchy snatch ... his talented tool planting in her head the worst kind of hold over a hostage—continued sexual desire. Resented by Pete for his talent and money even before they met, Will was the David Sumner avenger, turning the instrument of his delicate craft into a makeshift weapon. About a marriage that lasted only because Rona and Will stayed in neutral corners, what was to become of it now that her cocoon and his rest stop between concert tours was a wreck—peopled by sad spirits left broken.

Based on a factual crime, the crucifixion was obsessed on like a money-shot image. Either in visual replay or a repeated audio bird-like screen that echoed during the aftermath, the sequence was meant to haunt just as everyone who saw the commission of the act never forgot it. Hands and blunt objects killed Perry and the fence, but sharp utensils poked into flesh was proportionally proper justice for Pete and Stick.

Griffith Park was made to look like an accessory to Pete and Stick's invasion of the pad they "remodeled" by telescopes that could look into people's backyards.

The house where *Wild Riders* had been made was built by Cary Grant and was a home away from home for the Beatles and the Rolling Stones.

Arell Blanton co-composed and sung the moody tune "He's My Family." To make Will a convincing cellist, Ted Hayden took lessons from his musician wife, son and daughter so his closeup hand movements would appear believable.

Blanton and Alex Rocco had appeared in *Blood Mania* (1970). Cast as a slick blackmailer, Blanton was introduced and Rocco a featured actor playing an attorney. In *Wild Riders*, Blanton was "introduced" again! British Elizabeth Knowles played the dissolute, restless Rona like she was auditioning for a Pinter drama. Alex Rocco's arrival role was that of Moe Greene in *The Godfather* (1972). As Greene, he died from an eye mutilation just like Pete ... his effected by a bullet. A little boy Stick clowned with at a gas station was played by Rocco's son Marc, now a director.

Dirty Denney was the name used in real-life by Dennis Art, who played the story's Dirty Denney.

To help promote *Wild Riders*, Richard Kanter went on a cinema lecture tour. His true background was disclosed in the film's publicity, but John Burrows got some people thinking that he was Elvis Presley! John Burrows was an alias Presley went by during some of his covert business deals.

Wild Wheels

Fanfare 1969. Producer: Budd Dell; Director: Kent Osborne; Screenplay: Kent Osborne, Ralph Luce; Cinematography: Ralph Waldo; Film Editor: Ralph Luce; Music: Harley Hatcher a/k/a Paul Wibier; Camera Operator: Terry Forchette; Sound Mixer: Bob Dietz; Still Photographer: Hedy Dietz; Gaffer: Al Denny; Wardrobe: Gloria Betrue; Stunt Coordinator: Bobby Clark; Production Manager: James Kelly Durgin; Assistant to Producer: Aaron York. Color; Running Time: 81 minutes.

Cast: Don Epperson (Reb); Robert Dix (King); Casey Kasem (Knife); Dovie Beams (Ann); Terry Stafford (Huey); Johenne Lemont

(Cotton); Bruce Kimball (Boomer); Mac McLaughlin (Kraut); Bobby Clark (Gunner); Nancy Brock (Candy); Evelyn Guerrero (Sissy); Gordon Zimmerman (Bo); Lois Jones (Helen); Randee Jensen (Joy); Phill Bartel (Lt. Ryan); Lee Parrish (Wright); Byrd Holland (Rich); Mike Perrotta (Store Owner); Alex Elliot (Hank); Marsha Jo Sandridge (Bikini Girl); Willis Martin (Policeman); Billie and Blue, Three of August, Saturday Revue, Thirteenth Committee (Special Guest Stars).

Dune buggies made recreational inroads in the sixties, but didn't stir up the same amount of excitement as hot rods and motorcycles. Shot in sixteen-millimeter at Pismo Beach, Kent Osborne's *Wild Wheels* was generically titled either because he couldn't invent a name incorporating a reference to dune buggies or felt that Biker fans would automatically go to anything with "Wild" and "Wheels"—adjectives about as common in Biker titles as Angels or Hell.

President of a dune club, Reb Smith hangs with Bo, Bo's girl Helen, Bo's sister Sissy and Sissy's boyfriend Huey. Led by King, the Roadrunners Motorcycle Club kicks up sand at the coastal dune camp. Reb dates Ann, an amusement park ticket seller. True to Reb's fear, the Roadrunners return. On sand, the "kiddy car boys" reign with their more maneuverable machines. The Roadrunners invade the dune bar, where mama Cotton notices Reb and King meets Ann, who upsets Reb by going off with King.

At a private beach, King ogles Ann as she puts on a bikini behind some rocks. Startled Ann receives an apology from King.

Boomer and Knife fight over a girl Knife brought into the Roadrunners' camp until King breaks it up. Boomer, Kraut and Gunner are sent for booze while Cotton goes to score grass. Ann sees King

Bo (Gordon Zimmerman) and Reb (Don Epperson) clash with King (Robert Dix) and Boomer (Bruce Kimball) at the duners' bar.

again. Boomer, Kraut and Gunner steal liquor from store owner Baum, who receives a bad check. Cotton is impressed by Reb's singing at the dune bar. Baum reports the liquor theft.

Huey wants to see the Roadrunners' action on the other side of the murky dunes. Sissy insists on coming along. Drunken Boomer slugs Huey, then viciously beats Sissy. Bringing Ann to the Roadrunners' camp, King is shocked to hear about this. He orders a retreat, but Kraut knocks him out. Huey staggers back to the duners' camp. Cotton helps in calling the police.

Lost, disheveled Sissy collapses before the duners, who raid the Roadrunners' camp. King fights on their side. Fleeing Boomer gets enraged Bo on his tail. Bo strangles Boomer before Lt. Ryan cracks his pistol butt over Bo's head.

The cops take it from here. Put in Reb's custody, King may become a duner and kisses his special dune doll—Ann.

Wild Wheels was a likeable but naïve regression to the Beach gang's war with the Rats. Even the Roadrunners' name sounded passé ... like that of a fifties car club. Was the setting Pismo or Myrtle Beach? Reb and Bo, in particular, were more akin to Southerners than blue-collar Californians. Their names couldn't have been less obvious than if they had been Brits named Nigel and Clive. And Cotton and Candy ... come on! Problems in dialogue too. Wasn't the repeated phrase "dad" kind of old in the age of Groovy? And where did Ann get her sex ed, telling King her body was "only a biological mutation derived from a male and female—to be specific my mother and my father." (Boomer's parents must have been an ape and a magpie.)

The treatment of stereotype Baum was almost anti–Semitic. Not only did the bikers rip him off, but Ryan and Off. Wright mooched merchandise right in front of him, black Wright doing so in imitation of Ryan. Perhaps thinking it would be too rough for family viewing, the film kept rape out of Sissy's assault (the original rating had been X).

Long on pleasant music, *Wild Wheels* gave five songs to star Don Epperson. His dark, aging country boy looks ran counter to the kind of plastic prettiness Reb might have acquired in a differently cast version. Trouble was, he too closely resembled Gordon Zimmerman. They were like twin brothers.

Robert Dix had been a twin brother. He and his identical sibling Richard Jr. were born to Richard Dix and his second wife, Virginia Webster. Bob's ad-libbing in a school play of *The Prince and the Pauper* was a sign of real acting talent. He studied drama at the National Academy of Theater in Pleasantville, New York, did sundry odd jobs, including radio announcer, and enrolled at the University of California with Richard Jr. The latter was studying medicine—the career Richard Sr. wanted for Bob—when he died in a skiing accident in 1953. This left lasting emotional scars on Robert, who did movie contract work at MGM and Fox. A villain for Al Adamson in *Blood of Dracula's Castle* and *Satan's Sadists*, Dix was a hero in his Adamson-directed production *Five Bloody Graves* (1970) with Tara Ashton, the starlet Dix married.

A Mormon, ex-cop, teacher and professor, Bruce Kimball was a walking smokehouse of undisciplined ham as Boomer. He had done an unbilled bit as the Pismo cop who busted Angel in *Run, Angel, Run*, which *Wild Wheels* was paired with at drive-ins. Casey Kasem was Knife, looking genuinely humiliated as Boomer's "wet little bird," but pretty fierce waving a blade. Terry Stafford, who sang "Suspicion," had been a contributor to the *Born Losers* score.

Raven-haired Dovie Beams, much older than she looked (born 1932) became the mistress of Ferdinand Marcos. Evelyn Guerrero was the film foil of Cheech and Chong. While Guerrero was posing for *Playboy*, they startled her by crashing the photo set on a hog. Duly recorded, her reactions were put into the spread.

Bob Dix, Don Epperson and Bruce Kimball appeared in the next Kent Osborne picture, *Cain's Way* (1970), a/k/a *Cain's Cutthroats*, enacting the former comrades who murdered the family of ex–Confederate captain Justice Cain. Failing as a straight western, *Cain*—in a move Al Adamson and Sam Sherman would have been proud of—was partially updated by new footage of bikers terrorizing a modern town. The Cain story was meant to explain the reason. The bike scenes were cut for video, but Dix, Kimball and star Scott Brady, Biker faces all, survived the transition because they were playing nineteenth-century characters ... assistant director Dix even wearing his *Satan's Sadists'* eyepatch.

Chronology of Films

The Wild One (Columbia 1954)
Motorcycle Gang (American International 1957)
Dragstrip Riot (American International 1958)
The Hot Angel (Paramount 1958)
Ivy League Killers (Ivy League Films 1962)
Motor Psycho (Eve 1965)
These Are the Damned (Columbia 1965)
The Wild Angels (American International 1966)
The Born Losers (American International 1967)
Devil's Angels (American International 1967)
Hell's Angels on Wheels (U.S. Films 1967)
The Wild Rebels (Crown International 1967)
Angels from Hell (American International 1968)
The Angry Breed (Commonwealth United Entertainment 1968)
The Glory Stompers (American International 1968)
The Hellcats (Crown International 1968)
Hell's Chosen Few (American General / Thunderbird-International 1968)
The Mini-Skirt Mob (American International 1968)
The Savage Seven (American International 1968)
Savages from Hell (Trans International 1968)
She-Devils on Wheels (Mayflower 1968)
Easy Rider (Columbia 1969)
Five the Hard Way (Fantascope 1969)
Hell's Angels '69 (American International 1969)
Hell's Belles (American International 1969)
Naked Angels (Goldstone 1969)
Run, Angel, Run (Fanfare 1969)
Satan's Sadists (Independent International 1969)
Sisters in Leather (Sack Amusement Enterprises 1969)
Wild Wheels (Fanfare 1969)
Angel Unchained (American International 1970)
Angels Die Hard (New World 1970)
Black Angels (Merrick-International 1970)
C.C. and Company (Avco Embassy 1970)
The Cycle Savages (Trans-American 1970)
Hell's Bloody Devils (Independent International 1970)
The Losers (Fanfare 1970)
Rebel Rousers (Four-Star Excelsior 1970)
Ride Hard, Ride Wild (Phoenix-International 1970)
Angels—Hard as They Come (New World 1971)
Bury Me an Angel (New World 1971)
Chrome and Hot Leather (American International 1971)
Devil Rider (Goldstone 1971)
The Hard Ride (American International 1971)
The Jesus Trip (EMCO 1971)
Outlaw Riders (Ace-International 1971)
The Peace Killers (Transvue 1971)
The Pink Angels (Crown International 1971)
Sinner's Blood (Cinema-International 1971)
The Takers (Box-Office International 1971)
Werewolves on Wheels (Fanfare 1971)
Wild Riders (Crown International 1971)
Angels' Wild Women (Independent-International 1972)
The Dirt Gang (American International 1972)
J.C. (Avco Embassy 1972)
The Limit (Cannon/New Era Communications 1972)
The Loners (Fanfare 1972)
Sleazy Rider (Phoenix International 1972)

Index

Actor's Studio 15
Adam (magazine) 86
Adam Publishing 86
Adams, Beverly 58, 91
Adamson, Al 21, 23, 24, 102, 103, 106
Adler, Stella 15
Alex in Wonderland (1970) 20
Allen, Bambi 103
Altman, Robert 31
American Graffiti (1973) 72
American-International Pictures 2, 5, 52, 54, 61, 64, 86, 87, 92, 100
Anders, Richard 58, 92
Angel Unchained (1970) 2, 5, 7, 19
Angels Die Hard (1970) 9, 10, 11, 39, 40
Angels from Hell (1968) 12, 14
Angels—Hard As They Come (1971) 2, 16, 19, 20, 61
Angels' Wild Women (1972) 21, 22, 85, 103
The Angry Breed (1968) 24, 26, 27
Ann-Margret 41, 45
The Appaloosa (1966) 98
Arkin, Alan 14
Arkoff, Samuel Z. 32, 66
Art, Dennis 20
Ashley, John 70, 91
Ashlock, Stevie 23
Askew, Luke 72
Associated Film Distributors 87
Atkins, Susan 23
Avco-Embassy 38

Bad Charleston Charlie (1973) 23
Badlands (1973) 20
Baez, Joan 37
Bail, Chuck 92
Bain, Sherry 82
Baker, Joe Don 97
Balin, Marty 98
Banks, Emily 103
Barbarella (1968) 67
Barger, Elsie 92
Barger, Sonny 14, 87, 93, 95, 96, 97
Basil, Toni 72
Bassey, Shirley 103

Battle, Mike 45
Baumann, Kathy 49, 50
BBS Productions 67, 72, 73
Belmondo, Jean-Paul 87
Bembry, Maggie 23
Bender, Russ 92
Beymer, Richard 79
The Bicycle Thief (1960) 98
The Big Doll House (1971) 21
Biker's Heaven 73
Billy Jack (1971) 38
Billy Jack Goes to Washington (1971) 38
Bishop, Wes 46, 48, 49, 50
Black, Karen 72
Black Angels (1970) 2, 28, 29, 31
Black Diamonds m.c. 108
The Black Klansmen (1966) 87
Black Mama, White Mama (1973) 20
Blauner, Steve 67
Blood Freak (1975) 54
Bloody Mama (1970) 8
Blue Velvet (1986) 73
Bob & Carol & Ted & Alice (1969) 20
Bob Hope Chrysler Theater 75
Body Talk (1984) 101
Bonet, Nai 58
Bongo Wolf's Revenge (1971) 11
Bonner, William 106
Bonnie and Clyde (1967) 12
Borisenko, Don 109
The Born Losers (1967) 32, 35, 36, 37, 38, 105
"Born to Be Wild" 72
Botkin, Ted 52
Bracci, Teda 45
Brady, Scott 52
Brando, Marlon 191, 192, 193, 194, 195, 196, 197, 198
Brodie, Steve 52
Brown, Peter 49
Bruce, Paul 38
Buckalew, Oscar One Leg 101
Bury Me an Angel (1971) 39, 40

La Cage aux Folles 46
Caged Heat (1974) 20
Cagney and Lacey 8

The California Kid (1974) 11
Campbell, Robert Wright 87, 91
Candy 67
Can't Stop the Music (1980) 45
Cardos, John 92
Cardoza, Anthony 83, 85
Carlton, Rex 102
Carnal Knowledge (1971) 45
Carr, Allan 41, 44, 45, 46
Carr, Paul 59, 62
Carras, Nicholas 65
Carroll, Regina 23
Carrie (1976) 20
Cassavetes, John 54, 57, 58
Cassidy, Butch 55, 57
Cavell, Marc 58, 92
C.C. and Company (1970) 41, 44
C.C. Ryder and Company see *C.C. and Company*
Charolla, Frank 82
Chrome and Hot Leather (1971) 46, 48, 49, 50
Chrome Soldiers (1990) 50
The Cincinnati Kid (1965) 67
Citizen's Band (otherwise known as *Handle with Care*) 20
Clarke, Gary 65
Coe, Al 11
Columbia Pictures 58, 72, 73, 91
Commons, David 24
Compton, Richard 9, 10, 11, 39
Conan the Barbarian (1982) 50
Conceived in Liberty 73
The Contrary 32
Coogan's Bluff (1968) 8
Cooper, Jeff 38
Corman, Roger 8, 9, 21, 54, 59, 66, 104
Cover-Up 104
Craig, John 58
Cresse, Robert 46
Crime in the Streets 58
Crosby, Gary 78
Crosby, Lindsay 78, 79
Crown-International Pictures 86
Cry Rape! (1973) 23
Curb, Mike 27, 50, 52, 76
The Cycle Savages (1971) 27, 50, 51, 52

211

212 Index

Daley, Oscar 65; *see also* Ireland, O. Dale
Daly, James 8
Daly, Tyne 8
Daniel, Jody 106
Date Bait (1960) 65
Days of Our Lives 75
Dean, James 31, 37
DeBroux, Lee 59
The Delinquents (1957) 31
Deliverance (1972) 8
Dell, Gabriel 15
Demme, Jonathan 16, 17, 20
Denker, Foster 67
Dern, Bruce 50, 52, 67, 72
Deschenal, Caleb 20
Deschenal, Mary Jo 20
Detective Story 15
Devil Rider (1971) 52, 53
Devil's Angels (1967) 36, 54, 57, 81, 91, 105
The Devil's Brigade (1968) 16
Dexter, Maury 98, 100, 101
The D.I. (1957) 108
Diamonds Are Forever (1971) 45
Dickerson, Beach 9
Dierkop, Charles 70
Dinehart, Mason Alan, III 108
The Dirt Gang (1972) 59, 61
Dirty Dozen m.c. 8
Doc Savage (1974) 101
Dr. Strangelove: Or How I Learned to Stop Worrying and Love the Bomb (1964) 67
La Dolce Vita (1961) 87
Dragstrip Riot (1958) 1, 63, 64, 65, 106, 107, 109
Duffy, Dee 85
Dyer, Elmer G. 108

East-West Pictures 102
Eastwood, Clint 98
"Easy Rider" 109
Easy Rider (1969) 2, 7, 8, 9, 10, 11, 50, 66, 67, 70, 71, 72, 73, 79, 81, 82
Easy Rider—The Next Generation 73
Eggar, Samantha 14, 98
Ekins, Bud 16
El Dorado (1967) 91
Ely, Ron 78
Emergency 83
Ensign Pulver (1964) 91
The Escape Artist (1982) 20
Espionage 15
Estrada, Erik 49
Evans, Jerry 102

F Troop 27
Faces (1968) 54, 58
"Faker" 103
The Fakers 103, 104; see also *Hell's Bloody Devils*
Fanfare Films 5, 16, 87, 91, 93

Farmer, Mimsy 58
Fast, Howard 73
The Fast Ones 108; see also *Ivy League Killers*
The Female Bunch (1971) 20, 21, 23
Fighting Mad (1976) 20
Finian's Rainbow (1968) 109
The First Time (1969) 41
Fisk, Jack 20
Five Easy Pieces (1970) 72
Five the Hard Way (1969) 23, 74, 75
Fonda, Henry 73
Fonda, Peter 20, 66, 67, 71, 72, 78, 79, 93
Foster, Susan 38
Framed (1975) 97
Francis, Coleman 83
Francks, Don 109
Free Grass (1969) 66, 78
Freeman, Leonard 23
Frank, T.C. see Laughlin, Tom
Fulford, Fred 23, 24
Fuller, Robert 82

Gabriel, John 103
The Gallant Men 62
Garcia, Jerry 98
Garwood, John 65, 92
Gavon, Igors 109
Gaye, Marvin 49
Genovese, Kitty 31
Gibson, Mel 109
Gidget (1959) 31
The Girl in Gold Boots (1968) 106
Girl in the Leather Skirt see *Hell's Belles*
The Girls from Thunder Strip (1966) 104, 106
Glenn, Annie 20
Glenn, Scott 20
The Glory Stompers (1968) 50, 51, 66, 70, 76, 78, 79
Glover, Bruce 45
Glover, Crispin 45
Gorog, Laszlo 87
The Grateful Dead 98
Grease (1978) 45
Griffith, Charles B. 54, 55
Grimes, Tammy 37
Grinter, Brad F. 52, 54
Grollman, William Donald 11
Guess What Happened to Count Dracula? (1970) 30, 31
Guess Who's Coming to Dinner? (1967) 81
Gurney, Dan 12

Haggerty, Dan 37, 40, 49
Haig, Sid 45
Hall, Jon 46, 74
Hall, Tex 67
Haller, Daniel 54, 58
Handle with Care (1976) 20

The Happening (1967) 72
The Hard Ride (1971) 79, 81, 82
Hawaii 5-0 27, 50
Hawks, Howard 91
Haynes, Michael 49
Hayward, Brooke 66, 71
Hayward, Leland 66
Hayward, William 66
Hearts and Minds (1974) 72
Hefti, Ben 101
Heiser, Peter 67
The Hellcats (1969) 83, 85, 86
Hell's Angels m.c. 1, 19, 23, 37, 87, 88, 89, 90, 91, 93, 94, 95, 96, 97, 98
Hell's Angels on Wheels (1967) 5, 12, 14, 58, 67
Hell's Angels 69 (1969) 5, 93, 96, 97, 98
Hell's Belles (1969) 98, 99, 100, 101
Hell's Bloody Devils (1970) 102, 103, 104
Hell's Chosen Few (1968) 104, 105
Henderson, Don see Laughlin, Tom
Hewitt, David L. 104, 105
Hill, Jack 40
The Hills Have Eyes (1977) 31
The Hired Hand (1971) 72
Hogan's Heroes 15
Hollywood Man (1976) 49
The Honkers (1972) 65
Hopkins, Bo 97
Hopper, Dennis 50, 66, 67, 71, 72, 73, 78, 79
The Hot Angel (1958) 1, 106, 107, 108
The Hot Box (1974) 20
Hot Rods to Hell (1967) 58
Hughes and Harlow: Angels in Hell (1978) 91
Hunter, Meredith 19, 98
Huntington, Joan 31

I, a Man (1967) 11
I Crossed the Color Line see *The Black Klansman* (1966)
I Love You, Alice B. Toklas (1968) 20
Idaho Transfer (1971) 72
Ihnat, Steve 65, 98
The Incredible Two-Headed Transplant (1971) 76
Independent-International Pictures Corp. 21, 22
Ireland, O. Dale 63, 65
Ivy League Killers (1962) 1, 108, 109

Jagger, Mick 97, 98
Jaglom, Henry 67, 71
The Jailbreakers (1960) 65
James, Elizabeth 32
Jefferson, I.J. see Machu, Mimi

Index

Jefferson Airplane 98
Jeffries, Herb 49
Jessie 101
The Jesus Trip (1971) 48
John Goldfarb, Please Come Home (1965) 58
Johnson, Lyndon 67
The Jokers (1967) 96
Jordan, Marsha 86
Judging Amy 8

Kallis, Albert 106
Kallis, Stanley 106, 107, 108
Kananza, Ross 54
Kartalian, Buck 57
Kasem, Casey 50, 52
Keach, Stacey 8
Kelljan, Robert 92
Kempton, Pearl 15
Kent, Gary 92
Kessler, Bruce 12, 15
King, Joyce 67
King, Martin Luther 38
Kinoshita, Robert 104
Kinzie, Sharyn 85
Knightriders m.c. 11
Kovacs, Laszlo 87, 91

Ladd, Cheryl 49
Lafayette Escadrille (1958) 31, 37
Lanza, Anthony 78
Laredo 49
Latimer, Cheri 20
Laughlin, Tom 31, 32, 36, 37, 38
The Last Movie (1971) 66, 72
Lawrence, D.H. 71
Lawrence, John 76, 78, 79
Lewis, Paul 67
The Life and Legend of Wyatt Earp 108
Littlejohn, Evelyn 20
Littlejohn, Gary 11, 20
Look Homeward Angel 37
The Losers (1970) 46
Loughery, Jackie 106, 108
The Loved One (1965) 67
Lucas, George 20
Lucking, William 101

MacArthur, James 27
Macauley, Charles 59
Macbird 161
MacCarthy, John K. 104, 105
Machu, Mimi 91, 92
Machu, Sean 91
MacLaine, Shirley 58
MacLeod, Murray 27
McNally, Stephen 102
Macon County Line (1974) 11
MacRae, Meredith 45
Madden, Lee 5, 8, 93, 97
Magoo 93, 97
Mahon, Barry 52
Mahon, Sharon 52
Mahoney, Jock 78

Malibu Run 37
The Man with Two Heads see *The Incredible Two-Headed Transplant*
Manson (1973) 31
Manson, Charles 7, 23
Markland, Ted 16
Marley, Michelle 49
The Marriage 58
Martel, Arlene 15
Mary Hartman, Mary Hartman 45
Masterson, Bat 108
McBain, Diane 75, 76
McCrea, Jody 78
McCrea, Joel 78
McCrea, Joel Dee see McCrea, Jody
McEndree, Maurice 58
McKinney, Bill 8
McMullen, Robert G. 98
Medical Center 8
Mehas, Mik 106
Melvin and Howard (1980) 20
Merrick, Laurence 27, 30
Midnight Cowboy (1969) 71
Mignano, Dennis M. 31
Miller, Arthur 86
The Miniskirt Mob (1968) 1, 75, 83, 98, 100, 101
The Mod Squad 59
Mom and Dad (1944) 86
The Monkees 67, 91
Moody, Titus 104, 105
The Moon Is Blue 15
Moor, Cherie see Ladd, Cheryl
Motor Psycho (1965) 1, 14
Motorcycle Gang (1957) 1, 109
The Movie Maker (1967) 75
Mullavey, Greg 45
Murphy, Audie 26
Murphy, Jimmy 16
Murray, Jan 27
Murray, William 24

Namath, Joe 41, 45
Nature's Paradise (1955) 87
Never Too Late 15
New World Pictures 9, 11, 21, 40
New York Journal American 83
New York Times 50
Nicholson, Jack 66, 67, 71, 72, 73, 91, 92
No Communication 15
Noel, Chris 78
Nomads m.c. 87

Ocean's Eleven (1960) 93, 96
O'donnell, Erin 103
O'Donoghue, Michael 73
Of Love and Desire (1963) 87
Ohmart, Carol 102
Old Man Golden see Hefti, Ben
Oliver, Stephen 16

On Golden Pond (1981) 73
O'Neill, Robert 67
The Only Way Home (1972) 97
Operation M 102; see also *Hell's Bloody Devils*
Oswald, Lee Harvey 82
Otis Productions 32, 38
Outlaw Motorcycles (1967) 104, 105
The Outrage (1964) 16

Pando Company 67
Paramount Pictures 106
Parker, Joe 106
Parnell, Emory 108
Parnell, James 108
Passion Street U.S.A. (1966) 65
Pataki, Michael 59, 62, 72
Patterson, Melody 27, 52
Peabody, Dennis 40
Peeters, Barbara 39, 40
People 76
Peters, Gus 23
Pettyjohn, Angelique 101
Playboy 20
Polan, Claire Lynn 23, 75
Presley, Elvis 82, 85, 101, 106
Prince of Peace (1949) 86
The Proper Time (1960) 31, 37

Rafelson, Bob 67, 71, 73
Raggedy Man 1981) 20
Randall, Anne 102, 103
Raybert Productions 67
Return to Macon County (1975) 11
Riddle, Nelson 103
The Right Stuff (1983) 20
Riverboat 92
Road Racers (1959) 108
Roarke, Adam 91, 92, 101
Robbins, Leroy 67
Robinson, Chris 52
Romero, George 62
Ross, Diana 23
Run, Angel, Run (1969) 5, 8, 9
Run for Your Life 27
Rush, Richard 12, 15, 16, 67, 87, 91
Rush, Tony 16
Russell, Jane 38
Ryan, Robert 8
Ryan, T.C. 8

The St. Valentine's Day Massacre (1967) 91
Scharf, Sabrina 67, 72
Schiller, Bob 72
Schneider, Abraham 67
Schneider, Bert 71, 72, 73
Schneider, Stanley 67
Scream Free see *Free Grass*
77 Sunset Strip 41
Shadows (1960) 58
Shonteff, Lindsay 109
Slatzer, Robert F. 83, 85, 86

Smith, Maurice 50, 76
Smith, Roger 41, 44, 45
Smith, William 11, 44, 48, 49, 58
Sorel, Peter 67
South Pacific (1958) 31
Southern, Terry 67, 73
Spahn, George 23
Spahn Ranch 21, 23
Spector, Phil 72
The Spy Who Came In from the Cold (1965) 15
Star Trek: "The Gamesters of Triskelon" 101
Steppenwolf 72
Stooplemoor, Cheryl Jean *see* Ladd, Cheryl
Swing Shift (1984) 20
A Swingin' Summer (1965) 37

Tait, Don 93
Talese, Gay 97
Tall Story (1960) 31
Taltree, Luana 16
Tamblyn, Russ 79
Tea and Sympathy (1956) 31
Teenage Bridge (1960) 104
Teenage Rumble 65
Terry the Tramp 93, 94, 96, 97, 98
Tessier, Diane 75
Tessier, Joey 75
Tessier, Robert 37, 75, 78
Texter, Gilda 20, 61

These Are the Damned (1965) 1
Thirteen West Street (1962) 91
The Thunder Makers 59
Thy Neighbor's Wife 97
Tikonis, Gus 74
A Time to Run see The Female Bunch
Tiny 93
Titillation (1982) 101
Topper, Burt 54, 57, 79, 81, 82
Tracom Productions 97
Trans-American Pictures 52
The Trip 72, 78
Tucker, Larry 20
Twelfth Night 15
Twin Peaks 20

Ulee's Gold (1997) 73
Universal Pictures 8, 72, 91, 97

Valenti, Jack 66
Vanishing Point (1971) 20, 61
Van Stralen, Anton 65
Ve Sota Bruno 92
Viola, Joe 16, 20
Violent Angels see Angels Die Hard
Volante, Vicki 103

Walker, Ellie 72
Walker, Robert, Jr. 72
Warhol, Andy 11
Warner Brothers 38

Wayne, John 26
Wellman, William, Jr. 37, 38
Wellman, William, Sr. 37
West, Maria 8
West, Max 8
What's So Bad About Feeling Good? (1968) 8
Where It's At (1969) 93
White, James Gordon 76, 83
The Wild Angels (1966) 1, 5, 10
The Wild One (1954) 1, 57
Wild Wheels (1969) 5
Willis, Bruce 109
Winchester 73 (1950) 98
Winfrey, Oprah 23
Winter a Go-Go (1965) 37
Woelfel, Jill 103
Wood, Lana 79
Wood, Natalie 79
Woodstock (1970 98
Woolner, Larry 21
WW and the Dixie Dancekings (1974) 97

You Don't Need Pajamas at Rosie's see The First Time
Young, Carleton 49
Young, Tony 49
The Young Sinner (1965) 31
You've Got to Be Smart (1967) 15

Zila, John, Jr. 83
Zucker, Howard 73

www.ingramcontent.com/pod-product-compliance
Lightning Source LLC
Chambersburg PA
CBHW081554300426
44116CB00015B/2884